Studies in Jazz

The Institute of Jazz Studies
Rutgers—The State University of New Jersey
General Editors: Dan Morgenstern and Edward Berger

1. BENNY CARTER: A Life in American Music, *by Morroe Berger, Edward Berger, and James Patrick, 2 vols., 1982*
2. ART TATUM: A Guide to His Recorded Music, *by Arnold Laubich and Ray Spencer, 1982*
3. ERROLL GARNER: The Most Happy Piano, *by James M. Doran, 1985*
4. JAMES P. JOHNSON: A Case of Mistaken Identity, *by Scott E. Brown;* Discography 1917–1950, *by Robert Hilbert, 1986*
5. PEE WEE ERWIN: This Horn for Hire, *as told to Warren W. Vaché Sr., 1987*
6. BENNY GOODMAN: Listen to His Legacy, *by D. Russell Connor, 1988*
7. ELLINGTONIA: The Recorded Music of Duke Ellington and His Sidemen, *by W. E. Timner, 1988; 4th ed., 1996*
8. THE GLENN MILLER ARMY AIR FORCE BAND: Sustineo Alas / I Sustain the Wings, *by Edward F. Polic;* Foreword *by George T. Simon, 1989*
9. SWING LEGACY, *by Chip Deffaa, 1989*
10. REMINISCING IN TEMPO: The Life and Times of a Jazz Hustler, *by Teddy Reig, with Edward Berger, 1990*
11. IN THE MAINSTREAM: 18 Portraits in Jazz, *by Chip Deffaa, 1992*
12. BUDDY DeFRANCO: A Biographical Portrait and Discography, *by John Kuehn and Arne Astrup, 1993*
13. PEE WEE SPEAKS: A Discography of Pee Wee Russell, *by Robert Hilbert, with David Niven, 1992*
14. SYLVESTER AHOLA: The Gloucester Gabriel, *by Dick Hill, 1993*
15. THE POLICE CARD DISCORD, *by Maxwell T. Cohen, 1993*
16. TRADITIONALISTS AND REVIVALISTS IN JAZZ, *by Chip Deffaa, 1993*
17. BASSICALLY SPEAKING: An Oral History of George Duvivier, *by Edward Berger;* Musical Analysis *by David Chevan, 1993*
18. TRAM: The Frank Trumbauer Story, *by Philip R. Evans and Larry F. Kiner, with William Trumbauer, 1994*
19. TOMMY DORSEY: On the Side, *by Robert L. Stockdale, 1995*
20. JOHN COLTRANE: A Discography and Musical Biography, *by Yasuhiro Fujioka, with Lewis Porter and Yoh-ichi Hamada, 1995*
21. RED HEAD: A Chronological Survey of "Red" Nichols and His Five Pennies, *by Stephen M. Stroff, 1996*
22. THE RED NICHOLS STORY: After Intermission 1942–1965, *by Philip R. Evans, Stanley Hester, Stephen Hester, and Linda Evans, 1997*
23. BENNY GOODMAN: Wrappin' It Up, *by D. Russell Connor, 1996*

24. CHARLIE PARKER AND THEMATIC IMPROVISATION, *by Henry Martin, 1996*
25. BACK BEATS AND RIM SHOTS: The Johnny Blowers Story, *by Warren W. Vaché Sr., 1997*
26. DUKE ELLINGTON: A Listener's Guide, *by Eddie Lambert, 1998*
27. SERGE CHALOFF: A Musical Biography and Discography, *by Vladimir Simosko, 1998*
28. HOT JAZZ: From Harlem to Storyville, *by David Griffiths, 1998*
29. ARTIE SHAW: A Musical Biography and Discography, *by Vladimir Simosko, 2000*
30. JIMMY DORSEY: A Study in Contrasts, *by Robert L. Stockdale, 1998*
31. STRIDE!: Fats, Jimmy, Lion, Lamb and All the Other Ticklers, *by John L. Fell and Terkild Vinding, 1999*
32. GIANT STRIDES: The Legacy of Dick Wellstood, *by Edward N. Meyer, 1999*
33. JAZZ GENTRY: Aristocrats of the Music World, *by Warren W. Vaché Sr., 1999*
34. THE UNSUNG SONGWRITERS: America's Masters of Melody, *by Warren W. Vaché Sr., 2000*
35. THE MUSICAL WORLD OF J. J. JOHNSON, *by Joshua Berrett and Louis G. Bourgois III, 1999*
36. THE LADIES WHO SING WITH THE BAND, *by Betty Bennett, 2000*
37. AN UNSUNG CAT: The Life and Music of Warne Marsh, *by Safford Chamberlain, 2000*
38. JAZZ IN NEW ORLEANS: The Postwar Years Through 1970, *by Charles Suhor, 2001*
39. THE YOUNG LOUIS ARMSTRONG ON RECORDS: A Critical Survey of the Early Recordings, 1923–1928, *by Edward Brooks, 2002*
40. BENNY CARTER: A Life in American Music, Second Edition, *by Morroe Berger, Edward Berger, and James Patrick, 2 vols., 2002*
41. CHORD CHANGES ON THE CHALKBOARD: How Public School Teachers Shaped Jazz and the Music of New Orleans, *by Al Kennedy,* Foreword *by Ellis Marsalis Jr., 2002*
42. CONTEMPORARY CAT: Terence Blanchard with Special Guests, *by Anthony Magro, 2002*
43. PAUL WHITEMAN: Pioneer in American Music, Volume I: 1890–1930, *by Don Rayno, 2003*
44. GOOD VIBES: A Life in Jazz, *by Terry Gibbs with Cary Ginell, 2003*
45. TOM TALBERT—HIS LIFE AND TIMES: Voices from a Vanished World of Jazz, *by Bruce Talbot, 2004*
46. SITTIN' IN WITH CHRIS GRIFFIN: A Reminiscence of Radio and Recording's Golden Years, *by Warren W. Vaché, 2005*
47. FIFTIES JAZZ TALK: An Oral Retrospective, *by Gordon Jack, 2004*
48. FLORENCE MILLS: Harlem Jazz Queen, *by Bill Egan, 2004*
49. SWING ERA SCRAPBOOK: The Teenage Diaries and Radio Logs of Bob Inman, 1936–1938, *by Ken Vail, 2005*

50. FATS WALLER ON THE AIR: The Radio Broadcasts and Discography, *by Stephen Taylor, 2006*
51. ALL OF ME: The Complete Discography of Louis Armstrong, *by Jos Willems, 2006*
52. MUSIC AND THE CREATIVE SPIRIT: Innovators in Jazz, Improvisation, and the Avant Garde, *by Lloyd Peterson, 2006*
53. THE STORY OF FAKE BOOKS: Bootlegging Songs to Musicians, *by Barry Kernfeld, 2006*
54. ELLINGTONIA: The Recorded Music of Duke Ellington and His Sidemen, 5th edition, *by W. E. Timner, 2007*
55. JAZZ FICTION: A History and Comprehensive Reader's Guide, *by David Rife, 2007*
56. MISSION IMPOSSIBLE: My Life In Music, *by Lalo Schifrin, edited by Richard H. Palmer, 2008*
57. THE CONTRADICTIONS OF JAZZ, *by Paul Rinzler, 2008*
58. EARLY TWENTIETH-CENTURY BRASS IDIOMS: Art, Jazz, and Other Popular Traditions, *edited by Howard T. Weiner, 2008*
59. THE MUSIC AND LIFE OF THEODORE "FATS" NAVARRO: Infatuation, *by Leif Bo Petersen and Theo Rehak, 2009*
60. WHERE THE DARK AND THE LIGHT FOLKS MEET: Race and the Mythology, Politics, and Business of Jazz, *by Randall Sandke, 2010*
61. JAZZ BOOKS IN THE 1990S: An Annotated Bibliography, *by Janice Leslie Hochstat Greenberg, 2010*
62. BENNY GOODMAN: A Supplemental Discography, *by David Jessup, 2010*
63. THE LIFE AND MUSIC OF KENNY DAVERN: Just Four Bars, *by Edward N. Meyer, 2010*
64. MR. TRUMPET: The Trials, Tribulations, and Triumph of Bunny Berigan, *by Michael P. Zirpolo, 2011*
65. HARLEM JAZZ ADVENTURES: A European Baron's Memoir, 1934–1969, *by Timme Rosenkrantz, adapted and edited by Fradley Hamilton Garner, 2012*
66. WHAT IT IS: The Life of a Jazz Artist, *by Dave Liebman in conversation with Lewis Porter, 2012*
67. BORN TO PLAY: The Ruby Braff Discography and Directory of Performances, *by Thomas P. Hustad, 2012*

WHAT IT IS

The Life of a Jazz Artist

DAVE LIEBMAN

in conversation with
Lewis Porter

Studies in Jazz, No. 66

THE SCARECROW PRESS, INC.
Lanham • Toronto • Plymouth, UK
2012

Published by Scarecrow Press, Inc.
A wholly owned subsidiary of The Rowman & Littlefield Publishing Group, Inc.
4501 Forbes Boulevard, Suite 200, Lanham, Maryland 20706
http://www.scarecrowpress.com

Estover Road, Plymouth PL6 7PY, United Kingdom

British Library Cataloguing in Publication Information Available

Library of Congress Cataloging-in-Publication Data
Liebman, Dave.
What it is : the life of a jazz artist / Dave Liebman in conversation with Lewis Porter.
p. cm. — (Studies in jazz ; 66)
Includes index.
ISBN 978-0-8108-8203-4 (hardcover : alk. paper) — ISBN 978-0-8108-8254-6 (ebook)
1. Liebman, Dave—Interviews. 2. Jazz musicians—United States—Interviews. 3. Saxophonists—United States—Interviews. 4. Jazz—History and criticism. I. Porter, Lewis, 1951– II. Title.
ML419.L5A5 2012
788.7'165092—dc23
[B]
2011043588

™ The paper used in this publication meets the minimum requirements of American National Standard for Information Sciences—Permanence of Paper for Printed Library Materials, ANSI/NISO Z39.48-1992.

Printed in the United States of America

This book is dedicated to John Coltrane for the raison d'etre; my late parents Frances and Leo Liebman; my family, Caris, Lydia, Harold, and Natalie, for their never-ending support; all the listeners who love this music; and the artists who have accompanied me on this voyage.

David Liebman

"I know of no better definition of the word art than this: Art is man added to nature—nature, reality, truth, but with a significance, a conception, a character, which the artist brings out in it, and to which he gives expression, which he disentangles, sets free and elucidates."

—Letter from Vincent van Gogh to Theo van Gogh
Petit-Wasmes, Belgium, June 1879

Contents

Foreword by Richie Beirach xi

Preface by Lewis Porter xv

Acknowledgments xix

Timeline xxi

Chapter 1: The Delicacy of Youth: Beginnings 1

Chapter 2: The Call: I Find Music, It Finds Me 37

Chapter 3: Breakaway: Finding Myself 63

Chapter 4: Arrival: Becoming an Artist 83

Chapter 5: The Energy of the Chance: Going for It 105

Chapter 6: Guided Dream: Playing with the Masters 125

Chapter 7: It's Different Out There: On the Job with the Prince of Darkness 159

Chapter 8: Beyond the Line: My Own World 191

Chapter 9: Passages: The Ups and Downs 213

Chapter 10: Turn It Around: Solidifying Art and Life 249

Chapter 11: While We're on the Subject: On Others 293

Chapter 12: Tomorrow's Expectations: The Legacy 309

Appendix I: Selected Discography 339

Appendix II: Selected Educational Materials 347

Appendix III: Two Compositions by Dave Liebman 349

Index 353

About the Authors 363

Foreword

A man isn't made up of one facet but a multitude, and it's the combination of images that make up the complete man. Dave Liebman has been my friend for over forty years. I know him probably better than anyone. As a man, a musician, he's very complicated. He's a combination of teacher, philosopher, lawyer, warrior, and the ultimate fighter for what he considers the right thing. He's got a multiple personality in the best possible sense because he's a composer, a skilled teacher, a superior organizer, a great bandleader, and of course, a great instrumentalist. And a good friend!

So, Lieb is Mr. Multitask and he's still producing at a level that most twenty-five-year-olds would collapse from. Every day, he's working. And he's still vital, productive and playing great. Maybe the thing that he's going to be most remembered for is founding the International Association of Schools of Jazz, because it's a staggering accomplishment. He was the first one to pull schools from all over the world together in a kind of United Nations network. Nobody did that before, and he was the only one that could do it, because of his amazing stamina and organizational brilliance. It's still going on for over twenty years to the benefit of hundreds of students worldwide. Now he was given the National Endowmant of the Arts Jazz Masters award, the French Order of Arts and Letters, and a couple of first-place poll positions, finally. He deserves every bit of it because a lot of people who do that kind of thing can't play so well, if at all. And Lieb can play! In a way, he's really the Leonard Bernstein of the jazz scene. Lennie came in as a conductor and pianist, but with his TV shows he brought music to the people, recognizing the importance of education.

Lieb has learned over his life to soften his hard points and to develop his brilliance. The thing about Lieb is that you never have to worry about where you stand. He always tells you accurately, with complete honesty, what's happening. This is very refreshing, and it saves a lot of time. Also the older he gets, the sweeter he has become, losing some of that hard-core New York edge. We needed that when we were younger, as two young white Jewish jazz musicians growing up in the 60s and 70s in New York. It was like being a white basketball player today, you know? We basically had very good relationships with everybody, black musicians as well as white musicians. But the world was different then—there were LPs, there were almost no jazz schools except for Berklee, and jazz was a four-letter word you never mentioned in any of the classical institutions. I went to the Manhattan School of Music for theory and composition, and Dave went to NYU for American History. He never studied music formally.

We were lucky to be in New York at the time that that the giants were living. The equivalent of Bach, Beethoven, Chopin, Schoenberg, and Wagner were all alive: McCoy, Herbie, Chick, Bill Evans—whom I knew during the last five years of his life—Mingus, Monk, Duke Ellington, Trane, Stan Getz, Art Blakey, Cannonball, Miles. All the major guys were alive, and playing their best! We saw that every night in New York at the Village Vanguard, Five Spot, Village Gate, all the clubs. In your face—the best mo-fos in the world! And though some of them are still alive and playing great, most have passed. We saw it when it was happening, when jazz had gone underground in the late 60s. Miles's LP *Nefertiti* sold about five thousand records. I think Chick Corea's *Now He Sings, Now He Sobs* got a low review and sold maybe one thousand records. We got the chance to serve time with the masters. For myself, with Stan Getz and Chet Baker, for Lieb, Elvin Jones and Miles Davis.

Jazz didn't become really popular again until the 70s, but the time I'm talking about, it was seriously underground. There was no Internet and Facebook, etc., so it was kind of a homey, small community. Now, with the technology, any kid with five hundred bucks can record themselves and put it out and it looks like a real album. When we were making records in the 60s and 70s, the only way to make a record was if the guy called you from Blue Note or ECM and said, "Hey man, I want you to record." Then you went and made a record, and that was it.

Dave and I taught each other stuff. He taught me about melody and phrasing, and I taught him about harmony, composition, all the stuff I was studying. We worked together for hours and hours. People say, "Oh, you guys were geniuses." It's not true, if you think of a genius as someone who just has it and doesn't have to work at it. We were talented, and we had drive and we wanted it. Bill Evans was not a genius either. He and Trane—these guys were late bloomers. Sometimes, the young geniuses burn out fast, or they don't have anyone on their level to make music with. Lieb and I were fine with who we were. We grew up together and taught each other things.

When Dave told me about his plan to do this book, I said, "Man, why don't you wait a few years?" And he said, "No, I want to do it now." He's very impatient—he wants to get it over with. He should have that on his tombstone: "I wanted to get it over with!" On the phone he talks fast, and on his answering machine you have twenty seconds! But he does a tremendous amount of work, and always has. Even before the Internet stuff and all this Twitter and Facebook, he was sending out stuff like "Lieb's Log." He was doing the communications because he knew you had to do that to keep your name, your face, your accomplishments in front of people. He is a natural leader.

This book is an amazingly honest and detailed account of what it was like, not just as a musician but as a person, to grow up in those times. Dave tells the truth!

With love,
Richie Beirach

Preface

In 1968, during the summer, I think, I took the subway from my family's apartment in the Bronx to see that week's Sunday afternoon concert, part of a series presented by Jazz Interactions at the Red Garter on West 4th Street in Greenwich Village. That week the feature was a "youth group" with Randy Brecker, a long-haired trumpeter who was making a splash around Manhattan, and a tenor saxophonist named Dave Liebman, who played with memorable intensity. Around November 1973, I was visiting friends in Boston and decided to check out the famous Berklee School of Music (now College), which I had never seen. I was a bit cocky in those days and brought my saxophone with me in hopes of finding a jam session. I was primarily a pianist, but I'd experienced that it was way easier to sit in on sax than to get the pianist to stand up from the bench. Sure enough, in a small practice room I saw four or five student musicians jamming. I strolled in and immediately realized that there was a fifth person, Dave Liebman, playing the drums! Dave doesn't remember this, but he assumed I was a class member walking in late. So he didn't say anything when I took out my alto saxophone and started to play along. However, when we were playing riffs behind one of the other soloists, he did say to me, "Play long tones for backgrounds"—good advice, then and now. He sounded excellent on drums and then switched to the piano, on which he also burned. I don't remember him playing saxophone that day.

In April 1979, I met Dave in a professional circumstance. I was the first ever jazz band director at Tufts University (and soon to become the first at Brandeis as well). Dave was in town, scheduled to do a workshop at Harvard for students of my friend Tom Everett, the Harvard band director, and, I think through Tom, it was arranged that he would also do a clinic with my Tufts big band students. Dave talked, and played a bit—I have a cassette of it. My students found it highly inspirational, and they didn't mind that he used four-letter words!

Dave and I stayed in touch over the years. We both took part in a Coltrane panel at the International Association of Jazz Educators conference in January 1998. Dave was a guest soloist on my first CD in 2000. I remember running into Dave at Joe's Pub in Manhattan when our mutual friend Ravi Coltrane was performing there with his mother, Alice, in November 2002. Dave and I were truly happy to see each other, and it was clear that we were becoming good friends. We performed together as a duo in Tours, France, in 2007 and since then on a few other occasions.

So when Dave asked me in early 2008 to help him write his life story, I agreed. Quite frankly, I was not looking to take on any writing projects, and I wouldn't have done it for anybody else. I interviewed Dave for about twenty-five hours on various dates, from the spring of 2008 through 2010, and then had some of my graduate students transcribe the interviews verbatim. After that, Dave's wife, Caris, and their friend and professional editor, Mary Dorian, looked through the manuscript, and Dave himself worked on it in great detail for many hours. Finally, I spent much of the summer of 2011 with the manuscript, editing it and reshaping it (for example, there were many instances where the same event was discussed in two different places, and so on). I checked every name and date. I did new research on Dave's family history, uncovering documents and census data that even he hadn't seen.

With Dave's permission, I edited the interviews into this finished book in several ways. In many cases where Dave had said something like "Around 1971," I was able to establish an exact date, so I changed the words, with his approval, to "On September 25, 1971" (or whatever the exact date was). Similarly, I added exact names of persons and places to his text. I cut out many of my own statements, especially where I was simply reacting to what Dave said ("That's amazing!" "I can't believe it!" and the like). In a few cases I have added information in parentheses. Parentheses are only used for my editorial additions; Dave's words are never in parentheses.

Please understand that, as in any book of this sort, conversations that Dave recalls are not presented "verbatim"—Dave did not have a recorder with him every minute of his life! He has done his best to recall what he and others said years ago, but this book represents his memories, not some kind of "transcript" of his life.

For the most part, all technical terms are explained in the text. But it should be noted, for the person who is not a jazz musician, that jazz musicians use the word "changes" to mean "changing chords that underlie a song." We could simply say "chords," but the word "changes" has caught on, and, for better or worse, that's the word we all use.

The title of each chapter is the name of one of Dave's compositions. Each is poetically appropriate to the content of each chapter, as you will see. For the reader's convenience, here is a listing of what topics are covered in each chapter:

Chapter 1	Family, polio, childhood into high school
Chapter 2	Bob Moses, college, hearing Coltrane, studies with Lennie Tristano, Joe Allard
Chapter 3	Europe, Charles Lloyd
Chapter 4	Black and white, hippiedom, first love, spiritual search, teaching school, the first loft
Chapter 5	Ten Wheel Drive, macrobiotics, free jazz, Free Life Communication, Steve Grossman
Chapter 6	Chick Corea, Pete LaRoca, Ten Wheel Drive, Elvin Jones
Chapter 7	Miles Davis
Chapter 8	Richie Beirach, Eugene Gregan, Lookout Farm, Ellis-Liebman Band and California
Chapter 9	Back in NYC; Quintet with Scofield, marriage to Dina, mid-life crisis, Quest, teaching, focusing on soprano
Chapter 10	Caris, Lydia, IASJ, master class, chromatic harmony book, new band, European musicians
Chapter 11	Thoughts on Lee Konitz, Charlie Parker, Phil Woods, Cannonball Adderley, Bill Evans, Sonny Rollins, Wayne Shorter
Chapter 12	The Dave Liebman Group; other groups including Sax Summit, We3, Different But The Same, Duos; El Salvador and Mauritania trips, awards

Dave's website, davidliebman.com, is quite extensive and has a great deal of information that complements this book. There you will find more photographs, his archived newsletters, and many of his published interviews. Under "Education" he has placed many of the articles he has written, as well as the history of the International Association of Schools of Jazz. His "Recordings" menu includes a complete listing of his recordings, as well as a "Private Archives" section with recordings from his personal collection. Under "Media" you can see him in performance with Miles Davis, Mike Brecker, and others. In short, you will certainly want to bookmark his site and spend many hours there.

There will be new recordings to add to the list. For example, in September 2011, Dave and I recorded with some friends of mine, guitarist Marc Ribot and bassist Brad Jones, both of whom I've performed with occasionally since 1988, and drummer Chad Taylor. The CD will make a great complement to this book. Do look for it!

In fact, Dave is always looking for new projects and new people to play and record with. He maintains an intensive schedule of performances around the world, so it's easy to catch him in concert. And he's welcoming, easy to talk with, and involved with students everywhere he goes. But don't ever take Dave for granted just because he is so accessible. One example: I recently saw him in a band with five other saxophonists. All five were top New York players, full of fire and originality. But when Dave followed them, it was instantly apparent that he had twice the technical ability of any of them, combined with tremendous passion and creativity. Make no mistake—he is one of the masters.

But while Dave is indeed a master, he's also down to earth—an engaging storyteller, with a great tale to tell. Dear reader, please enjoy this book!

With Best Wishes,
Lewis Porter

Port Chester, New York
September 2011

Acknowledgments

Dave's Acknowledgments

My sincere gratitude to Lewis Porter for his time, humor, and sincere interest in getting my story down; to the transcribers of the conversations; to Matt Vashlishan for help in all ways; to Marek Lazarski for allowing me to use the cover photo; to Mary Dorian for her incredible editing skills and generosity of spirit; to my wife, Caris, for some heavy editing on this project and for everything, all the time.

Lew's Acknowledgments

The first few interviews were transcribed by Abbe Skinner, before she graduated from my master's program in jazz history. Then Gretchen Michelson took over, doing a great job on the bulk of the interviews. Another talented grad student, Jim Pepper, prepared the entire manuscript for "camera-ready" publication in a thoroughly professional manner.

For details about Dave's mother's name, Gottdeiner, thanks to William Gottdiener and especially Mark Gottdiener, both accomplished professors. For information about Dave's 1978 tour with Chick Corea, thanks to Ron Moss, Mike Fitzgerald, Masaya Yamaguchi, Agustín Pérez, Arild Widerøe, and Bryan Armstrong.

I would like to join Dave in thanking Mary Dorian for her work beyond the call of duty in helping to prepare the interview transcripts into book form. It was a pleasure working with our editor at Scarecrow, Bennett Graff, as well as his assistant, Christen Karniski, and production editor Sally Craley.

Above all, thanks to Dave for being such a great friend and for sharing his life story with me.

Timeline

1946:	David Liebman born in Brooklyn, New York, to Francis and Leo Liebman
1949:	Stricken with polio in left leg
ca.1956:	Begins piano lessons
ca.1958:	Begins clarinet and saxophone lessons
1962:	First time seeing John Coltrane—at Birdland, Manhattan
1964:	Graduates from Lafayette High School, Brooklyn
1967:	First trip to Europe, and first recording
1969:	Begins living in loft, Manhattan; joins fusion band Ten Wheel Drive through 1970
1970-2:	First major recordings with John McLaughlin (*My Goal's Beyond,* 1970); Elvin Jones (*Genesis*, 1971); joins Elvin Jones Group in 1971 through 1972
1973:	Joins Miles Davis in January 1973 through mid-74; records first major record as leader (*Lookout Farm*)
1976:	Lookout Farm places first in *Downbeat* as Group Deserving of Wider Recognition; forms Ellis-Liebman Band in San Francisco
1977:	First formal teaching experience at Jamey Aebersold clinic
1979:	Forms the Dave Liebman Quintet featuring John Scofield
1981:	Forms Quest with Richie Beirach
1986:	Marries Caris Visentin
1987:	First Saxophone Master Class held at East Stroudsburg University, Pennsylvania
1989:	Founds the International Association of Schools of Jazz (IASJ)

1991: Forms the Dave Liebman Group; daughter, Lydia born

1997: Honorary doctorate from Sibelius Akademe, Helsinki, Finland

2009: Order of Arts and Letters from the French government

2011: National Endowment of the Arts Jazz Master Fellowship

Chapter 1

The Delicacy of Youth: Beginnings

Lew: Let's start with your family history.
Dave: Let's discuss my mother's side first. My maternal great grandmother, Julia Weisz, was from the Alsace region of France, which was sometimes under German rule. Her daughter, my grandmother Carrie Weisz, was born in the United States. She had a sister, my great aunt Sally.

My maternal great grandfather was from Som, Hungary, which is about a seventy-five-minute drive from Budapest. His son, my mother's father, Samuel Herman Gottdiener, was born there September 1, 1884. He came over to the States from there—Ellis Island, the whole deal. He and Carrie Weisz got married in New York and they had my mother, Frances, in 1913, and later her younger sister, Beatrice.

Lew: I found Sam's World War I draft registration card, which tells us that way before you were born, back in 1918, your mother's parents, Sam and Carrie, lived at 474 Bainbridge in Bedford-Stuyvesant, Brooklyn. What about your father's side?
Dave: I don't know about my great grandparents on my father's side. But my father's father, Abraham J. Liebman, was born December 8, 1879, in Vilna. At that time I think it was part of Belarus, that part of Russia. Today, known as Vilnius, it's the capital of Lithuania. He had come to America in 1902. But he died when I was young and I don't remember him at all. Grandma Celia Liebman, his wife, was the same age, and had come over just a bit earlier (the 1920 census says 1899 while the 1930 says 1901), and I do have memories of her. She was Austrian. They

both knew Yiddish. They had my father, Leo, in 1907, and his sister Ruth in 1914, and then Esther in 1921 or 1922.

We had to visit Grandma Liebman every weekend, or it seemed like every weekend. She lived in Brooklyn, but in a completely different area than us, with a younger woman who I just don't remember but might've been one of my father's sisters—a spinster type. It was a very lonely, dark, ancient house, or so it seemed to me. I wasn't close with Grandma Liebman, and she died when I was young. But I do remember her. She was a little woman, very ethnic-looking, a babushka-type vibe.

Now, my mother's parents, Sam and Carrie, were very important in my life. By the time I was born, or soon after, they lived a few blocks from my home, Avenue O and East 14th Street. My family lived in two different places in my childhood, both in Flatbush, Brooklyn. First at 1047 East 14th Street between Avenues K and L, and then we moved to 1328 East 5th between Avenues L and M. The 14th Street home was a two-family. I remember because we had trouble with the neighbors upstairs, about noise or something like that. When we moved to East 5th Street, my parents bought that house for $22,000. I was about eight, so that has to be 1953, '54, something like that.

The place on East 5th Street was attached, but we had our own entrance with a basement, a first floor with a living room and kitchen, dining room, and upstairs, three bedrooms. That was where I lived from eight years old until I left for college. Eventually my parents again moved, not too far, to Ocean Avenue and Avenue S, where they stayed until my mother left for Florida after Dad died. This was all in the same Brooklyn area.

Growing up, we had a lot of contact with my maternal grandmother, Nana, and grandfather, Sam, whom I called Poppy. Poppy loved me. He would call me "butterball" and used to pinch me—I was a little chubby kid. I remember sitting and watching TV there. I was there a lot because my mother, Frances, worked, which was rather unusual for a woman in the fifties. At first she was a social worker in the New York City Department of Social Services. Eventually she became a teacher, which is where she met my father.

Lew: What are your parents' exact birthdates and full names, including middle names?

Dave: Well, first of all, we had no middle names in our family. In fact, at thirteen or something like that, I said: "How come everybody else has a middle name?" My mother said, "Pick whatever you want." But the names I liked were all the Italian cats, because they were the tough guys, so I wanted to be Vito or Tony or Tito, and she said, "You can't have that." That was the end of my middle name search. David "Tito" Liebman—I don't think so!

My mother, Frances, was born January 12, 1913. After Bed-Stuy, her family lived in Crown Heights in Brooklyn, where she grew up in a heavily Jewish area at that time. My father, Leo, was born September 30, 1907. Born in New York. He grew up in East Harlem. His father, Abraham, was a butcher with his own shop and also fixed up houses. They changed homes a lot from what I understood, but usually up around 3rd and 2nd Avenue, on the streets that were numbered in the 100s, until they finally moved to Brooklyn.

Lew: In the 1920 census, I found Abraham and Celia living in an apartment at 1404 Park Avenue in Manhattan, near East 104th Street. By 1930 they were in an apartment at 120 Powell Street, Brooklyn. Then in the '40s they were at 689 Bristol Street, Brooklyn—maybe that was the house where you visited Grandma Celia Liebman. Now, you have one sibling?

Dave: Yes, my brother, Paul, was born January 27, 1942. I was born September 4, 1946. So Paul was almost five years older. Eventually Paul went to Brooklyn College, and I went to Queens College and NYU. My parents were New York Jews, typical first-half-of-the-twentieth-century New Yorkers—going to a city school, getting a civil service job with a check every week or every month, basically New York City employees. I am a child of this background, rather typical in New York at that point in history.

Sam Gottdiener had worked as an auctioneer, and on that 1918 draft card you found it's hard to read the handwriting, but it seems to say that he worked in ladies' apparel, and definitely at 5 Lispenard Street in Manhattan, a street that sounds familiar from conversations I heard. But during my childhood he had a women's dress store around Seventh Avenue and 35th Street, Manhattan, in the textile district, called Globe Clothiers or Globe Furriers. I remember it because it was big—I guess a loft—with a gigantic globe on the top floor that overlooked the whole room. My brother, Paul, and I played on those clothing racks that you used to see the guys walking down 7th Avenue with, scooting around, having fun in this big space.

Lew: Your father worked in that clothing business for a time. But before that, maybe his father, Abraham, was already ill because, according to the 1930 census, he is unemployed, while Leo is already working as a

clerk at the post office and his mother, Celia, is working somewhere—I can't read her exact job title—as well.
Dave: I didn't know about the post office, but yes, my father, Leo Liebman, did later take a short foray with my uncle and his father-in-law Sam into that clothing business. Then my father joined the wave of guys who went to the City College of New York, which was the school for immigrants trying to better their situation. He got a degree in teaching and did that for the rest of his life and eventually became an assistant principal. He and my mother met in my Great Aunt Sally's school. She was my grandmother's sister on my Mom's side. She was a school principal at the time.

Aunt Sally was a special woman and, from what my mother said, she inspired Mom. These ladies were ahead of their time, for sure. My mother went to Hunter College at sixteen years old. Somehow she got out of high school early—she was a whiz kid. She was one of the first women to graduate from Hunter College. So you see, my family are real New Yorkers.

Lew: What was the ethnic mix in your Brooklyn neighborhoods?
Dave: My neighborhood was basically half Jewish, half Italian. I remember it more from the 5th Street house, where it was single-family homes. On the same block were Jews and Italians, not segregated. Vinnie or whoever was across the street and somebody like Mr. Rosenbaum or whoever was next door—all together. I don't know if we mixed much 'cause people tended to stay with their own kind. But you certainly mixed in school; although, of course, the truth was that a lot of Jews were in the advanced classes and the Italians tended to be more in the commercial or vocational programs. That's the way it worked. Of course, the gang thing—there was a sense of street gangs of some sort that were by and large the Italian guys. So, we were intimidated by them. We were the little Jewish nerds.

My father was an athlete. He loved all kinds of ball playing. He would drive his bike to Coney Island almost every day he could. On the weekends he would meet with other teachers and play handball. He was a big handball guy—black handball, a real city sport. Dad was in good shape, athletic, but he was also an intellectual. He read the *New York Times* from cover to cover. He read the *New Republic*. This is where I got my reading habits from, I guess. He and his friends were Jewish liberal intellectuals, Democrats for life—you know, real New York lefties.

Lew: Not only did Jews tend to be Democrats, but, maybe in a generation a little older than your folks, there were a lot of Jewish Communists.
Dave: Yes, though my folks weren't. But that was definitely in the line of what we're talking about. They were very liberal. I don't think they were Communists—officially. But certainly there was a lot of conversation about that because that was very obviously on the plate in the fifties—McCarthy and all that. You know, New Yorkers were not considered part of America. New York was, and still is, not part of America in a certain way. Now it's because of the world cultures, but then, maybe because of all the European ethnic communities in the northeast cities like Boston, Philly, and New York, which were very Irish, Italian, and Jewish. In general firemen were Italians, Irish were policemen, and teachers were Jews. As well, to a large degree, doctors, lawyers, and accountants were Jewish as well.

Lew: In New York City these patterns held true, while elsewhere in the country, there were no Jewish lawyers or doctors in many places.
Dave: It's who you knew—it was the milieu you grew up with—that's who the friends and family were. That's who your uncles were, who the neighbors were. In New York by the 1950s, Jews weren't laborers; they didn't drive buses; they weren't garbage collectors. That was the environment.

Lew: Now, your Mom's folks, you were close with them.
Dave: Yes, because I had to be taken care of a lot. Also because of my situation, which we'll get to, with polio, and the hospital stays and all that, my not having what you would call a "normal" childhood, certainly the first five to seven years. This basically dictated my life. My mother was teaching so it was always like, "Who's going to take care of David?"—that kind of vibe. We always had an African American lady helping out at the house who became like a second mother. I remember Rose—she was tall—I can picture her. Ethel was another. They came five days a week from Jamaica in Queens or somewhere like that with the subway, getting there by 7:30 a.m. because my mother had to go to school. My father had already left by then to teach, taking the bus. My mother drove to her school. She taught in Bedford-Stuyvesant for a while, and then when she became an assistant principal, she went to Rockaway, Queens, for years. I was in school till three o'clock and my mother got home at 3:30. When I came home from school, somebody had to meet me, to be there. Paul was nearly five years older, so he was on a different school schedule.

Teachers made a very low wage in those days. Until we had the strikes of the 1960s, teachers were really on a low peg economically. My father worked afternoons—he was in charge of afternoon centers at schools. He worked every summer at camps up in the Catskill Mountains, in upstate New York, where he would be the head counselor. I remember one summer he was in charge of a day camp in Coney Island in Brooklyn. There were always money issues. Not poverty—we had food—but they had to work hard. On the other hand teachers only worked 180 days a year. That's the other thing. A teacher's job was basically considered a kind of a pretty easy scene. This is before kids were coming to school with guns, before New York changed. It was a civil service job and you knew you always had a check. But because I was sick and there was a lot of stuff to do, there was always the thing of "take David to the doctor," and so on. We probably had more expenses than other families. I don't remember the insurance situation, but certainly they were insured because of civil service.

Lew: Your family and you first knew you were sick at an early age?
Dave: Well, the story from what I remember, or what I was told by my mother, goes like this: We were on vacation in Monticello, New York, up in the Catskills, during this summer of 1949. I swam in White Lake up there. One day I got a terrible fever. My mother thought it was something from swimming or being too cold—you know, a childhood type thing. The story is—I don't know if it was the next day or several days—I got out of bed and I just collapsed. A local doctor said: "We have no idea what's going on. You've got to go back to New York." She told me the story that she was going like 100 miles per hour with me laid out in the back seat—flat out!—with my brother, who was seven years old, checking to see if I was still alive. She got a cop to take her over the George Washington Bridge and escort us to Kings County Hospital Center in Brooklyn. It was like, one of these, "Get him in immediately, emergency room!"

Now, I was nearly three years old. Eventually I got transferred to St. Giles Hospital, which no longer exists. In any case, I was in for the next thirteen months. It was nine months for polio, and then I broke my leg in the hospital. I remember the moment I broke my leg. Of course, I'm three years old, so it's not like you remember that part of your life that much, but I do have images. One is of a balloon losing air and me crying about it, which my mother or somebody gave me, tied to the bed post. In the middle of the night I woke up and it was slowly losing air. My brother was not allowed in—he was too young—he would have been eight. I remember once being rolled in the wheelchair to the balcony, or something outdoors, and my brother waving to me from the parking lot.

I was in a ward. There was no private or semiprivate, so I was with others. I'm not sure if they were polio cases. I remember other hospital scenes. I wasn't on that oxygen tank thing that you see—the iron lung—but I do remember things like breaking my leg in the hospital. For some reason I was with another kid in a waiting room and there was a full-length mirror there. I said, "Let's fall"—like a game. Well, I completely broke my leg in the hospital—the one already weak from polio—and had to be in for another four months. That's where the thirteen months comes from. When I got out, my left leg had a full brace from the waist down.

You've got to remember that polio was considered sort of like AIDS in those days. When I did get back—we were living on 14th Street—people wouldn't come near the house. It was considered like a plague or something—even though Franklin D. Roosevelt famously had polio.

Lew: He tried to hide it when he was in office.
Dave: He did. By the fifties polio was more or less over in the United States. The March of Dimes became very important in my life, mostly because of Roosevelt I guess. The last great epidemic was '49 because by '54 they had the Salk vaccine. So, I'm the last of the last to get polio. As I found out, it's a virus—you catch it like a cold. A lot of people got polio in passing, without lasting damage, but in some cases it strikes the nervous system and that's how you get paralyzed. For me it was the left leg. It could have been worse. David Sanborn had something on his left side.

Lew: I didn't know Sanborn . . .
Dave: He had it.

Lew: But you don't see it . . .
Dave: You see the way he plays—you see his shoulder held in a different position than usual. Maybe this kind of pushes the mouthpiece up in a different angle and is partially responsible for the unique sound he gets. I don't know. Now, there's this Post-Polio Syndrome, which is a real thing happening to a lot of folks, a complete reintroduction of the symptoms. In any case, I had it in the left leg, which meant that I could not walk without the help of a full leg brace.

Lew: When you were playing that game with the other kid, you said that you broke your leg?

Dave: I fell down on the left leg, probably because it was weak. I don't know what I was doing without a brace. Maybe they were getting my brace fixed at that moment—I don't remember. But I couldn't walk without a brace. The knee buckled and the left leg couldn't support my weight. The main thing was my left foot pointed out. So, a brace kept my foot in line and gave me support so I could walk.

It was a straight brace up to the thigh. My brace now for the past twenty plus years is around the waist, but it was just the thigh then. I remember we went to an orthopedic shop called Winterkorn, 315 East 83rd Street, in Manhattan, which was always a major scene—we would spend hours there. I could only have one style of shoes for all those years with the brace, as a child. So, of course, shoes were a big thing for me as I got to be a young man and wanted to look good. As a kid I could only have Buster Brown shoes, or at least they seemed that way in my memory, because they were the only ones that fit the brace, until I finally found a guy who made styled orthopedic shoes in Manhattan, but that was much later.

The brace was present until I could have *the* operation that the docs said would get my foot straight and get me walking right. The procedure, quite common in those days for polio leg victims, was arthrodesis, some sort of stabilization of the foot, which would limit movement—I'm still like that—but at least the foot wouldn't point outward. But they couldn't do it until my bones were mature and more or less fully grown, I guess since the procedure limited growth, which is probably why my left foot is half the size of my right. That was supposed to be around twelve or thirteen years old. So, my whole childhood was like "Waiting for Godot," if you get my point. I had several operations because they tried a lot of things—I think three major operations, plus breaking my leg a couple times. But it was always, "You can't really have this operation until you are at least twelve, thirteen years old." I remember the magic day when it came. "You are ready!" I finally had this operation and it did basically make me able to walk without a brace. Then, coming more up to the past decades, I broke my leg yet another time in 1987, which we'll talk about, so I've been back to using a brace, this time around the waist, mainly as protection in case I fall again. Anyway, that was a ten-year period, more or less, with a brace as a kid.

Lew: Now, when you say you had several operations, you mean before that big one?

Dave: Yes. I had at least three. They did a couple of things that I really don't remember. There was a Dr. Dever at Bellevue, the famous Bellevue by the way, which besides being known as a loony hospital was known for rehabilitation. Other doctors were Monroe Schneider, Leo Mayer, and the final guy was Dr. Cooper, who I can remember what he looked like right now—it's amazing how I remember their names. But in my house, for my mother, the doctor was God. On days when we were going to the orthopedist I would be out of my school, going to my mother's school with her all day. At three o'clock we would take off from wherever my mother was teaching and go to Bellevue, where I would see Dr. Dever, who was this mythical heavy guy. When you got off the elevator on this floor there would be a gigantic wall map of the world. This is how I learned geography. I'd be there for hours staring at it with little pins and flags showing where people came from to this place 'cause it was so famous worldwide. That's why I knew where the Philippines were, where Japan was, where Australia was, because I would be there for hours just looking at the damn map, waiting for Dr. Dever to see me, or for me to pull a sandbag, whatever. In those days you pulled a sandbag with your leg for strength as part of physical therapy. My Dad strung one up at home, in fact.

I would go once a month at least, and "Mr. God" would say: "You've got to wait for the operation." It was always with my mother because my father would be working in the after-school centers or taking care of my brother. I remember that look on my mother's face. Here comes God, and God says: "No, not yet!" You know, I could vibe it even though I'm a kid. I didn't know much, but I could see it in her face that she would be crying—that I couldn't walk. The bottom line is that the most resilient stage of your life is your childhood. I mean specifically the whole pain thing. You only start to realize pain when you get older. The fear of pain makes pain worse than it is. Also as a child you're trying to always be Mr. Good Kid.

After an operation, I would be up as fast as I could. "Take the cast off," like I was a star pupil, the gold star for being the best student—well, I'm the best patient. "Oh, you're such a brave young man, David"—you know, that stuff. The nurses, the doctors—you're in the hospital and you get this pat on the head—a reward for being Mr. Brave—you know what I mean? So, I can't tell you that I suffered, that I was in pain, that I had a terrible childhood because I was handicapped. I know how it helped form my personality—that I can tell you because that's psychological stuff that comes later, but I can't tell you that I sat there in anguish and in pain—you know, like a kid in Africa has it a lot worse. I paid dues, I guess. I probably paid more dues than I realized.

Psychologists would have a lot of fun with this stuff—something I never really checked out, by the way.

Lew: I think what you're saying is, even though that's the case, your experience of it as a kid was not "God, this is a horrible life." That's not the way you experienced it, even though you know that you had it rough.
Dave: I am obviously an overachiever. Whether that is the reason or not—maybe I would have been anyway. But I was a star student. I even played ball with the brace. I was like a model kind of cat because I was overcoming everything. So I was a little bit of a superstar because I was able to do things, not letting my handicap get in the way. I was head of the class, president of my class, etc. I was an honor student. The teachers loved me, and, of course, when the music started, I was *the* musician. Truth is, I was on my way to wanting to be a doctor. That's where the whole doctor thing came from, I think, because they were my biggest image of what a powerful and respected person is. Now, this is psychological, I suppose, but this I believe is true. I saw the doctor as the all-knowledgeable saint-God-guru-whatever. Because when he would walk in and say: "Yes, you're going to have the operation," or, "No, you can't," that is probably where I got that from, so I wanted to be a doctor.

Lew: But it wasn't only power, it was also wisdom.
Dave: That's what I mean—he was the *man*. We were going to Mecca to see Allah. My mother looked at it like that. My father was not involved in the everyday thing, but to my mother, Dr. Dever was God because basically he was going to lay down the decision of when I'd have that operation.

I remember he had gray hair, distinguished-like. All these guys would come in with a white coat and stethoscopes hanging around their neck. You're impressed! Plus, they come to your bedside in the hospital before the operation asking: "Is everything okay, David? We're about to put you to sleep." Then in the recovery room—just the whole process you go through as a kid, with the operations, is like, you're a little bit of an army guy— you're like what you look at on TV—you're John Wayne. It all fits—you know what I'm saying? You grow up with this image of, like, "I'm a strong cat," or, "I'm different," or something. In a way, it specialized you. After all, you are paying dues for it. But I only remember it as just kind of happening. I can't say I was happy, but I can't tell you I was terribly upset or despondent. I had pain, yes, and I probably had more pain than I remember. I had a lot of X-rays, which who knows what's going to happen to me eventually because of that. I just don't remember it being an unhappy period, except the thing was that I had to be taken care of, I had to have somebody there, I walked slow—those kinds of things.

Lew: But during those years, you spent a lot of time at your grandparents. I still want to hear more about that.
Dave: Yes. I learned how to play the card game canasta with Nana. I watched a big TV, sat on the couch, listened to singer Kate Smith on the radio—my grandmother loved Kate Smith. TV—*My Little Margie*, *Lucy*, and *Jackie Gleason*. Oh man—I loved Jackie then. Sunday was *Ed Sullivan*, Saturday, *Perry Como*, I think. TV was a big part of my life. There is no question I watched a lot of TV. That was the fifties when it was new. Not music. And when I was six, seven, eight, etc., I didn't play that much ball, though later I did more. TV was a big part of my daily existence early on.

Lew: I guess you were home more than some other kids would be, inside.
Dave: I was usually in school. But when I would have operations I would be home for months at a time. That happened several times in my childhood. When I went to school, of course the teachers knew my situation, but I just remember being normal as far as I was concerned.

Lew: And Sam and Carrie—what would they do? How would they treat you?
Dave: They were very Jewish; in fact, kosher Jewish, which is even more so. You know, Passover is a four-hour meal, mostly read in Hebrew the whole way. My grandmother, she loved me. She made French fries for me, turning every one to get them evenly cooked, and soft scrambled eggs, which I loved. Food, food, food! She was a housewife, so she was always home. Poppy was eventually retired from his clothier business, and he would just sit on the couch. From what my mother said, Poppy was a rough kind of guy, not abusive but a bit cold. I don't know, but with me, he would just grab me and say, "Butterball, butterball," and I would be on his lap. That's all I remember from him—I guess a cigar also. I was very close to my grandmother because she was around a lot, and she and my mother had a lot of interaction.

Lew: Poppy, Sam Gottdiener, died when you were in the hospital?

Dave: I don't remember that, but it happened sometime in the six-seven-eight-nine-year-old range for me, I think. I remember him from early childhood, not from later.

Lew: So, you would still go over there, but Carrie—Nana—was just by herself then.
Dave: Yes, alone on Avenue O in Brooklyn. It was an apartment house. I can picture the elevator and the lobby of the apartment building like it was yesterday. Some things stay forever in your mind from the early days.

Lew: But you were a butterball—you were chubby?
Dave: I was chubby until about thirteen or fourteen years old. Then I decided to stop eating bread and cake for one summer, July and August. I wanted to lose weight and it worked.

Lew: Now, you said, the March of Dimes . . .
Dave: Well, the March of Dimes was a big thing because of what my mother did. She was famous for this. She collected $20,000 in dimes ringing door-to-door in Brooklyn. She became the head of the Brooklyn chapter. She went into it when I got polio. My mother was very dynamic. She was one of those real hustling, strong type women. There is a picture of me from the *New York Times*, November 10, 1951, with Justice William O. Douglas, the chief of the Supreme Court. I was the banner boy for Brooklyn for the March of Dimes and in the picture I'm with the banner children from the other boroughs. Justice Douglas had had polio at age three, and he supported the March of Dimes. I have a little suit on. I'm five, and the text underneath says that after thirteen months in the hospital I told Douglas "I can go to school by myself now." I seem to remember another one, I guess from another New York newspaper, where my mother is in the picture and it's "Frances Liebman raised $20,000." Mom was like a movie star because she did this. This was the folklore—this is what I heard.

So, the March of Dimes was always a big thing because of FDR. In my house, guess who the great hero of life was? In fact, Lewis, I used to carry a picture with me in my wallet of Roosevelt, a rare one of him with crutches, from 1924. Unfortunately I lost my wallet recently. My mother's rap was: "Look what he did. You can do it, too." I remember when we went to visit his home in Hyde Park, New York, it was like going to Mecca. Plus the Jews loved Roosevelt—you know, the whole Democrat thing.

My grandparents on my Mom's side were religious, but not on my Dad's. I did go to Hebrew school, to a Reform temple in Brooklyn, Temple Ahavath Shalom. I was bar mitzvahed and went twice a week to Hebrew school as well as Sunday school.

My father was—I'm not sure how you would call it—agnostic or whatever. He had no use for religion because, as far as he was concerned, it was a sham. The thing about my father was that he was a very straight-ahead guy, and he just hated phoniness of any sort, period. Lying, cheating—I mean, if you lied, that was the worst thing you could do. If I or my brother lied, that was when he got a little heavy with us. That was a big one. Honesty was a big thing with my father. As far as he was concerned, the whole religious thing was bull and a kind of rip-off of people. So, we were not brought up with any kind of strong religious thing.

Of course, when we went to my grandparents, we would do Passover and so on for the holidays. I was actually very good in Hebrew school. Good enough that the rabbi came on pretty strong to me and my mother at the *talk*. You know, when you get bar mitzvahed, you go into the rabbi's study when you're about three weeks from the bar mitzvah. You're deep into learning your haftorah—the section from the Bible that you recite—'cause you don't want to screw up on the biggest day of your life so far with everyone watching. "So, David, we would really love you to continue on in Hebrew school." And my mother is, "Yeah, go on." In fact, she's even thinking, "Now you're thirteen and high school is on the horizon—maybe you can go to yeshiva," which is a kind of private Jewish high school, "because you get a good education there." I say, "Mom, I can't take this Hebrew crap." I just didn't like the language. "I can't spend my life reading this language—it's just out of the question." Rabbi Alexander Steinbach says—I'm paraphrasing him of course— "You should continue. You have a strong thing—you're a good kid, you're a good student." And he was a famous rabbi who was high up in the Reform movement and wrote some books (among them *Prayer—A Pillar of Our Faith*, 1943, and *Faith and Love*, 1959). The temple was on Avenue R at 16th Street in Flatbush near where we lived. It was very beautiful with stained glass, an organ, singing, and women and men sitting together. (The temple is now in a different location, but the old building still exists and is the Prospect Park Yeshiva.) You didn't have to wear a yarmulke. In any case that was the end of my religious thing.

With learning in general I really dug the history stuff as a kid, Jewish history, American History, whatever. I read a lot of history biographies. With the Jewish thing, Abraham, Moses, King David, and, of course, my name is David so I felt a connection! I mean in my imagination I'm King David, slaying Goliath, playing harp. I was right in there, man!

Lew: So, your Mom—was she a little more religious than your Dad, would you say?
Dave: No. We did what was necessary. It was not a big thing. Hebrew school was around three o'clock in the afternoon two days a week after regular school. Sunday school, I think, eleven to one, which was more history than the Hebrew stuff during the week. You get going when you're about nine or ten. I remember when I was having an operation or something for my leg, I had special instruction—maybe when I broke it around thirteen years old—not sure. Someone had to come to the house and train me to get me up to speed for my bar mitzvah. Actually, when I was out of regular school I had home instruction. Remember, in those days when you were sick or not in school the parents had to take care you were getting educated by law. They came to your house two or three days a week. Rose or Ethel, whoever was helping us at the time, would let the teacher in at ten o'clock in the morning.

Lew: What were your mother and Dad teaching? What ages? Do you know anything about that?
Dave: They were both elementary level. My mother had first grade with young kids. For a large part, she was in Bedford-Stuyvesant, a complete black neighborhood, and later to Rockaway in Queens when she became an assistant principal. My father was a sixth-grade teacher—I'm not sure whether he taught English or math. He eventually also became an assistant principal and went to a junior high school in Brooklyn—Ditmas Junior High.

I remember the big thing in their professional life was "when are you going to take the exam?" *The exam.* Because the thing was, when you were a principal or assistant principal, you made more money than teaching. So someone was always studying for the big test. My father never really dug it. I remember when he was at Ditmas, he was responsible for scheduling. For the whole summer, there were these gigantic charts of classes and times on the table in the dining room, and he hated it. Plus he had a real asshole principal as his boss. My mother would say: "You've got to become a principal," and he'd say, "I don't want any more of this. Y'all got it?" That's my wording of course, not his! My father was very laid back; he didn't want to deal with it.

Leo was known as a great disciplinarian and, as I said, he ran the afternoon sports activities, playing basketball a lot. He would take care of the kids in the gym. In those days elementary schools often had afternoon things happening. He had a little posse of teacher friends who called themselves the Ben Franklin Society. They would have meetings every month at the house and shoot the breeze about the business. These were his best friends. The wives would have coffee and sit and kibitz (chat). My brother Paul and I would sit at the table while they talked about the system and teaching and so on. It wasn't an official society. They called it Ben Franklin because they loved Ben Franklin; they respected the man.

Lew: It was more like a social thing?
Dave: Yeah. It was made up of these guys who were also principals, assistant principals, teachers. It was a men's club. Let's see—Fred Greenbaum, Sid Glassman, Sam Romm—I remember them; I remember their faces.

Lew: You were welcome to sit with them?
Dave: Until bedtime. They'd shoot the breeze, and have cigars, coffee, and cake. Maybe a little nip of scotch, and that would be it. No beer, nothing like that—these were intellectuals. They were into politics and Democratic stuff. Adlai Stevenson was a big hero to these guys. He was their man; he was one of them. When Adlai Stevenson was running in '56 against Eisenhower, it was like one of them was in there. It was a big thing. I was ten years old then and I still remember these discussions today.

Here's an unrelated story about my Dad and teaching—my brother told me this story: My father was known to be good at controlling the kids' behavior. It wasn't gang war like it became in the seventies or eighties, but the kids were rough in his school in Borough Park. Some of the kids were like six-foot-nine, and he's five-ten or something. He was tall but not that tall. The first few weeks of school he would talk very softly. These guys couldn't hear what he was saying, so everybody would be leaning over, being quiet because they didn't want to miss anything important. It's human nature, especially at the beginning of a relationship with someone in authority like a teacher. Sure enough, after a couple of weeks, he would have them in his hands. As well, he could get tough so that they didn't give him any crap. Anyway, this is one of my great music lessons about playing soft, meaning that when you do that, you bring extra attention to yourself because everyone is going to want to hear what you are playing.

My father was very respected as a teacher and everybody loved him. He wasn't a macho guy, not like that. He could fix everything and was very mechanical—a kind of a street guy as it ends up, growing up in East Harlem. As a child he was the Jew who got beat up by the big guys. He wore glasses at a young age—they called him "four-eyes." He was bald pretty early, like me. He had something going on with the street—a certain kind of thing about him. But he was the nicest guy and would and could talk to anybody, whatever the topic—educated, well mannered, quiet, humorous, rarely raising his voice. When he punished us, it was very official, not an emotional issue. He did not get overly involved with it. He just made you aware that you had broken some ethical rule. He was a disciplinarian in the old-fashioned way if you did anything really wrong. But I remember it was only a few times that it happened, usually because I lied to my mother or something like that. Now, my mother, on the other hand, was a little more emotional. My father would just say, "Take it easy, sister, take it easy." Truth is, my mother had a lot of things to be worried about. She was a working woman, I was sick, the bills, you know—she was a tough cookie. People loved her—she was Miss Social—we had a lot of dinner parties—the dining room taken over. She would make roast chicken with pink rice that she had a recipe for—a typical Jewish cook. In general Jewish people weren't known for their culinary skills. But she had these dinner parties. We always had people around. She was president of my school's PTA—Parents Teachers Association—as well as the secretary or treasurer of our own family association, which was very common in those days coming from the immigrants landing in the States. It was called the B. Feldman Benevolent Association. It was made up of the family that came over from the old country.

The B. Feldman group was the first family organization to be chartered by New York State. In fact, where they're all buried in Queens is a family plot. That's where I go to see my parents' graves. On my father's side was the Caminetz Family Association. Jews belonged to family associations by and large, which were linked by tradition to what were basically burial groups, something you would find in a lot of cultures.

Feldman had nothing to do with Gottdiener directly, but there was some relationship through marriage or whatever, and somehow Gottdiener was part of the Feldmans, and Liebman was part of the Caminetz. I don't really understand it and never did. It's a tribe. When they came over from the old country, they formed an association to help each other financially, to socialize, and probably also to get the marriages going. You know, Jews should marry Jews, etc. As an officer my mother was always doing stuff for the B. Feldman Association, taking care of their plots at the cemetery, lining things up, and so on. Plus she had the March of Dimes and the PTA. She was one of these wonder women doing a million things, a real workaholic—probably where I get that from.

Lew: Tell us about your brother Paul.
Dave: He's around still, but he's out of communication with the whole family as we speak now, or what is left of it, which is my nieces, his daughters. He's a very bright guy who throughout his life had all kinds of businesses and did big-time gambling for a bit. It seemed to me he was always trying to beat the system. He was a hard worker at whatever he did, but with a very autocratic kind of personality, and went through several marriages. I tend to see people in some ways as a product of their times and to me my brother was a casualty of the fifties. He was a teenager in that decade and to me the '50s were a very repressive time. We know it now—strict is not even a strong enough word. It was a very conservative era. People were just getting back from the war, putting their stuff together; America was just really becoming the big power that it became.

People could finally own a home, the two-car garage, the whole advent of suburbs. By repressive I mean that if you were a teenager in the fifties, you had to be playing some kind of lying game. Lying about sexual things for sure. This is why the sixties happened—because of the fifties. I mean, in the late fifties there was Elvis, an out and out symbol of sex, wigglin' those hips and so forth—the bad boy. Why the Beatles with that long hair—as innocent as they look now? Not to mention the drugs, Vietnam, and everything like that—the whole hippie thing that happened. The '60s was in a way a reaction to the '50s. My brother, I believe, was a product of repression—not from my parents, not that way, but from the culture. I think he couldn't find his way out. In any case he had a gambling problem and his whole life seemed to be a search to make money, to outsmart the system. His drug was gambling, which broke up his marriages. My mother had to bail him out many times financially. At one point "they" were going to break his legs or whatever. It started with bowling, at which he was very good. He won tournaments or whatever.

Paul went to Brooklyn Technical High School. He was a good student. You couldn't get into Brooklyn Tech unless you were an A student, like Stuyvesant High School in Manhattan, and where you went, Lewis, the Bronx High School of Science. They were the three original technical schools for which you had to take a test, ostensibly looking toward engineering. No girls allowed! Meanwhile, he gets into bowling—I guess the team at Brooklyn Tech—and becomes a champion, like near 300-score stuff, the real deal. He competed in Albany for New York State and won something. But bowling alleys then were not the little social thing that they are now, where you take your date out and so on. They were where gamblers and the bros from the race track hung out. Eventually he became a guy to gamble on, meaning they were betting on him. So at sixteen, seventeen, already he was staying all night at bowling alleys. This is when the big split happened with my parents, and my father basically threw him out of the house around that time—not officially, but like that.

I remember plates being thrown. I'm eleven, twelve. He even hocked my alto sax at one point—no big loss, though. Meanwhile, he's at Brooklyn Tech, and then he goes to Brooklyn College for accounting, gets a degree in teaching, marries a girl, has two kids quickly, and then they're divorced. His life was by then a constant scene because of gambling. Nobody acknowledged it was an addiction then, but basically that's what it was. For him the track was the name of the game in life. I was a teenager and I didn't know what it was, but I could see he was really excited. He would put down a bet, check the paper, buzz around, etc. When I went with him one afternoon during the summer, I could see this is a different kind of environment because of the look on the faces there. This wasn't watching horse racing on television—this was the real deal. That's when I first got a glimpse that my brother was very different from me. Then I realized where the problems came from between him and our parents.

It was that way until the day my mother died—war and peace. With regard to what happened, my father had no use for my brother once he went to the dark side. You see, to my father, because of his honesty/work ethic thing, what my brother did was the lowest of the low, meaning the gambling. I mean, it probably would have been better if he had murdered somebody. They basically stopped their relationship somewhere around when Paul was sixteen, seventeen. I don't know if they ever talked or if they just acknowledged each other from then on. I think my brother might have thought of himself as some kind of big shot wannabe. He dressed like Mafia guys with the white sneakers, the jewelry, and so on. Like I said before, the Italian cats in our hood were always cool—so we thought. Then, it comes out somehow later on in my life that maybe my brother was suffering because I got all of the attention. You know the scenario: David got all of the attention because of polio, putting my brother in second place at eight years old. So he was psychologically injured for the rest of his life and never had the attention that a young boy should have, and therefore he was a victim. Maybe it's true. Who knows? Yes, it's true that I got a lot of attention, but it was no picnic for me either.

Lew: Now, with the five-year difference, how close did you feel with him?
Dave: We were not close. You know, older brother stuff. Some rough and tumbling, stuff like that. The closest we ever became was when he found out that Miles Davis dug Sly Stone, whom Paul liked, and since I played with Miles Davis, he could brag. When he saw me at Carnegie Hall in the seventies with Miles, suddenly he realized—this was much later, of course, than the days I am talking about—that I was some sort of personality, that I was some sort of whatever famous is. "My brother plays with Miles Davis," and so on. At that time I'm in my late twenties so we had some kind of relationship for a minute there. But he's a hard person to be around. Now he doesn't talk to his family. He's got two girls who have families of their own and he doesn't talk to anyone—a strange guy who always seemed to have problems, especially financially. He was bright with some attractive qualities I guess. He always had beautiful girls, which after all was part of his M.O. He could be very charming, obviously athletic and all that. But to my mind Paul was basically a classic underachiever. He just didn't want to do what you had to do. That's my take on it.

Lew: Did he stay around New York?
Dave: No. He moved to Jersey, Philly, Florida, like that. He was divorced, married again, a few times starting over—always a drama. I mean, my life is comparatively straight. He tried businesses—a restaurant, drove a cab, had a carpet store. He went in and out of being a teacher.

He had rheumatic fever as a teenager, which was just another thing for my mother to deal with—but no lasting damage. I can't say that he was a big part of my life or that he had any direct influence on me outside of any casual older brother stuff, because once the gambling and the problems started, he was just always doing something with money, money, money. My mother was into it with him, always about money. You know, her generation had a big thing about bread because of the Depression and all that. It was always a big topic in our house.

With Paul, it was never-ending—her bailing him out, him not paying, him needing money, him owing her money—I mean, it never ended with money. In fact, when I started my band Lookout Farm, I needed a van. My mother said, "I'll give you $15,000 because Paul has gotten hundreds of thousands of dollars over the years. In the will you'll be compensated." This didn't happen, but she did keep a complete book of every dime that went out of that house. He took a hundred or two hundred thousand over the years. You see, when my parents retired, they did very well with the pension stuff. Somehow even though teachers were underpaid, something in their negotiation with New York City led to great retirement benefits. I mean their generation ended up populating Florida with their money. Also they were the first to invest in bonds and things like that, which did very well in the '70s and '80s. My mother made hundreds of thousands of dollars because she kept bonds for thirty years. By the time the nineties came, she had a couple hundred grand because she had done this dealing in the seventies. That generation—that's what they did. They lived off of their retirement funds. That's the end of that now, as we know. We're not going to be able to do that because everything has changed.

Lew: They moved to Florida . . .
Dave: Eventually they started becoming "snowbirds" (people who escape the snowy northern winter by going down South), maybe in the seventies, going down in February. After my father died on January 12, 1986, Mom moved to Florida full time. He died from Alzheimer's at just about the time they were finally beginning to call it that. That was a disaster and drove my mother crazy—nobody knew what it was. We would yell at him, "What's wrong with you, Dad?" It wasn't pity; it was like "Something's wrong with you." He'd get lost in the neighborhood. It was very, very sad. By the time he died, it was a relief for my Mom especially. She recovered and hung in Florida. But she had another twenty years of life with a few male companions after my father passed. After all, she was good looking and active, the star of the show; everyone wanted to be with her.

She died September 2005, at ninety-two—until the end, a very strong-willed personality. She was from that special World War II generation. Like what Tom Brokaw wrote about in his book *The Greatest Generation*. My parents weren't in the war because teachers got exempted, but they were a product of the Depression, and that explains everything. Again, here we are back to context, the milieu that people live in. Teaching jobs were civil service jobs, and they were glad to have a steady job. If you had a civil service job in those years you were in good shape. They had money problems, so they had to work hard. They just didn't tolerate much. I mean, they were tough people, real survivors.

Like I said, my mother was a tough cookie on everybody around her. You loved her, but you also had to maintain a distance. Forget about bringing any women into the house! Especially if they weren't Jewish, which most times they weren't. Suddenly my mother was religious or something. Basically, who could ever be your son's wife unless their family were millionaires, and then Mom would be happy—you know what I mean? Look, I was supposed to be a doctor. There was constantly innuendo in this culture implying "not good enough." Jewish mothers—it's not just a thing, it's true. There comes a time when you've got to cool them out. We know this, Lewis. It has terrible negative aspects, this stifling kind of love. You just wish they could be your friend and tolerate you becoming an adult. But they can't. They are too tied umbilically to you and to what you become. That's why the doctor/lawyer thing is so important to them. It was part of the dream to have their son be a doctor and make a lot of money.

Lew: What age were you when you first started thinking about being a doctor?
Dave: Ten, eleven years old. I started reading books—especially *Understanding Surgery*, a pocket book edited by Robert E. Rothenberg. I read it from cover to cover. I knew what kind of anesthesia to use—I was into it.

Lew: And what got you interested? Going to see the doctor? Did your parents ever say to you, "You should do this?" Did it come up explicitly?
Dave: Implicitly—what I just said. That's what I mean. Jewish families wanted their sons to be a doctor: "My son, the doctor." And whether it was said or not, there was of course, the "you're going to go to college" bit. By the way, when the music started happening and I started playing gigs at thirteen or fourteen years old, it was with positive reinforcement from my mother: "You'll earn money on the weekend to get yourself through medical school." This was the premise.

Lew: As opposed to "this is your main thing"?
Dave: Music is just a hobby. But you can make money from it, so it's even better than a hobby. The whole premise of your life was leading toward going to medical school. The truth is that at that stage, around eleven to thirteen years old, I did want to be an orthopedic surgeon. What else? After all, those are the guys I knew—like I described, the guy in the white coat who had all the answers. The truth is if it wasn't for Coltrane, I probably would have been a doctor. I would have been a damn good

doctor—I know I could have been. Years later, when I had a stage we'll get to, considering becoming a lawyer in the eighties, part of it was: "You know what? I could have been good. I'm good at other things. I know I am." I could have done other things. Sure enough, when sometimes things weren't going great with the music, I would say to my mother, "I'm struggling a little bit," and she would say: "You should have done that. You would have been great. You should have done that." And sometimes I would say: "You know what, Mom? You're not wrong." Sometimes parents know best, in some ways that you don't consider.

Lew: So, you got into music how?
Dave: Piano lessons, because it was *de rigueur*. That's what a young person did in a Jewish home. There was always a piano in the living room in Jewish homes and in this case my mother played piano as a hobby—she played classical. We had an upright piano.

Lew: You don't remember a name on the piano—what brand?
Dave: Aeolian or Acrosonic? She would play "Für Elise." She took lessons as a kid. Once in a while, she would sit down—not every day, just once in a while. My father, he liked to sing along with Caruso—and he loved Tchaikovsky, I remember. I have the LP still—*Tchaikovsky's Fourth Symphony* with Toscanini on the cover conducting the New York Philharmonic. He liked to listen to classical. Meanwhile I loved early rock and roll. I cannot tell you where it started, but I was so into it that I had my own *Top 25* list of the week. I still have the lists, like: "Jerry Lee Lewis moved from three to one." I was a fanatic. I collected forty-fives. My very oldest friend has them now. I was a rock-and-roll freak and Elvis Presley was my number-one hero.

Lew: Now, around what age would you say this was?
Dave: This is "Heartbreak Hotel," "Rock Around the Clock"—eight years old, I guess, in '54, '55—the beginning of rock and roll. Maybe it was because I was sick, because of the radio—I don't know. Martin Block's *Make Believe Ballroom* was a big radio show for me. I didn't find out until later that Martin Block used to do big dances and stuff in the thirties and forties. I didn't know anything about it. On Saturday he used to have the *Top 25* and I listened to it from nine to twelve in the morning. And then of course all of the early groups, like the Monotones, the Del-Vikings, "Earth Angel" with the Penguins, etc. This is when I first heard the tenor saxophone because a lot of these singles had little

solos: "Come Go with Me" (sings tune), then "Earth Angel" (sings tune), which was my brother's favorite song.

We were rock and rolled out. That's where it came from. I loved the tenor sax. I'm sure I said, "I want to play the tenor sax." My mother says: "You've got to take two years of piano before you can play any instrument of your choice." Now, this is nine or ten years old. I started piano lessons with a neighborhood teacher, Luba Galperin. "Luba the tuba" I used to call her—big old Russian. I did "Für Elise," "Spinning Song," Mozart, and all that. I practiced every day. No big deal, no great talent, but I played the pieces. Finally after two years, because my mother would always tell this story, I said, "A deal's a deal." I continued for one more year, and then finally got to saxophone—well actually the clarinet, which we'll get to as part of the story. The main point was, I remember her saying that if you know the piano, you will understand music. You have to remember that in the Jewish home, music had a certain significance. That's why so many violin players, clarinet, etc., are Jewish. Music meant culture, pure and simple. Classical music was culture—it was part of the European tradition. You were being cultured when you studied music. Remember, basically Jews did not excel in sports. That was the thing—music had a place in that milieu of high culture.

Lew: Were you a radio listener in general before rock, or was that what got you into it?
Dave: Radio was on a lot in those days because they didn't have TV in the kitchen. There was one TV in the living room, which couldn't be moved because it was gigantic, like a piece of furniture. But in everybody's kitchen there was a radio. It wasn't news or talk shows in those days. It was dramas like the *Saga of Helen Trent* or whatever. These were daytime programs that would be on like a series. And music—Kate Smith—she was this big chick singer who went to television eventually. And of course, Lawrence Welk. This was what we grew up with. Music was like fine culture. We didn't have wine—remember, Jews didn't drink by and large. Music was the THING. If religion wasn't a big deal, which in our house it wasn't, what linked you to European culture? Bach. Mozart. Beethoven. Brahms. So, piano was a cultural thing as well as a hobby.

Lew: And the teacher, she would come to your place?
Dave: No. I went to Miss Galperin's. It was on 9th Street, between Avenues K and L, right across from the schoolyard of P.S. 99, where I went to elementary school. I would do an hour lesson once a week and took

part in little concerts and recitals. But I wanted that tenor from rock and roll, that solo on "Rock Around the Clock," the stuff that Duane Eddy's saxophonist was playing, and so on. Piano went on for two to three years. And, thank God. It was the absolute best decision ever in my life that anybody ever made for me. To this day, thank you, Mom. Because without that, I wouldn't be the musician I am, or maybe not even be in music.

Lew: That's how you can see the superimposed triads?
Dave: To say the least! That's right, exactly. Music is very visual for me through the keyboard.

Lew: So, you got the sax. I mean, she was good for her word.
Dave: Finally, yes, but clarinet first, because of the belief in those days that you had to play clarinet before saxophone because it was harder.

Lew: She actually said this?
Dave: She called somebody. The teacher said it's advisable to start on clarinet first because I'm going to play clarinet at some point. I don't know where this philosophy came from, where we were suddenly playing "doubles" at twelve years old. I mean, I wasn't even going to be a musician. I just wanted to play saxophone! I ended up at a little neighborhood school run by this family, the Bromleys, on 17th Street, between Cortelyou and Beverley Roads in Brooklyn. Faye Bromley, the mother, just died, but I spoke to her throughout the last years when she lived with her son. She was always happy to talk to me because, after all, I was one of the students from the school who went on to have a life in music. I spent all Saturday mornings there for the next few years from age twelve or thirteen—three lessons, eventually. First, clarinet/saxophone with Nat Shapiro, who sure enough started me on clarinet and then eventually saxophone. The second hour, I went to piano with Mr. Buster Bromley and learned chords. And the third hour was combo, with the son, Eric Bromley, who eventually went to Juilliard but ultimately didn't pursue a career in music. He played good, I remember, and was the first guy I saw play jazz. He would have all of the kids together in a combo and we would play from these books called Combo Orks, which were little half books with standard tunes—"I'm in the Mood for Love," I remember—all of the harmony written out, so three saxophones could play in thirds and everything.

Lew: Who would be in this combo?
Dave: Neighborhood kids. I don't remember any of them.

Lew: How about instrumentation?
Dave: Drummer, piano player, saxophones, trumpet maybe—you know, twelve-year-olds. Between combos on the hour Eric and his assistant would play, he on the saxophone and his assistant on drums. They would just start burning out. Now I'm putting my horn away or getting ready for my lesson, or my parents are picking me up, or I'm waiting for the next kids to come in, etc. I was mystified because it was the first time I saw anybody move their fingers without music in front of them.

This is really what it comes down to. In the end, something that gets your interest as a kid is usually about speed, energy. It's not that he played great deep lines with fantastic harmony. I wouldn't know what a great line was anyway, at that point. But here's a guy, eyes closed, no sheet music, and fast! That was the first jazz I saw, around twelve/thirteen years old. This is just me seeing it in this little break between classes. I was pretty good, I guess, and got to know him. So this is my Saturday mornings, nine to twelve, every Saturday.

Lew: Because you were into rock so much before you took up the sax, did you try playing a few of those tunes?
Dave: No. I never played them, and I never even realized that most of rock in those days was blues. I didn't realize that "Hound Dog" was a blues or that other tunes from that period were. I didn't even know what a blues was although I was singing Elvis tunes. I once sang Tennessee Ernie Ford's "Sixteen Tons" at an assembly in the fourth grade—a capella! I was into this rock stuff big time. I knew every word, but I didn't know anything was a blues.

Lew: And you didn't really have the concept that "I'm going to learn this at the piano."
Dave: No, and it wasn't like I wanted to be in a rock band, but I did get into this combo thing. It's a cute story. Mrs. Bromley used to get the students gigs at resorts in the Catskills in upstate New York. At thirteen years old, during July and August 1959, I played at a hotel in the mountains as a professional musician making $15 a week with my first band, which remained together for the next six years. The other guys were one year older than me—they were fourteen. The piano player was Mike Garson, the drummer was Bobby Katz—he's a psychiatrist in New York now—and the bass player was Gary Zehner, who committed suicide much later on. I'm still in touch with Garson, who played a lot with David Bowie and other rock groups, getting a rep as like the Cecil Taylor

of rock pianists or something like that. He lives in L.A. He's the first guy I ever really played jazz with. Somehow we formed this group and Mrs. Bromley got us a job at the Cedar Hill Hotel, which was really a bungalow colony in South Fallsburg, New York. We slept two to a bed, two beds to a room, and played in a small hall for the bungalow colony every night for an hour and a half.

People danced and schmoozed—on Friday and Saturday there was a show. That was when I first started to read show music for a comedian and singer. It was called "cutting a show." Of course, we were at the lowest level. This wasn't the Concord or Grossingers, the big hotels in the Catskills, but we were working in this top resort area for an absolutely Jewish clientele. So, here I am, sort of making money, playing in a tuxedo already—and joining the union. My mother took me to 52nd Street, up to the Musicians' Union, the famous Local 802, which is today on 48th Street. "My son wants to join the union." The guy goes, like, "How old is he?" "Fourteen." "Hmm, okay. Play a song." I think I played "The Lady Is a Tramp." He says: "Play a C major scale." I did it. "Okay. That's $120. You're in the union." I was in the union at fourteen years old! Imagine, now I'm getting an identity— I'm a person. I'm not a sports guy, I'm not a gang guy, I'm a professional musician at fourteen years old— man!

Lew: As far as getting your first band together . . .
Dave: I remember meeting Mike Garson very clearly. This has got to be the beginning of high school, so I am thirteen or fourteen. A friend of mine invited me to his audition with a rock band in the 'hood. I even remember the name of the drummer, Steve Gittleman. They were kind of rough-and-tough guys. My friend Elliot played first and then somehow I took his horn and got the job. He never let me forget that. So, I joined this first little band and the piano player was Mike Garson. By now, I had been in Bromley Studios in a combo for a while and I knew something. I knew that the piano player doesn't play the melody with you—they comp! C-o-m-p (accompany with chords). So we're playing and Mike's playing the melody with me. I go, "Mike, you don't do this." And he said, "Well, what do I do?" I said: "You comp." He said: "What do you mean?" Remember, I played piano a bit, so I showed him. That was the beginning of our relationship. He was my first close musical friend.

Gary and Bobby came through Mike. When Mrs. Bromley got me the gig, we named it the Impromptu Quartet. My first band—what a name. Now I needed a stage name. This is the time when everyone changed their names, especially in the fifties, 'cause you didn't want to have an easily identifiable name as a Jew. So, I thought, David Liebman sounds a little too square and I needed a calling card saying something like "Music for All Occasions," with my address and phone number. After all, this is part of being in the union and being a big shot, right? I picked "David Leeds." So, my first card is "David Leeds, Music for All Occasions." I'm fourteen and I've got my own card. It's classic.

Lew: So, you're up in the Catskills and you're playing for shows. Do these cats, the comedian or whatever, do they come with music and give it to you?

Dave: Yes, yes. You rehearse at four in the afternoon and play the show at night. They're doing three or four of them in the night, basically going from one to the other in this area, nine o'clock there, maybe eleven at another place.

They're carrying tattered music, handwritten, Scotch-taped, food all over it. Of course there's a lot of ethnic music, especially the Jewish thing with the clarinet. I'm already playing flute by then also. We worked the Catskills for the next five, six years, going up the line to better hotels as we got better. The Catskills is a whole other story in itself because that's really where I first started playing jazz on nights off and after the gig. That's where I first heard Arnie Lawrence play and Eddie Daniels, to name two known guys on the sax, because they were in the big hotels. We would go afterward to a club or a bar and cats would be playing. After the gig, when people were gone, they would jam, sometimes in the nightclub itself. These were New York–based musicians, up-and-coming jazz/studio-type players.

They would jam for themselves and anybody hanging out. There was a famous jam session every Thursday night at the Homowack Hotel in Ellenville or maybe nearby Spring Glen, New York. The nightclub would stay open, and Arnie Lawrence, who was the leader of the show band at the Homowack, led the jam session. I remember trying to sit in, which finally happened one summer. This was really the beginning for me, hearing live jazz right in front of my eyes with the other young cats.

We couldn't wait to play. We were a little clique. Trumpeter Steve Satten was one of the first guys I worked a lot with, and pianist Mitch Kerper, drummer Donny Fried, who sang real well. These were all talented guys from New York with whom I played in the Catskills, and around New York we played club dates (private parties, bar mitzvahs, weddings; known as "casuals" in L.A. and as G.B.—general business gigs—in Boston). We were also playing jazz and trying to figure it out. These were my hanging buds in these years. Afterward you would end up at an all-night diner. I always had French toast and a Coca-Cola, getting a reputation for wolfing it down in under two minutes. What a life!

Lew: So, you went to the Catskills during the summers for six years, from 1959 through the summer of 1965?
Dave: Not only that but weekends because the season started at Passover and went through Yom Kippur. So, you were there almost every weekend from April through October. It was a way of life. Friday afternoon, after school, we would drive up—can't remember who drove— getting there in time for the show. On Saturday night you would split after the gig and everybody would meet on Route 17 at the Big Apple rest stop and have coffee, getting back to the city by around three or four in the morning. This was really a way of making a living. In the summers you lived there full-time, from basically July 4th weekend. The four of us shared a room, two to a bed. Your last night was Labor Day eve. Everybody would go home on Labor Day, that Monday. The highway was mobbed. It was the end of the summer because regular school started the next day in New York.

Lew: So, the roads would be full of all the vacationers going home.
Dave: For sure. Folks who had spent the whole summer in the Catskills were most of them. A lot of people were there for the whole summer. The husbands worked in the city and came up on the weekends while the mothers would take the kids, who would be in these day camps, which is where my father worked during summers when I was a kid. Remember, teachers had the summer off, so we would be up there with the family all summer. My father was in charge of the day camp at a hotel and my mother would do arts and crafts. So, I was in the Catskills already as a kid in the summers before the music thing started. This was one of the advantages of being a schoolteacher in New York—you had the whole summer off. From age eight to when I started playing, it was like another home for me to go to the Catskills in the summer time.

Lew: Now, would you be in the camp when you were younger?
Dave: Sure. The big thing for me was swimming. Here we go with Franklin Roosevelt again. The best thing you could do for physical therapy was swim. I remember in my early summers—this is five, six, seven years old—my mother took me to Brighton Beach in Coney Island, near where we lived, every day. Often at seven in the morning I would take swimming lessons. When you see a picture of Brighton Beach with those chairs lined up, that's us. You would have a cabana—a place to put your

clothes, a shower stall, whatever—and you could lock your stuff up in a locker. We spent all day there because she wanted me to swim. At some point when I was about ten or eleven, we went to Florida for the whole summer so that I could *really* swim because there you could swim five, six hours a day and you didn't get cold. In the Catskills you got cold quickly because the water was basically freezing most of the year. I remember Florida well because I was in bad shape that summer. I couldn't walk too well; things weren't good for my leg. Sure enough, in Florida that summer I swam six to eight hours a day. We stayed at a motel called the Garden of Allah around 64th Street off of Collins Avenue in Miami Beach. The big thing was that I could swim as much as possible—swim, swim, swim.

My mother said I got much better. Look, I could move my legs in the water, which has to be good. The whole belief with rehabilitation was that it was just a matter of getting strength back. Oh sure, there was the *big* operation to really fix it up, but physical therapy was considered a cure for everything. The rap was your muscles are just weak, they're not nonexistent; they're just weak, so, therefore, physical therapy. I had a sandbag in my bedroom, rigged up by my father with a pulley screwed into the wall under the window. I would attach the rope to my leg, lying in bed across the room, and I would pull up the sandbag, like a couple of feet if I could—anything to get my leg working. So, swimming was also a big part of my summers and a big goal of my parents.

Lew: So, your Mom ran the arts and crafts.
Dave: Yeah. When my brother got older, he would be a counselor. Otherwise, he was also a camper. I remember one place—the Mayfair Hotel.

Lew: That's where the camp was?
Dave: That's one I remember. There were camps that had Jewish-themed activities, but we weren't part of that. This had nothing to do with that. These were hotels where mothers and children basically stayed for the whole summer. The fathers would come up on Friday and leave on Sunday. You know, they had their day gigs. My first girlfriend was up there, not counting Liliane Mager, my first crush in elementary school. I learned to dance in the Catskills. It was a big part of my upbringing.

Lew: You remember that first girlfriend?
Dave: Ellen. We danced to Sal Mineo singing "Start Movin'." Somehow I was a pretty good dancer. For some reason, I could dance, even with the brace, early on. I did the Lindy. This was the beginning of Dick

Clark's *American Bandstand* show on TV, which I watched every day. There was this chick on the show that everyone dug—Justine, the blonde, and Bob, her boyfriend. Justine was my first "teen crush"—blonde Justine from *American Bandstand*, which took place in Philly at three o'clock every day with guests like Chubby Checker doing the Twist, or Dion and the Belmonts, whoever would be on. It ended at four p.m. and I watched it religiously. Like I said, I knew every tune.

Lew: So your first girlfriend was Ellen.
Dave: Ellen was a Catskills summer thing. Because in the Catskills you always had little summer flings. We were teenagers. She taught me the New York Lindy, which was different from the Philadelphia Lindy. The Philly Lindy had a different spin to it which I knew from watching *American Bandstand*. I remember there was a distinction in the way you start—I can almost do it here—I can kind of remember, the way you're swinging your partner or something like that. It was a big thing, dancing, because it was a big part of your teenage persona—to be a good dancer was a big thing. That was like one of the trademarks of being cool, along with the leather jacket and the "DA" hair—you know, looking like a duck's ass with everything back from the part in your hair, and the rest maybe a little fringed or whatever, as well of course slicked back like Elvis with cream or gel stuff. The black leather jacket and Garrison belt were important. The belt was illegal because it was more than three fingers' width. It was basically a black leather belt with a pretty big buckle.

Lew: Why would a belt be illegal?
Dave: It was a weapon. The gangs used to use it to beat you, so it was outlawed. The whole thing was the images we got from James Dean and to some extent Brando—throw in a motorcycle vibe and there you go. This whole image is the fifties! This is what I'm saying earlier about my brother, who was dealing with this crap. I'm younger, looking up to it. When you're ten, you're not dealing with it directly, but you're looking up to the images of a teenage boy who is ahead of you. My brother was dealing directly with this macho crap—you know what I mean? It's interesting because it's more than just that they were the first modern actors or whatever when you study acting history. It was the sexual thing and that screwed up straight America, which is and was so hung up on sex. Chest exposed, provocative tight clothes, black leather coat, sunglasses, motorcycle—you know, threatening. Let me put it this way: This is not Clark Gable or Humphrey Bogart in a suit with a beautiful hat on.

These are cats with jeans, a black jacket with a belt, and motorcycle boots—the whole deal.

Every period has its way of rebelling in dress, behavior, mores, etc. I was after the James Dean era. By my time in the 1960s it became marijuana. I remember, in probably 1962, I had to work under a different name because you had to be sixteen for working papers. That summer I was "Mike Shorr." He was a guy from my high school who was older and was cool with me using his name for the working papers since my sixteenth birthday was in September, after the summer. I don't remember the exact details, but certainly we did what we had to do and security wasn't like now. You could slide through.

Lew: So, it wasn't like a stage name in this case. It was actually an assumed identity.
Dave: Yeah, exactly. Mike gave me his birth certificate. We actually got in touch a few years ago for a little coffee. "Mike, do you remember when I was you for a summer?" "Yes, yes. I gave you . . ." I think he might've been the first guy I smoked pot with in high school. He was a hanging kind of guy, a little different than the others. I remember one day we were on Ocean Parkway right where we lived in Brooklyn and went into the lobby of an apartment house where the buzzers are. As I recall that was the first time I smoked marijuana.

Lew: At that time, would you say that smoking pot—how common was it? Was it a certain group that mostly did it?
Dave: It was absolutely uncommon. It was, of course, as I found out, more or less musicians only. It had definitely not leaked through to the real world. Mike was a rebel kind of guy as I remember it. It did become more common in a few years.

Lew: Tell me about the pot bust in the Catskills.
Dave: We were dressed up and as the gigs got better, the more dressed up I had to be. Around 1963, a good gig was this one place we worked called Schenk's Paramount in South Fallsburg, where we played opposite Larry Harlow's quintet.

Lew: Larry Harlow, the famous Latin bandleader?
Dave: Yes, with Mark Weinstein, who now plays flute.

Lew: He's a friend of mine—we've played together. He also got a Ph.D. and is a professor teaching logic and philosophy at Montclair State University in New Jersey!
Dave: He was a trombone player at that time. And the drummer's name was Philly Newsome, I think. They were a real band. So, we, the Impromptu Quartet, are the so-called jazz band, and Larry is the Latin band, because in those days every club had two groups.

Lew: It was like a Latin combo?
Dave: Yes—for people to dance, cha-cha, mambo, rumba. And the legendary trombonist Barry Rogers was with Eddie Palmieri at Brown's hotel, and he used to come by in the late hours for jam sessions at Schenk's. That club in Schenk's got busted one night by the FBI for pot. I remember the whole scene, which of course was kind of scary for us. We were young kids; these were men. These were real guys, real New York cats who were in their twenties while we were sixteen years old, more or less. One night, I think in August, about one in the morning a whole bunch of suited cats come in to the bar: "Put your hands on the wall." The lights go on, the whole deal.

Lew: At that moment you guys weren't performing?
Dave: I don't know, but we were there because we shared the stage with Larry till 3:00a.m. every night—forty minutes on, then forty off while his band played, something like that. So, they go through the instrument cases. One guy at a time could leave after they checked your clothing. Harlow was one of the ones who was allowed to leave.

Lew: Did they go through your cases, too?
Dave: Everybody in that room was shaken down. For some reason, my bass player, Gary, who was a little bit of a wild character, I don't know how he got picked or whatever, but one cop took him and me back to our room. Anyway, Gary said that he or we had pot. I don't remember—maybe they pressured him and set it up. Look, we're sixteen, seventeen years old. Anyway, we go back to the room, and sure enough, he opens the drawer of the dresser and under the socks he's got some pot. Cop says: "Where did you get this?" Gary says, "Larry H." Now, somehow—I don't know how this happened—I am selected to go with the cops to the bungalow colony where Larry is living for the summer with his kid and wife. I don't remember all of this in detail, but as far as I recall they apprehended him right there in the morning, and I didn't see him for the rest of the summer—Newsome led the Latin group after that.

I found out later that Harlow spent three months in the county jail. I think it was in the papers—a big scene: "FBI Busts Pot Ring in Catskill Resort." This is in the sixties, pre–*Easy Rider*. You're up in the Catskills in South Fallsburg, Sullivan County, New York State! I mean, this is country beyond country.

Lew: And selling it to a minor—
Dave: You dig? This was a scandal. I remember it. That was basically the end of the summer. We did play till Labor Day.

Lew: Now, you didn't own any pot?
Dave: I guess we smoked it. I don't remember. We were just kids. I didn't do much; I was smoking cigarettes here and there, and I wasn't drinking. We did what was around. I was a good Jewish middle-class kid. I was on the road to being successful, you know, so you didn't do that stuff. You didn't want to mess up; you wouldn't do that to your parents—you get the picture. We were taught a moral code and we were supposed to follow. You were expected to be a good kid and not fool around. Do your job, get a good job, be a doctor, etc., etc. My parents were not so strict, but the message was clear.

Lew: At that point—this is still high school going into college—you were still thinking "doctor"?
Dave: Yes, but gradually, music teacher. Being a doctor devolved into music teacher once I saw that I didn't want to go through with the whole eight-year-plus medical school thing. Of course, the other thing was that I was getting into music then.

Lew: You were in high school. Let's get back to the school year now.
Dave: I went from K to 8 at P.S. 99, followed directly by high school at Lafayette High School, Bensonhurst, Brooklyn. The thing about Lafayette was that there were two main high schools in our area, Lafayette and Midwood. In those days, you were assigned to a school based on your residence—no choices—unless you got into Brooklyn Tech or Stuyvesant, those special schools that you were tested for where my brother went. Lafayette was mostly Italian and had a bad rap, while Midwood was predominantly Jewish and considered better—right around the block from Brooklyn College. Lafayette was in Bensonhurst, which is still an enclave of Italian guys, some runners, some captains. In a way, the Bensonhurst neighborhood was like *The Sopranos*. The dividing line between the "bad" Bensonhurst and the "good" Midwood neighborhood

was Avenue L. The streets in that area of Brooklyn were an alphabetical grid system with letters and numbers. So, which side of Avenue L you were on determined the high school you would go to. My house was on the "wrong" side! The discussion for families like mine was, should we use somebody else's address or do some shady business or whatever so that the kid could go to the so-called better school, meaning Jewish! In those days, you could get away with things—so the first thought was how to get "sonny boy" David into Midwood. Ultimately my parents decided that if I went to Lafayette, I would be in the advanced/honors/A.P. (Advanced Placement) track, and so on, whereas in Midwood there would be a lot of competition because you're in with kids all like yourself. So, I went to Lafayette, which had six thousand students. It was the third biggest school in the world at that time, or something like that. It had three different sessions with students starting at different times, going on all day from I think 7:00a.m. till 4:00p.m.

Remember, I was born in 1946—the biggest birth year in the history of mankind—the so-called Baby Boomers. When I graduated from high school in 1964, there were twenty-five hundred kids in my graduating class. I tell people this and they can't believe it. Some towns are not as big as twenty-five hundred! But, of course, we, the good kids, were about a hundred and on a completely different track from the twenty-four hundred who were earning what was called either a general or commercial diploma. Commercial was basically vocational training I believe, a trade. General was just get in and out, and academic was us—going on to college; once again, basically the Jews for whom a college education was culturally mandatory.

Music became a big thing for me there. The music department had six hundred kids involved—orchestra, concert band, dance band. A big show called *Sing* happened every year, and I was the bandleader for several shows. One time we did the music of *South Pacific*, meaning using the songs but with our own words to fit the story line, whatever that was. I had to write parts out and organize the music in a six- to eight-person group, gaining a lot of experience. And I was in the dance band, again with my first musical friend, Mike Garson, on piano, and I met the older guys who first took me to Birdland, the jazz club in Manhattan. On my website you can see a program from 1962, my last semester of high school, where I am listed as vice-president of the senior band—the concert band—and co-leader of the dance band.

High school—it's a big deal in a kid's life because it's coming of age. After all, high school is the first time that you think you know who you are, at least a little. Everything before this was for me basically polio, elementary school, and kid stuff with a high level of attachment to your home. High school is when your friends become your milieu.

So, now I'm the normal high school kid who is being exposed to everything, which in my case means of course music. Now is the chance to finally use music. In line with the Catskills gigs, which are coinciding with normal high school, music became more important. I was "the musician." That's my status. Every high school kid yearns for something to set them apart. I'm also starting to feel different because I limped and the girl thing starts to become a real pain in the butt. Now you get into troubled waters like any teenager does. In my case as I mentioned, it had seemed till then that the polio stuff was not a big personal deal, at least apparently. Now, as a teenager, I could sort of feel the effects of it on a personal level.

It was the music that saved my ass. That's the truth. It gave something that set me apart from everybody else. Look, I couldn't take part in sports. Although I did sports, I couldn't be on the football team, and as we know, sports is a big deal at this age. More important is how you looked and all the jock crap. It was high school, in Brooklyn, New York City, with thousands of other kids, competition on every front. The whole scene at that age was definitely ratcheted up a lot from my younger years. Thank God for the music!

Chapter 2

The Call: I Find Music, It Finds Me

Lew: Drummer Bob Moses was important in your early development. How did he get involved in your life?

Dave: It's a great story. I was invited to a sweet sixteen party by one of the girls in my class at Lafayette. I had to rehearse that night at the school for a show or something like that. I remember the girl's name, Nora Bauer, who has since contacted me and joked about what happened. It was the oddest thing at this sweet sixteen—a trio, with a saxophone, bass, and drums. I don't remember the bass player, but the saxophone player was from the neighborhood, Joel Peskin, who has been living and playing in L.A. for years since then. I think Joel attended Music and Art or Performing Arts High School—I'm not sure which one, but both were special performing arts schools in the city. Moses was definitely at one of those schools too, as I recall.

I walk in and see the drummer. He looks big, large, with an Afro, hair all over the place. I don't think I ever saw an Afro in my life—this is Brooklyn in 1962, you understand? In a little hall or something like that. By the time I got there, 10:30 at night, this drummer is playing like nobody's business—he's burning. I had my tenor because of the school show thing. I took it out and we started playing. The way Moses remembers it was that we played for the next hour and forty-five minutes completely ignoring the party. We just didn't stop; we went crazy. I had never played with anybody like that. He was a real drummer. "Who are you? What are you?" He was very ebullient, very outgoing.

It ends up that he was really kind of a "jazz baby." His parents were involved with jazz musicians, while his godmother was the singer Abbey Lincoln because she was very friendly with Bob's mom. They lived on

Central Park West and 101st Street in a building where there also lived several notable musicians at one time or another—Elvin Jones, Rahsaan Roland Kirk, and Max Roach—a real jazz building. It might be the "Central Park West" that inspired Coltrane's composition of that name. So Moses was already in the zone. He dropped out of high school pretty soon after I met him, it turns out. I just knew this was a guy I had to get with. This was the first real guy who knew the deal. He basically took me in over the next few years. Within a short time after our meeting, he began living in a loft at 110 Bowery near Grand Street. In these next years he got gigs with Gary Burton and then with Rahsaan Roland Kirk. He turned me on to everything, getting me to listen to stuff that I had no idea existed, not only jazz, but the Bulgarian Women's Choir before they were known, Ravi Shankar, James Brown, etc. This is 1962 and the world opened up. He was my guide to the other side—someone who takes you along.

Not a guru exactly, but someone who showed me another world. Whatever I knew about jazz was coming from records like Stan Getz's *Girl from Ipanema*, Horace Silver, Herbie Mann's *Live at the Village Gate*, and so on—whatever Mike Garson and I could conjure up in Brooklyn. Everything was starting to happen at the same time, like going to jazz clubs and trying to learn this music, but Moses was already in that world. If you lived in Brooklyn you might as well have lived in Nebraska. As weird as it sounds, being that it's New York City, still, it's not Manhattan. In that time, though it was only a forty-five-minute subway ride to midtown Manhattan, it was like crossing over a cultural divide. So, even though somebody said they were from New York, if they weren't from Manhattan, they were not really *from* New York, in a way. Although Brooklyn had its own world, it wasn't about art, culture, jazz, etc.

Bob was a New Yorker, born and bred, lived in Manhattan, in an Upper West Side pad that was beautiful. It was an apartment with gigantic rooms, African sculptures everywhere, and paintings. His mother and father, Greta and Richard Moses, were into art—great people. I slept over at their place a lot. Greta eventually became a travel agent who decades later booked travel for me and other musicians. I loved Greta. Richard was a quiet guy, a different kind of cat, but Greta was a real warm lady. She was great, great fun.

The father had had some business with Billie Holiday and others, from what I understood—there was some kind of attachment. To place it in context, his parents were from my observation the equivalent of, and I'm not saying this in any negative way, left wing New York liberal Jewish. They were very secular, of course, but Greenwich Village type, and in those days who knows, maybe Socialist leanings, things like that. I don't know for sure, but let's say that milieu definitely thrived in the Upper West Side of Manhattan in the fifties and sixties. They were a sophisticated crowd, liberals who were always pro-black and NAACP, life-long Democrats—like my parents but on another level since they were right at the source being in Manhattan.

When I was eighteen, Bob and I got a gig at an art gallery on 3rd Avenue and Tenth Street playing every Friday night. We found a bass player, whose name escapes me, but if I recall—or maybe I want this to be true—he looked like Jimmy Garrison, so I'll call him Jimmy. I had a driver's license by then. We would go and pick him up on Prospect Avenue in the Bronx, go downtown to play, take him back home, come back down and hear Coltrane or somebody, then go back to Moses's uptown where I would sleep. Significantly, it was also the first time I kind of got into smoking pot because Moses was already way in there. He provided my entrance into the subculture. Like I said, he knew the musicians. You know, having breakfast with Abbey Lincoln sipping coffee, that kind of thing. Meeting Moses was crucial to my future development as a jazz musician and even more.

Here's a great story that happened a few years later: The Impromptu Quartet had a summer gig lined up in the Catskills as we were doing for those years. Bobby, the drummer got a summer-long engagement at the World's Fair in some pavilion so we needed a drummer for the hotel gig. I invited Moses, who had no idea what the Catskills was or the scene or anything. This guy did not play club dates to say the least! Now, my memory might be wrong, but I think it was again Schenk's Paramount, the hotel I described earlier with the FBI bust. I seem to recall we returned there. In any case we played three times a day: at the pool in the afternoon, in the lobby after dinner, and in the bar from midnight to 3:00a.m. Now, of course, this is the sixties and you have to play cha-chas, merengues, bossa novas, tangos, frailachs, czardas, whatever—it was dance music. So, the first day on the gig I say: "Okay, 'La Comparasita,' a famous tango," (sings melody), and Moses says, "Tango? What's a tango?" Uh-oh! We are screwed. He knows none of these beats.

Lew: But you're already at the gig!
Dave: I didn't think about it. I figured everybody knows everything. Who knows at this age that guys play different styles? I figured you play and this is what you play. So, of course, everything turns into jazz. He completely takes everything and burns out on it. I mean, he could really

play already, so he's burning out. We're thrilled to have him. But of course, within a short minute, the owner comes running up to him: "What are you doing? They can't dance to the music!" Anyway, we somehow got through the summer. That's my Bob Moses story—trying to teach Bob Moses what a merengue is! It's hilarious.

Lew: With dancers, even if they don't know anything about music, if it doesn't feel right, they cannot dance to it.
Dave: It's got to be perfect. I'm talking about a period when a set could be a cha-cha to a waltz to a fox-trot to a merengue. You could do eight different styles in an hour—that was the job. Even though we weren't the Latin band, we still had to play basic stuff from that side, while the show band did straight dance music. So, to put it lightly, Moses was the beginning of seeing that there's another way. Of course we would see Coltrane together during these years, which was part of our voyage together.

Lew: Let's talk about Coltrane, the first time you saw him.
Dave: Well, there were nightclubs in Brooklyn—I remember playing a joint on Kings Highway called the 5000 Club—but mostly they were like Italian Mafia joints where'd they have a lounge group or something like that. Playing those places was basically a club date, but I didn't do much of it in any case. I mentioned in the last chapter that the older guys invited me out to Birdland, which happened during the Christmas vacation of my second year in high school. So I had no idea what a real jazz club was or anything like that. Now I'm backtracking a bit before meeting Moses—December 1961.

It was the Gerry Mulligan Concert Jazz Band with Bob Brookmeyer, from what I remember, and the Count Basie Big Band, both of whom I knew nothing about. We walk in and there is the famous Pee Wee Marquette, the emcee of Birdland. You hear his distinctive voice on an Art Blakey record, *Meet You at The Jazz Corner of The World,* introducing the group. Pee Wee was a midget or dwarf—not sure—but he was little, all dressed up in a tuxedo, with that voice. He used to stand on the street. The original Birdland was on Broadway, just north of 52nd Street, right near a restaurant called the Hawaii Kai, a tourist attraction with a Polynesian theme, torches, hula skirts, faux luau, and all that. Marquette used to stand on the street yelling, "Come on, ladies and gentlemen! Come on inside!"

He takes our five-dollar admission and you are led to what was known as the "peanut gallery," for young people, which was the last row of tables in the back where there were about twenty seats. If I recall correctly those tables were raised up in height a bit because it would be hard to see the bandstand since you were at the end of the length of the room. There was the bar on the left and in front, rows of tables. The bandstand was in front of this longish room—kind of like the Village Vanguard in a way—a long room with the last row being the peanut gallery. Of course, it was, as I remember it, blue, or pink, or red—very night clubbish—real garish, fifties—what we think of nightclubs. But more to the point is the scene. First of all were the waitresses dressed with their boobs hanging out, little frills hanging from the dresses. Then there are the cigarette girls coming around with the cartons on a tray hanging from their neck. And the photographer girl with the big flashbulb that you see in pictures from that era—you know, asking, "Sir, would you like your picture taken? Would you like cigarettes?"

First of all, I never saw a woman like that in my life. I'm like fifteen years old—like, "What?" Next awakening! The waitress comes over and I ask for a Coca-Cola. "That will be a dollar." "What?" Coke was five cents in Brooklyn. Talk about sticker shock! I looked at the other guys: "Yeah, that's right," and one of the cats kicked me under the table. They were older and cooler, but damn, a dollar—you know what I mean? A dollar for a Coke is like $20 now! In any case for that five-dollar admission and one-dollar Coke you could sit all night. They just forgot about us. So, my first real live jazz, and it really knocked me out. Like we all say as teachers, a kid has to *see* jazz in front of them to get the point. Well, I got the point that night, but more was to come shortly in that regard.

Shortly after, on February 10, 1962, came the epiphany night, the Coltrane night, on a date with girlfriend, Julie Gross. She was the flute player in the orchestra at Lafayette, where I played clarinet. You know, clarinet meets flute! Black hair—that's all I remember about her. Anyway, this is going to be a big night on the town. First we are going to a famous Italian restaurant, Mama Leone's, and then to Birdland. I have no idea who's playing. I didn't call or anything—I was just going to go to Birdland because now I'm kind of like, "Oh, I'm experienced. I've been to Birdland. We're going to go to a jazz club." Like that, you know? So, I look at the placard—you remember how it used to be in the old days when they would have these signs outside a club? It says Bill Evans Trio and John Coltrane Quintet—Eric Dolphy was in the band. First of all, I have no idea who Bill Evans is. I don't know Coltrane, except vaguely the name rings a bell because at this time I had started to read *Downbeat* magazine. I'm starting to get a little familiar with the names.

Lew: When you say starting to read, are you subscribing?
Dave: I don't know. It doesn't seem like it would be in the neighborhood store. Somehow I'm getting a hold of the magazine. Of course, when you're reading, you're starting to get into the names. I think, "Coltrane . . . Coltrane." And then there's a picture of him with the soprano, on the placard. I said to Julie, "Oh, he's the one who plays the soprano saxophone," which is a complete unknown instrument to me at the time. So that's my association before walking in. Now we go downstairs and, of course, there's Pee Wee doing his thing: "Hello, young man, would you like to sit . . ." We go into the peanut gallery, get the little Coke for a dollar, and all I remember is the noise level. After all, it's Saturday night, crowded and noisy. People chattering away like a Saturday night anywhere, anytime. This trio is playing and I remember the piano player—head down, hunched over—playing with the other guys like they're in a living room. I mean, you can hardly hear them or even take notice. I couldn't hear a note, or if I heard it, it was vague and didn't make any impression on me. Bill Evans with, I now know, Chuck Israels on bass and Paul Motian on drums. (A radio broadcast of the Evans trio from this night is available, and one of Coltrane's group from the previous night.)

Anyway, I'm probably talking to Julie as well. I don't recall if they play an hour and then off or whatever. But in any case, Bill's trio finishes, and this next group comes on and starts playing. I am completely shocked. First of all is the saxophone player, on tenor and then soprano. Now since Julie was a musician of sorts I could talk: "He's missing notes." If I had the horn right here, now, I would play it for you. You know what I'm talking about, Lewis—when you go for the altissimo and you kind of get that thing of missing notes. I said, "That's not right; that's when you miss a note." Then on the soprano all I remember is trills. Ten minutes of tremolos and trills—that's all. Plus they're playing real loud.

The alto player—the only reason I know who he was is that I remember this big bulge on his forehead that you see in pictures of Dolphy. Well, I understood him better, basically because as we know, stylistically, Eric played in a more traditional bebop rhythmical fashion, though the pitch choices were quite different than normal bebop, using wide intervals. I guess you could say Eric was more comprehensible to a novice like myself. So even to my rather inexperienced ear, I could get with that, whereas this other guy, Coltrane, he's like from another planet. I'm thinking to myself, *I can't believe it—this is Birdland, the temple of jazz.* I mean, I'm not thinking it's a fake, but I'm just thinking, like, *weird.* Then the upshot of the night is they go into a tune and Julie says, "That's from *The Sound of Music*." I say, "No way! Come on—these guys don't do that!" I think I'm so hip, they wouldn't play such a tune with someone prancing around the fields of Austria singing. This can't be possible. Well, of course, as we well know, "My Favorite Things" was Trane's signature song and his big hit. I didn't know it at the time, but this was the beginning of my life, the epiphany, and most important, going to see Coltrane from then on. As they say in spiritual affairs, once you see the light, you can never turn away again. You're always trying to go toward it. That was the night I saw the light. All the stuff that eventually came afterward started from that first night of seeing him and saying to myself, "I've got to go again. I must know about this."

Lew: But why did you feel you had to go again?
Dave: I don't know. This could be the story of my life and probably yours. What was it in him, musically? Because it certainly wasn't anything other than music. There was no flash, no smoke bombs, no teenage crazy stuff.

Obviously, the guys were good. I could tell that. But what was it that made us love him? Now, you wrote a book on it and I talk about it my whole life, but in the end, can we really ever express what it is that made us gravitate to that guy? To that music? To that group particularly? I certainly didn't know it at fifteen years old. To finish this part of the story, I went to see Coltrane from then on, anytime I could. He played New York three times a year, more or less, either the Half Note, Village Vanguard, or Birdland, for at least a week and often two. I could go on a Friday and Saturday night, so over five years, maybe fifteen to twenty or more times?

I'd get somebody to go with me or whatever. You have to remember I am fifteen, sixteen, seventeen years old and still don't have a clue about music. I couldn't believe that this tenor sax was the same instrument I had at home. That's the thing I remember. How can that be a tenor saxophone? This cannot be the same instrument that's lying in my house on 5th Street in Brooklyn that I just practiced, whatever practice I did. I wasn't a voracious practicer, but I played it every day. I said to myself, "This can't be the same instrument, the way this guy plays." That's what kept me going to see him. That was always the first reaction. The next would be about the drummer. That drummer! What the hell is going on here? What are they doing? How can you do that with the drums and the saxophone? How can you play like this? How can these four guys play like that? They don't even look at each other; they never talk! How can they get on the stand and play two hours in a row, and an hour and a half is soloing or duo with just the drums? You know, all the stuff guys who saw it talk about when they discuss hearing and seeing Trane and the group.

Lew: So, it's interesting that what happened that night was not "I love this—this is what I want to do." It was intriguing.
Dave: Intriguing and baffling.

Lew: You couldn't let it go. It wasn't, "I'm baffled, so forget it." It was "I'm baffled, but I need to know more."
Dave: That is exactly how I describe it to everyone. Usually when you don't like something, your first reaction is, "I don't like it. I can't use it." But on second thought you go, "Maybe it's because I don't understand it. Therefore, I really owe it to myself to understand it a little better." This translates to repeating the scene, and usually when you repeat something, you not only start to understand it, but somehow you usually end up liking it. I mean, if it's really something you don't like, well, you don't like it and that's not going to change, but usually with familiarity comes some kind of admiration.

Lew: Now, you saw Coltrane a lot, so at some point you really started to love it. How quickly did that happen?
Dave: Pretty soon.

Lew: Second time you went to see him?
Dave: I can't tell you. I can tell you one time when my friend Steve Lipman and I were there for a third set we were able to sit right in front of Trane because nobody was at those front tables. So we just left the peanut gallery. I can tell you about seeing him another time doing an hour-and-forty-five-minute duo with Elvin.

I remember being at the Half Note and the Vanguard seeing the quartet, but especially the Half Note. It was so great at the Half Note because you saw them right in front of your eyes. No matter where you sat at the Half Note, they were right in front of you because they were in the center of the room. That was at Spring and Hudson Streets. There's a great picture of the stage in the *One Up, One Down* live record. They were raised up over the bar in the middle. In other words, wherever you sat or whatever side you were on, they were equidistant to you. They were right there. I mean, you acoustically heard it. Birdland was different. You were removed by some distance, and the Vanguard depended on wherever you ended up sitting. I don't remember him playing the Vanguard that often. I remember seeing him more in the late stages with Rashied Ali at the Vanguard. In fact, the one time I met him or I got near him was with that version of the group at the Vanguard. But I think the Half Note was where I saw him more than any other club.

I went to hear other jazz, too. I didn't see Miles that much, but I know that Thelonious Monk worked a lot opposite Coltrane because I saw him a lot and did not enjoy it, feeling it was actually quite boring, at least to me. Then I became a little snobby. I became—only Coltrane.

Lew: Monk is amazing, but I could see that his tenor players could be boring.
Dave: It was to me, man. Charlie Rouse didn't get to me—and the tempos were all the same—I don't know.

Lew: And Monk had long walking bass solos.
Dave: It was a format that they just did over and over again. I couldn't wait to hear Coltrane. It was a double bill most of the time. But, in any case, I must say to finish this "epiphany" story, I have to at least credit myself for being open enough to be receptive to some degree. Is that because of my parents and upbringing? Is that because of my genes? Is that because the air was a certain way that night? Is that because I played saxophone? Is that because I saw Eric Bromley play the saxophone during the breaks on those Saturday mornings? What is it that made me go back for more and get entranced by it?

Whatever it was, I'll tell you one thing in retrospect. I didn't know it then or for decades, that there is more than meets the eye. This is a general statement that you can say about life, but in this case specifically, music. And even more specifically, jazz. This is not just some cats up there playing while you snap your fingers, move your body, groove, and have a good time, which is what I thought it was. This is everything you ever want to know. It's all the knowledge of the cosmos, of spiritual stuff, wherever you're at with that. It's just packed with information, feeling, humanity, life/death—the deal. And if it's *the* deal and it's there in front of you, you can't turn away from it. You are forced to have to find out what it is about.

It could have been a painting for somebody else. It could have been seeing an Ingmar Bergman movie. You get that hook, and that hook says to you, there's more. First, you think it's fun and all that. You move your fingers fast, and all that stuff I said about jazz in the beginning: "Oh, it's so interesting—the guys, their eyes are closed, they don't talk to each other—how cool, how hip." But no, it's more, and this guy made me see there's more. I don't think without Trane that I would have gotten it. I mean, this is a big statement, but would I have gotten it through Miles Davis? Or Bill Evans? Or, you can name anybody, and I'm not sure because still today I haven't gotten it from anybody else. Trane covers that place for me. But would I have gotten it another way? I'm not sure. And if I wouldn't have gotten it, we wouldn't be sitting here. It's the truth. I would not have gone on with this music. I would have loved it, enjoyed it, but I would have done something else in life. I believe that. And I really put it to the beginning at that night in Birdland, New York City. That was the seed that turned into a tree.

Lew: And what did Julie Gross think?
Dave: I don't remember, but I think we had a good time. You know, she was a nice girl. I don't remember anything about it. I probably didn't think about it much at the moment or shortly after. Look—epiphanies aren't necessarily noticed at the moment of their occurrence, but one thing was that I had been initiated to Birdland. I became like Mr. Hip Guy. "We're going to Birdland!"

Lew: This was before the sweet sixteen party with Moses?
Dave: Yes, because by the time I get with Moses, it was Trane, Trane! That was part of our hookup. We'd go see Trane after we played some of those Friday nights at that art gallery and took the bass player home. We would go back to see the third set by 1:30 or so because they played until three or four in the morning.

Lew: And, meanwhile, you were still doing music in high school as well.
Dave: When you have a handicap and you're a kid, you don't know it. But you're kind of special in a way. Everybody feels for you—you sort of stand out, for better or worse. But when you get to teenage years and the hormone stuff starts happening, girls are on your mind all of the time, and if guys around you are bigger and faster, you start feeling a draft. If you have a kid and the kid has some handicap, that's when the dues start. Because up till then you figure a kid doesn't appear, at least on the surface, to be really too conscious of it; he seems to be normal and well adjusted, etc. Then by the time of sixteen, seventeen, the kid is practically ready to commit suicide because of being so self-conscious and different. All you want is to belong. This can happen and it did for me. Music became the only way I had an identity. It was music that gave me my identity: "Oh, I do that. I'm in the *in* crowd. I know more. I'm special." With jazz, something that hardly anyone knew about, the fact that I was into it

made me hip—you know, a bit of the underworld, so to say, the whole subculture thing, and sort of being a member of it, at least in my mind. It sounds so ridiculous now, but then it mattered. So, even though those guys run faster and do everything and they get all the pretty girls, I'm cool because I'm the heavy guy, Mr. Underground Man!

Lew: Did it help to meet girls—having the music?
Dave: In some ways, yes, and when it happened, usually you knew you were liked for who you were because any girls into jazz were also definitely different from the mainstream. When you would go to a party, you pretty soon found yourself at the piano. I played for my own prom. I was the president of the class and I hired myself. If memory serves me correctly, I think it was my band. The thing to remember is that I was always working Saturday nights, Sunday afternoons, and of course there was the Catskills and hotels for the summers. My parents encouraged me to work and I loved it. I was dressing up in a tuxedo on a Saturday night, which made me feel like a big shot. I was with the Impromptu Quartet and my boys, Mike, Gary, and Bobby. Grandma So and So would come up and request that we play the "Anniversary Waltz." I felt like a mature person, and it really gave me an identity. This is away from the jazz stuff. What I'm talking about now is the function of music to somebody like me in that milieu and in my particular context and situation.

Another thing I have to mention about high school is that I really had the best academic teacher of my life, Marvin Feldman, whom I stayed friendly with for some years after school. The course was Advanced Placement American History, which eventually became my major in college. I just liked history, I guess. I read a lot of the Landmark series of American history books as a kid—remember them? They were biographies. By the time I was twelve years old, I had finished a lot of them. So, we got college credit for the A.P. course and Mr. Feldman was the teacher. He was a big guy with a kind of tough-love attitude. He made it come alive. Something as dry as history can also be great. Mrs. Rosenberg, whom I had in P.S. 99 elementary school, was also spectacular. You don't know until later that they instilled something in you beyond other teachers. It goes past the material—not really something specific but just a feeling of having had an extraordinary instructor who inspired you to learn, whatever the material.

Lew: That's great. And you had a circle of fellow students, a social circle.

Dave: Yes. We went to each other's parties. It was incestuous, almost—mostly Jewish and the same folks all the time. My very good friend Jed—Caris and I try to go to his Passover Seder every year. We've stayed in touch all this time. He was a part of that crowd.

Lew: What's his full name?
Dave: Jed Luchow. Not a professional musician, though he plays piano. He comes to a lot of my gigs. When I am playing Birdland, he's always there. He teaches disability kids, which is probably where I would have ended up, doing something like that.

Lew: So the class president thing is just an indication that . . .
Dave: We were all overachievers and expected to go on to college, which in those days wasn't the norm. There was no question about it. By the time I got to that scene around seventeen years old, I knew I couldn't leave New York. I was getting serious enough about the music to realize that there was nowhere else to go. Not that I knew the world. I hadn't been anywhere else really, but I knew, I just could feel it that I had to stay here for the music, even though I had no idea of a career in the field or anything like that. So, I limited my choices to schools in the New York area, although I did try Brandeis in Massachusetts, which I didn't get accepted to. I applied to Columbia and I knew that Brooklyn College was always in my back pocket.

In any case, I was getting to that point where you have to start making decisions. Am I going to be a club date musician? I don't think so. So, it appears to be teaching, especially since I came from teachers. So I'm thinking real straightforward—music degree, teach, play on the side. That's the protocol—that's what it's going to be. Queens College had an excellent music department, sort of famous for classical, and I could get there by car from Brooklyn. Remember, my parents were products of the city university system, in their case City and Hunter Colleges and my brother went to Brooklyn College, so it was the norm in our family—commute, free tuition, city school. I got into Queens College.

I got to the first orientation meeting at Queens College in the late summer of 1964 ostensibly as a music major. They gave me a list of required listening for the next four years beginning with Palestrina through Stockhausen or someone like that. Remember, I don't know anything about classical music. I don't know Mozart's *Jupiter Symphony* from his *Gavotte*. Beethoven what? Nine symphonies? What do you mean? (Sings theme from Beethoven's Fifth.) That's all I know. I'm completely under the eight ball, but I'm taking this seriously 'cause, after all, it's college. I take the list home and spend that first semester, every waking hour that isn't in class or driving, in the music library trying to catch up. Palestrina, lots and lots and lots of Verdi, etc. I hated it. I never liked that older stuff, and in fact, I still don't, although obviously from a musical standpoint I get it.

I wanted to listen to Trane. After all, I'm finally getting into transcribing. My lessons with Lennie Tristano were starting—we'll talk about that. All of this is coming together at the same time. I've been hanging with Moses already a year or two. I see that this music major isn't good. I switch majors in the second semester. Now, in those days, there were two majors that everybody took when they didn't know what they were doing: English literature and psychology. I mean, everybody was a psychologist, at least in their own mind. There was always some chick you could sit down with and talk about your problems. So, I took psychology for a semester, but that didn't work either.

I hated Queens College. I felt anonymous. Everybody seemed to know each other except me. It seemed a lot of the kids came from local high schools. Being from Brooklyn, I felt like I was from another country. I didn't belong, I didn't get with it, I couldn't talk to girls there. I couldn't stand the campus. I was driving every day. I hated it. I don't know how or why I got to New York University, but that became the next thing. I was accepted in the second year into what was then the uptown division, the College of Arts and Sciences, called University Heights, which was sort of the elite division. It was right off the Major Deegan Expressway with a beautiful campus—hard to believe in the Bronx. Years later, it became some sort of technical college, and now I have no idea what happened to it, but it had the feel of a real college campus, small but nice. There were these beautiful busts of famous Americans overlooking the highway—kind of a well-known historic site. We were close to Jerome Avenue, where it was much funkier, but here was this campus in the middle of the 'hood. American history became my major, thanks to Mr. Feldman at Lafayette, and now starts the next part of my life, which increasingly meant living two lives: jazz musician and college student, in the mid-1960s. I'm truly away from home for the first time. I'm nineteen and this is the beginning of living alone.

First I was in the dorm with a roommate, Steve Rowles, who actually worked out okay. It ended up that he loved Coltrane by chance, or maybe I influenced him right off—I don't remember which. We had a gigantic poster of John and a don't-come-in-the-room sign with blue lights all around—the Coltrane sanctuary—definitely a hippie vibe. Eventually we took an apartment, but the first year you had to be in the dorm.

I think NYU was $3,000. If it was $6,000, it was a lot, but it was nowhere near $10,000 or anything like that. It was another world from city universities, but my parents were very proud. NYU is and was a well-known private school. It was still a New York school that didn't have the panache that you would have if you went to Yale, Harvard, Dartmouth—out of town and all that. But it still was NYU.

Lew: When one first starts college, a lot of times you just end up with a roommate. Is that how you and Steve ended up—he was not somebody you chose?
Dave: Yes, I think we were assigned. We put in our preferences, I guess, and he liked music it seems. I don't know what he does now, but over the years he did get in touch with me and he became a bamboo flute maker in Vermont or somewhere like that. He later switched to making violins. He was one of these return-to-the-earth kind of guys. I think he came from a preppy kind of family and had a kind of upper-class background—maybe I'm wrong—but he was kind of well bred and quiet, a little mustache, a quiet guy with glasses, definitely not New York, but he loved Trane and we hit it off.

By then I had a car and started to live my two lives, playing and hanging with musicians till the wee small hours and then back to school. I was also starting to be around LSD and the whole hippie culture. After all, this was college in the late '60s with all the social upheaval happening, which I was definitely part of. A guy in college who played bass accompanied me on my first acid trip at NYU, probably around '66/67. We had talked about it for a while in a serious way. He said you had to have a "guide" to do it right. I remember doing it in that apartment I had in the Bronx, and mostly listening to music. I'd never heard music like that. I never saw anything like that, the way things were moving and flowing.

Lew: And around this time you began studying with brilliant blind pianist, Lennie Tristano (1919-1978).
Dave: I think it was my senior year of high school or freshman year of college. My connection with Tristano came through Mike Garson. Mike's father was a wholesale liquor salesman, who by chance sold to the Half Note Club. This is how life is—serendipity—amazing. One day in June 1964, Mike is with his father, doing the rounds, and they go to the Half Note in the evening and, lo and behold, Tristano is gigging with Lee Konitz and Warne Marsh. Mike started to study with Lennie, who is about the only known teacher of jazz in New York at that time.

Lew: Tristano didn't perform much in the sixties.
Dave: Well this was one time, and Mike started to study with him, and he suggested I do also. As I said, in those days there was no one who taught jazz. There was John Mehegan, known for his jazz piano method books, but he lived in Connecticut, and Hall Overton conducted public classes at the New School, where you could go once a week. They were open to the public, and I remember he would hand out onion-skin copies of Monk tunes, which I still have, I think. But it wasn't like you would go up to your saxophone teacher and say, "I want to study jazz." By this time I think I was studying sax with Joe Allard, which we'll get to, but not jazz, and by now I wanted to learn how to get it right. Lennie is the only one known as a teacher for any instrument, by the way. I don't remember the exact mechanism of how it came together, phone call or what, but in any case I started to study with him.

Lennie lived out in Jamaica, Queens, on Palo Alto Street, near 191st Street and Hillside Avenue. I remember pretty well because getting there was quite a trip. You had to take the subway D line from my stop in Brooklyn into Manhattan and change to go to 179th Street, if I'm not mistaken. Then you took a bus to 191st and walked across Hillside Avenue to a side street about a block or two up a hill—that I definitely remember. His house looked like it was out of a Vincent Price horror movie, like *The House of Usher* or whatever that flick was. It was an old Victorian. I see it now—you know, gables, big hanging low-type trees—most of all, *very* dark. You went up some big stairs to the front door and I can tell you, it was spooky.

I went every Sunday for about ten months or a year. I think it was \$15 a lesson, or maybe it was \$9. It was expensive for the time, especially in light of the fact that these "lessons" were no more than ten to fifteen minutes—at least for me, but I wasn't the only one. I traveled three hours round-trip basically to have a fifteen-minute lesson! On top of that, he was the first cat who ever did the following, which is actually a good idea: If you miss a lesson, you pay. Now, of course, I'm coming from neighborhood teachers and Mom calls them to say, "Oh, David is sick." Even Joe Allard, I don't think you paid him when you missed. But Lennie, you paid.

I'll tell you about my first lesson, which is a story I always tell because it was really an awakening. The first lesson I walk in, Tristano says: "Play a B-flat scale from the bottom of the horn to the top." Fair enough. First of all, I can't get the damn low B-flat out, the lowest note on the tenor.

Lew: You're not warmed up?
Dave: No. Finally after a few tries I get that note out and get to the scale. Lennie says in a very strong voice: "You go home and make sure you know how to play a low B-flat. Come back next week." End of lesson. That completely floored me the first time.

Lew: No way! And then you paid?
Dave: Or I paid before. That was it. He was tough. He didn't say: "Son, you're not tonguing right, or your chin isn't right." First of all, he's blind. The other thing is the way he looks, which was scary to me—kind of like Frankenstein. From what I remember, he never wore sunglasses. So his eyes were different, to say the least. Plus, he had scars on his face, maybe from acne—I have no idea. If you've seen pictures of him, you know what I mean. The room was gigantic with just a piano, and all white—if I remember correctly. In any case it was a scene! I don't think there was anything else in the room. It was right off the front door of the house.

He was a little cat who kind of crawled into the room. He didn't meet you at the door. Somebody else would open the door—all strange, it seemed to me, but remember, I'm just a teenager. When he came into the room, he just felt the wall. Anyway, that first lesson, needless to say, scared the shit out of me.

What did I do in later lessons? Singing with Lester Young solos from the famous Count Basie recordings of 1936 to '39. Then I moved on to singing along with Sinatra from the *Come Fly with Me* album, a whole record of Nelson Riddle arrangements. Maybe I got to Billie Holiday by the time I left him, but I forget.

Lew: He would say: "I want you to learn this Lester Young solo for next time"?
Dave: You had to sing along with Prez. I never got past doing that with Lennie, so I really don't know what was next, but from what I understand, he didn't do the analysis thing like I have students do now. But you had to play the solo on your instrument. So, singing was first in order to internalize the solo. You had to match it along with the record. And then with Sinatra I was singing along also. I'm assuming for phrasing in this case. I had to get the feel, get it into my whole being through this "saturated listening" that I tell students about now. You feel it and hear it before you even talk about playing it on your instrument.

Lew: So, Lennie would say to you something like: "You didn't match him, you didn't imitate him exactly, you were a little off; you should be so close that I can't hear the original"—stuff like that?
Dave: I don't remember the exact words, but in essence, yes to all of the above. You are a walking imitation—there should be no distance between you and the original.

Lew: But you didn't get to that point where you could do that on the horn?
Dave: No. I did later, but not with him. Then there was playing tunes. Pick a melody; play with the metronome beating on 2 and 4 without any reference to chord changes. I don't know if he said, "Don't listen to changes," or, "Don't take a tune that you know the changes," or if I even knew what changes were. "Just play off of what you hear from the melody." I remember doing "Pennies from Heaven" (sings tune). Then you're supposed to solo and hit the right notes, I guess. Truth is, I never got far enough to know why I was doing that particular thing. When I think about it now, it does get to the essence of, for example, Lee Konitz's playing, which in the final result is pure melody. I forget whatever else I did, if anything, but with Mike's lessons there were definitely piano voicings. Waiting outside, I heard Lennie yelling out numbers like "1 2 4 7, 1 2 3 6 10, 1 2 5 7" —whatever. You know, he would recite numbers for voicings and have the student write them down, and they had to obviously figure them out in all keys.

Lew: On the scale tones?
Dave: I guess so. They seemed especially like cluster voicings.

I'll tell you how my time with Lennie ended because it was on a sour note. It was a Sunday because that's when I went for lessons. This particular day I had seen Trane the night before. I just blurted out: "Saw John Coltrane last night. Oh man, it was fantastic." Lennie says something like: "He ain't playing nothing, and Elvin hasn't played good since he came to New York." Something to that effect. He just completely negated my whole life in one sentence. Now, this is Lennie Tristano, and truth is, I didn't really know how heavy he was, but I knew he was some sort of legend, and after all he was a jazz teacher, so that was heavy enough. Here he was basically barring my whole deal. I just couldn't face him after that. That was the end.

Now, here's the upshot of the story. I just didn't get past first base with him—that's the truth. I was loyal and went every week. I was just not mature enough for it. I was a kid. I wasn't ready for him. I wasn't ready for anybody. For sure I certainly wasn't ready for Lennie Tristano, who had a system, a method, as we know it now so well from Eunmi Shim's book on him and other books. At least ten years you were supposed to be with him, from what I understand, to get the "full monty," as Warne Marsh did. I mean, it was a cumulative, real-deal thing. So, there was no way for me in the first place, if only for that reason of commitment. It also appeared to form you into a certain kind of player, though of course not everyone who studied with Lennie plays the same way. I am generalizing, but point made, though I was not aware of it at the time, concerning style. But he was the only game in town.

He wasn't the nurturing type. No encouragement. There was nothing personal at all. I can't remember one personal word. Again, I'm young and I was a little intimidated and he looked so weird! He definitely didn't say: "Dave, how are you today?" There was no smile. I'm nicer to my students in the first second than he was in his whole time to me! He was the way he was, and probably very different with other people, but he was scary and intimidating to a kid—well at least THIS kid. To reiterate, I didn't know how heavy he was as a musician. Later I knew that he was a genius—a very far-reaching artist. In 1946 he was playing chromatic. In a lot of ways, he was way beyond everybody. He was way past Bud Powell in some ways. Intellectually, forget it! Rhythmically! It's ridiculous what he did and what he spawned.

You see, with a guy like that, you've got to sign up for the duration. He honed you and he owned you. He was the first teacher that I witnessed who demanded total dedication from the real guys who wanted it—total renunciation—you are mine, period! In the end, that's what a real great teacher says: "Don't ask, just do. Do everything I tell you to do and maybe I'll let you know something." That's what it's supposed to be. A student has to give himself or herself up to the master and trust the process. We don't do that anymore because we're so nice and so politically correct, but the truth is he was coming from the real strict tradition of, "If you study with me, you do what I tell you to do, and you're in for good." Look, you take eight or ten years with a classical teacher, right? When you get with a teacher in that world, if you are serious and so-called designated to be an artist, you'll start at twelve years old and you're there until thirty or whatever. He was coming from that, and I respect it. I just didn't know anything about it, that's all.

But check this out: The "lesson" I described from Trane, followed by this experience with Lennie, was that there's more than meets the eye—that this jazz thing is *work*, period. Naive as this sounds, it did not dawn on me at that time that you had to work to learn this music. It just seemed to come out of the guys. Learn jazz—learn what? I mean, classical music, yeah, you read. Jazz, you just do it, don't you? You pick up your horn and you do it. You have a good time. You call a tune; maybe you don't even call a tune. My ignorance was stupendous and nobody was there to straighten me out.

Look at the difference nowadays. Yesterday I was talking to sixteen-year-old kids, and by 3:00p.m. they were straight, meaning they at least heard the point of what they have to do. At least they know this is work because I can lay it out clearly. Nobody did that to me or you probably. We didn't get that. So, here I am with a genius musician who has a system—he's strict, the real deal—and I wasn't ready for it. But I did realize in my heart of hearts that this is no bullshit. That was the lesson. This isn't something that's just going to happen. This is not fun and games. So between that and Coltrane, by the time I was eighteen or nineteen, struggling with college and who I am with all the normal teenage and adolescent shit, getting out of my parents' house, etc., I am seeing finally that this is serious business. I'm starting to understand that this is different than I thought it was going to be.

Remember, originally I thought I was going to be a doctor or lawyer or teacher, like everyone else around me, following the models of what people did with their lives—the doctors who operated on me, or my parents and their community of teachers. That's who my role models were. Now I was seeing that I was going left, off the prescribed path. You've got to remember this is the sixties and the rebellion thing became pretty over the top and a movement worldwide. I am not my parents. They are straight ahead, loving people, liberal, good citizens, but they don't know what jazz is at all. "And that's going to be a life, David? And what are you going to do for a living? It's okay to do this in high school and on the side, but—." So, now the shit starts to hit the fan in a lot of ways. I mean, my generation was rock and roll and I added free jazz into the mix—I mean the jazz life style and ethos really. So, yes I'm trying to be Mr. Jazz, but I'm also kind of joining up with the burgeoning counterculture. This all starts to happen around the same time.

Lew: Around this time, you were already starting to see Joe Allard. How would you have heard about him?

Dave: We talked in the last chapter about taking Saturday lessons at Bromley Studios with Nat Shapiro. Somewhere around sixteen years old, I think, either I or somebody said, "It's time to look a little further." I don't remember it being negative, just obvious that I had to raise the ante, so to say. I literally looked in the Manhattan phone book under music instruction—I think it was listed that way. I also called some names that might be familiar from that era, like pianist Marty Napoleon. There was another guy, Garvin Bushell, who by the way plays bassoon on Coltrane's *Live at the Village Vanguard*, which is an incredible coincidence. I spoke to at least two or three people on the telephone because my mother wouldn't do it. She wanted me to take care of this, which was right. "What do you teach? How long is the lesson?" I don't know how I got to Joe, but he was one of those calls.

Joe was very friendly. He said it was a forty-five-minute or an hour lesson—I don't recall which—for $25, at Carnegie Hall Studios. Maybe that was the reason I went for it. You know the standard joke about Carnegie Hall. Guy gets in the cab and asks, "How do I get to Carnegie Hall?" Cabbie answers, "Practice." If there's any dream for a mother to have her son play somewhere in New York City, it's at Carnegie Hall. I don't know if that's the reason, but he literally taught right next to the concert hall on 57th Street. There was a little entrance and you went up to a small studio that Joe rented. He was there all day Saturday with one student after another. He even had a little cot where he would take a nap. This guy was relentless. He would teach fifteen hours in a row and was famous for it. He had seventy to eighty students a week. As well, he taught over the years at New England Conservatory, at Juilliard, at the Manhattan School of Music—incredible. He was the greatest guy, the most beautiful cat, and basically the saxophone guru in New York City for several generations of players from studio to classical to jazz guys.

He was a warm human being and we got along great. There were a few guys besides me he would always talk about to other students—Eddie Daniels, Dave Tofani—guys who were a little older than me. I guess we were among his star pupils. There might be some others I don't know about, of course. But especially Daniels and me, I guess, because we went on to some notoriety. Michael Brecker went to him; so did Steve Grossman. My relationship with him went on for fifteen to twenty years. He was my guru. For saxophone he was the main man. The thing with Joe Allard was that, in a way, he was a Zen teacher and the complete opposite of Lennie. Joe didn't tell you anything really, specifically. He told you stuff and you thought, "What does that mean?" Not that it was complicated, but that it was too simple! Like: "To breathe is to blow, to blow is to breathe, to blow is to sing, to sing is to blow"—stuff like that, often said in French—of course, I'm paraphrasing.

The whole idea with Joe was that playing the saxophone is an extension of what your vocal chords do every minute of life when you speak, when you vocalize anything, for that matter both literally and physically.

You are expressing yourself through your voice and through the movement of the vocal chords located in the voice box, in the larynx somewhere around the Adam's apple, and that's all there is. You don't have to *do* anything—the vocal chords operate below the threshold of physical recognition, like the knee-jerk response. In the old days when you went to a doctor, and maybe still today, he would strike your kneecap with a small rubber hammer to see the leg jerk up—I guess a sign that you are alive or something like that.

Now, Joe's simple concept means overcoming years of bad habits and, of course, physical stress, which impedes the flow you are trying to capture even before the creative act kicks in. I mean, the body is first in line when you play an instrument. You have to deal with the machine. His thing was, in a nutshell, "You're stressing—everybody's stressing; it's much easier than you think. You've got to break the bad habits. How can you play and create music in that state of stress?" So, Joe's thing was not so much about what to do as what not to do. That's why I call it Zen-like—it's that whole thing of less effort is more.

Again, I'm not perfectly sure as to when I started with Joe. It was certainly in full swing when I began Queens College as a music major and had to have a main instrument. There was no saxophone major at that time, so it had to be clarinet, one of my least favorite instruments, which I was still playing somewhat at that time on club dates. I came in to the first lesson with the Studies by Rose, a well-known clarinet book. I played the first line of page one and he stopped me. I did not get past line one for six months! Now, I'm coming from a teacher where the lessons were book after book, and if you don't do page two well, you just do it again and then go on to page three, etc., with Mr. Shapiro. Book, book, book, book—which was good because I learned to read pretty well, and Nat had me reading most of the stuff one whole step up, transposing concert key music for the tenor, which is a very necessary skill for B-flat instruments. So, I had a certain amount of technique, but I don't remember much discussion about tone or sound on the saxophone. You just put the horn in your mouth and moved your fingers. Nothing about what sound was about. Joe was all about sound and the physical aspects of getting a good tone. So, he takes out the classic *Gray's Anatomy* book used by doctors for centuries to describe the parts of the body.

Lew: At the first lesson?

Dave: Every lesson, to the well-worn page concerning the breathing apparatus, diaphragm, larynx, etc. All Latin words and intricate diagrams. After a few lessons of that, I'm saying to myself, "This is supposed to be the greatest teacher in New York." Here I am going to this great guru and I have nothing to practice except a low B-flat or something like that, and I am kind of freaking out. He goes on and on about the anatomy stuff and stories about Marcel Mule, the first great saxophone performer and teacher, and opera singers, and all kinds of tales: "Oh, when I worked with this opera singer, they breathed this way; they didn't breathe that way." Talk about teaching by metaphor and off the point! Joe was at one time the first clarinet player under Arturo Toscanini for the NBC television orchestra. And everything was "live" in the early days of TV. So, there were stories about the greatest conductor who ever lived and so on.

Every once in a while, I would play something and Joe would put his fingers in my mouth and move things around, saying stuff like, "Don't bite—chew—turn your lip out—put the tongue in the *Eee* position," and so on. So, here's the deal: It took me ten years to see the light, to understand his point, and of course now I am one of the leading advocates of Joe Allard's principles. I was once again, as in the case of Tristano, not mature enough, certainly musically, to understand his concepts. I did what he asked, that is true, but I didn't really understand what the hell he was talking about in general. Why is my tongue here, why are my lips like that? Because I was a good student, when the teacher said something, I did it. But I didn't really get the point until years later, and that's what my teaching and my book *Developing a Personal Saxophone Sound* are all about. I did go to him religiously for a couple of years. I don't know when I officially stopped weekly lessons with Joe, but I never really stopped going to him while he was alive.

Our relationship was great. I always tell the Miles Davis story that, to my memory, happened at the concert I did in 1974 at Carnegie Hall—how appropriate—when we recorded *Dark Magus*. I introduced Joe, and Miles said: "You taught Steve Grossman and Dave. I know you," and he shook his hand. He met Elvin Jones at the Village Vanguard when I worked there. Elvin picked Joe up into the air, the way he did all the time with people, and said, "Oh, you're the teacher." Joe was a very respected cat. Whenever I played in Boston, if he was up at the New England Conservatory that day, no matter where I was playing, Joe would have students bring him down. "Dave's in town," and they'd bring Joe to the first set. He was the only gray hair in the place, and I was so proud. At ten o'clock he'd say, "Now I've got to get up early. I've got to teach at six!" I was so happy. This was the closest I ever had to a master/apprentice relationship besides the jazz heavies I would eventually play with. It doesn't work like that much in our informal society, but that way of teaching still holds sway in other parts of the world and I love it.

Joe taught everybody. He didn't care about classical repertoire unless that was what you needed to do, if you were a Juilliard or MSM—Manhattan School of Music—student. For guys like us, he really didn't talk about any specific music per se. He knew what jazz was, and he'd even played in 1938 with the vibes player Red Norvo. I remember seeing a transcription of Trane's *Giant Steps* solo on his music stand for a while in the studio. "This is fantastic. John's so great. He came up for a lesson, and I talked to him." Guys went to Joe for remedial work. He was like a doctor when you had a problem. You didn't have to take more than a couple of lessons with Joe to get the story because he said, "You're doing this wrong. You're doing this too much. You don't need to do this." Basically he taught the same lesson every week. If you were ready, you could get it all in one lesson.

Lew: I should tell you I took one lesson with him when I used to double on alto as well as piano.
Dave: So, do you remember? He covered everything, right? He did it all in one lesson!

Lew: He taught me all the mystery of air. This is when he was already retired. I went to his New Hampshire place. I was living in Boston at the time.
Dave: So, you were where I went to visit him when I put the book together—his summer home on a lake.

Lew: Yes—I phoned and he invited me by around '84/85 and gave me an hour lesson. Everybody said that he hadn't played in years. He said, "I kind of like your mouthpiece. Let me try it." I had a Runyon—a metal mouthpiece for alto like David Sanborn used. He took my horn and said, "Let me just show you something." He hadn't warmed up and he certainly hadn't played since I walked into the room, and it was not his mouthpiece. So, he is sitting there like a half hour without warming up, and then he says, "I'm going to show you that the sound is all in your head, the notes are all in your head. It has nothing to do with the horn—the keys just make it a little easier."
Dave: And then he played any note on the same fingering like it was magic?

Lew: He fingered a low D, and then he played a D major scale starting on the D two octaves higher, up into the altissimo and back down—without moving a single finger!

Dave: He also did the opposite, play one note, say a palm key D, and then move his fingers all around without changing the pitch. I do this for the students, although not as well as Joe did, and that's when their eyes go buggy. "You see, now you know why the saxophone is an easy instrument. You just got the point." The thing with Joe was that he had one incredible lesson—that fingering didn't matter, it was a matter of the larynx—and that one lesson was the main deal. Of course, I'm exaggerating, but point made.

Lew: What amazes me all the time is that you need someone like Joe, as seemingly basic as it is, because most people don't teach that stuff.
Dave: He resented other teachers, by and large, who had systems of do this or do that.

Lew: Most teachers are doing like your teacher Mr. Shapiro—they're just saying it's this note, it's that note . . .
Dave: Or they're telling you to tighten up, or open your throat, or move your lip, or yawn, etc. Joe took it as a personal affront that so and so would ruin students with that kind of instruction, making them all stressed out. He had a real pet peeve about a famous guy whose book is all over the world and translated into a lot of languages on saxophone technique. Joe thought this was of no use. He thought that someone like that exerted a negative influence because it makes the player tense. The more directions you had, the more tense you are going to be, and how can you play music if you're tense? Then he would demonstrate, in a tense voice, "Hey, look at me—I can't talk, I'm tense." You can't talk like that and you can't blow like that and you can't play like that. With all the things you have to think about when you're playing music—hearing the note, expression, what's going on around you, the conductor—and you're going to be sitting there tensed out of your mind? No way. That was his view.

His basic vibe was if you're not relaxed, how can you play music? And to play the saxophone, in fact, to be musical, you had to be relaxed. If you're not that, it's because somebody along the line told you to do something that is unnecessary and promotes tension. Too much effort was counterproductive for playing music. That's why I call it Zen-like. He was about "Give it up. Don't strain. Just do what's natural." It was great, but not something an eighteen- or nineteen-year-old kid is going to get. He also worked on mouthpieces and reeds at the lesson, showing you all about that stuff. And as I said, when it was required, he did repertoire—tongue here, articulate there, and so on. But his general thing was the vibe of how to make a sound come out of the saxophone in the most natural and comfortable way possible. That was what I got out of him, and it took me, as I always say, at least ten years to realize it.

One day I heard Trane and I realized what it was—that his sound in the upper register, especially from A up to the palm-side keys, was, of all the saxophone players, the most satisfying. Why? Because it was even and emanated from the bottom register, the most vibrant part of the horn. I realized what Joe was talking about—that everything is a low B-flat. It all comes from there and it feels great. You go up to the high notes and they feel like they are coming out of the bottom of the horn. It is through the overtone exercises that you comprehend this principle, which takes a certain amount of time, period. You're playing with one feeling throughout the whole horn, rather than two or three different viewpoints or approaches.

Lew: Instead of hearing them as isolated high pitches?
Dave: Thank you. Exactly. Evenness of range. That was Joe Allard. And as I said, he was a sweetheart. Encouraging. After my initial few steady years with him, I would visit for a checkup, like a medical exam. Then I did the *Saxophone Sound* book with him by visiting his summer home in New Hampshire for a few days over two summers, armed with a recorder and with all the questions that I felt were not clearly answered—the reasons why, the real details that I was adamant about understanding, if only for my own teaching. The way my mind works is to get it down in detail, in a logical sequence, and then present the info in an orderly and logical way. I had notes from the lessons in the sixties, which I would write down after the lesson on the subway back to Brooklyn from Carnegie Hall, so those were a guide when I started the book in the early '80s.

Lew: Well, the book is great because that's his legacy now. Otherwise it would just be what people remembered of him. He never wrote a book of his own.
Dave: I know. It's him through me. What I did was amplify. He was a great teacher, but he didn't give you the reasons. I'm the kind of cat who wants to know *why* my lip should be in that position or whatever, not just accepting the info as doctrine. Why, if it's in a different position, will it not be as good? I like to know intellectually what's going on. I want to understand why because I think it enhances what you can do, when you have a foundation that's built on reason. So, when I went to him in New Hampshire, I pinned it down. I still have the tapes at home. I asked: "Joe, when you say use the V position for the bottom lip, or use your tongue in

the E position, or this or that, why? And what do you mean?" I pressed him and got him to put it on tape and then rewrote it in order to get it worded right. I was his scribe.

When I went to him, I said: "I'm going to be like Robert Craft was to Stravinsky. I'm going to be your guy." He was cool with that. For a minute he said that he wanted to do his own book, but eventually I just moved ahead and by then he was passing on. Unfortunately, he had Alzheimer's, like my dad, and I alerted his wife to that after a visit. It was so sad. There's a DVD of him called *The Master Speaks*, which a well-meaning guy cobbled together from a lot of takes because by then Joe wasn't too clear. If I had to list all the teachers I had in music—we have spoken about Lennie, Nat Shapiro, and we'll get to Charles Lloyd, just to name a few—I'd have to say that in a certain way, from the standpoint of a hands-on thing, I got the most out of Joe. In the end, he had the strongest effect on me because it was about playing the instrument.

Lew: Even while you were with him, even though, like you say, you didn't quite get it, you kept going back, so you were obviously getting something out of it. Maybe you heard your sound was improving or something?

Dave: Yes. This "clarinet major" charade went down pretty fast, thank God. As I told you, Queens College ended after the first year, so I didn't have to be concerned with the clarinet thing. Once that went away, as I was heading toward twenty years old and starting to go to jam sessions, playing more in the real world of jazz, I'm actually kind of on my own as far as teachers go. I'm picking things up from my friends. So, in a certain way, a teacher later on wasn't as crucial as it was at sixteen to eighteen years old, when I first got with Joe, Lennie, and Charles. By now I'm more independent. This was my "conservatory training," with masters like this, before the playing lessons began. I am forever grateful for what these masters gave me.

Chapter 3

Breakaway: Finding Myself

Lew: When did you really start performing jazz publicly?
Dave: In a certain sense, my actual jazz performing outside of the club dates and all that we've discussed really begins with the concerts I put on at NYU. Before that, in my teenage years I played concerts at hospitals, old-age homes, and public schools that my mother set up with my high school buddies.

Lew: Like Mike Garson?
Dave: Yes, and of course the guys in the Impromptu Quartet. We played whatever we thought jazz was at the time. Combined with all the club dates and the Catskills since thirteen years old, I had been getting in front of an audience for a while by the time I got to twenty years old. At NYU, I played a bunch of concerts at the student center up in the Bronx, some outdoors. I remember one concert with Lenny White, the drummer, who was sixteen years old. I assume we had met at jam sessions that we had at pianist George Cables's house in Queens. Unrelated, but it ends up that George's mom was a teacher also and knew my mother—small world. I believe it was in St. Albans, Queens, where we jammed with Steve Grossman, and Lenny, a bass player named Lanny Fields, sometimes Jimmy Sutherland on drums, and a piano player, Larry Shubert. I think I'm getting the names right. Anyway, I remember Lenny distinctly because he was so good, and not long after, he recorded *Red Clay* with Freddie Hubbard.

I did several concerts with members of one of the first fusion groups, the Free Spirits, which included my friend Bob Moses, and Larry Coryell, bassist Chris Hills, and saxophonist Jim Pepper. Through Moses, I was hanging out with them, going to college in the Bronx, and then going downtown and playing with the cats. In any case, this was the period where I really started playing and having to put together a set. I remember one concert in the South Bronx at a community center with Moses and Coryell. We did a long version of "Days of Wine and Roses"—I have a tape of it somewhere. We were kids and didn't think much about whether people got it or not, or even if there were any people.

Larry was one of my first heroes. He was very influential, the first guitar player to kind of move us into the modern age. He came from Galveston, Texas, and then to Seattle. I remember when he came to New York. Moses immediately got with him and called me one night: "You've got to come down to Café Au Go Go. There's a new guitar player in town." I walked in and this cat was burning, and so was Jim Pepper on Coltrane's "Impressions." I think trumpeter Randy Brecker, Michael's older brother, was there, too. Somewhere around '65 or '66, I believe. For Larry it was before he was with Chico Hamilton or Gary Burton, which eventually were the gigs that put him on the jazz map. I used these Free Spirit guys on concerts at NYU while they were living on the Lower East Side, maybe on Rivington or Stanton Street, which was pretty tough at that time. They were living in an apartment and I remember one time looking for them and there were like five guys I didn't know, sitting around the table, with one guy just hanging in the bathtub with his clothes on—a bit intimidating. When I asked where the guys I knew were, they said: "What guys?" in a pretty menacing tone. Needless to say, I split quickly.

Lew: Whose apartment?
Dave: I think it was Pepper and Larry's—I don't know. They were gone—M.I.A. It was crazy times. Who knows what was happening? But the point is that this was an important time for me because it was an opportunity to put music together, play, and keep up with those guys. They were definitely way ahead of me, no question about it. I was just not that good. They were already playing in the real world and getting gigs like, as I said, Larry with Chico Hamilton and Bob Moses with Rahsaan Roland Kirk, as well as both of them with Gary Burton.

I went to college because I wanted to, and it was expected from my background to do it. By the time I got to my senior year at NYU, I had enough for sure and wanted to really play and improve, etc. I went to Europe in my junior summer. So I'm nearly twenty-one—that's 1967. My parents believed that it was very important for a young man to see the world, visit culture, and all that. Going to Europe was not common in those days. But my parents said that I had to go. They gave me this famous book called *Europe on $5 a Day*. It listed all the student hostels and so forth, so that's why you can do $5 a day—plus a Eurail pass, which worked the same as now, unlimited train travel for a certain price because in those days air travel was not in the cards that much for travel within Europe.

I remember my parents handed me $1,000 in cash, a round-trip ticket to London, and the first night's reservation in a hotel, and said, "You will be glad you have the first night booked." I went on July 1 or 2, 1967, and landed in London. I got out of the plane, and I have to tell you, I was shaking—scared shit. I had no idea what I was doing, where I was, and of course the long plane trip with jetlag, etc. Getting into Heathrow and having to go to Victoria Station to go to Picadilly Circus right in the center of London—God—thank you, parents, for getting this hotel. So, I get to the room and I'm like, what do I do now? I'm completely alone in a foreign country. But I had phone numbers. The bass player Cameron Brown, who had lived in Sweden, had given me phone numbers. He played with Jan Garbarek and George Russell and knew guys. I don't know who I called, but somebody said, "Well, tonight all of the young guys are playing at Ronnie Scott's club after hours in a big band." Like a young guy's big band. So, that first night I went down and met the whole London scene. Among the musicians were saxophonists John Surman and Alan Skidmore, bassist Dave Holland, bassist Ronnie Mathewson, pianist Chris McGregor—they were all there. You have to remember this is '67, and a young American musician is exotic. I'm not Dexter Gordon or one of the expatriates who famously resided in Europe, but I'm from the other side and, of course, New York, which had a lot of caché even then. I'm a young guy who could play a little, so they were very open: "Don't stay in a hotel. Come stay with us." So, the next day I moved in with Surman and Dave Holland!

I stayed for a week or two in London, playing, hanging, living the life of a jazz musician—the first real taste. I know I'm going to be a senior in college, but this trip was the final nail in the coffin. I really didn't want to go back to school. After London, I went all over Europe for the next weeks, seeing museums and searching out jazz. I actually saw Dexter Gordon in Copenhagen at the famous Montmartre Club. I did it all. The rest of the trip was also interesting and even in some ways more important because I took part in my first recording session. I went across England to Newcastle, followed by a ferry to Bergen, Norway. Then I worked my way across Norway and Sweden by train.

In Bergen, I took a bus trip to the fjords and enjoyed Oslo, which was really pretty. I think I might've seen Jon Christensen and Jan Garbarek playing there. No other Americans anywhere, and I'm the only kid around on the trains or tourist buses. But now I'm feeling better than that first day in London. I go to museums, see the sights, actually fulfilling why my parents sent me there. I did the whole thing.

Finally, I land in Stockholm and once again I have the numbers that Cameron gave me. I call a guy named Lars Werner: "Cameron Brown gave me your number." He says to take such and such a train and immediately come to his house—to Bromma, a suburb of Stockholm. "Come and see us. Please be our guest." Completely hospitable. Before I shut down, he says, "By the way, do you know that John Coltrane died today?" So that's why I know the date, July 17, 1967. I started to weep right there at the train station. He said, "Come here—we'll take care of you—we're all musicians—you're going to be in good hands."

I get there and there's a house with a garden, instruments, records, the whole thing. The Werners were completely cool and I stayed for the next couple of weeks playing seven hours a day, eating flatbread, drinking beer, and experiencing LSD, 'cause that's what these cats were into. During that time we played a concert at the Kunstgarten in Stockholm and recorded, which was the first professional session of my life, after some high school recordings with Mike Garson. It's called *Och Hans Vänner* and it's kind of a famous underground record in Sweden since several of the cats have passed on since. Lars Werner was a well-known bebop piano player, apparently in the Bud Powell tradition, but also into free jazz, which was at its height in '67. The alto player was named Christer Boustedt, another very famous cat who died of a drug overdose. The drummer's name was Jan Carlsson, who subsequently became known as a comedian on TV. The bass player was Sven Hessle. The trumpet player was Otto Donner, who began his label, Love Records, with the release of this LP. A few years ago he re-released it on a CD commemorating forty years. Lars wrote a tune for me called "Ballad for Tenor Sax." It was kind of like a Naima-type tune—a spotlight for me. It was fantastic luck for me to hang with these guys who really took it far out as was the style those days.

I remember the concert in Stockholm, outside with a lot of people. The band started playing in different parts of the park, each guy working his way up to the bandstand. This was that period of history in the Western world—all kinds of experiments in art, drugs, happenings, and eventually political upheaval. In Europe, for example, 1968 was a pivotal year for student rebellions. But, at twenty years old, I didn't know anything about these things.

Besides the London and Stockholm adventures, I went to Paris, saw the Louvre, to Madrid and the Prado, all the way south to Alicante in Spain, to the Sistine in Rome, etc. I had my tenor with me everywhere. I didn't play soprano yet. I'm walking around with a tenor and a small valise. I did the whole thing, gladly fulfilling what my parents had given me money for, to see the world, so to say. There was no playing when I went south; the playing was over by August after Stockholm. I went back to London in the end and finished the summer with a party—coincidentally, on my birthday, September 4, 1967.

The point is that when I got back, I really realized that this is what I wanted to do. I saw the reality of what it was to wake up in the morning and only play, not to have to be a student in college. More importantly, to play no other music but jazz. So, this summer was a pivotal event in my life and I've got to thank my parents for that. This trip pretty well made it definite in my mind that after finishing my commitment to school, à la my parent's wishes, I was going to go for it. I mean, that was really it. The senior year was when I really started to play and hang a lot downtown.

Lew: So your folks didn't send you to Europe with the idea that you would become a full-time musician?
Dave: No, it was for culture. By the time I came back, things between my parents and me were kind of breaking down as a natural result of my changing and conflicts about the future, etc. I just didn't see the sense of school anymore but of course would finish what I started. But I really wanted to do this music.

My jazz life really started in that period, 1967-68. Even though I had done some concerts with heavy guys, I was pretty envious of the young cats who were already on the scene. By now, as I mentioned, some of my peers and new guys just coming onto New York were gigging. It seemed that guys coming from out of town got a better shot than guys who were in town, for the following reason, I think. If you were from New York, chances are you had already, somewhere along the line, probably played a jam session. Your reputation was shot because you didn't play that well. This is something you might do before you were ready, wherever you grow up, but in this case you were screwing up in the Apple. That's a disadvantage of being a native, at least it seemed in my case. Of course, you will have another day to redeem yourself.

In any case, for whatever reason, my senior year was fraught with a lot of difficulties. It was not a happy time for me personally as well as musically. Also I couldn't wait to get the hell out of school. So my scenario, in summation: I was about to graduate from NYU. Now what are you going to do with an American history major, a minor in sociology, and some teaching course credits? The only thing to do was teach. But I had to find a way to practice what I needed to do musically—so all of this was happening at the same time.

By then I also started to realize what I needed to do to get better. I needed a period of practicing and playing music only. That was my decision by January of my senior year with the last semester looming. I said to myself: "The day I graduate, I'm going to upstate New York or somewhere, and I'm shedding. I'm going to do everything I'm supposed to do," which I knew then was basically transcribing solos. The educational rap I give now to students all over the world is the same rap that was apparent to me by then. It was obvious to me that transcribing was the key to the kingdom.

There were no books; there was no other way to get it easily. Nobody taught it, and I realized that I had to know what Trane, for example, played, direct from the horse's mouth. There's not going to be guessing—that wasn't good enough any more. My ear wasn't the kind that sits down and hears everything immediately. I didn't have that particular talent. I had to sit and slow the phonograph down, go back, scratching the record, and so on. That's the way I did it.

With the end of college looming, my parents said that I would be on my own financially, so I had to figure things out for the immediate future. I needed a certain amount of money to rent a place in upstate New York. I figured out that I would need a couple of hundred dollars, which sounds like so little now, but I had it figured to the penny, what I needed for rent for six months and to eat. I figured I would do what I had heard other guys did, and get a taxi license. I took the taxi test and in my senior year I became a taxi driver. I got a hack license. And in spring break 1968, during Easter, I drove straight for seven days, eighteen hours each day.

The taxi experience was not the greatest thing in the world. Although I wasn't robbed, I did have a scary scene. I left someone off at a house in the Bronx and was told to wait for him by another guy, still in the cab. Next thing I see is this first cat running out, with a guy chasing him down the street pointing a gun. The guy in the cab says, "Split!" and I leave him off a few blocks away. He tipped me a dollar, which was a big deal, because he said I was cool! That kind of cool I didn't need, so being a taxi driver was definitely off my plate after this.

For my practice place, I knew I wanted to be around Woodstock, which had nothing to do with the event that happened there later on. It was just that I knew the area a bit but I didn't want to be in the hotel region where I had played for so many summers. I found a place near Kingston, New York, called Lake Katrine, with my girl friend of that time in college, Laurel, and a bass player I knew from school, someone I was familiar with.

I left the day after graduation, which in itself was heavy. I played Coltrane's "Naima" solo on tenor at the graduation, dressed in cap and gown, dedicated to Martin Luther King Jr. and Robert Kennedy, who had recently been assassinated. This was June 1968. It was a heavy time for the country—a lot of riots were about to happen and so on. All I knew was I was on my way to practice and get out of the school routine.

If you graduated school in the sixties, you really were in the middle of it. You felt it firsthand—the murders, the Vietnam stuff, the whole counterculture thing. We were the ground zero generation for big change, especially those born in 1946, the official beginning of the baby boom generation. Anyway, that was the end of school. I got my bachelor of science in American history and the day after I graduated, I got in the car and went to Lake Katrine. It was a little pad—I can sort of remember what it looked like. I was there until Thanksgiving. By November, when it got cold and snowy, I said, "Okay, that's enough. I'm out of here. I did my duty."

Lew: And you were there with your friends?
Dave: I was there with my girlfriend, Laurel, and this bass player. I did what I had to do to learn the music, which was basically transcribing from recordings. This is that whole rap I teach now, which comes out of what it did for me at that point in my development. It meant really copying *exactly* the feel, nuances, and general character of what someone great played, not just the notes. You could learn the notes from a book, but not the feel. I did Trane's "Impressions" playing along with the record using a phonograph—hard to believe now. I practiced eight hours a day. I don't remember what I practiced besides the transcription stuff, but I did something. I brought whatever I was working on or thought I should work on. This was the only really intense practice period I ever did.

We lived close to the bone—rice and veggies, etc—sort of a hippie existence. It was in the country and the whole nature thing was around me, which I had never really experienced before, not that I was paying that much attention to it. I could've been anywhere.

Lew: And your roommate?
Dave: He practiced bass, but he never continued on. I actually don't remember his name. He went there with me, which is why the money was cool, because of splitting the rent with somebody. Randy Brecker and Dave Holland came up to visit during that period. I remember us playing in different parts of the cottage at the same time. Dave Holland came to America to join Miles Davis in mid-August. Another visitor was drummer Pete LaRoca, with whom I had just begun playing. He came up with bassist Walter Booker and Anna Maria Booker, who was Wayne Shorter's wife's sister. She sang "Dindi" on Wayne's 1969 record *Super Nova*, where she is weeping as she sings—a very touching performance. They came up to rehearse and I will never forget Anna Maria singing the melody to "Bahia" in Portuguese, trying to help me with the phrasing. I will talk more about Pete later, but this was near the beginning of our relationship. After Thanksgiving, I went back to my parents' in Brooklyn before the next stage started, which is the first loft on West 19th Street, the beginning of my "real" life, so to say.

So, to summarize, these years were really heavy—the counterculture, being in school, away from home, the jazz component, the European tour, lessons with various masters, being on my own, the frustration I felt at not being part of the scene, feeling that I lost any kind of advantage I might have had, and so on. But something that took years to realize is about the educational component that I had finished. That is, if I look at myself, at what is unique about me compared to some others in the field, it's not a musical thing. It is education, pure and simple, exactly what my parents said, which is that you get a college education not necessarily because you're going to vocationally use it, not necessarily because you'll remember anything. I mean, does anyone remember what they learned on, say, November 5, 1967? Not really. The real point is that education adds to your reservoir of knowledge. It develops your mind, your level of sophistication, and hopefully equates to being a cultured person. That's the difference between you and a person who didn't go to school, who might be out in the field earlier and have gotten ahead faster. They will not have what you have when the dust settles—and it will.

Of course, when you're twenty-two years old you don't want to hear that explanation and even when you're thirty-two years old you don't want to hear it. But by the time you're a little more mature and you start to have some awareness of who you are, you see what the differences are between you and your best friend, or your neighbor, or, in my case, another player, your contemporary, or peer, whomever. You have to realize what contributes to one's singular personality, just as you have to equally realize what is common for all human beings. Now, in my case, the polio thing is one aspect, which we've discussed. But I think the fact that I had a liberal arts education is also important in my story. If you were to take a survey now of guys my age and ask them what their schooling was, I don't know, but I would imagine most would not have a liberal arts training, if they had any higher education. Not jazz education, because it wasn't widely available at the time, so a lot of guys just didn't go to college. It wasn't a big thing and it wasn't a priority.

Lew: Some conservatories weren't open to jazz at all. In fact, they were anti-jazz.
Dave: Exactly, so you had to do something else, and I found history, which I liked, and I feel that that's made a difference in my life. When I look back at those days, it was cool and the right thing to do.

Lew: At the time you weren't happy, but the results have been good. You are, as you said in terms of being different, not only a great player, you're a leading educator and an author. As an educator/author, it really helps to be college trained.
Dave: It comes full circle. Everything is for a reason.

Lew: Those are big parts of your career, the writing—
Dave: It is. I have to say that is because of the schooling. Also, the way I think about things is very related to history and human behavior, etc. It really does happen on a daily level that these things may come to me as part of my M.O. It's nothing unusual on my part, or any great amazing talent—just plain education—that's it.

Now, to backtrack slightly, I should discuss the role of Charles Lloyd, who is an important part of this period and really enabled me to get a bird's-eye view of what the lifestyle was like, what it was on a daily level to be a jazz musician. He was the first real jazz musician with notoriety that I knew personally. This is around '65/66, just when he was beginning his ascent, around the time of *Forest Flower*, which really put him over the top. That's the year I was with him. A reason why I can remember the date so well is that when he played Newport—July 1966—he asked me to drive his band—Keith Jarrett, Cecil McBee, Jack DeJohnette—to the gig in my car. I was the go-fer, the lackey, and glad to be.

Lew: Must have been a big car.
Dave: It was, in those days! It might have been a Chevy Impala, which was gigantic with the fins and had a colossal trunk. That was like my first college car. I don't know how they got the instruments to the gig. But I had the guys in the backseat, the three of them, and Laurel next to me. They didn't know who I was—I was just some guy. But the story of Charles and me is a great story—how I got to him. Again, it's Bob Moses and me trying to find something. I'd already been through Lennie; the Joe Allard thing was either over or coinciding, but that's saxophone only. So, what's on my mind is, who can show me the real deal. I mean somebody has got to tell you these secrets, you know. It's like this voodoo that you can't get; it's like some secret society that you can't break into!

You go to a club and you're actually standing at the bar next to the Great Man, and he might even answer a question, but nobody's saying much and anyway, who am I to him? So, I ask Moses, "Who plays the most like Trane?" "Charles Lloyd. He's with Cannonball Adderley." I get the record—*Fiddler on the Roof*—absolutely Trane. I go down to the Half Note Club to see the Cannonball Adderley Sextet. They are playing, and sure enough he's got that sound, old Trane. He's got the goatee, he looks fantastic, dressed to the nines, very elegant. After the first set, I go up to him at the bar: "Mr. Lloyd"—I might've introduced myself—"do you teach?" "No." Then he looked at me real deep and says, "But you can come over tomorrow." This is Saturday night. "Tomorrow afternoon." I said: "Where do you live?" He said: "West 3rd Street above the fire station." I said: "I know where it is." He said: "One o'clock." Bam—done!

I go over the next day, and for the next year I spend most Sundays with him and his wife, Joan. That's the Joan in his tune "One for Joan." They live right across from where the Blue Note club is today. I would take the subway down from NYU in the Bronx, or drive. We would have coffee or whatever, watch the Yankees—I don't know. I'll tell you that the lessons were not much in the formal sense, but the important fact was that here was a real guy, the real deal! This wasn't my friends, this wasn't standing at the bar next to a guy, this was Charles Lloyd, who was playing with Tony Williams at that time, on Lloyd's *Of Course, Of Course* recording—great record. He's happening—playing all over New York a lot, and really prominent on the scene. Pianist Don Friedman is on Lloyd's first record, *Discovery*. Like I said, he had Tony, and Gábor Szabó on guitar, sometimes Herbie Hancock and Ron Carter—basically

Miles's rhythm section. Later, there was Jack DeJohnette and Keith Jarrett, Cecil McBee—he had the best cats in New York. Really, that was when he was riding high. So, I was around a real bona fide jazz musician.

Charles had little African things around the pad. Outside of Moses, I had no exposure to this. It was a whole other world. As far as the lessons—what lessons? I mean, I have a couple of anecdotes concerning things he said, but that's all I remember. We didn't do much music per se, although I would bring my horn. He gave me the feeling, the vibe.

One time I played a little and he said, "You play better than I was at twenty-one. Your generation doesn't have to look back." He gave me the feeling I didn't have to get the change-playing down. Now at that time I'm completely into late Trane, the free stuff, as far as trying to play like that, and he's giving me the feeling that you don't have to learn the old language. One time I did say something about old Trane: "What about that stuff that Trane played on 'Oleo' and with Miles in general?" He said: "What do you mean? Like this?" He took the horn out, and he played Trane's "Oleo" solo. From what I could remember, he played the solo, or like it, enough for me to say: "Yeah, that's it. That's what I want." Then he went into what I just described: "You don't have to do that." This is funny, because that is why I originally sought him out, that he sounded the most like old Trane. Now the great guru is saying, you don't have to do that, because your generation's different. Remember, there's nobody else of that stature around to tell me that you're supposed to do it. I had already had this catastrophe with Tristano and I had nobody else guiding me, just my friends, and I don't know anything! So Charles Lloyd said you don't have to go back. That kind of convinced me that I don't have to do all that work with bebop. This is before I went away for the summer practice thing in upstate New York, when I straightened out change-playing anyway. In a certain sense Charles kind of misled me, not on purpose. I think he really believed that, as others do also.

I thought he was God, you know. He was so hip and cool and everything like that, and he played great—the whole package. Let me finish that story about driving the band up to Newport. I remember picking up Keith, I think, downtown; Cecil, somewhere in the lower East Village; Jack, I think, was living up on 88th Street. When we got to Newport, there was this big line of cars and they had to play in an hour, so they just got out and went ahead while Laurel and I waited in the car line. What stands out about that trip was that I saw Trane later that afternoon, July 2, 1966, playing with Rashied Ali, Pharoah Sanders, Alice Coltrane, and

Jimmy Garrison. There's a live audio recording of it, and a silent home movie of part of it by a Japanese fan. Trane is playing in, I think, a blue polo shirt. That's the only time I ever went to the Newport Festival as a listener.

Another incident I remember happened on one of those Sundays. I went to Charles's pad and he shows me an ad in the *New York Times* for a car. Next thing I know, we are driving over to New Jersey, somewhere near the Palisades. We arrive at this really elegant apartment house, obviously moneyed out, and it's a couple who are selling a Maserati. Charles buys it on the spot. I didn't even know what a Maserati was. Maybe he was trying to be Miles—he's got Miles's sidemen, he dresses great, he's crossing over to the pop world before it was fashionable. Charles is king of the world, man. So, there we are at this apartment overlooking the Hudson River, a black guy in a very white setting, and he buys this great sports car, and we drive back to New York. That was one of my Sundays with him.

These experiences with Charles Lloyd just gave me more incentive to make this jazz thing happen. What looked better than living in the Village—a great lady, artsy pad, great clothes, jazz with the best cats around, being on the covers of magazines, etc.? This ain't Brooklyn, man—definitely not Flatbush—I mean, this is the hip deal and I am a young, impressionable cat. So, between Charles and that summer in Europe, which is all coinciding within a year or two of each other, I am on my path to the future. These things were really more nonmusical in a way, different from seeing Trane and his influence on my spiritual and musical life. That had already happened a few years earlier to get me to this point in the mid-sixties—the idea that this could be a life, that you could actually do it. It was now becoming more of a reality.

I haven't seen Lloyd personally since this period. Bobo Stenson, the pianist whom I played with a lot in the '90s, worked with him, and one time we spoke on the phone, but otherwise I only know about him from what everyone else says—his time with the Beach Boys, making money in real estate in Big Sur, his resurrection in the '80s, and so on. He was very nice—I think he liked me. For a minute I was his boy. I was at the gig every night, being around and helping if I could. I loved it.

I don't believe I ever paid him for these hanging-out lessons. I think we just struck up a relationship. It was like the traditional master-apprentice system that has existed for centuries in all the arts and even the trades, and to some extent still does, albeit in a different context—the way it would be if we were in India. You help a young guy out. Like I have a saxophonist, Matt Vashlishan, who just finished his doctoral studies at the University of Miami, who has been helping me with books and so on and playing with me anytime we can. I helped him out on his first recording and so on. You know, that kind of thing.

Charles was a mysterious dude and apparently was experimenting a bit with LSD. In videos from that period, when the other guys are soloing—you see him moving his arms like a bird in flight. Some of the other guys may have been taking it also. After all, this was the period and jazz musicians were traditionally first in line for things like that. It seems they had it down to where they knew just how much to take—kind of like drinking alcohol just enough to get a little buzz. A full acid trip could take all day with recovery, but for a few hours that was a different story. People took it from a piece of blotter paper. It looked like a little dot, and I guess you could cut the dot up—something to do with micron measurements or whatever. Anyway, it meant you could sleep that night.

Charles was very charismatic—there's no question about it. He was one of the first, if not the first, jazz guys to cop a little of the hippie vibe, but in a clean and slick way. Miles was the man for all matters of style at the time and Charles seemed to give him a run for his money in that regard, even with, as we noticed, his choice of sidemen. It was like Charles's band was the warm-up for Miles, since Keith and Jack joined Miles later. Before that, Charles and guitarist Gábor Szabó were quite close. They really had a very empathetic relationship, the way the guitar played and weaved around the horn. The use of the guitar and saxophone was not a common combination, although Sonny Rollins did it with Jim Hall in 1961 and '62. I have discussed this at length with guitarist Vic Juris, who has been playing with me since 1991. Charles and Gábor were part of our model, and you hear it really great on Lloyd's *Of Course, Of Course*—also with Chico Hamilton's group earlier, in which they both played.

Also, he was an intellectual. Charles had been a school teacher in Memphis. I don't know to what extent, but he was definitely an articulate person. He got a degree from UCLA. He was not a jazz-musician-off-the-street kind of guy. He was well mannered and, in a way, very suave. He kind of represented a new wave. This wasn't Lou Donaldson or Sonny Stitt or even Dexter, with all due respect. This was the next wave of cats who were coming up educated, media savvy to a degree, and articulate in all ways. In a sense, it's the beginning of what we have nowadays with jazz education and all that.

Lew: During these days of hanging out, you would have your sax with you, but you were saying you wouldn't play.

Dave: Not much playing. I remember one day in particular. I had entered this history essay contest—one, because I was a history nut, and two, for the money award. It was NYU-wide, meaning any student in any program could write. It was called the Maas Essay Contest. I won second prize in my junior year and then first prize the year after, two years in a row. One paper was on the Battle of Leyte Gulf during World War II and the other on the Trent Affair, which happened during the Civil War. I did original research and a lot of formal essay stuff. I was into it. I went to the New York Library, looked at microfilms, the whole bit. I remember the day I was to go to the president of NYU's office to get the award in the Village, where the main campus of NYU is. Of course, I have a goatee and big glasses—I look older than I look now—my look in those days with the requisite long hair, but dressed in a suit for the occasion. I'm in the office of the NYU president, Dr. James Hester, and my mom is there and a photographer with the other two winners. NYU is right near Charles's place. I have my horn with me in the office and everyone's checking it out. After the ceremony, I was going down to Charles's pad. So, there on display were my two lives—the academic and the jazzer to be!

Lew: But again, Charles wasn't the kind of person who at some point during the day said: "Okay, now we're going to have the lesson"?
Dave: Absolutely not. No, I don't remember much formal stuff. He did say one memorable thing to me, which is one of my mantras to students—about the need for objectivity in evaluating oneself. I amplify the story to make it more telling. I don't remember his wording, but the extent of it was that when you practice, be objective. In other words, don't get into it. Don't practice with a vibe. Don't think you have to feel good when you practice. You're not supposed to feel good or bad. You're supposed to practice. If you're looking for emotional satisfaction out of practicing, you're in the wrong zone. Practice is just like hitting the nail on the head over and over time. There's nothing to feel about practicing. It's a four-hour neutrality zone. That's the only way to get something out of practicing.

Of course, you rightfully feel satisfaction if you've accomplished something. When I tell this, I say to the kids, "I bet you look in the mirror when you practice." They look at me with a surprised expression, 'cause I'm not too far off the money. Remember, this is near the beginning of the real serious process for musicians who want to get good. "Do you practice or do you play when you are in your house?" "Well, I don't know." I say, "You shouldn't be playing. Nobody's listening to you.

You're practicing." And there's my Charles Lloyd story. I certainly got something out of him in a lot of ways.

Of course, in the formal sense, someone like me or you these days teaches more material in thirty minutes than he did my whole time with him, but that's not the point. There are other things besides "facts" that can ring a bell. These concepts can be more important at a certain stage of development, which in my case was that time for me with Charles Lloyd. It's a drag that I haven't seen my great first influence over these years to hang a bit. But everything in its time, I guess.

Lew: What about the George Cables story concerning "Silent Way" that you mentioned before to me?
Dave: It's a sidebar because it's interesting about the process of learning. It has to do with my future relationship with saxophonist Steve Grossman, which we will get into. With George Cables and Lenny White and a few other guys, we used to jam a lot around this period, which I mentioned, in St. Albans, Queens. We used to play Coltrane tunes or whatever. One day we played in a car dealership on a Saturday afternoon in that area. I have no idea why or the circumstances. George had an electric piano, which was very new then—a Fender Rhodes. He comes in and starts to play this bass line that he tells us is from the newest Miles Davis release called "In a Silent Way." You have to remember that when a new record, as in LP vinyl, came out, it was seized upon by the musicians immediately to hear what was new, especially in the case of Miles. Well, we played on the bass line for the next forty minutes. That's the first time I heard a vamp on an electric piano. So, if there's a day or a moment when fusion raised its wonderful head at least to me, it was at a car dealership in Queens on a Saturday afternoon when George Cables came in with the title track vamp from "Silent Way." The beginning of something big!

Lew: The first time I ever saw you was at the Red Garter in the Village, 15 West 4th Street. They had a series, Sunday afternoons—this one was probably in the late summer of 1968. I remember Randy Brecker on trumpet.
Dave: Could have been presented by the organization Jazz Interactions.

Lew: Yes, Jazz Interactions, it was.
Dave: Definitely Randy, probably Cameron Brown on bass and Mike Garson on piano, and probably Lonnie Rutstein on drums. Lonnie was from the Catskill clique that I had played with and was one of the first

guys who really knew about jazz from that group. This is a guy who transcribed *Chasin' the Trane*. I remember sitting in his bedroom listening to Miles or Trane really carefully. He was an amazing musician and the real deal. A few years later Lonnie was found dead in a car near the 59th Street Bridge, the first real tragic death in my personal circle. It's a mystery—an unsolved murder, I think.

I had activity with Jazz Interactions because one day during lunchtime at my high school in Brooklyn years before, I was sitting in the auditorium playing the piano. Two guys are there setting up some equipment. "We're here to present something about jazz. We're part of an educational organization called Jazz Interactions." This was Allan Pepper and his partner, Stan, two Jewish guys who eventually ran the Bottom Line club in the location that had been the Red Garter, from 1974 to 2004. Two cats from Brooklyn, straight-ahead guys. I think I was playing "Night in Tunisia" on the piano. "You like jazz?" "Yeah, I love jazz." Anyway, that's how I got involved with Jazz Interactions, going to their events and so on. Remember, there weren't the numbers of young musicians like now, so anybody like that was sort of exotic in a way. The Red Garter gig you saw would've been a Jazz Interactions Sunday performance, probably with that band. I likely have a tape of that in my collection.

Lew: Well, they introduced your group as a youth award winner, so I guess it was the best youth band or combo.
Dave: Probably the only youth band! It was the same group when I did my first real major concert at Town Hall for Jazz Interactions on September 21, 1968. There's a photo on my website of me and Randy from that concert. I was chosen by Jazz Interactions to play opposite Roland Kirk's group and the Elvin Jones Trio. Allan and Stan produced it under the name Alstan Productions.

Lew: Randy was known because he was all over town. I remember he had long stringy hair. Later I went to see the Duke Pearson Big Band at the Vanguard and they said, "We've got young Randy Brecker on the trumpet." He sounded kind of Thad Jones-y, a little bit.
Dave: Randy had already come to New York by '64/65.

Lew: Once you were in college, how regularly would you do pot? How regularly LSD?
Dave: I don't remember. I don't know if we smoked every day, if it was like that. Certainly later on in the loft it was more prominent in everyday

life. The LSD thing definitely started then, but I didn't do it so many times. You were supposed to really do a trip right, think about it, have a day to recuperate and have the right music on—that's what Timothy Leary was talking about when he advocated LSD in the '60s. That's why you were supposed to have a guide. Leary wasn't talking about just freaking off, which is what, of course, eventually happened to a lot of people. Sometimes musicians liked to use it to put a little different spin on the music for a night. In general, it was supposed to help with the spiritual side of things and I think it did for me. I tried to get out of it what it was supposed to do, some kind of enlightenment.

Lew: When you were in Sweden during that Europe trip, you said the guys were doing a lot of LSD.
Dave: Yes, that might have been the first time I really did it a couple of days in a row. Then it was all music. We played for hours—you could just play and play. It felt like I was flying off the planet—sometimes easy to play, sometimes hard—sometimes it was great to play, then it wasn't. I felt good, then I felt bad—tight, loose. You know, it was like everything. This happened to be the Swedish experience. Everybody was completely stoned, but there was no pressure or bad vibes in that group. You went out in the garden, you sat outside, you went back in and played. Later on in the loft days, it was also like that.

Of course I had some bad experiences. One I remember was outside on the balcony of the apartment in the Bronx overlooking the expressway. I relived the whole polio thing. I was with Laurel and for a couple of hours I couldn't walk. I was crying. Maybe that's what a bad trip is like—I don't know. Somehow paralysis came back to me. Laurel was holding my hand and eventually I was cool, but you took a chance when you did that stuff, there's no question about it. We really were reckless. I would never do that now for a million reasons, because of chromosome damage possibly, because it really altered your state, because you don't know what is coming around the corner. A big thing was to be in a safe environment, not in midtown Manhattan, which I did do and it was horrible. Paranoia could be a problem when experiencing a trip. You couldn't handle somebody coming to the door—the postman, whomever—you know what I mean? You were hallucinating. At times everything was moving—you looked at a tree and you saw the rhythm in it. The lines in a leaf were fluid—movement—everything had movement. That's the main thing I remember.

I remember one trip I kept saying, "Time, time—there is no such thing as time. There are no endings, no beginnings." That whole thing of eternity became very clear to me—no start, no finish. You know, these are things you toss around in conversation, especially when you are young and just getting aware of these matters—the deep philosophical questions that are basically unanswerable. You say there's no beginning and no end and so on as a cliché, but I really zeroed in on it under the influence. And the music—that was the thing. This is why I love Trane's recording *Crescent* so much, especially the title tune. The time feel that the rhythm section gets on that track is unbelievable. For some reason that is the one that stands out among all the musical experiences I had on acid—with Elvin, Jimmy, and McCoy playing the beat like a ping-pong ball—so loose and relaxed.

And then the Bartok String Quartets—the music is like the history of life in front of you—biblical, dramatic, like a Cecil B. DeMille extravaganza all the time. Then, of course, Indian music, which really got to me—the spiritual side—God speaking. I really saw what music, and through that, what art is supposed to do. I didn't know it before and certainly wasn't ready for it. I'm just not sure that I would have gotten it any other way unless somebody sat me down and said, "Listen for that," etc. I don't see how I ever could have gotten to that understanding of what the whole creative thing is supposed to be about, especially the mysterious, impossible-to-define aspects.

Lew: It pushes you through. It takes you?
Dave: Exactly, exactly. Because to me, up to then, it was just good playing. I didn't realize the significance of it. Even Trane, as much as I loved him, as much as the late Trane moved me, did I really understand it? Did I really feel that, or was I just cognizant of what seemed to be a fact about it? The drugs opened the mind up to the possibility of these things, and you kept the memory for the rest of your life. In a certain way I am always trying to get back there, to remember what it was like. I understood why music is music. And again, as I say, understanding art in general, not that I know that much about other media, but the greatest art must all be talking about this same stuff. It has to be. This is what they mean. And that's worth putting your life into.

This is a blanket statement I will make, completely politically incorrect to say, but I don't think I would be the same person without the insights I gained from experimenting with drugs. I think that it made the difference in my life of who I am. It opened me up; it made me see there's more than meets the eye, the kind of insights I was getting through Coltrane and the like about art. I am not sure that I would've understood art, that I had it in me. I had other things, but not that. It really opened me up. Everything it's supposed to do happened, both positive and negative, but in sum I didn't have too many bad incidents from drug use. I don't have a terrible story to tell about addiction, and obviously I don't do it now or at all in recent decades. It's just not the time and period in my life, as it was earlier. I think drugs, especially the ones that stimulated your mind, basically LSD and smoke, resulted in a positive experience for me in total. Of course this is only applicable to me and obviously I don't recommend it to anyone. With drugs, things can change from positive to negative in a flash. I did not have an addictive personality. I was able to use these things, learn, and move on, but others were not so lucky. I am certainly aware of this.

As we have talked about Charles Lloyd, my trip to Europe, and so on, they all kind of fill in the answer to the question of why do this? Why do it—because you want to play saxophone? That's not enough. Why do it—because you heard a guy play and you'd like to be him? That's not enough. Why do it—because it releases you from a nine-to-five job? I don't think that's it. You need a meta-reason. You need something that's beyond the pale. And if you find that, you're lucky. I think that my experiences with LSD and pot helped me find it. I mean, of course, everything is part of the whole, and I might not have been ready if it wasn't for other things in my life that enabled me to be open to this whole process. Who knows? The drugs wouldn't have worked that way if it wasn't the right time and place for me. I was open and ready for it.

Chapter 4

Arrival: Becoming an Artist

Lew: We talked about your working with trumpeter Randy Brecker and drummer Bob Moses. These are fellow Jews. So, in terms of your peers, was it heavily weighted toward Jews?
Dave: Apparently so. Pianist Mike Garson and trumpeter Steve Satten, who was my main club date partner as a teenager, were also Jewish. There were not many African Americans in my scene for sure. My neighborhood was split pretty evenly between Italian and Jewish, as was Lafayette High School. As my interest in jazz grew, of course my idols were predominantly African Americans.

In the fifties, Jews and blacks had this relationship of being underdogs. There was a sense of simpatico on the surface in some ways, because there was prejudice against Jews in America, but nowhere near as much as blacks. In my home there was definitely some kind of liberal Jewish leaning toward supporting blacks. Certainly if we look at the civil rights movement of the sixties it is clear there was a lot of Jewish money and support. My parents definitely felt that blacks were getting a bad deal.

On the other hand, a case could be made that Jews were the landlords and blacks were the tenants. In Harlem, for example, many of the local business establishments were owned by Jews, and there was, as you could imagine, some tension in these situations. Also the Jews ran Hollywood and the record business, which had problems of its own vis à vis African Americans, as we know, in the jazz world regarding payments, royalties, etc. It was not la-de-da, but there was a bit more substance and interaction between Jews and blacks than there was, for example, between Italians and blacks. In that case they were equally suspicious of each other. Blacks did not enter Little Italy in Manhattan as a given. If you were black and you came into that area with guys hanging on the stoop or sitting in their little clubs, they definitely gave a bad vibe out. This whole thing I'm pointing out was part and parcel of jazz. You were entering, whether you knew it or not, a black world. And guess what? You wanted to. Why? Because they were hipper, they were cool, they looked better, they dressed better, they were flashier, they danced better, they looked like they had more fun, they hung out, and, most important, the majority of the jazz musicians were black.

Jews are not famous for their athletic prowess or dancing, activities involving smooth and graceful physical coordination. Musically speaking, outside of the classical world, Jews are not renowned for rhythm, which in the final result is one of the prime elements that differentiates jazz from classical music and most other musical idioms. There's no question that a young Jewish kid like myself would survey the situation in this regard and say, "Aw, man, I wanna be there!"

But there was something else driving me in the direction of music. I'll tell you the truth. I wanted to do anything but the nine-to-five drone I saw all around me. Thankfully, there came music and jazz as a salvation. Was the avoidance of a nine-to-five lifestyle more important than the music? I cannot tell you it wasn't. Was my being hip and cool more important than even the music, which I really had very little understanding of when I was sixteen, seventeen, eighteen? I'm not sure. I wanted to be hip, and I knew they, the brothers, were that.

Remember, the sixties was a bad period here. We're talking about the civil rights movement reaching its zenith, and the whole country changing in that respect. The voyage for me to the black world worked out because I got accepted by some of the chiefs. Later, being with Elvin Jones and Miles Davis, especially Elvin, was getting right to the heart of that world. We're talking drums, the root of the rhythm, and the king of the African thing was Elvin Jones. In the drum legacy he is one of the roots because of the way he played. And the raw power as well. When you think African drumming, it's Art Blakey and Elvin Jones at the top of the pyramid. All the great drummers have a touch of Africa in their playing, but these two were the epitome of those traits from my standpoint—power and energy. So I received some kind of benediction in my mind, a blessing from the chiefs.

To be in that world, I had to pay some dues for my entrance fee with both Elvin and Miles because there was flak in this regard. Look, Elvin's band was all white with me, Steve Grossman, and Gene Perla. I remember Elvin's wife, Keiko, one night saying that a well-known saxophonist made some disparaging remarks about the band in this regard. With Miles's band there was definitely some tension coming particularly from one guy in the group who couldn't abide that Miles had a white guy up there. After all, the colors of the Yamaha equipment on the stage were painted red, black, and green stripes, the flag of the Black Panthers—talk about making a point! Look at the pictures. Being white in the black world in those days was not a picnic. You were definitely a stranger in a strange land.

On the other hand you were privileged—you were an insider. I felt knighted, being with Elvin and Miles. "Hey, I earned my stripes. I'm living with these guys." And believe me, I wanted to be like them because they were so damn hip. They just were. In general, even though what I am about to say is a giant generalization, black people are just nicer people, more gracious and warmer than whites. They love to hang and relax. They know what life is about. This is outside of the terrible treatment that this country has inflicted on them—the prejudice and all that. Why is it that people are friendlier in the South? It's the Black culture. They're hospitable as a way of life, I guess like an African village. Jews, you know, they're arguing all the time. Let's face it. And they're on each other's neck. There's always the glass half empty, half full—and it's usually half empty! I feel like I went through a kind of socialization, besides the music, with Elvin and Miles. You know what I mean?

Lew: Yeah. There are white people, though—maybe not as many today—who grew up with jazz and yet, unlike you, it never really registered with them that it was black music.
Dave: Could be—I don't know. I wonder about the whites who were in jazz in the thirties and forties and were commercially successful. Were they looked upon like, "Oh, those aren't the real guys—Benny Goodman, Woody Herman's band. That's not the real thing. Basie's the real thing. Woody Herman is not!" I'm not sure. Anyway, who is the real deal? I think that's why the Tristano school got a lot of hard knocks. If anybody suffered from reverse prejudice it was them.

This is something that Lee Konitz could talk about, I'll bet. He certainly is qualified to talk about this, having gone through over sixty years of jazz history and being on the outside from the very start, if only because of the style he played. To some he appeared to not have embraced bebop in the standard sense of Bird and those guys. Of course we know that is complete bull as a criticism of Lee.

But, the masters were always cool. Miles was not personally prejudiced. Sure, he definitely knew the deal. When you read his autobiography, he pins the racism of the system, and he's right on the money. Of course he exaggerates, but Miles was okay with the racial stuff, basically. He told my lady during my time with him something like, "You know, the band don't like Dave because he's white. But I don't know what color he is. Dave has no color."

That's one of the great comments from Miles, and I feel very good about that statement: "Dave has no color." He's Dave. Miles didn't give a damn about that stuff, and Elvin was beyond it also. Not that they didn't know. They certainly knew what was happening in this country. But for them, music was first and they knew that music had nothing to do with color. It went way beyond that.

Lew: So, even at sixteen, seventeen, eighteen, you were aware that it was black music?

Dave: Definitely. It was apparent that the heavies were black. Who was white? Stan Getz playing bossa novas, Dave Brubeck playing in 5/4. They were popular at the time and great musicians, for sure. Was their popularity, which was a lot more than the usual jazz situation, because they were white and appealed to the general population, or was it because of the music they played? I don't know, but it was clear to me even at sixteen or seventeen that Herbie Mann was more popular than John Coltrane.

I could see that if I wanted this enough, I was going to have to deal with the black world—the good and the bad of it, and the fact that they really had been given a bad deal. They were probably going to resent me, and I was going to have some problems. I was trying to enter into that world and they were going to say, "You can't. You're not allowed in 'cause you're white." I expected that.

Lew: And when did you first start to work with black musicians or to be associated with them?

Dave: First was drummer Lennie White. As we discussed, he came around when I was in college and we played. In the first loft, a couple of others like bassists Clint Houston, Calvin Hill, and drummer Al Foster came by often. I was casually getting to know guys in the New York scene. So, it kind of just naturally happened. But with Elvin it was all white guys except for him; with Miles it was all black guys except for me. Sometimes with Miles the racial thing could get a little tense. Playing Chicago or Detroit, backstage was like a Black Panthers rally, definitely a feeling of being frozen out. This is '72/73, and they're looking at me like, "What are you doing here?" Seemed like guys Miles knew for decades. After all, these are cities he had played dozens of times. Let's put it this way—in Scandinavia or Europe or Japan, you never saw a black guy behind the stage, let alone in the audience.

But the audience was not heavily black. In fact, it has been noted that maybe one of the reasons for the *On the Corner* music and even the drawings on that LP cover was a purposeful attempt on Miles's part to reach out to the black youth. By and large, African Americans were not as involved in jazz in the '70s as in prior decades. They were into the Ohio Players, Earth Wind and Fire, Stevie Wonder, etc. Not until the eighties when Wynton Marsalis came around did young blacks get a little bit back into it.

But backstage there was a vibe in cities like I mentioned, or a place like Howard University. I mean, obviously, you're in their land. With Miles, the road manager and I were the only white guys of the eight or ten of us in the troupe, and there was a definite draft.

Lew: Was there ever something specific about not just being white, but being Jewish?

Dave: Not specifically, but as I said, Jews were part of the power structure in ways that impacted blacks' lives, especially represented in the music business. At least I had New York going for me, since I was from Brooklyn and there was a little bit of the 'hood vibe in there. I wasn't from the sticks. New York was the center of jazz in the fifties and sixties and I was a native New Yorker at least, for whatever credit that accrued to me. You had to at least have street smarts. That was the thing. Black guys were about the street and learned the music from the ground up, like we all did at that point. As far as they were concerned, they attained success through hard work, hanging out and being there. It wasn't a book that taught them to play. So, they definitely took a hard look at guys like us, who were middle class and more obviously intellectually trained. I went to college. I couldn't hide that I was college educated, no matter how "down" I tried to act.

Lew: Was being interested in black culture part of the counterculture during this period?

Dave: It was different in the sixties. The counterculture was the Vietnam, hippie, LSD thing, which was mostly white, middle-class kids who could afford to be that way. We got away with murder. We were not ghetto kids worried about our next piece of bread. The hippie stuff was basically a middle-class movement by kids who just couldn't stand it anymore. "I'm sorry. I'm not gonna do what my parents did, so I'm goin' completely out and different," and so on. You really didn't see blacks involved that much in the counterculture at all, except of course for the civil rights movement and how it naturally related to the hippie-freedom thing.

Lew: It was really civil rights for African Americans, not so much the counterculture.
Dave: Yes, exactly. At a certain point, I was entering two subcultures. Talk about rebellion. I was doing the white anti-everything—anti–my mother, anti–my father, anti-anything that's happened before—and I was trying to be a part of the black thing, which was obviously much hipper than the white vibe. Musically it was really like that also because we had Jimi Hendrix, Cream, Beatles, etc., standing next to Coltrane. This helps to explain the whole eclectic attitude that I and others of my generation display even now because of that time in our lives. From age sixteen through my early twenties, these were the important artists who were changing pop music upside down, kind of at the same time as what was happening in jazz, vis á vis the free movement. Jimi Hendrix was happening, Cream was happening, and the Beatles—*Magical Mystery Tour*—when that came out, we flipped! It was unbelievable—*Sergeant Pepper*—I mean, we flipped out! Alongside, you had Trane, so because of timing, my generation was really poised on the precipice of a few different movements.

Lew: Interesting. That counterculture, the so-called hippies, the drugs, all that—how did you move into that?
Dave: College, and the fact that it was the period, '64 to '68. You couldn't escape it, from anti-Vietnam protests to the drug culture to spiritual aspects like Hare Krishna. So you checked all of it out. You were naturally interacting with peers and picking things up. Although our campus at NYU in the Bronx was small, there were a few folks into this thing, though nothing like at big schools like Berkeley, California, or Columbia.

But you have to remember that this was a minority. Nobody should think that this hippie thing, this sixties revolution, was widespread. In the beginning it was like a little cult on the campus, and of course we were the weirdos. But when you see the anti-war Washington, D.C., demonstrations of 1969 and you see two hundred to six hundred thousand protesting against the war, it appeared to be quite massive, which it was by '69. The 1969 movie *Easy Rider* was very true. I will never forget it. It was like the national anthem of the hippie movement. In *Easy Rider*,

Nicholson and Fonda are hippies on a motorcycle experiencing the deal. They're basically drugged out, but harmless. Of course at the end they're killed by some rednecks on a country road. So, you couldn't leave New York City. In fact, even in parts of New York, if you had long hair or a tie-dye shirt—the uniform of our movement—you were looking for trouble. You didn't go to Long Island like that, or New Jersey. You didn't walk around Lodi or Paterson in New Jersey like that. They didn't like us. They didn't like us doing this stuff.

When you consider the movement retrospectively, the whole counterculture premise has evolved, or devolved, depending on how you look at it. In some ways we were ahead of our time: women's lib, the pill, the whole drug culture, don't trust authority. And, sure enough, Nixon ended up being a criminal anyway, so we were right at least about some things. On the other hand, we had our fun in some pretty extreme ways and maybe that's why some of the children of our generation are running around like idiots. I mean, did we help destroy the education system by looking for freedom and so on? This is complicated and not the place to discuss it, but for every action there is a reaction and for the past decades it seems my generation has been dealing with the effects of our trip. But at that time we were counterculture and the mainstream was threatened and did not want us around. The cops stopped you, saying they were looking for drugs, and they would beat your ass up. *Easy Rider* was true.

Talk about being paranoid! Especially if you got high and you went out in the street, you were afraid of getting busted. It really was a small little rebellion. Then the war dragged on, and by '68/69, which is a little later than I'm talking about, with Woodstock and all that, more people got involved. It became a political thing against the war, and then you see mass protests on the mall in Washington and so forth.

Lew: You didn't have to be as brave to join the movement in 1969. But when you were involved in 1965 or so, it was really a statement.
Dave: Thank you. It was a statement. And by the way, it ended with violence. In December 1969, when the Hells Angels killed that guy right in front of the stage at Altamont, in clear sight of everybody, that was the end of peace and love. Why were the Hells Angels there—some say for security? And the Rolling Stones are supposed to be so cool and all that—right! They are using these cats to police the stage, and they go and kill a guy, right on the ground there. That was it—peace and love was a complete lie.

It was the official end. There was the summer of love in '67, and Woodstock, which was just a few months before Altamont, was the zenith of the movement—the festival, in the mud, love, peace, everybody cool. When you see the movie it looks so cool. Everybody's dancing, waving, chicks don't have their shirts on, you know, nobody's acting weird, everybody was happening—half a million folks united by Jimi Hendrix, Richie Havens, and others from the folk/rock scene of that period. But after Woodstock it got sour, just like everything does eventually.

You know why? The mainstream culture got hold of it. It became, "Oh, this is it, so we'll join up." Then the idiots enter. It's only when a subculture stays pure that it can really keep its integrity—but that's pretty impossible, actually. The integrity of a movement is going to always be compromised when the main culture gets hold of it. By 1970, it was losing its power and meaning. But there were positive statements happening, despite the excesses. There were some people who didn't come back from their LSD trips, it's true. There was a lot of sex that was really just sex for its own sake, of course. There was a lot of passing around of drugs that turned bad. But there was a minute when it was positive.

Lew: And when you were involved in it early on—in the early and mid-sixties—just the way you looked, people could tell you were part of it.
Dave: Yes, by the hair. If your hair was long, you were the enemy. And clothes—tie-dye shirts and scarves, jewelry and beads! Hey, for me the bandana on my head during my time with Miles was because I was going bald and I didn't like the look of it! That's the truth. The bandana was usually part of the hippie thing, but I just thought it was a way to dress.

Lew: So your hair started to go in your twenties?
Dave: Twenty, twenty-one. Oh, it was terrible! It was a disaster! I mean, that, with my leg—damn, I would never get a girl. I couldn't compete. I was not handsome. It was not a good time. The only thing I had was the music. I knew that for me to meet a woman, she would have to be really special. It wasn't going to be a bar pick-up thing. I wasn't necessarily going to meet the prettiest girl. It obviously had to be someone like me, who was a little bit off, which most of the time is what it was, you know.

My father was bald when he was a kid—same age, he got bald. It was understood that it would be me and/or my brother going through the same thing. I went for treatments. Man, that's a funny story. I'll never forget the name. It was called the Wybrant System, and it was down on J Street in Brooklyn. I was living at home, so this must be my first or second semester at Queens College, since I commuted that year. I was going for three treatments a week for forty-five minutes. You look at the before and after pics of other cats and you get roped in. My mother was like, "So what are you doing?" You know, I had the money, so what the hell. "Hey, you're losing your hair, so face it." I would go in and sit there while they put this stuff on my head. Then a cap and under a dryer, and I was thinking it was great. It was burning so much that something must be happening! So I went—I tried everything, and nothing worked.

I was a young guy and being bald was not cool—stylish in some circles maybe, but it was not like I was Yul Brynner in *The King and I.* That was my mother's shtick: "Look at Yul Brynner. Look how handsome he is!" He was a movie star and he got away with no hair on his head, completely bald, which at that time was very odd. Okay, Telly Savalas—Kojak—he was next. Suddenly it became sexy and kind of cool. But that was in the '70s and it didn't help me.

Lew: And what about glasses?
Dave: Well, I tried contacts. I am the contact trial king. I must have spent the equivalent of thousands of dollars on contacts, 'cause I thought glasses were a drag. I wore glasses from ten years old for reading, then eventually all the time. The drag was that one of my few positive physical assets were my blue eyes, but you couldn't see them with glasses on. So, okay, contacts. And in those days there were only hard lenses and they were a drag. They hurt, you couldn't get them in, you couldn't get them out. Every new development in contact lenses, I tried. Only after a couple of decades did I give up on them. It doesn't matter now. But I tried everything, and I wanted them. I hated glasses and I hated the fact that I was bald, so I really didn't like the way I looked. And I limped. So what the hell? What kind of package is that? So for me, contact lenses were about vanity—what this whole discussion is about—being a young man trying to be attractive to women.

Lew: But you did meet a lady?
Dave: I did. First of all, in high school there was Julie Gross, who went with me for that first time seeing Trane. Then there was a girl in the neighborhood, who was, shall we say, a well-built young woman. Also, I had interaction with a girl from my neighborhood in high school who helped me toward feeling better about myself in relation to women. She was very supportive. We had a platonic relationship. She was my best friend in some ways—at fifteen, sixteen years old, we'd talk for hours. She was very mature for her age. She was a great lady who went to Yeshiva High School of all things and had very strict parents, but she was

hip as could be. Any girl problems, I would talk to her. It was easier for me to talk to a girl than to a guy at that age. She was the equivalent of the older woman, as bright as could be.

And then at NYU was the lady I mentioned earlier, Laurel. The first day of class, this girl walked in and I went right there. She was blonde and tan, had a kind of Marilyn Monroe swagger or something. Check it out—I think every man and woman has an image of what is beautiful, sexy, somewhere along that line, coming from movies and TV. In my case, it was definitely Marilyn Monroe, 'cause that's my generation. Also, I loved Kim Novak in Hitchcock's *Vertigo*—I fell in love with her. I was into blondes. I'm a product of the fifties and blonde was sexy. That was my image.

So, this girl walks in with blonde hair and she had a beautiful dress on. She looked great. From there it was right through college with her. She was my first real love, and she told me later that she had spotted me across campus before the first class, or something like that. It was a bona fide love affair, I guess you could say. She was a bit different from the norm too. That's the point! She was like Miss Psychiatry and she ended up working in that field. She wrote a book that she sent me a few years ago and I couldn't understand one word. She lives in California and we have talked on occasion—a nice memory at this point.

Lew: When she walked into that room, how did you react?
Dave: I don't remember. I just think I became bold. Pretty quickly the music became part of it. She was a counterculture type—not a hippie, but she was into some different stuff. I got her into Trane. I was living up at NYU in the apartment with Steve, the first year. Eventually she and I got an apartment together. She was my main girl for that part of my life, sophomore year through the end of school and slightly beyond into my loft period. It was a long relationship and really got me through college.

But I remember, after my first time in Europe, the summer of '67, when I got back into Kennedy Airport, she was waiting for me and I knew something had changed. I could just see it on her face. It was the beginning of a terrible year. That basically was it. We were still sort of together that whole next year, but it was a drag, you know. Steve ended up with Laurel for a time. It was a kick in the face when she started seeing my former roommate. The same scenario happened another time in my life.

I think that my personality was to take women for granted after a while. I would just get into my work and all that. I know that women need attention and I would do it for a minute, whatever that minute would be, a year or a couple of years, but then eventually I'd just get back into my world, which was this music thing. I'm not without guilt in this regard. That's part of my personality, it seems—after a while when things get comfortable, to take things for granted and just say, "Well, where's the coffee?" Not the greatest thing in the world, but this is what I or maybe we're guilty of—I mean men as a group—work has a habit of taking precedence.

Lew: Especially when you are a musician.
Dave: I was obviously obsessed. Especially after my career started happening, there were a lot of things I had to do. It gets complicated. It was not the time to have anything more than fleeting relationships.

Lew: So, when you came back from your trip to Europe—after a while . . .
Dave: I forget in my senior year what exactly happened. The relationship did go through to the next summer because Laurel went away with me up to the Woodstock area, when I went through that practicing period I described right after graduation. Then she got into the Sufis, which was very interesting. Pete LaRoca became my first real heavy mentor at that time, and by coincidence they both got me into the Sufis.

I went to some Sufi meetings and met the main guy. This is all kind of tied into this period where I'm getting into Indian philosophy, yoga, and macrobiotics. The Sufi thing was very appealing at that time. It was a universal-religion-type deal. I went once to their Sunday service. They had all the religions represented like a UN-type thing. Sufis are very ecumenical, although they're an Islamic sect—Persian, Turkish. People know them from the dervish dances they do.

They do believe in the universality of religion. Not us-versus-them stuff. The founder of Sufi-ism in the West wrote a series of books that I got into. His name was Hazrat Inayat Khan (1882-1927) and I saw his son speak once. Khan had written twelve books, on every subject: health, government, education, a lot of stuff. His book on music was the heaviest I have ever read.

When I am finished with a student, when they graduate from the so-called "Liebman Academy" and I've nothing more to show them, I give them the Sufi book on music. I've photocopied fifty pages of it. By the way, he mentions jazz in there, which he hated. The book was written in the 1920s. He probably heard Dixieland by some guys who didn't know what they were doing. He says it's cacophony; it's not real music. But outside of those ridiculous statements, it's really dead on about music, that the rhythm of life is music, music is life—all that great stuff.

The hippie thing kind of led straight to mysticism and directly to Indian philosophy, which led to macrobiotics, which is close to Japanese thinking, and so on. Basically if you were open to it during this period, you were led to the whole Eastern thing because Catholicism and Judaism were not making it. That's really what you were counterculturing—the Western world. You looked East and there were these prophet types—with the nirvana and satori rap, Buddhism, and so on. But mostly it was the Indian stuff that was on the table in those days.

I read a lot of books, which I still have and probably should review at this point of my life. Swami Vivekananda was an Indian cat who came to America in the 1890s or so—one of the first cats to come over to give lectures here about reincarnation, karma, and associated topics. The Tibetan Book of the Dead was very important to me. The main premise was that when you die you will see light of different shades depending on your karma. You have forty-nine days to get into the light while you're in a state of bardo. You will keep reincarnating, keep coming back, until there's nothing left for you to do. You see the "clear" light and you are in a state of satori with no need to come back again to this wordly suffering existence. Meanwhile, you may reincarnate as an ant, or as a saint, based on the karmic activity you created in your life, the sins you committed and the good deeds you did. I am of course completely simplifying, but it just all made sense to me.

Everybody seemed to be into it at that time. The hippie thing, if you followed through, naturally led to that. The implications of taking LSD inevitably went in this direction. It was to find the truth within you, which was certainly new to me, coming out of the Jewish-Christian space, even though guys had been talking about it for decades. There were these guru chiefs who were coming over, like the Beatles' guru Maharishi Mahesh Yogi, and Sri Chimnoy that John McLaughlin famously got into. The Sufis were less known, but it was part of that time when guys like me were looking for some explanation. We were into, "What's life? Why?" That was it. You're in your early twenties and you have to get some answers.

Lew: Were you into the philosophical stuff, or were you also into the reincarnation? Were you into the details of it, or the general message?

Dave: I learned about it. I read about reincarnation. Something a few years later happened in this regard. Around 1977, when I lived in Berkeley, California, for a minute, I went to the Berkeley Psychic Center, where they read your aura, life signs, whatever. You know, past lives and all that stuff. I had a feeling about my past lives. I think I still have a tape of the session. There were three people behind curtains, if I recall correctly—semi-voodoo stuff. After their so-called reading, you asked questions. One of the questions I had was if they saw in my past lives something to do with the desert and sun and white light, playing a straight horn of sorts. I always had a thing with the desert and sun and heat. By that time with all the self-exploration and readings, I had this feeling that in a past life I had played some kind of straight horn in a desert setting. I started playing soprano sax in '69 with Ten Wheel Drive, and by '77 I'd been playing it a lot and had gotten a reputation on that horn particularly. This is before I went to Israel, before I'd been to the Middle East.

I feel that somewhere in the past I was in a desert setting because something about the heat, the white sand, and the sun transfixes me. One of the people that day said something like: "I see you with a horse or chariot, a sword, some kind of King Arthur time, 1100s, something like that, England." Then another one said: "But I see the past before that. I see you in white robes, surrounded by people, and you're dancing. You're in the middle of the circle. It's definitely white, desert, blinding heat. I do see that in your past lives." Well, pop psychology aside, that just reinforced what I had always felt, which was that there was something there in my past lives where I was definitely in some desert environment, playing a horn of sorts.

The point is that I do believe in some ways about the whole idea of reincarnation; that I've had past lives and we definitely come into existence with something already having happened. This is true of every human being, but as artists, it is our job to find out who we are and use it to express our feelings. That's our work, like another guy's job is to build a good car. So, we go a little deeper into who we are. You're not just walking out of the womb, an empty plate, etc. I don't see how you walk into this existence with nothing, coming out of the womb, besides the DNA code from your parents.

There's so much happening before, it seems. It just doesn't make sense any other way. Energy doesn't disappear. So, for a variety of scientific, spiritual, and philosophical reasons, I do believe in past lives. I'm not sure what that means—that I'll come back as an ant or as a tall person—I don't know. But people love when I play that little wooden flute, which I have been doing for some years now and I'm pretty good on it. Everybody comes up after the set and says: "Oh man, that flute, when you played that flute . . ." Well, I think the next lifetime or so it will be only a flute for me, sitting on top of a mountain, rice and water, and one note at a time. Or at least I hope so! Not this life—my next lifetime. I don't know if that's ten years after I die or a hundred years after I die, but I think I've earned my stripes. And I am ready to not have to be dancing around the world doing this whole deal again. Come to *me* if you want that thing that I do well.

By the way, here's a great Zen koan about the flute and the message of music that I like to tell. You know, Japan was very on China's case. They wanted to learn anything they could from Chinese culture. So, the Emperor of Japan says, "We must learn the wisdom of China, and I appoint you, Mr. Yushu, or whomever, to go there. You're gonna be the cat." So he went to China and was gone for fifteen years. They didn't hear from him—you know, no cell phones and so on. Finally he came back. He went to the court, to the emperor, with the whole country watching what he will say about his visit. This is A.D. 900 or some time like that. The Emperor asks: "Okay, Yushu, what did you learn from the Chinese culture?" Yushu takes a flute out of his pocket and plays one note—then he bows.

The point is that within anything the universe exists. Even for teaching, I tell the kids they don't need to know everything, just know *something* well. Thomas Blake noted that in a grain of sand you can see the universe. It's an expression to remember—that it's up to you to add the creativity. You don't need the whole beach; you just need a grain of sand, and the beach will appear if you are on the case. So, that's a Zen koan, and that is my next lifetime. We shall see.

Lew: I love that.
Dave: The warrior, the leader, the teacher. I've been through all this—don't you think it's time for me to take a rest? When my master's students are graduating from the Manhattan School of Music, I say, "Okay, you have your master's degrees. Some of you are going for a doctorate, which we can talk about later. You people are in New York City—you all want to stay, right?" Of course, they all raise their hand. Then I start this kind of rap that I hope they are all figuring out how to stay here because they're smart enough now to figure it out. That they have been here for at least two years if not more, and with all the stuff that is descending upon them when they finish school, bills due, where to live, parent pressure, etc., they should really put the search for meaning into high gear. Find out who you are. Look around at other things and experience the world. Try everything, because after that, you will have more responsibility than you can imagine with family, whatever, that just naturally occurs as you get older. Your mid- to late twenties is your time to

be who you are. This is your time to experiment. If you want to be a Jehovah's Witness, now is your time! Everything's on the table. There are no rules, except don't get arrested and don't hurt anybody. That's all! Take advantage of this time in your life. For me, it was the loft period, when I experimented—every kind of weird stuff from drugs, to philosophy, to diet, to doing headstands, whatever. Some good and some bad, for sure. Musically, the same thing. That period of my life, the loft period—I'm still living off it. Those two to three years segue right into Elvin, which I guess you could say was the official beginning of my career. It is those three or four years of self-investigation that are the bedrock of who I am.

Lew: In terms of forming a lot of your beliefs?
Dave: Yes. Of course, that's filtered through seventeen years of living with my parents, through the experience of being who I am in New York City in the 1950s and 1960s. But that's true for all of us. What I'm saying is whatever uniqueness I have was planted in those years right after college. It happened in the loft where I was able to experiment and able to look at Sufis, go to Hare Krishna meetings, whatever. I was trying to find the answers. This "quest" was on everybody's plate. Among who I knew at least, young artists looking for answers, this was very fashionable then. Now it's not, at least as we speak. Back then, we were all looking and searching and trying everything, from drugs to diets to religion.

This is the Bohemian period. It's *La Bohème*—it's Puccini. It's that time when you go for it. It's *Rent,* if you've seen the play. It's that time when you are supposed to be trying stuff. If you don't do it, by the way, you've cheated yourself. You will probably never have an opportunity like that again. You won't have the energy, or the circumstances will not exist. If you don't get that little time—at least a year or two—then you really haven't fulfilled who you could have been. Soon you're working nine to five or whatever and becoming a so-called citizen of the world.

Most of us join the world at large—predominantly the middle class. That's fine. But, man, you have to go through that period when you have like one pair of jeans, living off of McDonald's or whatever it is—when you do not need a lot of money. If you're not going to use this period for self-discovery—if you're not going to movies, plays, museums, if you're not in deep discussions with your friends about the meaning of life, the same questions that Aristotle was dealing with—if you're not doing that, then you're not fulfilling your responsibility of being an artist, and I think that's not fair, especially after you've been in school for twenty plus years. You deserve it, you know. So that was my period, and that's why this all happened in that time.

Lew: This loft was an important thing. How did the loft come about? When did it start?
Dave: In late 1968, after the practice period upstate, I went home to my parents' house to figure out the next period. During my time practicing in Lake Katrine from June to Thanksgiving, I had realized that I wasn't the super talent that some others around me were. I was just starting to understand what talent was and how that affected what you did. I had already met Steve Grossman, who definitely was what you called talented. I didn't have that kind of natural ear. I did not have that kind of natural talent, but I was a hard worker. I was fairly disciplined and had energy and emotion and expression—these aspects were never a problem. I knew that I had a story to tell. I could compel people to listen to me, but I wasn't that kind of guy who could hear something and play it back at you, which is the heaviest thing you want. I knew that for me to be good, I had to play and play more. There was no shortcut. It was hands on, hours at the wheel, and the only way to do that was to have a loft.

At the same time, I made a musical decision to play no more club dates. If I needed money, I had, after all, the right credentials and credits from college to be a substitute teacher in the public schools, which was a familiar scenario because of my parents. With substitute teaching two days a week, I could swing enough bread to be cool. It paid $35 a day and you were done by three in the afternoon.

I knew about the loft situation through my experiences with Bob Moses, who had introduced me to that whole world before. I knew that was the situation I needed in New York to get good. I knew how you got one—a real process. You got the *Village Voice* on Wednesday morning at six a.m. at Sheridan Square—direct from the printers. Then you got on the phone, ready to go immediately to see an advertised loft. You had to beat everyone else.

Lew: You mean you would buy it?
Dave: Exactly. It was called key money, which was basically a payoff. In other words, someone "owned" the loft who had ostensibly put in the fixtures—stove, fridge, toilet, shower, whatever. He might want $2,000 just for you to have the right to go to the landlord to negotiate a rental lease. I mean, you still had to pay monthly rent and a sizable deposit for security. It's hard to explain, but in a way you were paying them, or someone before, who had put money into the building to make it livable.

Now, we are talking *very* basic in some cases, although when lofts became fashionable in the seventies and eighties, they could be like palaces. So, if you wanted it, you paid what the guy asked or whatever you could negotiate.

Lew: And it had nothing in it?
Dave: Well, maybe a toilet, but these were former industrial spaces, often for the fashion trade, which was centered in New York City during this time, especially in the Chelsea area on the West Side.

Lew: This is before SoHo lofts?
Dave: Before SoHo. That came a little bit later, and they were generally bigger and fancier—much more expensive than what I could ever afford. This area I'm talking about consisted of former industrial spaces with heavy machinery and the like. In one of my later lofts, above me was the constant thumping of clothing presses or whatever, but it all stopped at five p.m. and on weekends and holidays. *Chunk, chunk, chunk*, but at five o'clock, done!

Lew: Who lived in lofts?
Dave: Painters, photographers, and musicians. Painters needed room for canvases. Photographers needed light. A lot of these lofts had big windows with a lot of light—floor-to-ceiling windows, twelve-foot ceilings. Musicians needed a place to play where they wouldn't have trouble with neighbors. With these places deserted at night, holidays, and weekends, you were cool. Nobody cared. It also fit the musician lifestyle, which was hanging all night and sleeping during the day, though depending on the situation, it could be rough with the factory noise. Often I didn't get up until two in the afternoon, after having gone to bed at six in the morning.

That loft I found was on West 19th Street between 6th and 7th Avenues. It had been a tie-dye fabric factory, which is really kind of ironic in light of the hippie thing. I paid $1,200 in key money and the rent was $125 a month. The building was three floors and I was on the top walkup. The landlord's name was Saul Lieberman, similar to my last name. When I turned over the loft to Mike Brecker a few years later, I got $2,500 in key money. Later on, when I turned over my last loft to saxophonist Bill Evans, I charged him $8,000, which I think was double of what I had originally paid, but by then it was the early '80s. This key money thing was considered fair game and no problem. These were good deals. Guys were charging whatever they could. Like I said, once you paid the key money, the tenant was gone and you had to deal with the landlord with a lease and all that.

Lofts were illegal to live in. These were commercial buildings, so the first sentence in your lease was that you would not live there, which of course everyone knew was a sham—the landlord and you—and the fire department, etc. These were all fire traps, but that was the way it was. Guys would have a hot plate and a cot maybe, saying you were heating stuff up or just napping, but most of the time nobody cared. In the case of this first loft on 19th Street, I went to the landlord and he said, "Oh, your name is Liebman," meaning obviously Jewish, so at least there was some rapport. "What do you do?" "I'm teaching school and trying to play music." He remarked, "Yeah, yeah. I guess that's why you're here." You know, he was hip to it.

This was a very small loft, 1,200 square feet—one long room with a little room off to the side for a mattress. There was a small room at the back, if I remember right, with a toilet and a shower. The previous guy just left all this tie-dye material, so the day I took over I got out a staple gun, got on a ladder, and stapled all that cloth into the ceiling, which was only about eight feet high. The ceiling looked like a rainbow. I went around with three cans of spray paint and did the walls in about ten minutes. Then I got a refrigerator. I bought a piano, got a drum set from someone, and now starts this next period of my life.

Lew: Did you have an upright piano?

Dave: No. I had a George Steck baby grand. I'll never forget it because the movers couldn't get it up the narrow steps, so it was hoisted up from the roof. We were lucky the whole damn building didn't collapse. These big black cats came in, the moving brothers, saying, "We can't get it up the stairs. We'll bring it from the roof." And I'm like, "Forget it. I don't know nothing. Do your dance." The next thing I know, there's a cat on the roof with a hoist, and I see the piano coming in through the window—sideways, legs off. That piano never moved again. It's probably still there. I could never get it out. I bought it for $600, I think.

So, that became my first of several lofts—January '69. The building is still there, but it's not a loft anymore. I don't know what it is. That was the beginning of my real life, I would say. No more school, and definitely no parental stuff anymore.

Lew: What about Laurel, for the time you're in the loft?

Dave: She's around, but it was dissipating. I'm in the beginning of my real life as a musician. I'm jazzed out though teaching as a substitute

Monday and Tuesday, meaning putting a tie on and doing that whole deal. Talk about straight life! Tuesday afternoon, I would come back from whatever school I was in that day and get to my music work. I only needed two days to make a living— $70 a week. I had it down to $280 a month.

My name was on the substitute teachers list everywhere from the Bronx to Queens. When they'd call on Monday, I'd go. This could be anywhere from Howard Beach to the North Bronx or wherever. I was on the subway by six-thirty, quarter-to-seven in the morning. Of course, I had some difficult experiences. Even a good kid would take it out on the sub! Lewis, don't you remember when you had a substitute teacher when you were in fourth grade, fifth grade?

Lew: Yeah?
Dave: Did you go, "Hmmm—we're going to have fun today"? When I was a kid, I was a ringleader, so I was the one saying, "Let's really have fun today, guys!"

Lew: Uh-oh.
Dave: Yeah. So here I am going to schools everywhere—the South Bronx, Bed Stuy, etc. The public school system in the late sixties into the seventies was completely broken. There was a major strike and a whole lot of stuff happening. There was decentralization, meaning local boards of citizens would decide on who the principal would be, the assistant principal, whatever. It was called community control and it led to a breakdown. The teachers' strike of 1968 was very famous, and a big deal nationally, concerning pay and community control. Albert Schenker was the guy in charge of the teachers' union. Remember, my parents and their friends were all teachers and administrators. I think by then both my parents were assistant principals, so I heard all these discussions going on around holiday dinners. Nonetheless, it didn't prepare me for being a substitute. I walked into one school and the principal said, "You got class 6Z today? Make sure they don't jump out the window." I was like, "Uh, okay." He said, "Good luck."

Sure enough, by two-thirty in the afternoon, I was standing at the door with my arms extended, blocking the exit. The kids were throwing stuff out the window, screaming, yelling—all minority kids, going nuts! Three o'clock—bell. You're finished. You're done. I tried to be hip, so I would take Coltrane records to schools. These kids had no idea who Coltrane was. They couldn't care less—didn't mean a thing.

The best time I ever had was with a kindergarten class for two weeks—all young kids, so I played Trane all day! What did they know? They were cool. Anyway, that was my job in that period to make a living.

Lew: So, it could be any grade?
Dave: Anything. You could have kindergarten to high school. You didn't teach biology, algebra, or any subject—just basically babysitting. You told the kids to take out their notebooks and do what they did yesterday. No real teaching, of course.

I hated getting up in the morning and putting on a tie. I hated authority. I hated people telling me what to do. Plus, it was a very unfulfilling job because basically I was a babysitter. This was not education in the positive sense of the word.

When I got home Tuesday afternoon by five o'clock, I'd rip off the sport jacket and tie. I would smoke a joint and play for the next twelve hours, and then for the next five days. Then Monday morning, I would start all over again. This was my routine until I got the job with the group Ten Wheel Drive, which is the next subject and was a real salaried musical gig.

The big thing with playing in the loft was that I told everyone who wanted to play to come over to my place any time, day or night. In the case of this building there were no factories so it was open ended as far as when I could play. I had drums—maybe a bass—vibes, and that Steck grand piano. And I had a tape recorder. There was a kitchen area and a living room area, all covered in linoleum, and a nice oriental rug, stereo system, a big picture of Trane, and LPs. In the little anteroom was my mattress with a shower and toilet near the kitchen somewhere. There was stuff everywhere. I was already starting to collect flutes from all over the world. It was hippied out with a jazz vibe—like that.

I had a little pouch for throwing the key down and everyone knew how to open up and come upstairs to the third floor. It was wonderful. But let me finish the living situation because it's apropos. Dave Holland, playing with Miles Davis, was living in a hotel or something like that, so I told him that the second floor of this building was available. I went to the landlord, Saul Lieberman, and asked him. He said, "Can he pay the rent?" I told him that Dave was working with one of the most famous musicians in the world. Saul said, "Well, you've been paying the rent, so I guess it's okay." So Dave moved into the second floor with his wife, Claire. Their daughter, Louise, was just a baby then. I used to babysit her.

The next tenant in that loft building was Chick Corea, who also was playing with Miles, and getting divorced at that time. This was the period of his influential LP *Now He Sings, Now He Sobs*, recorded in '68. I drove out to Chick's house and I remember hearing the mix of that record before it was released to the public. It had no name at that point. I remember being very struck by the music. Of course, eventually it turned out to be the pentatonic scale bible—especially the "Matrix" solo, for sure.

I didn't know Chick personally at all. His house at the time was in Middle Village, Queens—row houses, real suburbs. I couldn't believe that this was where Chick Corea lived. Joan, his wife, was the subject of that tune "Tones for Joan's Bones." I think he had two kids, Thad and a daughter, whose names together made up the title of one of his tunes, "Litha." In his basement there was a piano, tape recorder, and phonograph.

People already knew Chick Corea. The 'hood knew—the community knew him. He was definitely *the* piano guy in New York. So, he asked me if I thought he could get the first-floor loft. I went to Saul and we went through the same rap—can he pay? Yeah, he works with Miles Davis. Ok, you guys have been good, etc, etc. That was how we had all three lofts in the building on 19th Street—Dave, Chick, and myself. That's the beginning of a lot of stuff—scientology, macrobiotics, psychedelics, the group Circle, and the Free Life Communication project.

Chick had a big influence on me. First of all, just the physical aspect of living with Dave and Chick since they were playing with Miles. Informally, as it turned out, because of the proximity, I was privy to their reactions and what was going on with the incredible music they were creating in that band. In fact, Miles came up to Dave's loft for dinner one evening, so I formally met Miles for the first time. I had met him backstage previously because of Lennie White, who was on some of his gigs and played on *Bitches Brew*. When Miles came to the loft, the guys made a macrobiotic dinner for him, and the three of us were sitting there on pillows, legs crossed, Indian style. Miles was cool. He ate the rice. We were very strict with the macrobiotic thing. Miles said the food wasn't bad—we actually had a very civil evening. I don't remember much. I know that I didn't talk and I remember that Miles was a very soft talker. He was very nice and it was a pleasant evening.

The 19th Street loft was truly the beginning of my creative life. Everything was preparation up to that point.

Chapter 5

The Energy of the Chance: Going for It

Lew: So, moving into 19th Street was a real beginning of the next part of your life.
Dave: Right. Now I'm in the real world in New York City and part of the young jazz community. A lot of activity is taking place in this loft building. I lived alone, but people would hang, and I had an extra mattress.

Lew: And during that time period, your relationship with Laurel just kind of fell apart.
Dave: Yes, and then I was with nobody for a while. But career-wise, the big thing was getting the gig with Ten Wheel Drive. The significance of Ten Wheel Drive is that it got me out of teaching, because they had the band on salary. Here's the story of that period:

It's the late 1960s. Miles's *Bitches Brew* was around. Blood, Sweat and Tears' music was being heard, as were the groups Chicago and Tower of Power. This is the beginning of the horn band/fusion era with the premise being that a horn section can have a place in a rock band beyond James Brown–type backups, with some improvisation á la jazz.

There was a whole population of mostly white musicians who had played the Catskills, including some of the guys I mentioned earlier. These guys were typical New York–based players, freelancing on club dates and studio work, Latin gigs, etc., whatever was around at the time. With this horn band concept, suddenly there was a whole new viable thing for a studio player to do— quasi-jazz, with real written parts, but popular music. So, you were rock, but you were also jazz. Studio-type guys could work in something akin to creative music, because they weren't going to get into the jazz world. In fact, the late sixties was the worst period of jazz business-wise. Also the white-black thing was definitely a little bit of a fly in the ointment then because of current events happening in the late '60s.

One of my oldest friends whom I have mentioned, trumpeter Steve Satten, was my mate for a lot of club dates and the Catskills gigs during my teen years. He was a very talented guy who became a singer-songwriter type in a Randy Newman style, eventually recording for Columbia Records. He got the gig with Ten Wheel Drive and recommended me, so I went for an audition. The instrumentation was two trumpets, trombone, and saxophone, with a standard rock rhythm section and singer. It was an interesting band with two guys leading it. Mike Zager was the composer and keyboard player who got real popular later on during the disco era in the '80s, while Aram Schefrin, the guitar player, was a Harvard Law School graduate. (Schefrin, before he died in November 2010, put up a Ten Wheel Drive blog with photos, text, and music.) They formed this band and found singer Genya Ravan, who had some success with an all-girl band, Goldie and the Gingerbreads. She had a Janis Joplin vibe to her singing—a powerful presence on the stage, more sexy than Joplin, but as strong. In fact, she was a Polish Jew and her parents were in the concentration camps. I liked her. She was funky and soulful. The band was signed to a major label at the time, Polydor. So I auditioned and got the gig, which was when I first got a soprano sax.

They wanted me on tenor, clarinet, flute, baritone and soprano sax. Those were the days of reed players having to double, triple, quadruple on different instruments. The soprano was relatively limited in jazz at that time aside from Sidney Bechet, then Trane of course, and in the late '60s Wayne Shorter started on it. The king at that period on soprano was Steve Lacy, who went to Europe around '67 and stayed there for the next several decades. The soprano was starting to be recognized as a viable voice in the sax section.

Zager, from what I understood at the time, studied a bit with Steven Sondheim, which is pretty heavy in itself. Mike was very sophisticated and if you listen to Ten Wheel Drive, it's pretty happening. The voicings are good and the words say something. It's rock and roll—it's not funk, but it is well done for sure.

Lew: But that's the great thing about those bands during that period. You could be making money, but the music had some challenges.

Dave: True. I was the main soloist playing my Coltrane stuff over the rock rhythm section. This was around the time of the band Dreams with Mike Brecker, Sanborn, Billy Cobham, and John Abercrombie. Everything was all happening at the same period. There was competition, of course. Blood, Sweat & Tears was the most successful by far, but we were all doing it. So I joined Ten Wheel Drive making $125 a week. You were on call every day, either rehearsing or doing a gig. We rehearsed on 27th and Broadway in a little studio they rented. It was a real band with a solid record company behind them. The manager was Sid Bernstein, who brought the Beatles to Shea Stadium in '64. This was the big time—the height of the days when that was happening. When I got the gig, I took my tie off, let my hair grow, and considered myself finito with the middle-class world. Done!

Lew: Now, during that time from January '69 when you moved into the loft until you got this call, were you doing other music gigs?
Dave: I don't think I was gigging, because I refused to play club dates. I really wanted to be pure. We started Free Life Communication, which is a whole other story that we will get to, but the point is that there was a lot of overlap in my activities from Ten Wheel Drive to teaching to Free Life, eventually to the band Sawbuck and finally Elvin Jones's group—quite an intense period. The bottom line is that the Ten Wheel gig released me from the equivalent of nine to five, which was my substitute teaching. I was now living off an acceptable music gig, which was considered cutting edge at the time.

Lew: So the leader said you'd need a soprano?
Dave: I went to Manny's music store and bought one—the first time I'd played soprano. Like I said, I played everything with that band! I was Mr. Doubler. I bought a Selmer soprano like Trane—there wasn't much choice then in sopranos.

Lew: Anything else notable during that period?
Dave: At that time, we were all into the macrobiotic diet and quite strict about it. Certain foods were yin; certain foods were yang. There was some logic meaning this or that food was positive, one was negative, and so on. You had to mix the two—it was all about balance. You could only buy certain foods.

When I went on the road with Ten Wheel Drive, I carried my own cooker, a little Bunsen burner, with tahini spread, rice cakes, and always a leather bag attached to my belt with nuts and raisins. Sure enough, on the recording I did with Ten Wheel called *Brief Replies*, my nickname was the Illustrious Raisin. Cute! Yeah, I was seriously into this diet for a minute.

Chick Corea turned me on to it. It's definitely a 19th Street thing during that period. He was the man at that time, always into something. You could smell the bread being cooked by the three of us every night. We used to go to a food store at 125 1st Avenue near 8th Street called Greenberg's Natural Foods (Mr. Greenberg later became a founder of Snapple), and buy forty-pound bags of brown rice, millet, bulgur wheat, soy sauce, vegetables, everything to be self-contained. This was not easy to do in those days. If I went home to Brooklyn to visit my mother she had to get a macrobiotic chicken for me—talk about culture shock!

Here's the story of why I stopped the diet after a year or so: Ten Wheel Drive was playing a rock festival in Gainesville, Florida, opposite Sly and the Family Stone and other groups. It was hot as hell and everyone was hanging at the pool, having a good old time, and there I was cooking rice on a little cooker in the motel room with my door open, looking at them partying, sweating like a pig. "Something's wrong with this picture." And that was a big shift because then I realized the obvious, which is, when in Rome, do as the Romans do. It was a big lesson in life, you know, because I was very, very strict about things like that—no one was going to deter me from my path of righteousness—you get the picture. The band was always cool with me. I had my nice little scene together and everything like that, but of course they were thinking it was weird. Really, I ate only rice and vegetables on the road in 1970 and you can imagine that there was not much opportunity to get that kind of stuff in America, in those days especially.

Lew: You were missing out on the party.
Dave: The question was, was it so important for me to keep to this regimen and by doing that not be part of the experience going on around me, whatever that was, and most important not to have a good time? They were hanging out and I was sitting there in a motel room sweating my ass off, boiling rice! But that's how fanatic I was.

Lew: Yet, you've described yourself as an occasional smoker.
Dave: In the early years—and very, very rarely in the past decades. I wasn't the kind of guy to smoke at home. It was just when I was around music and the association with the club environment and the bandstand. There are pictures of me on the bandstand with a cigarette in my hand, on the side. It was kind of hip in a dumb way, like Bogie (actor Humphrey Bogart) with a cigarette. It was never a thing that I enjoyed or got hooked on. I just did it 'cause it was part of our life, part of the milieu. To think of all the smoke that we lived through up until the last years or

so—cats smoking in front of you right in your face while you're blowin' your ass off! No air. No ventilation. And we used to play in the fog and even smoke while we were on the bandstand. We did it without a second thought. That's a big change in our world—this nonsmoking thing.

Lew: That's true. We look at talk shows in the sixties, and people have cigarettes in their hands—in the television studio! Seems like a fire hazard, too.

Dave: In any case, that was an interesting time. Ten Wheel Drive got me out of the loft and into rock and roll again, my real roots. So, now jazz, rock and roll, all happening at the same time. This whole rock experience morphed into a band called Sawbuck, which we will get to soon and that will bring me to meeting Eleana.

Lew: I'm a little confused about whether Free Life Communication was before, after, or during Ten Wheel Drive.

Dave: It was more or less simultaneous. It was Ten Wheel Drive in '69 into '70. We'd go out on tour, but it was never for long. We played every weekend pretty much, but they were mostly bus gigs, although on occasion there was some flying. It was an East Coast band, and I would say in general the Boston to Washington loop. Ten Wheel didn't make it to real prime time in terms of popularity. They tried, and they certainly wanted to be, but it never got to that level.

Meanwhile, Free Life Communication was an outgrowth of the whole loft thing. To recap, Dave Holland, Chick, and myself were in the loft building at 138 West 19th Street playing all the time, night and day. There were times when there were three sessions going on at the same time. For me, it was very clear that the way I worked, to make musical progress I had to play, play, play. I needed hands-on playing to get better. That's not anything that anybody else wouldn't say, but in my case, I knew that the only way I could get better was to be on the spot "in the coal mine," working on it.

As I said earlier, I encouraged anybody who wanted to play to come in any kind of way—two saxophones, three drummers, anything. By the way, that is part of the reason I can play drums and piano a bit, because we would switch around a lot. You'd be hanging out for hours, and someone would go over and play the drums or whatever. Bob Moses was very important at this point for me, as he was earlier. He also had a loft on the East Side—I think 7 Bleecker Street. Bassist Gene Perla had one on Jefferson Street near the Fulton Fish Market. There were a few places with a lot of activity in that respect. A small group of guys—Lanny

Fields, Karl Schroeder, sometimes Al Foster would be around to play—Gene Perla, certainly Mike and Randy Brecker, Steve Grossman with whom I was very, very close, Calvin Hill the bass player, another bassist named Clint Houston, Bob Berg, Terumasa Hino the trumpet player, and many more. We were basically playing for each other—no public at all. I taped a lot of it. I have forty, fifty, sixty reel-to-reel tapes of these things—each tape seven, eight hours at three-and-a-quarter speed. It was almost all free jazz. I don't know if we ever played a tune or a set of chord changes.

In addition to my private tapes, there is an LP that documents this scene. In February, 1970, I recorded an LP called *Night Scapes* for CBS/Sony with a poet friend of Chick's named Carvel Six—we freely improvised while he read his poems—and the band was me, Richie Beirach on piano, Frank Tusa on bass, percussionist Armen Halburian, plus a friend, Nancy Janoson, on flute.

There were, because of what was happening around us musically, some forays into fusion stuff, the very beginnings of that style as it would be eventually known. I remember one taping session with Hal Galper on piano, maybe Gene Perla on bass, and Moses, with me, Randy, and Michael on the lead. We did two of my tunes, "Sam's Float" and "Porpoise," odd meter vamps and so forth with a rock beat. Actually, "Sam's Float" is on my first ECM record done a few years later, *Lookout Farm.* We were beginning to fool around with electric stuff. Randy was coming out of Blood, Sweat & Tears, and the band I mentioned before, Dreams, was starting to happen around the same time as Ten Wheel Drive. It was in the air, this fusion stuff, after Miles laid it out in *Bitches Brew.* As far as jazz goes, at the time the main thing for us was free, à la Trane's *Ascension* recording, meaning a lot of guys playing all the time together—chaotic, loud, intense, like Dixieland gone crazy, in a way. Then there'd be a point somewhere in the session when everyone played with the spoons on the tables or whatever was around—you know, sounds of life stuff. That music was very black or white; there was no gray.

Lew: Yeah, that's true. Like Chick's album *Is* from 1969, with Woody Shaw, Hubert Laws, Jack DeJohnette, and others playing totally free, playing percussion, etc.
Dave: Like that, yeah, exactly. That's exactly what it was.

Lew: Why not any tunes? Today we tell the students, "You gotta know the tunes, man." Did you guys already know the tunes, and you were out of that?
Dave: No. I did not know the tunes. We were inspired by late Coltrane. When I played with Steve Grossman it was like he was Trane and I was Pharaoh Sanders. We sort of had this understood relationship, with Moses playing like Rashied Ali. This was the music that inspired us to play in that fashion. You have to remember we were young guys, outside the school situation. Young cats usually do what's hot at the moment. The past is studied formally now in jazz schools where young folks get their so-called experience. But in general, young guys are into what is hot *then* and not *when*. You wanted to be hip. You didn't look back to play like Horace Silver.

Lew: At that time, the only time you'd be using old tunes is if you did a club date—and even then, not really the hip tunes,
Dave: That's true, because before the Top 40 format came, you heard mostly old standards at club dates. But our jazz situation was quite separate from the older cats and from what a typical jam session might normally be like. In some ways we were an anomaly, though there was precedence before us. We were white, mostly middle class; I won't say all Jewish, but quite a few were; not all New York, but definitely coming from urban centers. Speaking historically in jazz terms, we were different than our predecessors, who were uniformly or for the most part African American and came from a whole different life and working situation. We played club dates, Latin gigs, and some of us were into rock—all of which was not the typical M.O. of a jazz musician in previous periods. I'm not sure why, but I know we just loved playing free jazz.

I do remember one of the regulars, bassist Lanny Fields, coming in one day saying something like, "Have you heard this record?" He was referring to Wayne Shorter's *Speak No Evil* recording. We spent the next day or days transcribing the melodies, trying to get the chords, and so on. Remember, this is with the phonograph and needle, which meant a very scratched LP. "Wow, this is unbelievable music." It seemed I'd missed something and was just not aware of Wayne's music or, for that matter, the incredible period of Miles with *Prince of Darkness*, *Nefertiti*, and all those studio records. I was Traned out and pretty oblivious to the sophistication of the mid-sixties Miles group and the sidemen's work. I wasn't familiar with *Miles Smiles* or *Juju* or *The All-Seeing Eye*, all made in the mid-sixties. On top of that, I, maybe we, had an attitude that playing a so-called tune was below us. Talk about being young and foolish!

Lew: That was considered old school.
Dave: Right, like you're into the new thing and you don't go playing tunes with changes. But, of course, once we started transcribing and listening to these records I'm mentioning, we realized that there was a lot we certainly missed. Slowly, things started to change by the early seventies with my joining Elvin, the Brecker brothers joining Horace Silver, Gene Perla with Nina Simone, etc. Slowly we started joining the mainstream in a way, both physically as sidemen and musically as to what we played. But this period in the loft that we're talking about that leads to Free Life Communication was pretty exclusively about free-energy jazz, with a vengeance. Nobody talked to us from above. This is me with my friends—or, my contemporaries. It wasn't like anybody came in and said, "Hey, you guys don't really know what came before, etc. You really should get your shit together." Of course, some of the guys were playing in more straight musical situations at the same time, but I wasn't because I had quit playing club dates. What I wanted to do was just wail and scream.

Lew: But obviously you guys already knew how to play changes. You can't just show up for Horace Silver and say, "Let me see if I can figure out how to play changes."
Dave: In Michael or Randy Brecker's case, they could definitely play changes. They had gone to school in Indiana with David Baker and were somewhat trained. I didn't have that stuff down. Sure, I had what I had picked up from the various teachers we discussed, but I had no formal training. I was already hanging with my future bud, pianist Richie Beirach, but even he was going to the Manhattan School of Music for composition—not jazz but at least something. Even Steve Grossman was at Juilliard.

Lew: At Juilliard with Joe Allard?
Dave: Yeah, but not for jazz. What I'm saying is that I really was not that equipped to play on changes. I really had to do my work eventually. I did a little and through some kind of osmosis, eventually it came. But Randy and Lanny Fields, they certainly knew how to play on changes in time. When we got to the loft—at least my loft—the green light was on to go ahead and play in this very energetic post-*Ascension* style.

Lew: The reason I'm focusing on it, just for a minute, is because you are one of the masters of playing changes.

Dave: It got better!

Lew: What you teach is the advanced changes playing—that's what your book is about. So obviously you *way* got there at some point.
Dave: Well, I got there somehow, but I'll tell you right now that playing changes is still a mountain to be climbed by a musician, forever. I can't tell you that I'm as comfortable on changes in general as I am in more open harmonic situations. Playing on E minor or an E pedal was preferable for sure, because changes just weren't natural to me. I'm going to discuss this when we get to Elvin, but there are definitely generational differences concerning what is natural to you and what you can and cannot account for. What you grow up around and hear, and how natural that feels compared to things you have to learn—they're always going to be separate and not really equal. I don't care how good you get, what you came up with is your hometown. Where you travel to, you are a stranger. In our case, generally we were looking back at bebop, because we were on the precipice of fusion, which was generally modal-based. We had come after Trane's stuff already. By the late sixties, it was already five years after *Impressions*. In other words, for us to play rhythm changes, I vi ii V was a trip compared to *Impressions*, for example. So, how adept I've become at it, or good at it, by hook or crook, yes, sure. But it was never something that was easy to do—and I have to tell you, not that enjoyable to do. Maybe that's part of it. You always like what you feel comfortable in more than what you don't feel comfortable in.

I certainly had very little formal training in this respect and knew that I was weaker than others. Besides which, I had an attitude, which goes along with being at that stage and age along with the generation and that time period, which was like, "Hey, I don't need that!" I talked about Charles Lloyd and how he said to me, "You don't need *that,*" *that* being this tradition thing, and how I took that as the word from up high. It was later on that I realized he could've said, "You don't need it, but you should know it." You know, he never said *should—should* know. Now as I talk to students—to get back to your main point—yes, you should know it. You have to. But in those days there was nobody to say that, at least directly to me, in a manner that I could hear.

In any case, we got to this point where Bob Moses, who was more in touch with the community and what was going on, said: "You know, there's this group called the AACM." These were the Chicago guys—the Association for the Advancement of Creative Musicians—Muhal Richard Abrams was the chief. There was also a cooperative in St. Louis, and in 1964 in New York there had been the so-called October Revolution of free jazz.

Lew: Right. Organized by the late trumpeter and composer Bill Dixon.
Dave: In other words, there was momentum toward playing this music and doing it yourself—grass roots. Why? First of all, because it was not commercial and it never was or would be. Number two, from a political standpoint, from the black side, free jazz had an obvious relevance. From our side it was playing for each other and the lifestyle that accompanied it—drinking tea, smoking pot, maybe dropping psychedelics, listening to tapes for eight hours, going to Chinatown to eat, coming back and playing more, having a wonderful time. Basically we were stroking ourselves in a way, because we were not getting any feedback and we had little awareness of what was going on in the real world.

This is the beginning of something in my life that has recurred a few times, which is some sort of organizational/administrative capability that I seem to possess. I'm the guy who says, "Okay, let's organize. Let's get together." So, I called a meeting in my loft and I remember ten, fifteen guys sitting on the floor, with invited guests being violinist Leroy Jenkins and saxophonist Anthony Braxton, both from the AACM.

It was Bob Moses who knew these guys. I remember we got together early in the evening—seven o'clock, seven-thirty—and Leroy Jenkins came trudging up. He saw a sea of white people and he completely went off, because he basically said if you don't have a cause like the brothers do, forget it. The vibe was like, you've got nothing to organize about so there's no reason for you. Thank you very much and good night. Then Braxton came up a couple hours later and he's like peace and love—like yeah, organize, grass roots, free jazz, go for it, love each other, you know—all that stuff. Anyway, that night we talked and I don't know how the discussion exactly went, but it came down that we should organize and put on our own concerts. And that we had to have a name.

Remember, almost everybody who was there had long hair and a beard, tie-dyed shirts—the whole counterculture outfit. It was '69—this was right after Altamont, toward the end of that whole thing. We concluded that we needed the word *free* because of the emphasis on free jazz. We needed something about the fact that it was not just music—it was about life and communication. I think it was Bob Berg who said "Free Life Communication!" Yeah! And that was it. Epiphany—it was great! Beautiful! So, next, we had to get down to brass tacks. I found a lawyer.

Lew: Was Chick a member of this?
Dave: He might have been there that night, or not—same with Dave Holland. As a real active member, no, but he was definitely aware of it. He lived in the building so it was a given, but he and Dave were with Miles and in another league. Anyway, we organized. I don't know how it happened, but I became president. Moses eventually pulled out, which he has been known to do.

Lew: Because he's just not an organization guy?
Dave: Yes, but there's more to it. Mose is somewhat of a contrarian. You say yes, he says no. But his purpose was served—he helped me get it going. I had Richie Beirach and Frank Tusa, my future band mates, who took over leadership with me. Cameron Brown was involved. I think he became treasurer. We actually incorporated with a lawyer as a 501c non-profit organization, eventually getting a grant through the New York State Council of the Arts for $5,000. We tried to follow parliamentary procedure at meetings as outlined in *Robert's Rules of Order*. My mother was up on how to run these types of things, as an officer of the PTA in my school and in her duties for the family association. *Robert's* book was a gold mine actually. I took it very seriously. We had meetings and we had dues.

The main thing was that we wanted to put on concerts. So, we spent the whole next year performing in churches like Judson or Washington Square Church, for example. We played in all different combinations, mostly free music of course. I always tell this story, which kind of epitomizes our vibe: We would meet at my loft at midnight. Frank had a car, so we would drive around with a pail, brush, flour, and water. You weren't supposed to put signs and posters up, so we did it after midnight, splitting Manhattan up into zones, as well as putting posters up in health food restaurants, clubs, anywhere they would allow you to put something up. It was each guy's responsibility to get his zone done, so people would know about the music. There was the Lower East Side, Midtown—which was kind of off limits really—and then there was 72nd to 96th Streets around Broadway. We'd meet afterward and ask each other, "How many posters did you put up?" We charged $2, I think, at the door, and we did a lot of concerts.

Then an opportunity came—I can't remember through whom, but it might've been the accountant. It seemed there was a philanthropist and his wife—Rubin was the family name—who were, I believe, big contributors to the National Symphony in Washington, D.C. They were financing the renovation of a building on West 36th Street, a former church, which was to be named the Space for Innovative Development. In this space were Alwin Nikolais and Murray Louis and their well-known Nikolais Dance Theater; also the famous theater guy Joe Chaikin. There was also a videography type of project, which was of course kind of avant-garde in those days.

They needed a music group. The Rubins put a million dollars into this project with each group on a separate floor. They wanted to meet and hear us play first. So, one day, me, Richie, Nancy Janoson on flute, maybe Moses—I forget—came to my loft, definitely at a civil time of day. The Rubins came in a limo, walked up the funky stairs—no throwing down the key this time!—and sat on my couch. We, of course, refrained from any off-color activity and so forth, just playing completely free for forty-five minutes. We got the gig! I think I served them tea and we talked. They were very nice and appreciative. It was rich benefactors visiting the starving artists. We got a full floor in the space—maybe two thousand square feet with a grand piano on permanent loan. All we had to do was find chairs or something for seating. Now I'm telling you that this floor was pristine. Beautiful. It was completely new, as was the piano I believe. Oh yeah—the piano was ours for one dollar a year. Nice!

Lew: That's because they had to have some number. I mean, they were really giving it to you for free, but they wanted it official.
Dave: Yep—I signed the lease; it said one dollar. With the grant money from New York State, we went and bought pillows somewhere in Chelsea. I had this bright idea that I wasn't going to get chairs, so I got these gigantic pillows. All the crazy fabric mixed up, and folks would just lie on them. We bought forty pillows or something like that. Our room was set up, and we gave three hundred concerts the first year. Double quartet, double trios, a bunch of saxophones, etc. Basically, anybody could do whatever they wanted.

Anyway, that was the height of this period. It was 1970 and more or less simultaneous with being in Ten Wheel Drive. The bottom line was that a bunch of young cats were running Free Life Communication, with all the pitfalls you could expect from egos and so on going unchecked. Soon enough it became, "Who's going to get in or not? What kind of music is acceptable?," etc. The seeds of the end were right there from the beginning, if for no other reason than we were young, all trying to do the same thing. It's a setup for an unpleasant situation—peers are judging peers. What can you do?

Guys would come and play for us, like an audition basically. I think it was $15 to join Free Life. We had sixty members at one point. It was obviously getting out of hand. Free Life Communication took its own course, and eventually after I had it running for two years and got the gig with Elvin, I couldn't really put any more time into it, so the next cats took over. It survived for a couple of more years. A drummer named Shelly Rusten kind of took over for me, but eventually it faded out. Still, at the height we did do three hundred concerts the first year. We really had a great time.

You'd get anywhere from twenty to sixty people or maybe more on occasion, pretty much the way it would be now for that kind of music with no real "name artists." But we had progressed from community centers, churches, and little museums into our own home. They even wrote about us in the *New York Times*. Before the Knitting Factory, the so-called downtown scene, we were one of New York's avant-garde collectives. On my website there's a picture of us.

It was exciting because we were doing something on our own. From the positive standpoint there were two important things. First of all, musically: Free jazz was, outside of a few "stars" like Cecil and Ornette, persona non grata. It wasn't really a viable style for any kind of public consumption, even for musicians themselves who weren't playing in the moment. But the fact is, it really made me go places on my instrument that I would never have gone otherwise. The second thing, from a very personal standpoint, with Free Life, was developing organizational chops and leadership—how to call a meeting, delegating responsibility, using authority to get things done, etc. That is real-world stuff that I didn't know. I was twenty-four, twenty-five years old. When would I be able to use these talents, if indeed they were talents? I got a chance to use them at a very early age with a group of people. I made mistakes, obviously, but this was a very good lesson for me, and it remains as probably one of the pinnacles of my self-learning. That was what was good about it.

Lew: Tell us more about what you learned from playing free jazz.
Dave: There's no question that you had to develop some avant-garde techniques and unique ways of playing that you wouldn't come up with if you played only the blues, for example. I have listened once in a while over the years to the music from that period and I see that I played extremely legato with very little articulation. I never marked off the time in the typical way or tongued much. My fingers were like glass. I mean, they were just fast. I've never been that fast since—seriously.

Energy, youthfulness, stamina, and some technical things—the way I moved my fingers. It was just the way it was. A certain kind of mouthpiece I had also. I'm not going to say we were out of control, but I never had to think about pulse or harmony. As you know, one of the guidelines when I teach is this so-called slack theory. This means if one element is exaggerated, or the opposite left out, that means other elements will be more emphasized to fill the void. So, if you don't have pulse-type time and direct harmony to be concerned about and there's basically no melody, what is left? Color, texture, sound, and form. Color becomes, let's say, 99 percent, which is not the same if we go and play a tune with changes. Color is of course an aspect in straight-ahead playing, but it's not usually *the* aspect. I am exaggerating, but the point is that what was being musically emphasized in that period I never experienced in that way again. So that was of value, though I didn't recognize it then. I wouldn't have been able to say this to you until at least ten years later from that period.

In fact, there's one tape I play in the chromatic harmony class I teach at Manhattan School of Music. I call it the "Five-Horn Day." It was Bob Moses on drums and Calvin Hill on bass. The horns were Michael Brecker, Steve Grossman and myself on saxes, with Randy Brecker and Terumasa Hino on trumpets. For some reason, those three hours just really happened. I've listened to it since and edited it a bit. I bring it into the kids like a joke, asking who they think is playing.

Lew: Can they recognize it?
Dave: They can't recognize anybody! No way! I use it for a kind of joke, because it's players they know, but they've never heard them play free. But also I use it from a pedagogical standpoint, because one of the things we do in this class is they have to write me a suite, and I use Coltrane's *Meditations* as a model, with the analysis I published years ago, which is now on my website. One of the other things discussed is about the rhythm. I want them to understand what non-pulse rhythm is about. So we discuss drummer Rashied Ali's playing with Coltrane. I bring in that tape to show what we were doing in 1969, playing no pulse, and so on.

Really, that's a period of history that is a time capsule. We were young, and to us it was amazing music. Trane was already dead two to five years. This style was pretty much finished and subsumed by fusion by '73. Way gone. Even some of the guys who did it originally wouldn't touch it with a ten-foot pole, let alone talk about it. In any case it petered out and ran its natural course, with some guys remaining with it. It was a great era for some of us. I just remember how it felt—how free we were!

Lew: That's great. That's a nice way to say it. Now, what about LSD? You said that was part of that scene.

Dave: For some people it was very important, because it was a major part of that period. Mescaline too and mushrooms.

Lew: Some people took LSD and it really worked for them. Other people took it and said: "Man, I don't dig it. I had a bad trip." Or nothing happened, you know. It didn't work for everybody.
Dave: For sure, but there was another thing about it, which was that once you experienced it and reinforced that experience a few times, there was really nothing left to it. From the artistic standpoint, once you heard and played music in that state of being, you basically got the point and doing more of the same was coming from another, not a positive place.

After that, it's another story. This was a period when guys were dealing with it. There was no alcohol, I can tell you that. Nobody drank—I don't even think there was a beer. It was not on the table to drink—there was marijuana, obviously, but more psychedelics. Somehow you could play this free stuff for hours and enjoy it. I think that it was an important thing for that period of time.

Lew: And for you, it didn't get to a point where it became bad.
Dave: I'm not an addictive personality. I never have been. I never ended up with problems like that. I could smoke a cigarette or not smoke it. I'm compulsive and intense, but I'm not addictive. I'm too busy to stay on one thing. There are too many things I have to do.

Lew: Well, you're also very focused, and if you don't want it, you don't feel like, "I have to take it even though I don't want it."
Dave: Look, other guys, some brothers from that period didn't fare so well. I don't want to mention names, but they were or are casualties of war—someone has to go down, unfortunately.

Lew: I understand. Now, you've mentioned Steve Grossman coming to the loft a lot.
Dave: Steve was friendly with the bass player I've mentioned, Lanny Fields, and a drummer named Danny D'Imperio. These guys were in the Army band, as was my very good friend Mike Garson, whom we have spoken about. They were at Fort Jay in Staten Island and they played a lot. Mike told me, "You've got to hear this kid who's really young." I don't remember exactly how young, maybe sixteen, which would make it 1967 when I first met him. I went to a jam session at the Army base in Staten Island and sure enough he was killing, playing Trane modal tunes and everything, definitely in there big time. This cat was way beyond

me. He was a great musician. I said it then and say it now. You know how things change when you get older and you hear guys you thought were great, but as you get better, you realize that guy was just so-so. Well, not in Steve's case—he was truly happening. He was a quiet guy with a little bit of a "'tude"—slightly arrogant, as would be expected. But because we shared certain friends, we had to have interaction. I mean, I wanted to kill him because he was so good and also a pain in the ass! And he knew it. He was in high school, for God's sake!

The story is that his brother Hal, who has since passed, was a trumpet player teaching at Berklee. He got Steve going real young, doing the right things. They say that when he was nine, ten years old Steve was transcribing Bird, just sitting in the basement. That's what he did. He didn't play ball. This was a good-looking, normal, straight kid. He wasn't a nerd, he wasn't handicapped in any way. He was talented and had a brother who directed him, it seems. By the time I met Steve at this jam session he had already been through Bird and had Trane down! We're talking the middle period *Impressions* on tenor and the *Afro Blue/Promise* stage on soprano. As well, he played bass, trumpet, and piano and seemed like he knew a million tunes. He was a phenomenon! He had worked on it, that was for sure.

So, our first encounters were not pleasant—ego and youth and all that stuff. I don't remember the details, but eventually I took the initiative to say, "Steve, look, we've gotta talk. This is not cool." He said, "Sure." I went out to his house. "We both love Trane—that's why we are here. We are better together than not. We have to get our act together." He said, "Cool." Somehow I needed to make peace with him because he was a fact of life, and I really wanted to do Trane and Pharoah Sanders or Trane and Eric Dolphy. I really wanted to have another cat there. There weren't a lot of saxophone players around, let alone cats who could play. There was some personal motivation here.

Lo and behold, we became the best of friends—like brothers. Steve eventually went to Juilliard at seventeen or eighteen and also studied with Joe Allard. By 1969/70, he was coming to the loft every day, living with me the whole weekend. He would be there all the time, sleeping over, going to Chinatown with me or Ratner's Deli on Delancey Street where you could eat late and cheap. He's on most of those tapes I mentioned in my basement, more than anyone else except maybe Moses. He got into the macrobiotic thing with me, actually staying with it longer. We would smoke, some weed, whatever. We really were a team, which had its denouement in the Elvin Jones group a few years later. The funny thing is, this is '69, and he gets the gig with Miles. We did a Free Life gig at a club on West 45th Street called Danny's Hideaway, and Miles came down. I had met Miles earlier when he had dinner with Chick, Dave, and myself in the loft. And I had been backstage a couple of times at some Miles gigs during this period because of Chick and Dave.

It was a Sunday afternoon featuring a double rhythm section with George Cables on piano, Lanny Fields and Dave Holland on the two basses, Bob Moses and Lenny White on drums, and Steve and me. Miles came down, probably 'cause of Lenny, who made some fast progress as a drummer, already playing on *Bitches Brew*. Lenny was in with Miles, and he must have told him about Steve, and of course Dave was already playing with Miles at the time. So, the Prince of Darkness came down to this club. We played a matinee. I remember it well, because it was pretty soon after he was shot at in his Ferrari in Brooklyn, which had happened in the early morning of October 9, 1969. He was sitting with us in the break and suddenly said, "Come outside. I want to show you something." Parked on the street was the famous red Ferrari with bullet holes in it! "Look at that—they tried to get me!"—kind of proud in a way. It was great.

We played two tunes—one was mine, called "Slumber"— for an hour plus, and for the second set we played only one tune. We were seriously into the late Trane thing. Steve got the gig. He first recorded with Miles in November 1969, and joined the band on a regular basis in March thru August 1970. He's on *Jack Johnson*, *Black Beauty* at the Fillmore West, the Fillmore East, and some others. This was the period when we were partners, friends, and then incredibly we were together with Elvin and separately with Miles. A year and a half later I got the gig with Elvin. Then he left Miles, we worked with Elvin together, and then I went with Miles. That's basically a three- to four-year period, 1970-74. It was kind of a changing partners dance we had going. Steve was my tightest friend, before Richie Beirach took that place. We had a really great rapport. He was four to five years younger than me, from an upper-middle-class Jewish family. His younger brother was named Miles—not bad! He was a privileged kid who took the ball and ran with it.

Lew: When did you become aware that drugs were really becoming a problem for him, or was that not until years later?

Dave: That's after. When I left Elvin's group for Miles in '74, Steve stayed on for another year or two. But Steve was changing and hanging with a certain group of guys by then. I could see what was going on. Something went on between him and Elvin from what I understood, and they kind of fell out. Maybe a year or two after I had left Elvin for Miles,

Steve called me and said he was in Detroit working with, I think, Lonnie Smith. I hadn't heard from him for a while. It appeared that he was working the "chitlin" circuit—black clubs with an organ trio. He said something like, "They took my horn." I said, "Who is they?" That was about it. The word was around that Steve was strung out, or something like that was going on. I could hear that his voice wasn't that good. Maybe he was at some rooming house and somebody took his horn—who knows?

I didn't talk to or see him again until 1987, when somebody in Italy set up a gig featuring us near Rome. The club was called Birdland, I think—a weird place, as I recall. Steve was living in Italy, so we picked him up and he immediately said to me something like, "I'm straight, I'm cool!" as he got in the car. He seemed okay. And all I know is that we went to dinner and the cat drank a lot of wine. That's all that I can tell you.

We went to the gig, and this was when I was playing only soprano. There was a rhythm section from Montreal that I had heard about who had come to live there with Steve. He attracted certain kinds of people to play with. We played, I remember, "Naima," "Impressions"—tunes we used to play. I was just shocked at how he sounded. I mean, he sounded really like Sonny Rollins—okay, but nothing particularly special, almost like a time piece. I had heard about the way he was playing in those years, but it was a bit of a shock to hear it in front of me. I had progressed a bit by that time. I remember by the end of the night the club was very smoky. I got paid and was ready to split. Meanwhile, Steve was walking around the anteroom, the lobby outside the club, coming up to everybody with his horn and playing little snips of tunes and saying, "You know this one?" Of course, he was playing the most obscure bebop tunes in the world. I was in the bathroom and he went up to a cat in there and said, "Hey, you know this one?" The cat had no idea what he was talking about!

That was the last time I had contact with him until a couple of years ago, when one of my students transcribed the whole *Live at the Lighthouse* recording, which is published now as a book. You know, that was the most famous recording we did with Elvin, and it was quite something what a former student, a wonderful saxophonist from Norway, Petter Wettre, did. I was with some guys in Milan and we called Steve and spoke—nothing notable, just about the transcriptions. He asked me to resend the Trane at the Half Note "One Up, One Down" track, which had been passed around for decades until it was finally released on CD. Then two years ago or so, I played in Bologna where he lives, and I borrowed a tenor like I always do—"tenor du jour"—and it happened to be from the guy who lives with Steve. I called him up and said he should come down. I mean how often am I in Bologna using his roommate's tenor? He said something like he was watching TV and maybe he would come down, which he didn't. Those are my interactions with him since the mid-1970s.

Lew: That's too bad. That's sad.

Dave: I hear he's doing good now, which I hope is true. I heard a record from 1990/91 with Art Taylor, and it's great. It's more Sonny Rollins than Sonny himself—that particular Sonny style from the fifties.

Lew: I have one from Italy around '97. Sounds like Sonny, but, like you say, excellent. It is good, but it was surprising for me, too. I was like, "Wait, I thought he was the Trane guy."

Dave: He was more than that. When you hear *Jack Johnson*, when you hear stuff he played in the loft, and, of course, *The Lighthouse*, you know he was into something unique that could've continued developing—I mean, the lines and choice of notes. But he was not that kind of guy. He was just very talented and very good by the time I got to know him. I don't think he sat down and did any sort of deep figuring out of the stuff. He somehow had a way of playing lines that was different than Wayne and Trane, and with a lot of passion, for sure. In my opinion it could've definitely been a bigger thing if he had taken more responsibility. I'm no expert, but it seems that his life style waylaid him off a path that might've really been innovative—who knows? The plate was full when he walked in during those years with Elvin and Miles, with the great reputation he had. Remember, in those days there weren't as many teen-aged whiz kids walking around playing great as there are now. It's not my business, obviously, because he followed his path on his own free will. But for me, he had a lot of promise and it's a bit sad. And then the expatriate thing. . .

Lew: You're right, the expatriate thing, meaning people around here don't even know he exists.

Dave: Well, he's around and he works, from what I understand. Europe has that ensconced jazz club situation, which will never go away. It is part of the culture, an extension of the café vibe, harkening back to another period of history. Every joint has a picture of dead brothers on the wall—Chet Baker or whomever. They exist in places like Italy or Germany—little subterranean joints—"kellers" or whatever they're called. A guy like Steve can work there forever and play music that is really what people want to hear in that specific environment. That's his thing at this time, it seems. I keep hoping that he will return to the Steve I knew, for which he'd probably get a lot of recognition.

There are other connections that we will get to when I talk about my relationship with Eleana Steinberg. Her sister Bonnie was with Steve during those Elvin years, when I was with Eleana. So we were all hooked up for a minute. This is a whole family thing. Steve's story could end like Frank Morgan's or Art Pepper's or Dexter's did—the triumphant return of the "clean" expatriate, ready to burn and play his tail off like he used to. You know, the return of the prodigal son and all that. The press loves that sort of thing. Anyway, that's the Steve Grossman story.

Chapter 6

Guided Dream: Playing with the Masters

Lew: Let's talk some more about Chick Corea.
Dave: I remember one time Chick wrote this tune "Waltz for Bill Evans" that is really a masterpiece, with polychords and some time signature changes. He would come upstairs and play drums with me and the guys. I guess we were in a way friends, for a minute. He's five years older, and I definitely looked up to him on a lot of levels. Chick was—this is the pre-Scientology Chick—a nice guy, a friendly guy, as he still is—not an overly warm guy, always keeping a distance, but friendly enough. Dave Holland also was the same way, but I attribute that to his English background. They are generally more private and reserved, by custom. But in the end, Dave could get down when it was right—Chick, not so much. But he was certainly ahead of me, and somebody I looked up to. I mean, he was like *the* guy!

Lew: He had already recorded with name cats.
Dave: He was practicing Monk and Bud Powell stuff next to music of Charles Ives. His tastes were very wide. Like I said, he was the first person I knew who got into macrobiotics and soon enough Dave and I followed suit. I remember another time when he rented a little house in Warwick, New York. One day I drove up and spent the day with him. He was into playing Spanish classical guitar. We sat all day basically in one room, just hanging. There might have been some LSD around—not sure. Chick was calm and cool all day, like in a meditative state of mind. He was "gurued out," if you know what I mean—truly searching for answers, meditating and stuff like that. We were all searching, using any means possible across the spectrum of philosophies, methods, anything.

We were all into it. "Did you read this? Did you check out that?" Chick was a leader and I followed him.

Lew: When you went to see him in Warwick, was that just the two of you?
Dave: Yeah. I spent like six hours with him, sitting around while he was playing guitar. He was just sitting there, cross-legged and playing, and we just talked—or didn't talk—I don't remember. But he was in that zone. He was definitely looking for enlightenment. He was searching—I mean, musically, psychologically, spiritually. Maybe some of this was because of the breakup of his marriage, but it was obvious that here he was on his own, and he was going to find himself one way or the other. His musical career was obviously taking off. This was his incubation period. He wasn't from New York and, like most guys who come from elsewhere, they get things together in a different way than a native does. New York guys—they have to do the same work, but they sort of have had a little bit of it here and there because they have grown up in it. Chick was clear as the day is long when you talked to him. I definitely idolized him. He was amazing, and it was obvious that he was an incredible musician and could play anything. This is pre–*Return to Forever* and pre–*Crystal Silence*. This is just around the time he did those first solo records for ECM in 1971.

Lew: Sure. And he had already recorded with Blue Mitchell. He's on a live album at the Vanguard with Dizzy—
Dave: With Miles he is playing with DeJohnette and Holland, one of the most burning rhythm sections of all time. Then *Circle* with Anthony Braxton and Barry Altschul, leading to *Return to Forever* with Flora and Airto, and finally the electric band—quite an intense period for him.

Lew: *Light as a Feather* was big.
Dave: *Light as a Feather* was a hit. It seemed like the breakup of Circle was a little tense when he decided to do the Flora-Airto thing. He moved out of the loft around that time, I think to the Upper West Side, and then eventually to California. So, I lost track of him til '78, which is getting a bit ahead of the tale, but let's do it now since we are on the topic of Chick. I was playing duo with Richie at a club called La Bastille in Houston. I remember this very well because it was Superbowl Sunday—I looked it up; it was January 15, 1978—and we were watching at the promoter's house. The phone rang and it was Chick Corea: "Dave, I'm doing a three-month tour and I would like you to do it. Joe Farrell can't

make it." This was an offer I couldn't refuse. It was perfect timing for me. But we have to backtrack a few years to Scientology.

Lew: This has to do with his trying to find himself?
Dave: It appears that way. Among all the things he tried, there was yoga, meditation, Indian philosophy, macrobiotics, and here comes Scientology to the rescue, roaring down the track like a tsunami. He was introduced to it by another musician and sure enough Dave Holland and I got into it. There I am, holding beer cans hooked up to the truth-meter or whatever, paying 1,500 bucks for six weeks of "instruction." When I stopped doing it, all I remember is that Chick was gone to California. I have no feeling about Scientology one way or the other. I can see he really got into it deep. Anyway, both Dave and I couldn't use it. It was no big deal. It wasn't the political thing it is now.

Lew: So it wasn't for you, but you weren't thinking, "Oh, that's a crock," or whatever?
Dave: No. And I must say, to be fair, that I read that first book that Hubbard wrote.

Lew: *Dianetics*?
Dave: Yes. That is a book that should be read. It was twenty or thirty years ago, but there's nothing wrong with what he says, from what I remember. My take on it is that this is a religion for the technological age. Hubbard had figured out some key things—symbolic gestures with great appeal to intellectual people. This was for sure. This is not something you could sell to the masses. You definitely need the Chick Coreas, the John Travoltas, and the Tom Cruises of the world. Being wealthy doesn't hurt. This is not for everybody. You need guys with a high intellect who are searching and looking and are possibly a little confused, in the sense of discovering the meaning of life, like all of us. Because of that, Scientology definitely represents some kind of path toward figuring out questions of that sort, existential stuff and so on.

At this point, it was just another thing, a modern fad, but not for me. During the world tour with Chick in 1978, the upshot of this thing is him telling me that the reason my episode with Scientology was not as positive as it should've been was that the people who were dealing with me weren't the right folks. In fact, they were eventually banned from the movement. So, according to Chick, I got the wrong impression, which is why I was turned off. Anyway, I said yes to the tour, and a few months later, we all met in L.A., I'm pretty sure in early April, to rehearse for about two weeks.

We were playing the music from three of his records: *Leprechaun*, *My Spanish Heart*, and *Mad Hatter*. It was a string quartet, plus brass, and rhythm section. His wife, Gayle Moran, was on keyboards and vocals, with Rick Laird on bass and Tom Brechtlein on drums, Al Vizzutti and Bob Zottola on trumpets, Jim Pugh and Ron Moss on trombones—Ron was also his manager—a big operation. They were all relatively unknown folks at that time. I suppose I was the only one who was sort of known, and maybe Rick Laird a bit from the Mahavishnu band.

Lew: And it's interesting, because there were a couple of graduates from the Eastman School of Music, Vizzutti and Pugh.
Dave: I know he held auditions for the strings, at least. The viola player, Judy Geist, eventually went to the Philadelphia Orchestra. The lead violin was Charles Veal, who, I guess, did studio work in L.A. The other two, Carol Shive on violin and Paula Hochhalter on cello, I don't remember where they were from. After the rehearsal period, we had gigs all over Europe, then Australia, Japan, Hawaii, and back to the U.S. mainland.

Lew: I managed to reconstruct some of your itinerary, with the help of some friends. You played in a place near Barcelona, Spain, on April 21, 1978, and I don't have exact dates for the gigs before and after that, but you also played in London, Zurich, Geneva, Hamburg, Vienna, Munich, and elsewhere in Europe, into May. Then you were in Australia during May, playing in Brisbane, Perth, Canberra, Melbourne, and Sydney. Laird had lived in Sydney, so he was thrilled to be back there. Your first gig in Japan was on May 30; after Japan, you played Honolulu.
Dave: Thanks! So, now I'm back with Chick, whom I admire, who was an influential part of my life five years earlier. This is 1978 and I'm already done with Miles; I've done my own band, Lookout Farm; I lived in California for a while doing the Ellis-Liebman band and so on—thirty years old. If I talk about the loft now in our interviews with such enthusiasm, thirty-five years later, imagine then what I was saying. The loft days, how great it was, the music that we played, macrobiotics—the overall scene. You know, so I'm excited to see Chick! The guy was my man, my teacher. It ends up that he is a completely different person than what I remember from five, six years earlier. It was something that is hard to describe. He was very impersonal—there, but not there. He was looking at you, but he was not looking *at* you. It was obvious that his

support of Scientology was entrenched, and he felt strongly that everyone around him should be on board.

Here is what happened, which I found out later. There were more than a dozen people on tour, with sound guys, equipment, PR, etc., besides the musicians. Almost to the man and woman, everyone was into Scientology or close to it, at least as it appeared to me. They all had to sign a paper that there would be no drugs or uncaring love—sex, I assume. I never signed that and no one said anything to me about it, maybe 'cause I was kind of the main soloist besides Chick, and they needed me? They could have had anybody, but there I was on flute, tenor, and soprano. I memorized all the music the first two weeks of rehearsal. The music was what it was. Of course, it was well written and happening on a lot of levels. We did a duo every night, either "Lush Life" or "Crystal Silence." This, of course, was a highlight for me.

But Chick was so different and really corny with the audience, like, "Turn to your neighbor and say hi," or whatever. He sounded like Jimmy Swaggart, like that. So, being the way I am, I couldn't help but say to him, "What's with you, man? What's wrong with you?" We got into it—nightly discussions, hours at a time, friendly, but a bit contentious. I'm not sure why he even put time into it with me, why he even cared. Maybe he thought he could win me back to the Scientology fold? I have no idea. I was pissed at him, or maybe more than that, disappointed in him. And, of course, I was a little rebellious, so there's an attitude on my part that I'm sure you could probably cut with a knife! He can really get into it, 'cause he's a talker. We would go for what seemed like a long time. "What happened to you? I mean, you're not the same!" I can't tell you the details of the conversations because I just don't remember them, and probably because I blocked it out after the ending incident.

We were on the road. Everything seemed cool—we were doing the gigs and so on. Strange as it sounds, on occasion I would leave notes for him in the hotel mailbox about the music the night before—nothing much, just communicating. "Last night was great." "You have to do that again," etc. The band was getting together for what, I guess, were Scientology sessions—not every day, but when they could. I certainly didn't go to these meetings. It seemed like kind of cultish behavior to me. The last gig was the one in Hawaii, and then we went to L.A. in early June. In Hawaii I had friends, so I partied and enjoyed myself, especially since we were going home the next day, after over two months. We got into the airport in L.A., stepped out of the plane, and Chick turned around and said, "I never want to see you again! You were against me, you started trouble, you fermented rebellion"—like that. He really went into it right in front of everyone—pointing his finger at me.

I was shocked. I had no idea this was coming. He knew how I felt since we had communicated on the tour in those talks. I wasn't hiding anything. I just didn't know it was such a major thing. He went out on me. I stayed at somebody's house that night. I called the violin player, Charles, who had always been cool with me. "Charles, what the hell?" He was like, "I don't know, man. He's really pissed off. I don't know what went down with you guys."

Lew: Was he raising his voice? Was he actually yelling?
Dave: Well, he's not the kind of guy who raises his voice. He was very controlled, but obviously pissed off!

Lew: The rest of the band heard it?
Dave: Well, whoever was listening, whoever could hear it. I mean, just the night before we had had what appeared to be a truce of sorts. I just felt that things were understood. When this happened at the airport, I was shocked because I didn't know that it had affected his attitude toward me in such a way. I felt terrible. I lost a friend, I lost a pal, one of my gurus, *and* I lost a gig! I mean, a gig was a gig, you know.

Lew: But when you landed after the Hawaii gig, was there a whole other leg of the tour that you were originally supposed to be on?
Dave: There were a few more gigs coming up, the U.S. part of the tour. Joe Farrell came back for those gigs, including the Hollywood Bowl. I think it was a week or two off, and then there were other gigs like a "Newport in New York" gig at Lincoln Center on June 30, and so on—summer things I think.

Lew: And it was just understood that you weren't going to play with Chick again?
Dave: Oh, yeah. "Don't ever talk to me again." You know, like that! Like I was an errant kid! That was it until I saw him at a hotel in Tokyo in '80 or '81, where he was completely cool. By then I had done that record *Dedication* with a string quartet, Richie on piano and Eddie Gomez on bass. Inspired musically by the Chick tour, I studied the string quartets of Bartók, Ravel, Debussy, and Beethoven. This is one of my favorites of my own recordings, by the way. Anyway, somehow Chick heard the record. I think I sent it to him with a note: "It's because of you." For

me, that tour with Chick was a revelation because I had never heard strings so close or played with them, and of course it was a turn on.

So, he saw me in the lobby in Japan and said, "I really enjoyed that record." His wife, Gayle, always liked me. I get along with the wives. I don't start any problems and I'm nice to them, like with Keiko, Elvin's wife. Gayle was always nice—a motherly Midwestern type, very sweet girl. So Chick and I had a little communication then, and we've had on and off communication since then. Somehow during the last decades every once in a while we have some interaction, especially by e-mail. One night, playing with Pete LaRoca in the '80s, Chick came down and sat in, which was nice. But I can't help thinking that in his head he is still a little pissed off at me. I asked him to record and he said absolutely not. I know he has recorded with other guys, so I take it personally. Maybe I'm exaggerating, but that's how I feel about Chick. I just feel like he's still pissed off at me, which is a drag, especially because Richie Beirach was really following in his tracks at one point. He's a lot like him in some ways from the musical standpoint, especially in the intellectual sense. A lot of classical background—a lot of similarities there. Chick was a powerful force in my early years and I hope someday we can play together. We had a great time musically. The one record I'm on with Chick is *Merry Go Round*, one of Elvin's recordings.

So, that's the Chick Corea story. To sum it up—to get back to the loft thing—he was very influential in my life, very important, and a real model of what an artist should be. He is—and I say this unabashedly—the best musician I have ever known. This means to me a musician who can do anything. He has absolute control of music without even lifting a finger, it seems. And not just that he could do anything, but do it deeply. In my opinion, Chick had the chromatic language down better than anyone—plus Monk, Bud, Cecil. Piano players are always at the top of the food chain. They have to be because of their instrument, its history and the implications. Chick had it all, *plus* the electronic stuff. Sure, Herbie, Keith, McCoy, but for all-around, I have to give it to Chick, at least the way it was in the late sixties into the seventies, for me. He could swing, play free, write, whatever. This is *the* cat. So, I hope that someday before we both pass, I can play with him again.

Here's my final thing on Scientology, which of course I have an opinion about, just like everybody does, but even more so in this case. My take on Chick is that here is a guy who only wants to do good for all. This is what separates Chick from most others. He really is a United Nations kind of person who wants to help the world, which was very clear to me in the loft days in the early '70s. I still think his basic M.O. is that he wants to be a force of good, and Scientology apparently appeals to a certain kind of personality that was very much Chick. He got into it, and once you're in it, you become it, and of course he's one of their heavy assets now, though I imagine the proselytizing days are long gone. We all mature, thank God. He's past that point, I have to think. From what I understand, he lives on the campus of Scientology—one of the centers worldwide, I think. But like I said, I doubt it comes up now when he has musicians working for him. Hey, we basically got along. He even wrote a tune for me when we had a week off in the middle of that tour in '78. It's called "Blues for Liebestraum." Joe Henderson recorded it with Chick in 1980. That was a hard tune—suspended chords, plus fives—like that. I have to record it someday. I even wrote a shout chorus for it.

Lew: I guess he wrote that tune before he got angry.
Dave: We were on a break during the three-month tour. Before the airport. I look upon this incident, this whole thing, as unfortunate, and a deficit in my character. He was being who he was and I should've just ignored it, instead of personalizing it. I just couldn't stand who he had become, but who the fuck am I? I was wrong, and I admit it. So he, let's say, "punished" me through banishment. I don't know.

Lew: I know what you mean. You can be with somebody who you totally disagree with, and you can choose to just let that person be.
Dave: Living in a marriage or any relationship, you've got to be like that. We do this every day. There's a point in life when you accept stuff and it's no skin off your back. What do you care? But I cared. And it wasn't like it was hurting anybody else. It was just my ego, I guess.

Lew: All right. Now, throughout the early '70s you continued to work with Bob Moses, on and off.
Dave: Yes, I had the Open Sky Trio with Moses and Frank Tusa or sometimes other bass players—Steve Swallow or Miroslav Vitous in particular. That trio was an outgrowth of the free jazz beginnings we were involved with in the late '60s, early '70s. It was the first organized music of mine with my peers. We put out two records on Gene Perla's label, PM Records. Gene was one of the first guys to start his own label, obviously ahead of his time. *Open Sky*, our self-titled recording, live from WBAI public radio in 1972, was his first release, followed by *Spirit in the Sky,* which was recorded in '73 and '74. So, besides the Swedish recording I did in 1967 in Sweden with Lars Werner, these two Open Sky

records were really my first recordings, even before *First Visit*, which I made as a leader when I was in Tokyo with Miles in July '73.

Lew: Another drummer you've mentioned several times is Pete LaRoca. I met Pete in '66 when he was driving a cab. He introduced himself at a little Mensa "jazz interest group." He said, "My name is Pete LaRoca," like I wouldn't know who he was. I said, "Pete LaRoca!" I was fifteen and I knew my jazz already. At his suggestion, the Mensa group went to see the Thad Jones-Mel Lewis band, and Pete drove me home from the Vanguard in his cab and told me he was planning to get a law degree.
Dave: Great story! Pete was crucial to my development, big time. I mean, Miles and Elvin and Pete! That's the triangle for me, musically. I started working with him early in 1969, when Bob Moses told me that Pete was looking for a saxophone player. Jim Pepper was on call but couldn't make it, so I went to Steve Swallow's brownstone in Chelsea to basically audition. I already knew Swallow through some gigs with Moses. Chick was there as well. Of course, by then he was living on 19th Street. I walked in and Pete said, "Thanks for coming. What would you like to play?" So, just as I would do with Elvin a few years later, I called "Softly as in a Morning Sunrise." After a chorus or two, he stopped and said, "Let's rehearse!"

This started my relationship with this guy, who, as you know, is a unique person. He is singular in every aspect. I have never met a guy like this—mind-boggling brilliant, intellectual, sophisticated, well-read, irascible, and so frustrating because he is such a perfectionist, which is maddening. I have been through so much with this guy, whom I have such love and respect for. It is one of the most frustrating relationships I've ever been involved in. He can't help but be himself. He is just the way he is and actually has as part of his multifaceted personality, the true mind of a lawyer, for better and worse. I did legal things with him over the years. You want to talk about crossing the t's and dotting the i's—this is the chief of this stuff.

It's hard to believe he is a jazz musician. Pete is like split personalities—not clinically, I wouldn't know that, but just as a person. He is among the loosest drummers I have ever seen, meaning physically speaking. There was a period when it appeared that he was experimenting with psychedelics when he played, but just enough to be cool, not more than necessary. He literally seems to dance when he plays, smiling away, oohing and aahing throughout, and is one of the greatest musicians I have ever known, with a perfect ear, time, swing, and creativity. So here's the epitome of a jazz giant, combined with the nit picking perfectionist lawyer side. There's no such thing as a simple sentence with this guy. In any case, he took me under his wing. I knew this was a real opportunity—the real deal. He told me that he didn't want to be a sideman anymore and wanted his own band, so that was what I was signing up for. This is the guy who was among Trane's choices as a drummer, who played with Sonny Rollins, Freddie Hubbard, everyone. It was my chance for sure.

Eventually we got a pretty steady gig at a club called La Bohème on 69th Street and Broadway. I had played there already with a drummer named Jimmy Lovelace and other guys, so I knew it. We basically played there for the next six months, maybe five nights a week. During that time I played with everybody in New York because the bass and piano chairs kept switching since the gig only paid $5 a night. Pete was Pete and he got the best, but of course only if a guy didn't have a better-paying gig. For me, it didn't matter because I was doing the substitute teaching thing then and supported myself that way. We were playing his music mostly and a couple of standards, like Chick had an arrangement on "This Is New." But it was mostly Pete's tunes, very simple tunes.

Lew: Chick's arrangement—was Chick there to play that?
Dave: Yeah, Chick was on the gig a lot. Other pianists were George Cables, JoAnne Brackeen, even Mike Garson did it. On bass was, besides Swallow, Dave Holland, of course, and Jimmy Garrison, Charlie Haden, Miroslav Vitous, etc. This was my first exposure to the real heat. Everything before was with peers, friends, acquaintances, basically my age or so. Here was the real deal. I wasn't with anybody ahead of me until I got to the loft with Chick and Dave, and then with Pete and whomever else was playing on a given night. So he was my first real mentor-teacher. As a musician, first of all, he can sing everything perfectly in tune, even the bass line. Most of all he would sing the melody to a tune in a way that you wish you could play it, with incredible nuance and feeling. I learned more about melody playing from Pete than from anybody else besides Miles. He would say, "Phrase it like this," and sing it perfectly. It seems that he had a perfect ear and perfect time. He was an unbelievably natural musician. His writing was pretty basic, harmonically speaking, but he had guys like Chick translating the chords, so it didn't matter. But if the bass played a wrong note, he would let the guy know what note it should be. Pete was somethin' else, man!

Lew: Did he have perfect pitch, or did he just know from the context?
Dave: He might have perfect pitch, I don't know. But, boy, the way he played those drums—he's one of a kind. Great, so musical, so heavy, so

happening. I learned so much from him that it's incalculable—things that can only happen on the bandstand—no words. His goal was to get Max Gordon to give him a gig at the Village Vanguard. Sure enough, on Thanksgiving weekend in '69 we played there opposite a singer named Novella Nelson. That was my first time in the "temple of jazz," for three nights, no less. We had the "A" band, meaning Chick and Swallow. I remember Chick didn't get there on time, so we had to start trio, playing this fast standard "Hindustan." It's like a tune Sonny would play—fast as lightning! Pete can play fast like nobody. And I was up there, my first time at the Vanguard, trying to keep up without the help of the piano. Finally, on the second tune, Chick sneaked in. I have tapes of that night and others from La Bohème, and I can tell you that I have never heard more piano playing than Chick with Pete. The rhythm especially was amazing. You can't believe the way these guys played together—Chick and Pete and Swallow, or even Dave Holland, but especially with Swallow. It was a rhythm section to behold. You know, they loved playing with each other.

Lew: Swallow and Pete—they did a lot of stuff together. They were a classic rhythm section for George Russell, Paul Bley, Steve Kuhn, Art Farmer, and others.

Dave: I learned a lot because Swallow was always very open, and as I said, I already knew him through Moses. I was very young and green. I went home from this gig every night and wanted to kill myself. This was like a major thing in my life. I was a nervous wreck. Pete tried to cool me out: "You wouldn't be here if you weren't good enough." I said, "Pete, I have to count every beat. When I'm off the stage and I don't count the beat, I don't know when to come in. I'm the only horn!" He said, "You're thinking about it too much. Think in ones, the whole measure; don't think in two-three-four." I asked him, "Why do you like Swallow? What makes a drummer like a bass player?" He said, "When I go to my bass drum, he's there already." So, you don't have to do it—you can find something else or nothing to play, 'cause everything is accounted for. Makes perfect sense.

Swallow was and is always great. We'd played free stuff with Moses, completely different than with Pete—no problem. Remember, this is Steve Swallow on upright bass, before the electric. He always takes care of business. We finished the Vanguard weekend, which was fantastic. That's the last time we played together in the quartet format. Next thing I knew, Pete went to law school after that. From what I understand, he decided almost concurrently with the end of that gig that he wanted to go to law school. Obviously, he was thinking about it. The next time I saw him was a couple of years later in an NYU dormitory. He was living in a room with books piled up to the ceiling. Amazing—Pete LaRoca in college.

The rest of the story with Pete is that he did indeed become a practicing lawyer, but as you know, on occasion he will come out and play. Every couple of years we would strike up the band and do a few nights at Sweet Basil or some other joint. He got into this thing about having three horns, which wasn't exactly my cup of tea, but of course I followed whatever he wanted to do with full support. He is a stubborn kind of guy, which is what I mean about frustrating. I even got close to helping him record for ECM. After all, it has been said that one of the inspirations for Manfred Eicher to start the label was the *Footloose* trio, that great record with Paul Bley, Swallow, and Pete. And he was my lawyer on several occasions. He even did something for my mother or brother as a lawyer, and in the 1990s when I was being stalked by some maniac, Pete was involved.

Lew: Yeah, the stalking incident is on your website, that horrible dead fish incident.

Dave: Pete came in and helped me out. I think with my mother it was that a waiter spilled hot coffee on her shoulder or something like that, and she had first-degree burns. I don't remember the details, but he had something to do with that case. He's retired now from law, and seemingly from music. This is a loss. This guy can play! Drummers would flip if they could see him now. He, Elvin, and Jack DeJohnette are also the best drum soloists I've ever heard. He had his own way of playing, incorporating timbales technique. He had some experience playing Latin music on timbales. Pete was the house drummer in Boston at the club Storyville, where I have to imagine Tony Williams must've been peeping him, since he is from there.

I would love to play with Pete now. It was sometime in the eighties, doing these occasional gigs, that I realized I could finally musically keep up with him. He's the kind of drummer who when you play a rhythm, you're going to get an answer. It's not just going to pass by unanswered. He's going to take the idea you tossed out and absolutely make something out of it. You could really have a rhythmical dance with this guy, in real jazz, in 4/4 time.

There was an interesting discussion apropos free playing that went on with Dave and Chick and Pete outside La Bohème one night. That was when they had been doing the group Circle, which as we know played quite free. They were asking Pete why we didn't play some free time—you know, no steady pulse: "Why don't we play free? Come on—stop the beat. Let's play some free!" They were imploring him. Standing against the car, Pete said: "Well, you know, the truth is, guys, I'm free in 4/4." And you know what? In his case, that was right because the way he played 4/4 anything could happen. He was really a genius in that respect.

Lew: But what's so exasperating, as you say, about him?
Dave: This streak of perfectionism. Like with the possible ECM deal, he started asking about tour support and things like that. They don't give tour support. He said, "Well, it's not worth making a record unless they give money for tour support." I mean, unreasonable. No compromise—that's what I mean by perfectionist. This guy would not give up an inch. And because he is brilliant, with incredible reasoning power and logic and, of course, verbally, with words, you cannot win.

The story of how Pete got to jazz drumming is kind of legendary from the folklore. He was a New Yorker, born and bred. Supposedly one night he cut Tito Puente on timbales at Birdland on a Latin night jam session. You know, "whiz kid arrives and cuts the master" deal. The other supposed story happened in the Catskills with a drummer named Lenny Seed. Pete was in the Latin band at one of these resorts and Lenny was in the show band. Pete asked Lenny if he wouldn't mind letting him sit at the drums during the day and fool around a bit. In three days, he was playing drums like crazy. It must be true, because I can tell you one thing: When Pete has come out and played sporadically in these last decades, I'm not sure if he touched the drums in between gigs, but it never mattered. He just gets up and plays. He is not a technical player anyway, so it works because his concept is so strong.

Lew: Great. Now let's pick up the story of Ten Wheel Drive and its aftermath, 1969, '70, '71.
Dave: To get back to the pop world, right around the end of 1970, we, the horn section for Ten Wheel Drive, had a union strike, so to say, the girl singer versus the band—typical power play about material, record company stuff, fairness, whatever. The instrumentalists wanted a better deal, and she and the management wouldn't give in. As a horn section we even wrote some sort of manifesto letter to the *Village Voice* about musicians' rights in relation to management and so on. You know the routine—nothing new. It was a whole scene, because it came down to us versus management and, of course, they were going to prevail, so a few of us quit Ten Wheel. To be honest, I don't recall the details, but cer-

tainly the trumpet player John Eckert and myself split. To try and bring in some revenue, in January and February 1971, I ran a classified ad in the *Village Voice* to get some improvisation students.

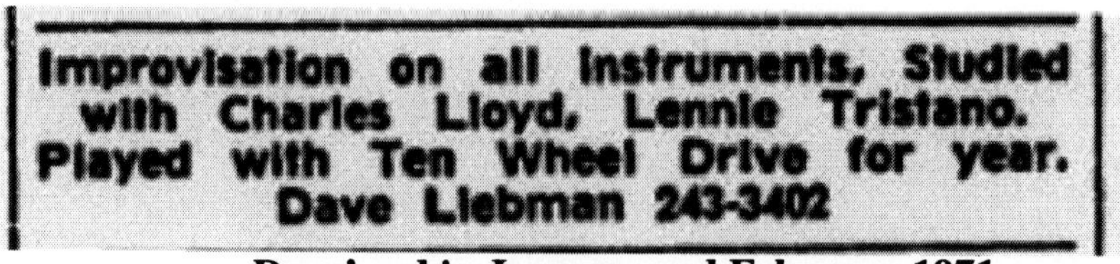
Improvisation on all instruments. Studied with Charles Lloyd, Lennie Tristano. Played with Ten Wheel Drive for year. Dave Liebman 243-3402

Dave's ad in January and February 1971

Also, right around this same time, I had discovered a tiny bar up in Port Chester, New York, called Rapson's, which had jam sessions. It was known because it was on the New York side of the border and Connecticut kids could come over and drink because it was a lower age limit than in their state.

Lew: I live in Port Chester now. The older cats all tell me that there used to be this scene.
Dave: This was it: Rapson's. I got up there somehow and found myself at a jam session. It was that first night that I met Eleana Steinberg. Eleana, who as we speak is and has been married to drummer Jimmy Cobb for quite a while, was a big part of these years. Her sister, Bonnie, is presently with Al Foster. Guess who introduced them to the world of jazz?

Lew: You. Right?
Dave: Right. I also met this guitar player named Linc Chamberland and a drummer, Jimmy Strassburg, who was from that area. So I started hanging out there every week and eventually I met saxophonist Pee Wee Ellis at the club. Anyway, this all morphed into the band Sawbuck. Rapson's became our home. We ended up with a manager and a contract with a Motown-owned subsidiary, Natural Elements. This was the first white group with Motown, from what I remember.

It was 1971 and this band became like the whole rock-and-roll family thing, real personal and on a mission. Linc, who was the main cat both playing and writing the material, was a jazz guy but played incredible rock. He found this amazing, soulful singer with the name Sky Ford. I have no idea where he came from. I never really got to know him well, but he could burn—screaming, bluesy singing that was compelling. Two trumpets, two saxophones, bass, guitar, and drums—no keyboard. It was mostly Linc's writing, and it was a kick-ass, raw, burning band. Of course, I was Coltraning out all over the music. Remember, this was new at the time, playing that crazy stuff over a rock vamp. This was the rock-fusion band that you wanted to have. So we got this contract, and of course, we were very close—rehearsing, hanging together, a rock-band vibe, playing all these funky gigs, trekking around, the whole rock thing.

Finally, we got this chance, this shot. Sure enough, right when we were about to record for Motown, I got the gig with Elvin Jones. I will never forget that day. I walked into the rehearsal and said, "I've been hired by Elvin Jones." I was in tears, or near tears. The cats all looked up and were like, "Man, you've gotta do that. This is the chance of a lifetime." And eventually they went on without me and recorded the LP *Pass the Butter,* under the new band name Gotham. Great band.

Lew: Sounds like it! Now, you were the only one in there who was from Ten Wheel Drive?
Dave: No. John Eckert and John Gatchell, two of the trumpet players, were in this band. We definitely came out of Ten Wheel Drive looking to do something. We found Linc Chamberland and he was perfect. We were a working band and I think on the precipice of what could've been a famous group, but of course everyone thought that in that period; this horn band fusion thing was in the air.

Lew: After you left, they must have gotten another tenor saxophonist.
Dave: They did. I think that's when Frank Vicari comes in. I think he took my place.

Lew: He passed away in 2006. That was too bad.
Dave: I agree—he was a beautiful cat who could really play, very natural. But Sawbuck was where I first met Pee Wee Ellis and that would come to the fore later in the tale when we formed the Ellis-Liebman band in San Francisco in '76.

Lew: So you left Sawbuck for Elvin Jones. How did Elvin know about you? How did he make the offer?
Dave: There's a good Elvin story with Pete that happened at La Bohème. One night with nobody there, we were all sitting around the bar, Elvin walked in with Keiko. I remember because he had a big fur coat on—striking—magisterial, really. I don't remember who else was playing that night with Pete and me, but we were sitting there. It was during the period when I was substitute teaching and doing this $5-a-night gig. Pete

was depressed. Elvin came up and asked, "How is it going?" I didn't know Elvin, but maybe he recognized me because I had done that big concert opposite Elvin's trio in 1968 at Town Hall. Pete said, "Oh, not that good. My saxophone player's gotta leave, 'cause he's gonna get a job," or something like that, and he pointed at me. Elvin turned around, came up to me, put his face in my face, and said, "Let me tell you something. You stay with Pete. Do you understand me?" This was like gunfighter shit. This was not like, "What are you doing, son? I know it's difficult out there to make a living." This was an order. "You stay with Pete. You got me?" So, did Elvin remember me in '71? I don't know.

Lew: Why did Pete say that? Had you been saying something like: "I need to find a gig that pays better?"
Dave: Yeah. We had been six months into the La Bohème gig. This was frustrating. It was night after night, and nobody came there. It was a lonely place. You'd get a $5 bill at the end of the night.

But the Elvin story basically starts with bassist Gene Perla, who, I have mentioned in connection with the loft thing because he had one down near the Fulton Fish Market and moved in the circles I was in. He was a bit older and had played with Nina Simone, Woody Herman, etc. He was experienced and a great musician. Well in '70 or '71, Gene got the gig with Elvin. I absolutely remember this because it was the first heavy gig for somebody from our small peer community. The fact that one of our guys was going to be Elvin Jones's bass player was big news. It was a major thing. Nobody had a break like that. Gene was from Jersey and had gone to Berklee in Boston. He definitely knew Chick from before and other guys like that. So, he got the gig and it was a big thing. I remember he said to me: "I'm going to get you and Steve Grossman in the band. Watch me."

Gene is also a very entrepreneurial guy. He was taking Wilbur Little's place in the band, which had Joe Farrell and, at different times, Frank Foster or George Coleman, most often in a trio or quartet, pianoless group with Elvin as leader. One night in probably February 1971, I was at 19th Street and at 11:30 p.m. the phone rings. It was Gates, that was Perla's nickname, for the "Pearly Gates." He said, "Now!" I said, "What now?" "Elvin wants to hear you now. Come to Slug's. Come right now."

I took a taxi from 19th Street to Slug's, over on the Lower East side. There were maybe five people there. Elvin was standing at the bar with Joe Farrell. I walked in—he looked at me and asked: "Are you ready?" He's so dramatic, you know. I said, "I think so." Joe was just looking at me. "Get your horn out." So it was me, Gene, and Elvin on the bandstand. Joe stayed at the bar. Elvin said, "What do you want to play?" Well, it worked once with Pete doing "Softly," so that's what I called. We played it, and then we played "Yesterdays," and then "Night in Tunisia." We played for about thirty minutes. After each tune, Elvin asked, "What do you want to do next?" When we finished these three tunes, I got off the stage, and Elvin said, "I'm recording next week. Do you know where Rudy Van Gelder's is?" Yeah, of course I knew Rudy's recording studio in New Jersey. He said, "Ten o'clock in the morning, and bring a tune." That's it. Just a few months before, I had recorded *My Goal's Beyond* with John McLaughlin. These are my first two heavy recordings.

So February 12, 1971, I walked into the recording session at Rudy's, the most famous studio on the planet, and of course it was like entering the temple where so much music had been played. There were just two overhead microphones on the drums, from what I recall. Elvin came in. Everything was set up for him. "What do you got?" It happened to be that I had this tune "Slumber," which is on Chick's *Sun* record with Grossman. It's kind of based on Wayne's "Speak No Evil," and the truth is I wrote it with Elvin in mind for that certain tempo, medium slow, which he is the master of. Think of Trane's "Tunji" and you get the tempo I was thinking about. So, I pulled it out and I don't even know if we ran through it. Anyway, we did one take, and that was it! You can imagine how nervous I was. By the way, the take is screwed up. Gene and I are in different places. I'm at the bridge, and he's on the last eight or something. It's fucked, and I knew it but couldn't do anything about it. As I subsequently learned rather quickly, it wasn't like you go back and fix it. Nope, it's, "Next!" Talk about learning a rough lesson. First take is it!

Lew: Yeah, right! Plus you're not the leader.
Dave: Time is money.

Lew: They like to finish the session according to union rules—one three-hour block, sometimes two, and overtime is expensive.
Dave: There's one take to make it. You'd better get it right. If you're, for example, out of tune, you're screwed. I learned with Elvin, man, that you gotta be on, 'cause you've got no second chances. Same with Miles—no second chances. And it's not your solo they're worried about. If you took a bad solo, the hell with you, brother. You had nothing to say about what takes were going to be used. This was not a democracy! And don't try to "save it" for the next take, 'cause there may not be one.

Lew: Did you know at the end of that "Slumber" take that you screwed up, or only when you heard it later? Sometimes it's hard to know.
Dave: I don't know if I knew, but it was definitely not together. I'm not sure we even heard it back, but Gene and I were definitely in different places in the form. It's hardly noticeable, but we are just not in the same harmonic place. The tune had an ABCA form. It was something a little strange and we screwed up. Also there's another weird thing about this session, which became the record *Genesis* on Blue Note Records. It's the reverb. I don't know what the hell Rudy did—it's like he lost his mind. He must have put on the Taj Mahal reverb. It's terrible.

So, anyway, we finished the tune and I remember Joe Farrell and Frank Foster came in. Elvin had a guitar with him and he strummed out something to Joe, saying he should arrange it for the horns. That ended up being part of Elvin's book for a long time, "Three Card Molly." Joe put it right together there with harmonies. We played it slow, too. It was the first time it was recorded. We also did "Simone," a great waltz from Foster, and a ballad by Gene, "P.P. Phoenix."

Lew: So, it was three saxes?
Dave: Three saxes. Three tenors, though I think I played the soprano on "Three Card." There's a big picture of Elvin on the cover. By coincidence, Frank Wolff, the famous co-founder of Blue Note, had just died, and the producer was a young cat named George Butler, who would eventually go on to be pretty big at Columbia Records. This was his first date, so we had something in common! Poor guy! Elvin was like, "Who the fuck are you? You're taking Frank's place?" Over the years when I did see George, we would joke about it and how Elvin scared the shit out of him. Elvin could definitely be rough, that's for sure. So, that was that record date. Elvin didn't say anything to me at the end.

Lew: He wasn't saying: "Now you're in my band and we're going to play a bunch of gigs?" It was really only for the recording date?
Dave: It was for the date only, at that point. However, a few months later in September, living in a loft on Warren Street right near the World Trade Center with Eleana, the phone rang at four a.m. This was a big loft and the phone was way on the other side. I said, "Screw it. I ain't getting it." Eleana got it and said it was Keiko Jones: "Elvin wants you to come to Chicago, first flight out of LaGuardia. There's a ticket waiting for you, and you'll have to play with him at twelve o'clock noon at a school. Okay? Seven a.m. flight." That's it. I got my horns together and took a

taxi to LaGuardia. Someone picked me up and I ended up at some high school at twelve o'clock with Gene and Elvin. We played a set and went to a hotel. I remember the name clearly—the Croydon Hotel—which must have been a musician's joint. Elvin said, "After you check in, come up and see me." I didn't know if Joe couldn't make the gig that night or what. I didn't know if I was taking the next plane out. In any case, I went up to the room and Elvin was in his bathrobe: "I'd like you to join the band as of right now. You've got anything you need to do?" I said, "No, sir!"

Lew: So, just to be clear about the sequence—earlier that year in February 1971—
Dave: I was doing Sawbuck. This is all that same time period.

Lew: So you started with Elvin.
Dave: After joining in September 1971, I did the next couple of months, on occasion trio, or with Joe Farrell, or Frank Foster, maybe Clifford Jordan, George Coleman, and sometimes with pianist Jan Hammer, who was friendly with Gene. Even Hank Jones, Elvin's oldest brother, did some gigs with us on piano. Joe was still on gigs, but he was on his way out. It was a transition time for Elvin's group, it appeared, until Steve got in the band.

Lew: What was the material you played?
Dave: Elvin's book was a combination of standards and some modal tunes. What was interesting, and a real lesson to me, is something I tell the kids about in relation to one's milieu and what they are used to. It has to do with how these aforementioned great saxophonists played on the modal tunes compared to me. When we would play "Yesterdays" or "Night in Tunisia," they would play great—after all, these were original be-boppers. But when we played an open A minor tune, for example, something called "Shinjitsu," they sounded like they were trying to play a ii-V progression over the mode.

Lew: They couldn't really think modal. They had to find a turnaround.
Dave: Exactly. They could not make A minor good for eight bars without it being some kind of modulating progression. This was very interesting to me, because here were these giants and this tremendous respect I had for them, but when they played that material, I as a young cat was in a better position from the musical standpoint. It was because I came from a different context and period obviously. For me, "Impressions" is where

I started. For them, it was "Confirmation" where they started, or something like that. Of course, I'm generalizing now, but you understand my point. I realized that this is the way it always is. It's like these kids today who are playing in meters of seven or nine or thirteen. They don't even look a second time at the page, the rhythm section cats especially. And I'm up there counting 1-2, 1-2, 1-2-3, whatever, just to keep up. It's like that same thing. You are a product of your time and what is in the so-called "air" when you are at your formidable stage, somewhere in the teens to twenties age-wise—that's what will always feel most natural to you.

By the time Steve Grossman got in the band, because of our relationship, the vibe really came together. Steve was a bro; Gene was a bro. That's partially why the *Live at the Lighthouse* recording is so known, I think. It wasn't just because of the music, but because there was a vibe in that band. It was me and Steve and Gene, who were definitely united in a generational thing. We were buds. Elvin was happy as a pig in shit. He had a bunch of guys who idolized him and wanted to really play. He said years later that this was one of his best, if not the best, band he had, and one of the great records is *The Lighthouse*. He was really WITH us, not just the leader with sidemen, and I think that's what comes across on *The Lighthouse*. It isn't just that we're playing the pentatonics or whatever post-Coltranisms we did, which is what saxophonists love about the recording. It's that there was a vibe in that band, which was special.

Lew: What was it like playing with Elvin on a nightly basis?
Dave: The first thing is that it was really a dream come true because I saw him so many times with Coltrane, and I was just very familiar with his style, at least in the aural sense. In fact, six of my ten "Desert Island" records have Elvin playing: *Speak No Evil*, *The Real McCoy*, *Inner Urge*, *Coltrane Live at Birdland*, etc. He's ubiquitous in my musical life. As a sound, it's the way I heard jazz drumming as it should be.

Of course, the emblematic thing about Elvin was his ride beat and his ability to play so far behind the pulse. Added to that was the triplet filler stuff that would be played all over the drum set. All of these aspects would combine with a powerful and sustained energy. There is a difference between sustained and explosive energy; explosive in the sense of Tony Williams, for example, where the power curve would go up and down dramatically, turning on a dime. Elvin, with Coltrane, had to sustain for forty-five minutes, an hour, hour and a half sometimes, at a pretty heavy level of intensity. Put all these things together, and it was like playing with the ocean and the earth and the sky at the same time. It was just such a massive thing to be playing over.

Now, of course, coming into his band at twenty-five years old with so much of my training and listening concerned with Coltrane, I can't tell you that I wasn't thinking that I'm going to be the next Coltrane. I'd be lying to you if I didn't admit to thinking, "Well, I'm with *the man*." I'm with the engine of the train, so I'm going to play long duos with him and get down on my knees because of the intensity and so on. That was in my mind and in my dreams. Obviously, first of all, I certainly wasn't Coltrane, and Elvin was a different Elvin by the time I was with him. He was already six years removed from Coltrane. He was now a bona-fide bandleader with a working band that had been going on since '68 when he first started with Joe Farrell and Jimmy Garrison. He was playing a different body of music; it wasn't that heavy, intense Coltrane thing.

We played standards, some little modal things, and a ballad each per each set. There was no way he was going to play the way he did with Trane. The truth is that he had matured in all ways, which as a bandleader is a necessity. By that I mean he really had that pacing thing down by this time. In other words, he wouldn't go to sticks until he was really ready. He wouldn't get intense when YOU were asking for it—it was when he was good and ready. That doesn't mean that you wouldn't get it from him or that he wasn't playing *with* you. That took me a minute to understand. I was ready from note one to be burning and he'd just be coasting on the cymbal, as if it were the first chorus for five or six choruses. Sometimes I would be very frustrated because I felt like I was just left hanging in the wind, burning out, while he'd just be playing like it was a walk in the park.

Lew: You felt like you weren't getting the support.
Dave: Exactly. Of course, it was Elvin Jones, so it wasn't like he couldn't do it; it was just that he wouldn't do it. After I got past the fact that this wasn't personal, because for Steve he did the same thing, and that it was obviously a musical thing, it made more sense. I mean, we weren't Coltrane; it was his band, and the truth is it was a drummer's band. If the drummer has a band, he's got to pace it, because if he just starts exploding, what else is there to do? He was thinking about when to play slow, when to play soft and play loud. I'm not sure if he was thinking literally, but it all made sense. In a well-rounded presentation, you're going to pace things out, which is the responsibility of the bandleader anyway. So, it took me a minute to realize the obvious.

The other thing was this behind-the-beat thing. Now we know in jazz—just a short primer here—that the beat has a distance around it that's like fat on the bone. You've got the middle of the beat, which is the metronomic center according to nature or whatever. Then you have slightly before it and slightly after it. We call that ahead or behind the beat or pushing, laying back—all kinds of descriptions. We certainly don't want to be dragging, which is a negative, or rushing, which is equally negative. Of course, there's that very thin gray line between what is dragging and what is behind. It has to do with circumstance—with whom you're playing, the context, and a bunch of other variables.

For example, as an aside, it was such a big facet of Dexter Gordon's style to be behind the beat, but when he played up tempo he was on top of the beat. A good musician will be able to go everywhere in this respect. A really artistic improviser is constantly playing with this paradigm. It really makes for a very subtle feeling range and means of communication to the rest of the band. But also the listener is feeling something without knowing it, because a guy who places his beat in the same place all the time will be predictable. I'm talking about a very small thing, but it's definitely felt by the listener whether they cognize it or not. A great player who plays good time metronomically, absolutely accurate, is commendable, but not necessarily desirable. And a band that plays that way would rightfully be seen as excellent because they have such accurate time, but it might not *feel* that good. In my judgment, a rhythm section that agrees to disagree—in other words, you're my bass player and you feel it a little under the beat; I'm the drummer and I feel it a little bit over, at least today with this tempo and this tune—this can work great. In fact, that can even be much more interesting for the soloist and for the listener, up to a point. This is what I mean by "agree to disagree." If it becomes "I'm right, you're wrong, and I'm not gonna shift," then we've got a problem. It's that tension and pull that I think is interesting and definitely challenging to play over, for a horn player especially.

This is really a daily question if you're in the rhythm section and by the way, the same band could be different from night to night. It could just be dependent on how much sleep the guy had—whatever. There are no rules, just degrees, and it should logically fit the environment and the soloist. A good rhythm section will shift. You'll hear a different way that Ron Carter and Tony Williams played behind Miles than with Wayne or Herbie Hancock. You'll hear a slight difference with Trane playing than when McCoy solos, as far as Elvin and Jimmy Garrison played. This all means that a sensitive drummer and bass player should be responding to differences of innuendo and mood and, again, the immediate environment. They may be tired or happy, or just had a drink, or didn't sleep—this is life.

My main point is that being able to play around with the beat is an accurate depiction of the human condition, which implies that the heartbeat is constantly changing. You cannot be at sixty-one beats now and think it's going to be sixty-one a minute from now. So, we're really talking about something that is very interesting and very subtle. Most musicians don't necessarily talk about this. I teach it and make a big deal out of it. I make students very aware of it when they do transcriptions: Do you hear how he's behind? Do you hear how he's ahead? Because this comes down to matters of articulation, and of nuance, and more. The whole curve of your line is, in a sense, dictated by your placement of the beat.

In Elvin's case, he was the king of playing behind the beat and, to an extreme at certain tempos. You hear it clearly on the Coltrane tracks "Crescent" and "Wise One." There are so many tracks with Trane that you hear these things happening. This was how Elvin heard. When we played fast, Elvin was really on top of the beat. Sometimes I couldn't even keep up with him. When Elvin played fast, he didn't play what might be considered the clear and normal articulation on the cymbal, like let's say Max Roach, for example. He played over the bar line and I'd be like, "Where's 1-2-3-4?" He was playing in kind of larger groupings, meaning each individual beat was not articulated as such. When he played slower tempos, it was much clearer.

Now, this whole thing about laying back that I got from Jones is not too easy for a musician to duplicate because it's about relaxation. Maybe it's naïve to think that because Elvin or Dexter Gordon ingested so many substances and alcohol into their bodies, they just ended up being super relaxed, but maybe this is at least part of the explanation concerning their ultra laid-back time feel. By the way, they weren't the only ones. There was Hank Mobley, Chet Baker, and others also who exhibited this relaxed feel, really coming from Lester Young in the final analysis. It seemed these musicians could just get on the stage and from the first beat lay it down so far behind, yet so comfortable and so relaxed, that you'd say, "Whoa!" It's certainly a great feeling to play like that, and in jazz to feel that little beat pulling back is just a unique physical sensation.

So, in any case, Elvin was known for it, and he did it every night. And I, at age twenty-five, was aware of this, but I could not get it. For at least six months I was rushing. These were the beginning days of cassette machines and I would tape the gig. I would hear myself rushing night after night. Now, rushing to the degree that it was inoperable or wrong? No. Would a listener think, "Oh, that saxophone player is rushing"? No, because then I'd be wrong and I wouldn't be there. But enough to know that I certainly wasn't laying back.

I really wanted to get this—I knew this was the nut. This was the crux of the matter with Elvin Jones. This was what you got from Elvin Jones and it took me a while. In retrospect, of course, as with everything in music, it takes years to really get what you observe and cognize to become natural. You have the awareness, but it doesn't happen the next day. You learn a new line today and it won't come out for maybe six months or whatever time period. I don't know what the lag time is because it depends on the activity, who you are, etc. But I've got to tell you that the ability to lay behind the beat is something that took me years to be able to do on call, with no thinking. And to recognize it, to be able to describe it to another musician: "Could you lay behind?" I could do it a certain amount on the cymbals myself, which definitely helped. So, this was lesson number one from Elvin musically: how to make the beat lay behind. There's another little magical thing about it. When you get that beat behind, it becomes fatter and wider, by nature of it being stretched. A wider beat means you have more room for nuance.

Now, on top of the time, Johnny Griffin, for example—there's an excitement inherent in that kind of motion. There's an edge to the beat and the music reflects the energy of anticipation. That has its value for sure. To reiterate, great musicians can, should, and must be able to go to all places on the beat, but they will have a predilection for what they like the most because it's their body and their mind and their persona, meaning you are who you are. Elvin's basic home was behind the beat, but as I point out he could go in the middle or ahead at will. A guy like Griffin seemed to feel the beat more on top from what I could deduce, although I never played with him.

Miles was famous for his metronomic time—probably the best time I've ever heard. He was like a metronome, right there in the middle of the beat. When you see the videos of Miles directing, almost conducting in the time I was with him, he's imploring drummer Al Foster to keep the beat up. Just think about the drummers he had over the years—Philly Joe Jones, Max Roach, Jack DeJohnette, Tony Williams—all on top of the time. I think it's because with Miles's sense of time being so metronomically accurate, anything that wasn't slightly ahead felt like it was dragging. The worst thing you could do to Miles was drag because his whole style was predicated on the upbeat. With Elvin it was a lesson, a primer on a night-to-night basis for me of what it meant to have a wide, relaxed beat, something that I don't know how many other people were fortunate enough to receive because you can only learn that from the horse's mouth. You cannot learn that from observation. You may learn a certain amount from transcribing and accurately duplicating a solo, because you're doing what so-and-so did, but for you to go out and do it, you need a drummer who does it. Sure, the piano and bass are crucial, but it is the drummer's cymbal beat that's going to control this aspect. If you have that behind or under your beat, you have many more rhythmic and emotional places to go. That was a big lesson.

Lew: So you're saying that after six months or so you felt like you were getting it?
Dave: I finally realized that I'm starting to relax a bit. A lot of it, again, is mental cognition that this is a thing you want to do. But it's also a physical thing for each instrument. For the saxophone it's the tonguing, timed with the breath and fingers. It has to do with the air stream, the tongue attacking the reed, because tonguing is rhythm, and at the same time your fingers are going down on the keys. For the piano, it's kind of the motion of the wrist and the fingers. For trombone players, it's going to be something different. We all have our particular characteristics on each instrument that we have to deal with. Once that starts to come in line, that's when you start to think, "Oh, I'm starting to feel this thing." But you've got to get your body into it.

This is a fine-tuning thing. You're just getting your body to slow down. I might be articulating with a little bit of a lighter tongue motion and a little slower than normal to pull this off. It can't be analyzed in detail because basically it's a feeling. And it's a feeling that most musicians, again, unless they are trained in this, or they play blues—because a blues musician will naturally go there as a result of the feeling of the blues—unless you've done music like that, it's going to be a challenge to get it. Maybe that's why African Americans more naturally have this thing, because of gospel. When you hear gospel, certainly if you've heard it from five years old on, you're hearing a pretty big, fat backbeat on two and four. That's the essence of what I'm talking about, just that in jazz we articulate it with eighth notes. If you've been hearing that from when you're young and in church every Sunday, by the time you get the horn in your mouth, you've probably already got a good feeling for behind the beat, because a lot of African Americans do have a better feel for this. I have definitely seen that. It's the dancing thing. It's the body and the physicality. The African root is sun, outside, relaxed, no coats, no sweaters, you dig. You're behind the beat because everything is relaxed. European cats are not in there the same way, nor Asians. Obviously, I am generalizing, but I think the point is well made. This physicality is not a direct outgrowth of the European culture. For whatever reason, that was the big lesson with Elvin—the major musical lesson for me.

Finally, the most important thing I learned from Elvin and later on with Miles as well as before with Pete—in essence any great musician with whom I have played—is that once the count-off is finished, this is serious business. It was as if there was no past, no future, and any fooling around or anything less than a dead serious attitude was not cool. Once we sat down and got started, it was 100 percent business. That was very powerful, because I was doing it on a night-to-night basis. As I said earlier, before Pete, I basically played with peers. I mean, who has the authority and the weight of your peers to do that? We were trying, but we were not Elvin Jones, Miles Davis, or Pete LaRoca. My peers as well as myself couldn't command that sense of authority because of lack of experience in both music and life. With Elvin, I was in the presence of somebody who did this as his job every night. You could feel it. The downbeat would start and it was business. It wasn't ugly, it wasn't terrible, it wasn't mean, and it wasn't anything negative. It was business, and it really made me see that this music is serious.

You're in the zone immediately or at least you try your best. That's not easy for anybody. I was basically a fledgling. I didn't know about that commitment at 9:30 p.m. in, say, Dayton, Ohio, with five people in the audience—that you are expected to play like your life depends on it. I had to learn that it doesn't matter where you are, this is your job, and just like anybody, you do your job. You hope the guy who drives a bus has the same attitude, because in that case your life depends on it. Music is not life or death, but it is serious, and I really have to say that this was an awakening. That was very important for me.

Lew: Now, tell us about Elvin as a human being.

Dave: Elvin was a great cat. You could really talk to him. I could discuss Elvin forever and I've written a lot about him. He was a very warm person, the most human of folks. He knew the score. He had been through ups and downs, but he didn't use it as a power thing at all. It was part of who he was and his experiences as a human being, outside of the music. He was a seasoned warrior. He didn't dwell on it, but it was in everything he did. There was a humanity and depth to him that other people didn't have. This was something that certainly Miles didn't have, at least in that way. I've never encountered anyone with more depth of feeling than Elvin in my life. He was the top guy. I was around him a lot and watched how he treated people and interacted with everyone from waiters to bartenders. He was not an angel. He could be a drag at times, do stupid things, and there was some ugly shit, but no question about it, his humanity and his passion for the human condition was tangible. You could feel it. It was palpable.

The way Elvin handled people was extraordinary. He did not suffer fools easily. If you were jive, he'd call you on it. But he was the most open, congenial sort of public person I've ever known, and accessible beyond belief. Elvin would be sweating and dripping, drinking all those Lowenbrau beers. He would sweat when he *saw* the damn drums, let alone play them! He'd be in the back changing his shirt and somebody would come to see him. There wasn't any security in those clubs. "Oh, I love your music, Mr. Jones. I saw you with John Coltrane." Elvin would respond, "What's your name? What do you play? Do you go to high school?" I couldn't believe this from a guy who was such a heavy drummer, a heavy musician, a heavy person.

Lew: He was very physical, too. He gave me a big hug the one time I spoke with him. He'd give you a hug and lift you up!
Dave: At the least! As well, he was very verbal, very evocative and colorful in his language, if you get my drift. This all made for a very charismatic personality, but beyond that, it's about his depth of character and humanity, and that, I think, is why he played the way he played. When we think of Elvin Jones, yeah, he played triplets across the drums and all that, but man, it's the feeling. When you get to that level, you absolutely cannot separate the music from the man. He really taught himself how to take care of business.

Lew: What about Keiko, who seemed to be there all the time?
Dave: I feel that without her, he would not have been around as long as he was. She could be tough to musicians, but I got along with her and never had a problem. A lot of people didn't. I guess she could be a little tricky with money. He also was smart because he let her do stuff that he wouldn't do. He wanted us to wear T-shirts with "Jazz Machine" written on them. The name of the band was the Elvin Jones Jazz Machine. I flipped: "What is this, a goddamn rock band?" He said, "Well, that's what Keiko wants." He knew he could use her for something like that. Clever cat! From what I understood, Keiko helped get Elvin out of jail in Japan for a drug bust, something like that. It seems that she was with him forever.

Lew: How did she control Elvin?

Dave: I mean, really, how could she control him? He was a giant of a guy. Sometimes he would just split, and though I am not positive, it seemed that he had some personal business in Frisco. I would get a frantic call from Keiko: "Do you know where Jonesy is?" When I saw him next time, he would kind of wink at you and say he had had things to do. No doubt he could be ornery, but as a human being, he was the most human of humans.

I didn't know him in the old days, but the stories about Elvin were legendary. I mean, he was a bad boy, like Philly Joe Jones was supposedly a bad boy. These guys, what they needed, they needed, and they didn't spare anybody. Charlie Parker would take your horn and be gone. I guess this was the way it was, and Elvin had been there, seen and done it all. That he could come out with such a positive and gracious attitude toward the world was very impressive to me. Also, he had a great smile. He had those big white teeth that would light up the room. He was very dark and the teeth really stood out. When he was playing, he would smile, and he had that sound that we hear so much on record, a kind of growl. He was a real salt-of-the-earth guy who, it seems to me, just educated himself to be a better person. By the time I was with him, and later on in the eighties and nineties, he had it together. He wasn't like Max Roach, who was so dignified and scholarly. But he was a version of that, and he really took it upon himself to become this kind of person. I have a lot of respect for what he accomplished as a human being.

Lew: Is it possible that Keiko had something to do with that?
Dave: Absolutely. She was a tough lady and a real businesswoman. She took complete care of him. He didn't lift a fork. If he put his underpants on, I'm amazed. This woman did everything. She set the drums up, famously. She'd tune the drums in intervals of a fourth and she wasn't too bad. She kind of got it down while he'd be in the back drinking beer. He lived like a king. In the morning, he'd be in those long Japanese cloth robes and she would have a raw egg and orange juice ready. "Elvin, you must drink this." That was the first thing he drank. He'd sit there with his glasses on, his long legs laying out there, and reading, because he loved to read. I gave him a bio of Pablo Casals once and he loved it. I don't think he got dressed until four o'clock in the afternoon if we were in a hotel—and always smoking one cigarette after another. He was carefree. She definitely was the enabler. Thank God, because the gift of Elvin Jones being around, and the opportunity to hear him and play with him, I don't think would have happened without her taking care of him.

Lew: And on the other side, when you were with him did you see any of that bad boy element?

Dave: Well, he was on methadone during this time, which was pretty controllable, so it seemed. Of course, the three of us would occasionally smoke pot and once in a while he would take a puff. Check this out. It's very interesting because both Elvin and Miles, from what I saw during my time with them, didn't like to smoke. That made them crazy! It's unbelievable. The other stuff they did didn't make them crazy, but this made them crazy—who knows? Sometimes somebody would give Elvin a joint, and he would give it to us.

Elvin wasn't supposed to drink. He would have his beers, but once in a while, especially if he was exhausted, he might imbibe some rum. This happened several times when we would do two weeks straight—say, the Village Vanguard in New York to the Jazz Workshop in Boston. The workshop started on a Monday, so we went to the Vanguard from Tuesday to Sunday and then directly up to Boston and played Monday through Sunday. So we had a straight two weeks, fourteen days. On that last Sunday in Boston, we had our two sets in the afternoon for the matinee and then two sets at night. We were pretty tired by then and Elvin might drink a bit of rum. I learned something about drinking, or about this kind of condition. He would drink and be completely cool, let's say one drink, but the next drink could bring on a complete change in personality. I've noticed that kind of thing in Finland, for example. Like that one more taste just puts a guy over the line. With Elvin, he wouldn't know you. It was scary. It was like a spark had been ignited. Once we were in Ottawa, Canada, in the dead of winter, twenty-five degrees below zero with snow up to your head. I wasn't there when the following occurred, but from what I heard he said something to Grossman and threw the trap case at him across the room after the gig. The next day at nine in the morning, Elvin was at the door of our room: "I'm sorry. I didn't mean to do that." It seems he walked back to the motel two miles in the snow after the incident. Elvin was a big guy and strong physically. He could be a menacing-looking cat and look pretty mean at the drop of a hat, with a growl in his voice to match.

But I've got to say that generally there was a great vibe in that band. He was with us—he loved us and knew we loved him. We were just knocked out to be playing with him. This was the gig of life for us! It wasn't just playing jazz; it wasn't just that we had a gig. We were with a genuine jazz hero—Coltrane and all that. It was a dream, and he knew that we were appreciative of the opportunity. He felt very comfortable with us. We had nicknames for everybody—I was "Lush Lieb." I never drank before, but I drank with Elvin. I drank boiler makers, gin and beer chaser. I don't know why or how. I didn't get drunk, but I would drink, so "Lush Lieb." And then, as I said earlier, Gene Perla was "Gates," as in the pearly gates of heaven, while Steve was always "Gross Man." By and large, during the first year or so of the gig we all got along with Keiko, too.

Before I forget, I have to mention the presence of conga master Don Alias with us for about a six-month period. Don, who had played with everyone and was a great trap drummer as well as congas, was part of our circle and especially close with Gene. In fact, a few years after this period, the band Stone Alliance with Gene, Steve, and Don was around. He knew how to play congas in a jazz setting without getting in the way. Imagine that Elvin would actually include a conga player in the band, so you know it had to be right. When this period of the band was happening, the rhythm section was like thunder. Unfortunately, there are no recordings except some live tapes, but we had a ball with Don and the vibe got even better. By the way, Don's nickname was "Lungs," obviously for his capacity to hold in a certain type of smoke—you get the point.

Lew: Ha—yes, I get it. Now, you already mentioned a couple of times that there sometimes were not many people in the audience for this group. You were playing basically acoustic jazz in '71 and '72. That was notoriously a time period that acoustic jazz was not doing too well.

Dave: It was a low period, yes. It was the beginning of fusion, but it wasn't the explosion of fusion that would happen a few years later, because you've got to remember that it was really only Miles as far as notable jazz guys who were successful with it that early. Return to Forever, the Mahavishnu Orchestra, and Weather Report were just starting. There were the horn bands on the pop side like Chicago, Blood, Sweat & Tears, and Tower of Power, most notably. There were some commercial attempts by jazz guys to cross over with the CTI label coming into its own, but this whole movement was still in its infancy in '71/72. Acoustic jazz was not in the best of shape as far as clubs went, though.

The late '60s was a kind of low point for interest in jazz. First of all, rock and roll had such publicity, and with the Beatles, Hendrix, Joplin, Woodstock, Altamont, etc., the whole drama of pop music was just too much of an onslaught for jazz to keep its head above water. Rock was on everybody's mind. Not that jazz was ever on the public's mind as much as it was in the swing era, but whatever there was became minimized even more so in this period. Did we ever have full houses? Sure, on a weekend. Did we have empty houses? Sure. When I saw Coltrane in the sixties at Birdland, did I sometimes see only five people there? Of course. But besides clubs, you had college concerts and festivals, especially in Europe, which was just really starting to get hot in the seventies.

I came in at the tail end of the real jazz era, meaning steady six-nights-a-week gigs. Thank God. Obviously, we lament the passing of that period for the opportunity to play and to work your stuff out. It was the last wave and I caught it, the tail end. There's a story that I always tell my students about working every night and repeating things, sometimes ad nauseum, even though you are trying to sustain interest for yourself and the band. If you have an opportunity to play the same tune a couple of nights in a row, let alone a couple of weeks or months in a row, how do you come up with something different on that D-minor chord in the same tempo and the same context? It was about a year into the gig with Elvin. Steve and I each had a ballad feature nightly. My choice at this time was "I'm a Fool to Want You." At some point, I also played "My Ship" on flute. This "Fool" on tenor was a dramatic ballad—talk about dragging it out of your heart. It was famously Frank Sinatra's ode to Ava Gardner. When I say *ballad*, that means *slow*, and with Elvin, slow meant that sometimes his brush playing was so soft, you would be searching for the beat. I mean, the bass was just on one and three, if that, and Elvin was sliding the brushes like across glass! Your two hands rubbing together would produce more sound! Remember, Elvin was a master of dynamics, and though he was famous for bashing, he could play softer than a baby sleeping—incredible dynamics.

One night after the gig—and remember, we didn't talk much about the music at all, none of these guys did from that era—I said, "Elvin, I don't want to play this ballad anymore. I can't stand it. I can't play different on it and I'm just so stuck." Well, to paraphrase his reply, he didn't minimize it, but he said something to this effect: "Oh, you're stuck and it's the fault of the tune!" Point made—obviously, it was my attitude that was the problem. The basic conversation was that the audience doesn't know you played it yesterday. Your job is to get them on your side and for them to believe you. They have no past experience of hearing you play this or that tune, for the most part. It's just like, if you do Shakespeare, are you going to change those lines night after night? You have to make it feel good and convincing on a night-to-night basis. I had never thought of it from the standpoint of the audience. I was just concerned with *my* creativity thing, not the communicative aspect of what we were doing on the stage, which was kind of the point in the first place. The bottom line is that we had a gig, people were paying for it, and our job was to make them feel good, period.

Elvin said, "You think you have to play something different all the time to feel happy, to feel satisfied." I said, "Yeah, isn't that what it's supposed to be? That's improvisation! Aren't we supposed to come up with another combination? Isn't that the whole quest, the whole search, from night to night?" He said, "Maybe, if it happens. But there are many other things. For example, something that was hard to play yesterday could get easier today. Refining is the name of the game! You refine." I don't know if he used that word exactly, but Charles Lloyd had once said to me something to the extent that you will spend most of your creative time editing out unnecessary gestures. Of course, I am exaggerating all of this, as I do for teaching, to make a point. For these guys, whatever they said to me was very casual and nonpedagogic to be sure, but over the years I have expanded on what these things meant. He was saying that you may play the same phrase that you played last night, but you can always execute it cleaner. You can always make it more meaningful. You can always play it better, which is like the classical player's game. I never thought of it like that. Anyway, at the end Elvin said, "Just keep playing that goddamn ballad!"

There's another equally important story in this respect that happened years later. There was an Italian promoter who loved the original *Lighthouse* band, and he wanted me with Elvin in one way or another. In the mid-eighties he would put Elvin and me together with different combinations: John Scofield and Steve Swallow; German trombone great Albert Mangelsdorff and French bassist Jean-Francois Jenny-Clarke; bassist Palle Daniellson and saxophonist Courtney Pine, etc. In fact, on You Tube you can see a tune or two from a workshop in Italy with Sco and Swallow. It's interesting because my other drum mentor, Pete LaRoca, who had become a lawyer in the intervening years, was using me on some gigs every once in a while in New York during the eighties. So, I was back with my teachers on occasion, fifteen years later, and I was definitely a better musician. There was no question about it. I could finally play with these guys. I wasn't Coltrane, but I could by now stand toe-to-toe with Elvin and Pete, in the sense that I could deal and feel good about it rather than feel like I wasn't cutting it. Therefore, these gigs were just great.

By then I was a bit more confident in general about myself and could actually play and talk to Elvin man-to-man. We were on the train in Italy enjoying some Chianti, just the two of us in the compartment. I said to him, "Elvin, I've got a question, and this is one of those stock, cliché things, but I've got to ask you—how many times did you play 'My Favorite Things' with Trane? I saw you from '61 until you left John, about ten to twenty times at least. And you played 'My Favorite Things' every night. I'm just curious." But of course there was the underlying question: How do you play something different when you're doing the same tune over and over?

Now, we know Trane changed the arrangement in some ways, which is a great study in that process happening over years. Basically it just got more and more intense and dissonant. But still, it was three-four time for the drummer, which didn't change, and it was E minor to E major. So here comes Elvin, real slow and dramatic-like: "Well, you know, I was with John for six years, and we played forty-five weeks a year average. We played three, maybe four sets sometimes. Could've been we played the tune twice in a night." All true, since this was Coltrane's hit tune. Then he looked at me and said, "You tell *me* how many times we played Favorite Things." So, I did a quick calculation of three hundred times five. "Fifteen hundred," I said. With that voice and face that only Elvin could do, he leaned over and put his face about half an inch away from mine, that gigantic look, those white teeth and eyes, so dramatic, and he said, "I don't know how many goddamn times we played it, but I'll tell you one thing: Every time we played it, it was like there'd be no tomorrow." Then he leaned back, looked at me with that smile and just put his hands in his lap: "You know what I'm talking about." Point made! For the students I add, "What would you play like tonight if you knew it was the last gig of your life?" A little tough, but it makes the point.

Outside of that period with LaRoca, playing with Elvin was the first and last time for that kind of playing in my life. It went on for a year and a half to two years. You had to get your horns and reeds together, know the music and be ready. Here it was, finally. I was a working jazz musician and I didn't do anything else. I didn't play any other music except what I wanted—the gig with Elvin and the loft sessions. This period was all music, and it made me what I am today. In the final analysis, this is basically why we're sitting here.

Looking back on that period, when I did the liner notes for the Mosaic release of Elvin called *The Blue Note Years*, of which I'm on four out of eight CDs, I was really impressed. Somehow this guy who appeared to be a bit loose—I wouldn't say disorganized, but certainly not the demeanor of a bandleader in the sense of a Max Roach—somehow he pulled it off. Sure, he depended on the guys to bring the music in, which they did lovingly and gladly. But there is so much diversity in this boxed set, it's incredible: two or three saxophones, synthesizers, and timpani on the last record, electric piano, electric bass on a couple of tunes, etc. Somehow, Elvin, in that five-year period, '68 to'73, pulled off incredible records that really had a concept. He could have gone in and just played the blues and standards with an all-star band. There would have been no problem. But he actually had concepts.

There were a lot of things that I was exposed to by being with Elvin on a steady basis that were realities of what it was like to be a jazz musician from a different period than we were in. These were considerations from the forties, fifties, and sixties. This was the jazz life. This is really what it was. You slept all day, you were up at three or four in the afternoon, you got yourself together, ate something—but not dinner—you'd eat something later at night, 'cause then you'd hang. You were in the same hotel room, same bar for a week, so you got to know the waitress and the bartender and the hotel guys behind the desk. Relationships inevitably formed. The movie *'Round Midnight* captures it a bit.

I felt special to be let into another world. I was a stranger in a strange land. This was not the world of my parents or my milieu, nothing like that, and here I was with the greatest drummer of all time—the cat who played with the greatest saxophone player ever, and I was there with him on a day-to-day basis. I had to pinch myself. Who got a chance like this from my generation? There weren't many of us. There were only a handful of guys, but I was lucky, big time. I had waited in line. I had earned my way. There were guys who got ahead of me in the sense that they got things faster, but now here I was. I had landed *the* gig for a saxophone player, with Elvin Jones.

Chapter 7

It's Different Out There: On the Job with the Prince of Darkness

Lew: Where were you living during the time with Elvin?
Dave: Eleana and I had been living in that loft on Warren Street. Then, around the middle of 1972, we moved to her family home in Greenwich, Connecticut. This was an out and out mansion on over twenty acres, in one of the most expensive areas in America, Fairfield County. Down the "road"—really quite a bit more than a road—were the families of Gimbels (*sic*) and Macy's, which were at one time the two biggest department stores in Manhattan.

Her Aunt Jean lived in this gigantic house, along with Eleana's oldest brother. Her parents had died. Her father, from Poland, had made his money in real estate, at least partly. Her mother was beautiful, and she and her sister, Jean, had been friends with movie stars. In fact, the day after I met Eleana in Port Chester, we first were at her pad in Woodstock, then drove to Greenwich, and lo and behold Mr. and Mrs. Robert Mitchum were there for lunch with Jean! We were there maybe two years—all through my Miles period. We had the horse barn completely renovated as a studio for me, and there was a gigantic swimming pool. No question, this was a house for the books. I had some great hangs there, I can tell you!

Lew: And around this time you first heard from Miles.
Dave: Yes. The first specific event was June 1, 1972. I happened to be staying at my parents' house, visiting in Brooklyn, and had an appointment at a doctor's office in downtown Brooklyn, Hoyt-Schermerhorn

Street to be exact. I think it was an allergy doctor. Out of nowhere the secretary shouts, "Is there a David Liebman here? It's your mother on the phone." My mother says, "Somebody named Teo Macero said you should come to the studio to record now with Miles Davis." Teo was Miles's producer for many years. This was like eleven-thirty in the morning. I happened to have my soprano with me—talk about good luck. I knew what this meant, because I knew that Chick and Dave were doing sessions with Miles in the mornings. As well, I knew that it was probably a ten to one p.m. session and it was going to end soon. So I high-tailed it out of Brooklyn like a maniac and parked my car right on 52nd and Madison in Manhattan, where the studio was. It didn't get towed, by the way.

So it was about twelve-thirty when I got there. I walked in and stood in the hall between the studio and recording booth, looking through the glass at Miles and everybody. There were like nine thousand people in the studio, all sitting, quiet—John McLaughlin, Chick, Don Alias, Herbie Hancock, Michael Henderson, Colin Walcott, Larry Young, Jack DeJohnette, Billy Hart, Badal Roy on tablas, and another keyboard player named Harold Williams. Miles signaled me to come in.

Miles was standing next to Jack and was whispering in his ear the way he used to sort of sing something in that gravel voice. Everybody was really still, at attention. There was a big boom microphone in the middle of the studio—obviously Miles's mic. He said, "Let's go," and they started playing. You've got to remember that everybody was electric, all plugged in—keyboards, guitar, organ, bass—and I had no headphones, so it all sounded like clicks! All I could hear were the drums and a little tablas and congas. Basically, I don't think there were any actual amps in the studio. Miles made a motion moving his fingers, like, "Get your horn out." I took the soprano out, and he signaled me to come over to this gigantic microphone and nudged me up to play. He literally put his hand on my back to go to the microphone.

Anyway, that's the title track of the *On the Corner* record. You hear me fumbling around because I couldn't hear what damn key I was in! I couldn't hear anything. I couldn't hear a root. Nobody said a word to me, and everybody was pumping along on their keyboards and drums. I didn't have time to think, but I played okay. Anyway, that's it. The take kind of peters out because, as I learned, there were no beginnings or ends to any of these tunes during that period. It was a little bit awkward. I could feel the presence of Miles just put a freeze on everybody. The session seemed over and everybody was putting their horns away or whatever. I didn't know what to do. Nobody said anything to me. I put the horn away and I went into the booth. I thought maybe I could hear back what we did—which of course never happened. Teo communicated with me: "Here, sign this paper and you'll get a check." Something like that. Then I saw what I learned was pretty much the ending process on all of those recording dates. Miles got the cassette and was gone. The limousine was waiting for him, evidently. As he passed me—he hadn't said a word to me yet—he said: "You should join my band." Very offhand.

Lew: That was a funny way to say it. It wasn't like, "You're hired."
Dave: Yeah, it was weird. I didn't know what he meant, and of course I didn't know the guy, although I had been around him a little bit and I knew the way he was. He was mysterious, so you didn't know what to read. I didn't know if he was serious or joking with me. I just said, "Well, I'm with Elvin. I can't leave him." He said, *"Baaah,"* or some similar guttural type of response, and he was gone.

Lew: But those other guys must have had headphones on or they couldn't even—
Dave: Well, they did, I guess, but I didn't. Like I said, no one uttered a word in the studio. In any case I was not about to leave Elvin.

Forward six months or so, to the second week of January 1973. I was with Elvin at the Village Vanguard that week. On Tuesday night, Miles showed up right at the beginning of the gig. Max Gordon asked him, "What are you doing here?" "Just hanging out." He was very cool, alone, no trumpet, no entourage, no girl, no nothing. He said, "How are you doing, Dave?" Steve Grossman was in the band by that time and he didn't talk to Miles, which was weird since Steve had recently worked with him. I don't remember if they had any words at all. My girlfriend at the time, Eleana, was sitting with Miles when I was playing. He was very personable, very cool. This was just a few months after he had broken both ankles in a well-publicized car accident when he ran into a traffic island on the West Side Highway in October. He said to me during a break, "We're gonna play Friday and Saturday night." I can't tell you what we talked about—it was just very kind of like, "You've got to join the band." He was there to get me. Wednesday night, he was there again. He said something like, "You don't wanna play this corny shit no more."

You have to understand that these guys were like plantation owners and they were bartering their cats. It was funny in a way—you were like a piece of meat. So he was there again, and Elvin saw him. Elvin said into the microphone: "Now ladies and gentlemen, Miles Davis is here." Keiko asked me: "What's he doing here?" Elvin said, "What's that little black motherfucker doing here?" You know, the way they were to each other. The next thing I know—now this was Wednesday night—he said, "I want you to join the band." I said, "Miles, it's up to Elvin." He said, "I'll take care of it." So, he left. I drove home to Greenwich, Connecticut—and at around four-thirty a.m. the phone rang. It was Miles: "Elvin said it's okay. You play with me Friday and Saturday, then go back and finish with him next week in Boston. Then you're mine."

Lew: Wow! So, it was a very specific deal?
Dave: Oh yeah. "I'll send a car for you tomorrow night. You'll come and hear the music." The next night, Thursday, I walked in at eight-thirty since I always liked to get there early. Elvin was there, standing at the bar. He looked at me and said in a very dramatic way, "Lush, if Miles Davis wants you, you gotta go." This was followed by a big Elvin Jones bear hug. That's the truth. "He's got one set Friday, and one Saturday. You do that—then you come back here and then finish the week. Next week in Boston, you'll do it with me, then you're done." I said: "Are you sure it's cool?" He said: "Hey man, it's Miles Davis." I had to go. How could you not go? But it was beautiful, the way he said it to me: "You've got to go." This was the chance of a lifetime—it was the top of the line. It was *the* gig. So that was it. The next two nights, I did both gigs, because the thing with Miles was just one set each night.

Lew: Even when Miles came up to you at the club, it's not like you said, "Yes, I want to go with you. Absolutely."
Dave: No! I was very loyal to Elvin and it had been nearly two years. I was comfortable with him. Of course, this was Miles Davis, but I also knew he was playing some strange stuff—not jazz at all. The point was that I was in a jazz band with Elvin, and I knew that Miles was not playing anything remotely like jazz, at least the way I conceived it. I felt torn. My first reaction was I have to get approval from Elvin, just out of loyalty and because it was the gig of my life.

Lew: And as you say, the type of music mattered too?
Dave: I think this all factored in. I'm telling you that now. I can't tell you what was going on those nights in my head, but it all must have filtered in. The point was that Elvin was *jazz*, the most you were ever going to get, and Miles was—well, whatever.

So, after I finished the gig at the Vanguard on Thursday night, the night after Miles talked to Elvin, I went up to the building that Miles owned, 312 West 77th Street, at two-thirty in the morning. Eleana was with me. I went upstairs to the so-called living area and he yelled from the bedroom, "Listen to this track." He had an LP on—Sly Stone's *Fresh.* When one track came on, he said, "Keep playin' that." It was the track "It's Time." He was in his bedroom, which was attached to the living room, and he kept yelling in to play that track over and over, which I did. "Put it on again!" I must have played it fifty times.

Lew: Did he greet you in the living room first?
Dave: No, he was in the bedroom. I didn't even see him at first. He came out later. The place was dark. I don't remember if it was that night or later when I saw the bedroom, which had like four thousand pairs of shoes, with a circular bed and a mirror on the ceiling—freaky deaky! The living room was crowded with stuff—completely a mess. But it was kind of a nice-looking brownstone. So, I put the track on, and Miles said, "Yeah, that's the shit we're playing. You gotta call the road manager tomorrow and get a pickup." I said, "Pickup?" He meant a pickup mic. "Yeah, or you ain't gonna hear nothin'." Then he asked, "How much you want?" I mean, cut right to the chase. No pleasantries, nothing.

I said, "I don't know." Because with Elvin we made $300 a week, if that. I never thought he would ask me that question. With money, I learned later on, he was another kind of personality. Money was a special thing. So, it wasn't like having a little discussion—he had a kind of agenda or something. What was I supposed to say to Miles Davis, for Christ's sake? He'd come out from the bedroom by this point, and he said, "I'll give you $400 every time you play, and you can bring her," pointing to Eleana. That was it—done.

I didn't ask if it was different for a steady club gig, but we didn't do many of those anyway. It was basically pretty good money for that time. If I did three gigs, it was $1,200, and he would pay for Eleana's travel 'cause he knew we were tight. I think he could see that.

Lew: He would pay for her for out-of-town gigs?
Dave: Yeah, flights—very generous. She was talking to him all that time I was playing, and who knows what she said. Her relationship with him went past my time with Miles. That's another story. I'm not sure of the details. She got involved with some well-known cats in one way or the other over the years.

Anyway, this was the beginning of the Miles period. The next day, Friday morning, the roadie called and told me I had to get a pickup for that night at Manny's or whatever music store—maybe Sam Ash. I went into the store and when they told me they had to drill a hole in the necks of the soprano, tenor, and flute, I almost died. This was the Varitone that Eddie Harris and Sonny Stitt played. You attached the actual pickup on the neck of the horn and the wire leads to the amp. I was flipping out. I think the road guy was there—Jim Rose. "It'll be fine," blah, blah, blah.

In the evening, I went to the theater. This was formerly the famous Fillmore East, Second Avenue and 6th Street, which had closed in June 1971. Now it was reopened under the name the Village East, with new owners, and there were two groups, Miles and the Paul Winter Consort. I went backstage and saw drummer Al Foster and Badal Roy—some familiar faces at least. Next thing I know, I plugged in and my sound was coming out of like seven hundred watts of Marshall amps. I had never had this experience in my life, with a wire coming out of my horn. Miles arrived and didn't say a word—didn't talk to anybody.

We were in a semicircle, and Miles was in the middle. I don't know why we were in a circle, but a Japanese director named Teppei Inokuchi actually videoed the gig because he was doing a documentary on Miles called *Prince of Darkness*, which I never saw, but I got hold of the gig footage. It was so dark in that theater, and everybody was dressed in black. Miles had gigantic sunglasses on and a cape—he looked like some alien from another planet. The music was deafeningly loud and chaotic. Now, there was also Cedric Lawson on electric organ, Khalil Balakrishna on electric sitar, Al and Badal as I mentioned, Mtume on congas, Reggie Lucas on guitar, with Michael Henderson on bass. I had no idea what I was doing. When Miles put his hand out and pointed to me, I played, and then he cut me off. That's all I know, and that was it. The gig was short, maybe an hour and a quarter, if that. Nobody said a word to me.

I took a taxi to the Vanguard across town and stood on the inside steps. This was Friday night, January 12, my mother's birthday. I just stood on those famous steps that lead down to the Village Vanguard listening to Steve, Gene, and Elvin playing. I'll never forget it. I savored the moment. Here I was just returning from a twenty-first-century *Star Wars* vibe, back to the root. It was the old world and the new, and I would experience both that one night. I must say, that is one night that stands out above all nights for anything to do with music because I played with both of them and it was the beginning of another life for me. I just stood on those steps to listen, reflecting. Nothing overly dramatic, just standing there and saying to myself: "This is really something, Dave." Talk about being a jazz musician! Being with Elvin Jones meant you were accepted. But I was going with Miles Davis, which meant in a way that you were in the line of Bird. You were taking Trane's place. You were taking Wayne's place. Of course, there were others—Gary

Bartz, Grossman—and Carlos Ward, whose place I actually did take. But this meant a certain kind of legitimacy that speaks for itself—the top of the sideman food chain, so to say.

I went downstairs in the middle of the set and took my customary place with Elvin for the rest of the night. Everybody was like, "How was the gig?" I sort of mumbled, "It was cool." We went to Boston and I played the next week with Elvin, then joined Miles as promised the following week. It's a very dramatic, great story and I remember pretty clearly the details because it stood in my mind forever—the whole getting hired by Miles, the Vanguard, Elvin's graciousness, and that first night playing that music.

Ad for Dave's first gig with Miles Davis

Lew: Let me ask you just a couple of little details—with all that noise in Miles's band, what about earplugs? Did anybody wear them?
Dave: I don't think anybody did. In those days, nobody thought like that.

We should have, but we didn't. It was the loudest band I ever heard.

Lew: And Miles's gestures—did you find that a little funny, the way he conducted?
Dave: Yeah, it was funny! There's nothing elegant about it. He was like throwing you a piece of change, you know. He was very offhand, beyond casual—kind of rude-casual. But he wasn't thinking about rude or not rude. He couldn't care less. The amazing thing was that he remained on stage when he wasn't soloing. You have to remember that this is the guy who famously walked off stage and supposedly turned his back on the audience. Here he was turning his back, but he was conducting. You can see in the videos, cutting the band in and out—stopping the rhythm section like the old cut-time routine. He was the absolute producer of every move. It was all about him doing it, and he wouldn't let it go on without him.

You had to be focused. Your attention was on him physically. That was the big deal, to be able to see when he wanted you to do something. I was in front with him, only like five feet away. When he would point his trumpet at me and throw it up in the air toward me, that meant I was supposed to play. Some of the time, which you see on the videos, he would just start to play, or signal someone else to start, before I was done—not all the time, but enough. Remember, we didn't have choruses, we didn't have thirty-two bars—it was all vamps.

Lew: Would you say that part of Miles's concept, and part of the reason it was different, was that the music didn't need this thing of, "We have to make a grand statement"? It was more kind of like, "You played enough. Stop now."
Dave: Yes.

Lew: In fact, you couldn't even think about building a so-called statement because you didn't know when he was going to stop you!
Dave: Right. There were no real dynamics or storytelling possible to a large extent, and little if any direct communication between the soloists and the rhythm section. At first I had no idea what the hell we were playing. I didn't know what to make of it. Now it appears to me, years later, that it was a concept.

I couldn't help thinking that I wished it were ten years earlier and I was in Wayne's place because of the music they played, compared to what we were doing. Not that I could have been in that group of the '60s—I wasn't up to that level at that time, to be honest, but in any case I felt frustrated. After I got used to Miles, nine months or so into the gig I sort of got the point, but still felt like, "This is great, but really not that great." Because, musically, it was not really challenging.

One of my famous Miles stories is when I asked him why he even had a saxophonist at all during this period. This was electric music, real loud, not subtle at all. Basically it was guitar and keyboard, electric bass, drums, percussion-oriented stuff. Obviously, there had to be a trumpet there, but it seemed to me the saxophone was superfluous. So, I asked him once why he had a saxophone. He said, "Because people like to see you move your fingers!" As nonsensical as that sounds, when I thought about it years later, as in most of what he said to me during that period, he had a point. When you think of Bird, Trane, Wayne, etc., the saxophonist was the foil to Miles's trumpet style. He played slow and you played fast. Opposites—tension and release. *Right!*

One thing was definitely true about the music we played. When Miles hit the stage, man, it was serious business. Like I said earlier about lessons learned from Pete, Elvin, and Miles, there was nobody smiling up there. I mean this was a level or two up in seriousness from Elvin, basically because Miles never really laughed or joked, at least not the typical way. To me the music itself was chaotic and disorganized, but it seems to me now that Miles had a scheme, just that I didn't really get it—although I sort of understood what was happening better after awhile. We always listened to the cassette of the gig afterward. One night it just made sense to me in some way and I said to him, "I think I got it. I know what you are trying to do." He looked at me like I was an idiot—like, "Of course, you moron." This "awakening" made it better, but still I was musically frustrated, mostly because the music didn't allow for the kind of interaction I was expecting and used to in a typical jazz situation. When you think about the Herbie/Wayne band—that was the ideal.

But there was always one high spot in the set. If there were two sets, the tune that has become known—in those days there were no titles—as "Ife" (sings tune) would start the second set. It was slow and started soft. Miles would build for five or more minutes. It seemed like forever. This was the real Miles Davis—the lesson of the gig. He'd play and he'd peck around—play one note and then he'd play another note—then he'd play off the key—then a blues phrase—then a gigantic space. He would build way up with the mute and then take it out and Al would get real strong with the sticks. It was like having an orgasm, musically speaking. *This* was Miles Davis. Once a night, I saw the Miles Davis that was the great teacher for thirty years of music because of his storytelling ability. The rest was loud and crazy.

Lew: And in your own solo, he could cut you off, so you didn't really have the luxury of being able to build like he did?
Dave: Absolutely. I did sometimes get to it, as I see now on some of the videos and bootleg stuff. But in general there wasn't enough time to build 'cause you didn't know when he would cut the band out or start soloing or point to the guitarist for him to solo. When he cut the band, it wasn't like the traditional cut-out stuff, meaning an even four or eight bars. He would just bring the band back in whenever—and then maybe cut them again a few beats later. In a way it was dramatic to the audience, I guess, but a pain in the ass to play with. It was like stop, come back in, stop, come back in, stop for a long time, come back in. Now, do you play time or you don't play time? I don't know what I did.

When all the music was starting to get re-released in the past ten years and I wrote liner notes for *Dark Magus* and *Get Up With It*, I had to listen to the stuff again. Also, many of our gigs were recorded by audience members, or I recorded it from the stage, or, especially in Europe, we were broadcast on the radio. But I have to tell you, it ain't bad. Some of it was really good, and on some of it the band was really smokin'. Most of all, Miles played great. I must say that sometimes I sounded good too. I never really played bad. I played a lot of stuff—pentatonics—blues shit—out-of-key lines—all very strong and in a continuous stream of notes, of course. Some of it was happening and it was somehow a bit unique at the time. I really never heard anybody else do it, at least up to then. Also, I had the C flute and, for a minute, an alto flute, which he dug. I have to note that in retrospect, the music sounds better than it did when I was there, which is nice to be able to say.

Lew: And maybe this whole thing of cutting off and everything, maybe the idea is that in his mind, it wasn't so much about the solos as it was about the real ensemble thing.
Dave: Exactly, but it was hard not to take it personally. I did feel like, "Oh my God, was I that bad?" But after a while, I thought it had something to do with continuity. But, as I said, I couldn't help thinking that I wasn't playing shit. On the positive side, I had some solo space since the only soloists were Miles, Pete Cosey, and me. Pete was added on guitar in April 1973. Once in a while, Reggie, the second guitar player, soloed, but very rarely. There was a long conga thing at the end where Miles would leave the stage and let the congas and drums finish up. So, I invariably soloed two to three to four times a set.

But sometimes I wouldn't solo that much. He would just point to

Pete instead. It seemed capricious. Also because he was so drugged out sometimes, I'd think like, "Oh shit, he's out." You didn't know and you couldn't read anything with him because he was so mysterious in the way he worked, and he had those damn sunglasses on, these gigantic dark-as-hell sunglasses, so you didn't know if he was looking at you or not! This was weird. I'm talking about a very small thing, but the truth is you had no idea how to read his mood because he had those glasses on. Now once in a while, he would lower them on the bridge of his nose. His white eyes would be staring out at you and he'd do something expressive with them. Once in a while, if he played something he liked, he would push his glasses down and give that look like, "I played some great shit. Did you hear what I played, Dave?" Well, of course, I heard! I was standing there and that was all I was doing.

Miles was very in the moment and very serious about it, that is for sure. Like I said, it was business even before the hit, in the dressing room. In those days he was with the band, not like the eighties where he was separated from the group. We were all together, and you knew with him, somewhere, five minutes or so before the hit, there would be this quiet time. Nobody would talk or play. He'd just be sitting there, not meditating, no corny chanting or hold-hands jive—just silence. Then, seemingly out of nowhere, he'd say, "Let's go!" Sometimes the house lights were still on and people were still getting into their seats. They weren't even ready for us. The music was supposed to start at eight o'clock and we'd start at ten minutes to eight. On the other hand, sometimes we'd start at ten o'clock, or he wouldn't show at all. This happened a few times.

Anyway, we'd get on the stage and Miles would point to Al, and off we'd go, loud and boisterous right from the start. He was definitely the boss, and when he would say something to any of the guys, it was minimal, but it seemed to be meant to suggest something. He never wasted words. He didn't talk for talk's sake. He had a different relationship with each cat. Michael Henderson, he didn't seem to talk too much. Pete Cosey he didn't talk to either, it seemed. Reggie Lucas, he was on his case all the time, making him always a little nervous. Al, he was kind of like the big kid in the band, and Miles was like, "Oh, how's Al tonight?" because Al really loved Miles. The other guys knew how important Miles Davis was, but in Al's and my case, we knew every record. We were New York guys, after all. Miles was our life and had been for years—the real jazz deal.

Lew: Mtume, who is Jimmy Heath's son, was named James Forman, Jr., after Dizzy's pianist James Forman (often misspelled "Foreman"), who raised him. But Jimmy Heath told me that Mtume had never met Miles until he was hired. Miles's tune "Ife" that you often played was named for Mtume's little daughter, Ife.

Dave: Interesting—I didn't know that. I do know that he was seemingly quite militant. I had heard he was active with the civil rights stuff—I don't know for sure. I felt that maybe he was uncomfortable with me, a white guy, in the band with Miles, but that could have been in my head. Mtume and Miles definitely had a unique relationship from what I could see, although, as I said, Miles did have a different scene with each guy. Look, these are the times, '73 and '74. We were in the middle of the civil rights movement then in America. The amps and equipment were painted with black, red, and green stripes. When you see the videos, that isn't just haphazard; that's the Black Panther party flag. Yamaha painted it for Miles. Talk about making a statement.

In this period, everyone had dashikis, Afros, and all that stuff, and I had my tie-dye shirts and scarves. I was *the* white hippie! Hey, I had a right to be there, period, because of my jazz cred with Elvin. I was validated. But it didn't quite feel like a warm bath with that group, and I think Mtume's strong personality had a lot to do with it. There was a chill in the air, one way or the other. And you know something—I could dig it. After all, here was the Prince of Darkness, the embodiment of all that was black and hip, and he had a white saxophonist in a period that was wrought with racial tension. I probably would've thought the same thing if I was black. And I took the place of a brother who was let go—Carlos Garnett.

I was the only white guy in the band. The roadie, Jim Rose, was the only other white guy around, at least on the road. And the "freeze" was on in some places, when we played Chicago or Detroit, Howard University—places like that. Not in Europe, obviously, and Japan, but I could feel the vibe. In Detroit, I got the hell out of the dressing room quick after the gig, right back to the hotel. There were some real bros definitely in the room.

Lew: What would they do at that time—ignore you? What would Miles do?

Dave: It wasn't like a scene, but you could feel it. I think even Miles was uncomfortable sometimes in these situations, but who knows? I told you that he said to Eleana that "Dave has no color." He was like that with Bill Evans, too, in the fifties. He didn't care, as long as you played. He certainly knew the score, and he knew what was going on in the world and politics. But he would never make it an individual thing. Music was music, and that was what it was.

So, there was an underlying tension that I felt in the band, of course. Reggie was Mtume's guy. Later on, they became successful pop producers together. Michael didn't communicate with anybody too much. He was on his own and just stayed in his room taping, overdubbing and stuff. He also went on to have a successful pop career as a singer. I don't know how he did overdubbing in the room in those days!

Pete Cosey was pretty much on his own too, with his sunglasses and big dashiki, a big Afro, and a big black beard—he looked a little imposing, and nobody talked to him much. The truth was that he was the nicest guy—not that I had much communication with him at the time, but in the past few years we have played together for this or that Miles thing. Pete has a grandfatherly, uncle-y kind of thing—very softspoken. But in those days you could get a threatening vibe from him, even though from what I could tell, he didn't want anything to do with that stuff. All I can say is there was a feeling of unwelcome, that's all. I can't say we had a good time and talked and hung out much at all, though I did a little with Michael and Al, but that was the extent of it.

Al and Mtume had a rather intense relationship. After all, Mtume was raining on his parade. Truth is that often congas are in the way of the drum set. With Elvin, when Don Alias was in the band with the congas, it was one of the few times I saw it work in a jazz setting—albeit Miles's thing wasn't jazz, and a case could be made for the role of the congas, but not if you were Al Foster. A drummer's worst nightmare can be if there's a conga player on the gig. This would be under normal circumstances, let alone with Miles Davis. Also Mtume was using some kind of drum machine, which he would put on—*clickety-clackety*—some very basic drum synthesizer sounds. He also had log drums. In general, it seemed Al didn't dig his presence, or the way Miles seemed to kowtow to him. You could see Miles treated Mtume a little bit differently. Not a musical difference, just personally it seemed.

But you know what? Miles dug it I think. In his group, everybody was fighting for a piece of territory. I'll bet there's never been a band of his where things were cool. It's the nature of the heat at the top, and also Miles's persona. He kept you on edge. There are leaders like this in the world. There are even corporation guys like this.

We know this from psychology. I have no way of knowing if he did this on purpose. It was just his way of keeping everybody's attention. You could never relax, because of him, or because of the situation, or because somebody in the band didn't like the way you played, or because somebody was getting ahead of you in line. There was always something in the air that made for tension, and I think he liked that. He kept you on your toes. That was his way to keep things happening. Or maybe just because he was the most bored person I've ever known in some ways, and he had nothing better to do then to stir the pot. Outside of playing, in my opinion that's why he had such weird stuff going on with women, drugs, and everything like that. I never saw a guy more bored than Miles Davis.

Lew: He didn't keep himself busy reading books or anything like that?
Dave: No, though it appears that in the '80s when he returned, after his hiatus, he had a sketchbook with him. Actually he was quite a good artist it turned out. But in my period you have to remember he was sick a lot and not feeling good—he was on pills or whatever. So he just looked for things to occupy his time. When he played, it was business, but for everything else, whenever anybody was around him, they eventually paid for it one way or the other. I think he sometimes did it just out of boredom. For example, he would say something, and because Miles Davis said one word to you, you were like, "What did you mean?" He'd say, "You know what I mean," and that was that. Guys like that say two words and walk away. You're supposed to know what they're talking about. A lot of those guys from that era—Paul Bley, Steve Lacy—all seemed to have come from the one-liner response school of thought, leaving you to figure it out.

I think it was a Ginsberg/beatnik/Jack Kerouac thing that came out of the cool period—meaning to be understated, don't say much. If you said anything, it was only meant as an allusion, and your Zen third brain was supposed to understand what the hell they were talking about. On the other hand, it leaves you to figure it out, which can result in learning something better than you would with more direction. Miles: "Play less." What do you mean play less? Play less what? Less harmony, less notes, less rhythm? Play less volume? For example, Miles never said a word to me about what to play behind the little fragment melodies he played during that period. So, one night I asked him. He said, "Thirds," and walked away. Now what does that mean to a musician? Literally, to harmonize in thirds? That was the whole discussion of what to play behind him. In a way, he treated everybody like that—to keep you on edge, out of boredom, or because it was his basic personality? I can't tell you. But it was somewhere in that combination, in my mind.

Lew: Did you try playing thirds?

Dave: Yes, I did! On a couple of tunes, I did play thirds. I mean, he never said anything to me. I learned from LaRoca, one of the things we discussed earlier. If they don't tell you anything, you're doing good. Don't expect a rose garden, but as long as they don't tell you you're not good, you're cool.

Lew: It's very refreshing when somebody actually says you sound good.
Dave: Thank you! Or if somebody says, "That line you played was right." But those guys, forget it. LaRoca actually would comment here and there, but Elvin, no way. I don't know if he had anything to say about the actual details of the music, and the same with Miles. He would just say these three words and stare at you like you were from another planet. This was the way of the aural tradition, I'm assuming, which is where these cats came from. In general, these musicians didn't do school or do the kind of things that are commonplace now. I was in the transition period between the aural tradition, or what is referred to as "the street," and the academy.

Lew: You're right—because maybe to sit there and parse it out intellectually would have been like, "Oh man, don't make me do that!"
Dave: Yeah, like: "How unhip."

Lew: "Don't make me get academic about it."
Dave: Exactly. That's that anti-anti thing, especially among this generation. In any case, with Miles, there was always a tension of some sort. Even if it wasn't me, it was between the guys in the band somehow.

Lew: Now our friend Badal Roy was in the band, but he didn't stay?
Dave: Here's the chronology, as I remember it, and checking with Peter Losin's online discography. Right away after I joined in January 1973, we were touring all over the United States and Canada. Pretty soon, Lonnie Liston Smith replaced Cedric Lawson on keyboards, and at the beginning of April, Pete Cosey was added. In May, Balakrishna and Badal were gone. Smith was also gone, and Miles played keyboards himself from then on. So basically the group I was in for the remaining fourteen or so months was Miles, me, Cosey, Reggie Lucas, Michael Henderson, Al Foster, and Mtume. That summer we toured Japan and Europe. For the last few months of my stay, May thru June or early July of 1974, there were three guitars because he added a French guy named Dominique Gaumont, who did the Hendrix thing.

Lew: During your year-and-a-half with Miles, how was his health?
Dave: He was not in good shape. He was on all kinds of drugs and definitely in pain. He had crutches at one point because of trouble walking, and took a lot of painkillers. These days this would've been recognized immediately. He was taking ups and downs, snorting coke like it was going out of style. This was not a great period for him and stories about the drugs are really not for publication, but it was tough—I can tell you that.

Lew: On the videos of Miles, especially from this time period, it looks like he has discomfort in his TMJ, the jaw joint that's just below each ear, because he stretches his mouth and touches that area.
Dave: It seems to be some jaw stuff, pressure maybe? I don't know if it was an affectation or if it was pain. You see a picture of him with Lester Young from Europe in 1956 where he is doing the same thing. I don't know. Also, during my time he had a lot of phlegm and he would often let it go on the stage. That could be a bit rough, to say the least. When he stopped playing after 1975 and I visited him one time in the hospital, he told me that he had walking pneumonia all that time. It seems you can have that condition and be walking around with it. It's in your lungs. In general, he was in bad physical shape during my time with him. That's the other thing, going back to the disorganizational factor I brought up in the musical sense. How much of the musical disorganization was planned, how much was not, and how much was just a by-product of the cat being really ill?

I stayed with him a lot—up all night at times, or Eleana or Al would be there. Look, this is Miles Davis and if I could hang with him under whatever conditions I was going to be there. I didn't know what he was saying half the time. He would talk and I would just nod my head.

Lew: He'd be mumbling?
Dave: Yeah, plus that raspy voice made him hard to understand. He would say something and I wouldn't know what he was talking about. In any case, I was there with him and I would do whatever he wanted. Like if he needed cash to get some drugs, I might front him the money, and get it back the next day from the road manager. The truth is Miles never had money on him.

Lew: He'd actually give you your money back? That's good.
Dave: Miles would tell the road guy, "Give him the money he loaned out."

Lew: So, cocaine was present during this period?
Dave: I had been around some previously of course, but with Miles it was definitely there more. And pills—I had never taken Percodan or Tuinal or "black beauties"—a kind of amphetamine—or whatever, which I did a bit with him. I thought this was what you do when you're with Miles Davis. It's idiotic—I sound like a jerk—but there I was with one of the heaviest guys in the history of music, and he wanted company—he didn't want to be alone. Women were sometimes there, but not many, and as I said, this band did not hang much. If there were pills and Miles said, "Take this," I would not question it. He gave me something once that knocked me out for two days. Eleana wanted to kill him: "What'd you give him, Miles?" "I don't know."

One thing I learned from Miles was deflection. Anything he did that he was guilty of, he would deny. He was one of those cats who would say, "I didn't do that." I mean, not that this happened, but he was the kind of cat that if you found him in bed with your old lady he'd say, "That wasn't me." The kind of guy who said, "I don't know what I gave him." Maybe he didn't know, but the truth is he took most of what was around, without discretion, it seemed. The big thing was Percodan. He needed them for the pain, so he said. This became a thing when we went on the road. There was a doctor who would help me out for pain with my leg, which occurred on occasion. In those days you didn't need a triplicate prescription for Percodan. That was the drug of choice for pain. The doctor gave you a script and that was it. Miles would start off a tour with a big bunch of Percodans from his stash and mine.

Now maybe I had already taken one, or whatever. It seemed that Miles was taking eight, nine, ten a day! He hardly ate anything. Miles would pop a couple in the morning right away. By the second week, I guess he ran out and hit on me, which of course I gave him. I would get that call in my room, to bring up my supply. Then after a few more days he'd say, "You got more? 'Cause I know you got some." I'd say, "No, man. I gave you everything, Miles." I don't know how he went to the bathroom. Percodan makes you completely constipated. All morphine-based things do. You just can't move your bowels. That's what I hated about it most, actually. So, we would do whatever, then have a beer or something like that. I'm not proud of it, but I learned a lot, in a strange, convoluted way. Sometimes we would get into a nice discussion, but usually we would just be drifting.

Then there was another thing, which is the doctor scene, which could be pulled off in Europe, but not here or Japan. We would land in a city and the road guy would tell the promoter, "Miles is in pain and he needs a doctor." In a couple of hours in the hotel, I'd get a call to come to his room. The doctor would be there with his black satchel. House calls—amazing. Of course, they knew it was Miles Davis. Miles would tell the doctor that I was not well and needed some pain killers, so he could have more around. In some countries, they prescribed morphine for Miles. Whatever he could get, he would try. Some doctors were thrilled to give Miles Davis what he wanted; others would say: "I can't do it."

But when we toured Japan, where you couldn't have any drugs, when we landed, Miles had a woman there. She knew him, it seemed, and was with him the whole time. She'd cook soup for him, massage, whatever, and he was completely together in Japan. He was like another person—really together. We played at six-thirty in the evening, done by nine, and he was very congenial. Somebody was taking care of him, and he was cool.

But in general when we came back from a tour, he looked like he had been out there living hard. Then a week or two later, I'd see him and he was transformed. He lost weight if he had gained any. He was strong and he was going to the gym. He was like a chameleon. Stan Getz was like that—Dexter Gordon too. These guys had like thirty lives. They just would take it out and come back! They'd have some nice soup, they'd eat good for a couple of days, they'd go to the gym, and they looked like a million dollars. It was extraordinary. I'd say, "Miles, you look so good." "Went to the gym, eating some soup, eating my vegetables, no drugs, not drinking, nothing." It was just the road life taking its toll, but since we weren't really doing clubs, it was probably a lot better than previously for him, in the sense of less opportunity to debauch. We did mostly concerts and were done by eleven o'clock at the latest.

Lew: It wasn't about hardship.
Dave: No, not by then. He was getting paid five to ten thousand dollars a concert, and in those days that was a lot. We were in good hotels. When we were in Scotland, they picked him up at the airport in a Bentley. He told me to come with him and that damn car was like a house—better than what I was living in at home. He was treated great, like a king. When he went through customs, he whizzed through. He'd come to the airport a few minutes before the plane was leaving, and it would be fine. Try that now, whoever you are. You know, this was another time.

When we played a club just a few times when I was with him, it was Paul's Mall in Boston with the Lenox Hotel across the street. We literally just walked across the street. The other club we did was the Keystone

Corner in San Francisco where Todd Barkan was in charge. In general, besides the rare club gig, we might have two or three concerts in a row, and then a night and/or day off. In the clubs we played two sets, but the concerts were one set, and not that long usually. If there was an opening act, we always played first. I found out it was in the contract that Miles played first—actually a very good practice.

Lew: Because he just didn't want to have to hang out?
Dave: Maybe, but you know what? He was right. He was the headliner, but he didn't care to go last. We were done sometimes by nine-fifteen and were in the hotel by nine-thirty. There was always a spread of food in his room for the guys. Some of them would eat a little bit, then leave pretty quickly. There was enough food left over to feed India! Miles himself hardly ate, just picking a little. I don't know if it was the drugs or his metabolism, but he didn't seem to eat much of anything.

On drugs, he could be paranoid, crazy—and he'd be tough on people. I saw him do stuff to people that I just couldn't believe. One cat came up at two or three in the morning with coke, put it on the table, and Miles said, "Pour it out." He poured a good sized mound. Miles took a matchbook and scooped up enough for a small army. I'm not talking about a little snip—we're talking a pile. Then he would ask someone in the room to test it, as if whoever he was knew the difference. The so-called "tester" says, "I have no idea." Miles: "Shit's fucked. Get out of here." I don't think the cat got paid, or maybe he came back the next day, I don't know, but it was tough. Maybe he was just running a game on the cat. Here we go again—this is Miles Davis, so everybody was intimidated, I guess.

Once saxophonist Sam Rivers came in and Miles was really weird with him: "What are you doing here?" Sam said, "I just wanted to say hello." Miles replied, "Well, you said it." He could be rough, especially with women it seemed. He did some stuff to the woman who was with him during some of this period, who really seemed like a nice girl. I don't know what the hell she was doing with him—African American woman, sweet, young. We were in this hotel in Paris, a fancy boutique joint called L'Hotel. I was with Eleana, he was with the girl, and we had a couple days off. Every room is called the Versailles room, or the Louis XIV room, and so on, decorated beautifully—maybe eight rooms total. In the seventies it was a big deal to stay there.

So, we were in the hotel and the next thing I heard is some screaming and yelling next door. I went in and Miles was standing over this woman on the floor pouring champagne on her. "Bitch" and all that stuff. She had a black eye. I said, "Miles, what are you doing?" He said, "It's none of your goddamn business. Get out of here." Eleana was screaming: "You gotta do something or he's gonna kill her!" Next thing I know, the woman was put into a separate room, I guess to recuperate, and Miles was in his room huddled over. Yeah, he could be tough. He really had a Jekyll-Hyde personality, which the drugs of course brought out.

Lew: But being around all those drugs with Miles, after you left him, didn't that stay with you a bit?
Dave: Well, things definitely needed to be changed after this experience.

Lew: You got used to doing it?
Dave: Let's put it this way: In some ways, I sort of became Miles. I copied his style—I talked like him—in some ways I had an attitude like him. I was a real drag, you can be sure, because it wasn't me. It was me trying to be him. It was because I was obviously very impressionable. Maybe I'm exaggerating now, but it seems that he had some kind of effect on everybody who worked with him. He just rubbed off on you—his way of being, whatever—because it was very clear what it was. There was no wishy-washy. Miles was Miles, and the personality, for better or worse, was clear and unmistakable. Talking here in retrospect, maybe I'm exaggerating some of the negative points, but let's just say it was no picnic. What you saw was what you got.

One cannot help but be affected by a strong personality—well, at least at a young age. That doesn't mean you're a weak personality. It just means you're susceptible in some way, or you're open to it, or something like that. Furthermore, when you're in a subservient position, which you are because he's the boss, you're immediately not as confident. Therefore, you're already kind of a yes-man, and how far you go with that is, well—remember, this is jazz, and it's a way of being and a way of life, and he's Miles Davis. He's the history of jazz. I've got to say that it definitely affected me then and after—maybe not the most positive stuff in some personality ways. But musically, it was as you would expect, the most monumental experience I had in these learning experiences with these masters. For sure it had a gigantic effect on my music, and to some degree personality. This took years to be understood by me.

Lew: Plus, you were in a situation where the other guys in the band were not really hanging-out guys, and Miles actually needed you to hang with.
Dave: It seemed for that period I was the favored boy. What a privileged position! I was Miles Davis's yes-man. I spent more time with him than

any of the other guys, and I figured, geez, what an opportunity. Every once in a while, there was a little musical tidbit.

When it came to music, he was really on it. Like when you finished a recording session, he'd call you—"This shit is a mother-fucker," or something like that—and you had to listen. He would put the phone on the cassette machine and come back every so often: "Are you still there?" He'd make sure you didn't go away. He wanted us to hear what we did. That would be the last you heard it. After that Teo Macero took over; he did everything.

Lew: Teo did have a lot of leeway, but there is a written memo—my grad student Ryan Maloney found it—and an audio outtake where Miles tells Teo which themes to splice together. That's not generally known.
Dave: That's interesting. But I can't see Miles sitting in a studio saying, "Hmm, let's see if we can splice this note." I don't know for sure, but I just don't see him doing that stuff. I don't think he ever did any of that. Maybe Teo got it to him for approval or something like that. I don't know. But it appeared to me that Teo did everything and Miles had very little to do with so-called postproduction. Once Miles was done with something, it was history. He was just into present time. It appeared that way to me. I can't tell you for sure.

Lew: You toured all over the world. You must have some stories.
Dave: We did Japan, Canada, Europe of course, and Baalbeck in Lebanon, Tabarka in Tunisia.

Lew: Baalbeck?
Dave: Baalbeck is an old Roman ruin in Lebanon, near the Syrian border. July '73—it was a very dramatic gig—five thousand people. Unbelievable—playing in front of a temple—guys with guns all over the place. I think it was traditionally a classical music festival, and this might have been the first time they had jazz. Tabarka is the most northern point of Africa, where the tip comes up that you see on the map. Somehow, we were there through the French government. The electricity blew out in the middle of the gig. We couldn't finish and people were pissed. I guess we blew out the whole electrical grid of the town. I remember I was standing out in an open area after this happened, and we left the stage. There was kind of pandemonium for a minute. I had my horn, and Simone, a very famous promoter who booked all the guys, came by in a car with Miles inside: "You better get in the car now. We've gotta get out of here and back to the hotel." People were pissed off, throwing stuff.

For a minute, when it happened in the middle of the set, we played acoustic, but obviously that meant just congas, drums, trumpet, and saxophone. Miles gave it a try. He looked at me and put his hands up in the air like, "What am I going to do?" So we left. Talk about a "Night in Tunisia"!

In Brazil, we had an incident when some chick slipped him LSD or something and he was in the hospital for a couple of days. Our concert scheduled for May 31, 1974, had to be canceled, so we added an extra one later. I'll never forget when I saw him after the hospital, June 1, on the stage in São Paulo. He whispered to me, "That was close." Meanwhile, he played some of the best stuff I ever heard at that concert.

And one night after one of the concerts in Rio, I went out to clubs with the local cats and sat in with bands all over the place. I came back to the hotel and saw his light on and went in to his room. "I just went around playing that samba shit. Man, it's hard!" Miles: "Bird used to play 'Tico-Tico'—the first tune of the set—fast as a motherfucker. I used to scuffle. I couldn't play on it. Only Bird could play that." Then again, one of those one liners: "One and three." I said, "What?" He said, "One and three." That's it—end of story. What I think he was saying was to feel the downbeats in cut time on beats one and three, to keep up that momentum and the pace—kind of opposite of jazz in a way, where we emphasize two and four.

When I gave him notice toward the end of the Brazil dates in '74, he had some, let's say, interesting comments. Probably the last night or whatever, I went to his room after the gig and told him I had to split. He said, "What are you doing?" I said, "I got guys ready"—I meant, for a band of my own. "What are you going to play?" I said, "A little of this, a little of that." Miles, with an attitude: "You're gonna play them corny eight-bar forms?"

I think what he was getting at was how dare I pass on his great, hip shit to play "jazz." Here's what I said and I use this to make a point in teaching: "Yeah, you're right. But you know something, how many years did you do that? How many years did you play straight ahead? Twenty or thirty? If I would skip that, what would I say to myself? How could I face myself?" He looked at me scowling: *"Baaa!"* I knew this expression. If you made a point with him that he didn't want to agree with or you one-upped him and he didn't want to acknowledge it, he would just go, *"Baaa!"* He didn't laugh and say, "You're right."

Lew: He couldn't disagree.

Dave: No, no, he *couldn't* disagree because I was right, period. Anyway, while we were on tour in Brazil, Duke Ellington died on May 24, 1974. I remember this because one night when we were about to play, Miles said, "We gotta do something for Duke." That's the last thing I played with Miles in the studio a few weeks later, June 19: "He Loved Him Madly" from *Get Up With It*, that thirty-two-minute track. Remember, that was Duke's closing line at concerts: "We love you madly."

Lew: How did you know it was time to leave Miles?
Dave: Well, I had this first record with ECM, *Lookout Farm*, already released and had just recorded *Drum Ode*, the second one, in May. ECM albums were released on Polydor in America, so there was some action, and I had a guy helping me manage it all. I had the band together; we had music. I was rehearsing when Miles wasn't working, and I knew that the industry perception was that after you served time with Miles Davis, you were expected to do something on your own, step out and declare yourself, so to say. I could have stayed a little longer, probably, but the truth is that things were moving fast, and again, the music didn't compel me to stay. My time had come. I was among the hot guys in New York on saxophone, and the fire was burning for me. I had just finished being exposed to everyone who knew jazz worldwide with Coltrane's drummer, Elvin Jones, and incontestably, the greatest bandleader who ever lived, Miles Davis. This was the top of the food chain in jazz as a saxophonist. In a way I was in the line of Trane and Wayne, even Bird in a sense. My cred was high, both officially and on the street. I had a new prestigious artsy label from Germany that nobody really knew yet, but Keith Jarrett and Chick Corea were also on this label, ECM. I was in a very good position to work and to start my own career. The main thing was that in those days the system still worked. When you were with Miles Davis, there was nowhere to go up anymore. You had reached the top of the apex.

Lew: There was no other person to work with, as a sideman?
Dave: There was no other gig. Everything would be a down from there. You would be perceived as less if you did not go out on your own and have music ready, or just stupid not to take advantage of whatever notoriety you had earned by then.

Lew: If you just went as a sideman with somebody else...?
Dave: If I went to Art Blakey or Elvin asked me to come back, it would have been a retreat career-wise. I'm not talking music, although that may be true depending on the specific situation. From a career standpoint, I

felt that I had a chance that would never happen again, which was true. I had a band, I had a record label, and I just had more or less four years with Elvin and Miles Davis, not to mention Pete LaRoca. What could be better?

Lew: You did keep in touch with Miles some, in later years.
Dave: In '75 Miles went into hiding, and he was not in great shape. I saw him a few times, once in particular in either '78 or '79 on New Year's Day in the hospital. Actress Cicely Tyson was there also, though she and Miles didn't marry until 1981. I spent a couple of hours with him. Remember, the hospital is my domain. I'm a bit of an expert, sad to say. When I visit a hospital—how can I say—I get a warm feeling. I don't mean warm in the fuzzy way—let's just say familiarity.

Lew: It's interesting, because for most people it's like, "Oh, God." But you had to deal with it.
Dave: I can scope it out as soon as I get out of the elevator on a floor—the nurses' station—the cleanliness—the organization, etc. Miles was in a hospital gown, and really skinny. His legs were like toothpicks and he had stubble all over his face. I think he was there for pneumonia, like I said earlier about all the phlegm he had. I said, "Miles, you've gotta get up, you've gotta walk, you've gotta move." This is before blood clots became a thing to be aware of in hospitals, but I knew he had to walk.

We walked down the hall and he hung onto my arm, really haltingly, step by step. He was weak. I remember very clearly the nurse situation, because, as I saw that day when the nurses would come to his room, he was like the most charming, nicest, funniest, most polite guy you could ever see. He was kidding around and kind of flirting with them and everything. I couldn't believe it was the same Miles Davis. Nurse: "Miles, you have to watch your step now." Miles: "Oh, yeah. Why are you always talking to me like that?" They were bantering! Of course, they knew who he was. His sister Dorothy called while I was there. I had spoken to her a few times in the past when I was with Miles. She was his older sister and he listened to her. I remember one time when I was in the band, Dorothy being real emphatic about making sure Miles didn't do drugs and all that. Richard Pryor called during that hospital visit also. You have to remember Miles was more than just a jazz musician, especially to the African American community.

There's another thing that happened that day. I told him that everyone was asking if he was ever going to come back and play. And he said to me—I'll never forget this—he either pointed to his head or his heart or his ears—I don't remember what the order was: "What happens if it don't go from here to here?" I assumed he meant, what do you do if you don't hear it, like a rhetorical question. I said, "Well, I guess you've got to wait." He said "Voilà!" Hey, the guy was straight as an arrow in a lot of ways.

The next time I saw him was around '80 or '81. I was living in a loft on Sixth Avenue and 28th Street. The phone rang. I don't think I had talked to Miles for a year or two, but immediately it was that voice. No hello, no nothing, just, "Who do you got?" I knew exactly what he wanted, which was a saxophone player. I said: "I've got a kid who lives around the block." Now this is Bill Evans, the saxophonist.

Bill followed me around. He had gotten a hold of me at a Jamey Aebersold summer jazz camp and had more tapes of me than I had. He came to New York and lived around the block from the loft I had had on 6th Avenue and 28th Street. He was in the jazz program at William Paterson College—now University—in Jersey. He played the tunes I played and sounded a lot like me. He was a real protégé of mine and some kind of wunderkind—extremely talented for sure.

Lew: So, he studied with you?
Dave: Well, not formally, because I wasn't doing that yet, but he hung around me a lot. In fact, there's a nice story about the mentoring thing with Bill. He was so into me that I had to put a halt to it. Look, guys were into me and Steve Grossman, but really they were trying to decipher Trane through us. Anyway, he sounded more like me than me. I said, "You've got to stop this. Have you listened at all to Sonny Rollins?" He answered, "I don't like Sonny Rollins." I said, "Oh, you don't like Sonny Rollins?"

I talk about this now to my students. I say, "First of all, I don't care what you like or don't like. You're gonna do what I tell you to do, because you don't know what you like or don't like." I didn't talk exactly like that, but this is the bottom line. I said to Bill, "You know what? I know why you don't like Rollins. It sounds less serious to you than Trane." It sounds sometimes trite or whatever, with Sonny's sense of humor, sarcasm, or whatever it is, as compared to Trane's super serious stance. But as we know it is MUCH deeper than that with Sonny. I told him to get past the surface and get into Sonny, and Joe Henderson, who was an extension of Newk, as they call Sonny. So Bill did, and within three months, he had it down, really down. He was grateful, because you learn things from Sonny that you will not from Trane—things from Hawk—Coleman Hawkins.

So I said, "Miles, I've got a kid around the block." He said, "What's he play like?" I said: "He plays like me and Steve." "Tell him to call me," or I gave him Bill's number—I don't remember. Either way, within the next five minutes, I called Bill or Bill called me. "Was that Miles Davis on the phone? He wants me to come up to his house. Now!" I said, "Well, come over here first." I gave him a little primer, and off he went. Some hours later he came back, and that began the next stage of Miles Davis's life, because Bill became his aide-de-camp. He drove him around in the Ferrari; he took him to the clubs, and of course he became Miles's saxophonist upon the return to playing.

You know the story with the Thad Jones-Mel Lewis Band that happened in June 1981, on one of those Monday nights at the Village Vanguard, when Miles tried each cat's trumpet and sat in? That night, Bill brought him to the Brecker brothers' club, 7th Avenue South, where I was working with my band, John Scofield, Kenny Kirkland, Adam Nussbaum, and Ron McClure. That's where he heard Sco for the first time. We were finishing up and I was talking to Miles. Of course, everybody was nervous with him there listening. He told me to come with him to the limo outside and Adam begged to come too, which Miles said yes to. That night turned out to be pretty wild, but that's another thing. Anyway, I asked Miles if he liked the guitar player and he said no. I boldly said, "That's your next guitar player." I said, "Just don't let him comp." He looked at me like I was from another planet. But I turned out to be right.

So, I recommended Bill Evans, who became Miles's guide dog, in a way. Bill met guitarist Mike Stern on one of my gigs in Boston around this time. I was playing with Bill, drummer John Riley, and bassist Ratzo Harris, just a one-off at Michael's Pub or another place like that. Marcus Miller, who later worked with Miles, was on one of my recordings in 1979, the fusion record that we are using for the title of this book—*What It Is*. The point is that guys get gigs through other guys, by networking. Some leaders would have auditions, but usually it's: "Who do you got? Who do you like?"

Lew: By the way, I was at the first gig that Bill did with Miles, at Kix disco in Boston, June 26, 1981. The local news were there, and they aired a piece on it at 11 p.m., with, among others interviewed, me saying, "Miles Davis is the Marlon Brando of jazz!"

Dave: Ha—I certainly wanted to hear it too. In July, Miles also played the Savoy Theater in midtown New York. I got in because the roadie was the same guy, Jim Rose, who was with Miles in my tenure. Out of impulse I just walked on, grabbed Bill's soprano, and started playing. Miles was at the keyboard, and when he turned around, he got up and hugged me. I have a beautiful picture of that taken by Julie Coryell, Larry's wife of the time. Mtume sat in as well, and there is an audience recording of this. From what I heard later, no one ever sat in like that before. I had balls—that's for sure—but look, I knew all those cats and had something to do with putting it together in a way, so what the hell. It was my boy on saxophone, and even the soprano was mine. I sold it to Bill when I started with a saxophone company in the late seventies. I told Bill I might just jump up. He said, "Do what you want. Miles loves you."

During this period the three of us had gone to the gym a little bit together, because Miles was as always into the boxing thing. It was Gleason's Gym, at that time located on 30th Street and 8th Avenue in Manhattan. I got into boxing a bit then, and Bill definitely did in a big way. I was working out there, training for a minute. Miles was a celebrity in the gym. There were times when we went, the three of us, to be around the boxing, which I still love. I still have a speed bag at home. I have a theory about the boxing and Miles. I think it was really part of his thing—the jabbing style, the rhythm, the in-and-out, the up-and-down, the feinting, the moving back, the dancing, the not-really-hitting but actually hitting—and the timing, above all. I really believe it was tied up with how he played. That's why he loved boxing, and he loved ballet also, and African dance of course. Dance and boxing, if they're about anything, are about timing. Miles's thing was timing, both as a trumpet player and as a bandleader in how he coordinated musical events on the stage or recording.

Lew: And you got into the boxing through him?
Dave: Yes. I had done karate, I had done judo, I had done martial arts as best as I could over the years. I have a high regard for the martial arts because of the learning process, which is master/apprentice. With Bill the boxing was positive because it gave us stuff to talk about besides music, and a kinship with Miles, who by then was feeling better, no question about it. This was all happening at the beginning of Miles's resurgence.

Lew: What did you think about Miles's music in the '80s?
Dave: As the eighties went on I kind of lost touch with the New York scene on a day-to-day level. And in the case of Miles, I didn't really follow the music he was playing. I didn't know the revolving cast of players outside of Bill Evans, Scofield, Mike Stern, Bob Berg, and then Kenny Garrett. For guys like us who had followed Miles since the fifties, it was

great that he was playing and all that, but it wasn't something that you needed to hear.

Lew: It was very different from the early fusion Miles stuff. The eighties stuff was more pop, you could say.
Dave: It was certainly more so than before. There was no mystery as to how and what they were playing, which had always been more or less true of Miles's music and bands through the years. You didn't need a degree in rocket science to figure out what was happening. The main thing for a musician is that when you hear something you don't know, you naturally want to figure it out. I always make a point of this for students: It's not your first reaction to like or dislike that is important. Obviously, we have opinions, like with food or whatever. But this is a little different. You're a musician and you're supposed to know what it is before you pass judgment. You can't have ignorance or lack of comprehension determine your opinions because it is self-defeating—you will never understand it if that's the case. Usually, once you learn about something, you can use this knowledge in some way, if only for the mistakes. With limited time and so much to learn, you of course have to make priorities, but what I am saying holds true, at least philosophically. Don't let your personal taste get in the way of learning more.

With the Miles music of the eighties, there wasn't much to figure out, so I listened to him more out of nostalgia. But I must say he was still burning when he soloed—that was for sure, no matter how mundane the music was. I felt the same with seeing Elvin in the decades after my time with him. The music was nothing special, and in most cases the sidemen were good enough, but Elvin always burned it up himself. That's why you go see the masters when you have the chance, because they rarely if ever let you down. Getting older makes your time more valuable and you can feel this in a mature musician, whatever the style.

After Bill Evans left him, I lost contact with Miles. I don't think I saw him much in the next years until 1987, the night of the concert in Tokyo that I did with Wayne Shorter that's now kind of famous. It was the last time I saw him.

Lew: The tribute to Trane that's available on DVD?
Dave: Yes. *Live Under the Sky*, twenty years since Trane died. I had broken my leg again a month before the gig in Berkeley, California, in a parking garage working at Yoshi's with Quest. So I was on crutches for this gig in Tokyo. I was with Caris, my second wife, whom I'd just married a few months earlier. Miles played in the afternoon. I went down-

stairs to his dressing room and there were three bodyguards there—big brothers—like football kind of guys, and it seemed something funny was going on in the back. I heard Miles say, "Dave! Come in." I walked in on crutches with Caris: "What are you doing here?" I said, "I'm playing with Wayne." "Wayne's here?" "Yeah, he's upstairs."

Miles said, "What happened to you?" He knew I had broken my leg a couple of times. "Well, I broke my leg again." Then out of nowhere he said, "Who's she?" I said, "That's my wife." Quick Miles reply, "Another one?"

Lew: Ha, ha! I'm sure she loved that—not!
Dave: She is so sharp. She says, "The last one." Miles winked and gave a nod of approval. Classic Miles. And then he motioned me to the back with him, but I went back to the cats upstairs. That was the last time I saw him.

There's one last story that I have told a lot about Miles, because it shows a more human and generous side, which he definitely had. Much like the stories about Sinatra helping Sammy Davis or somebody who was sick—these kind of bigger-than-life guys sometimes get a bad rap, vis á vis how they treat other people. Of course, they were maniacs in some blatant ways, but they were also brothers to their friends. In the early '80s, I moved out of the city to Peconic, Long Island, and I broke my bad leg badly the first day there and had a cast. I was getting divorced from my first wife, Dina, etc. Shall we say a mid-life breakdown—I was all of thirty-five years old. In my convalescence period, Al Foster came out to visit me, among others.

The next day after Al's visit, the phone rang—and that voice: "You need any money?" Once again, I immediately knew it was him. I put two and two together, and I figured Al told him what was happening. You know, it was hand to mouth in those days—no playing, no money! I said, "No, it's cool. It's okay." Miles: "Yeah, Al told me about you." Then, out of nowhere: "I'll tell you a story." This was most unlike Miles Davis, an out-of-personality thing, telling a story to make me feel better.

It was very short: "When I was a kid, my father took me out to the backyard, pointed up to a tree, and there was a bird up there. He said, 'See that bird, Miles? That's called a mockingbird. That bird imitates what you say. You don't ever want to be like that.'" Miles to me: "Nice story, huh?" I said, "Yeah, thanks." Miles: "Take care of yourself." A mysterious, beautiful three-minute conversation. I mean, this guy never made conversation that wasn't about him. This was completely out of character. I wrote a tune called "Mockingbird" about that conversation, because I don't know whether he was just making me feel good, filling up the space, or trying to say something to me. I don't know what he meant, but it was a generous act of kindness. The main thing was he offered me money, which was right to the point, something that every musician can empathize with.

Lew: How would you sum up your relationship with Miles?
Dave: I don't know if it was the music, if he even liked the way I played. I kind of assume it, but the main thing with Miles was that it was macholand. Those guys from his generation, it was about man-to-man stuff—how much you could drink, get high, fuck, play, how fast, how strong, how much you could hang. All that stuff was part of the code. I could see it with Elvin and Miles so clearly, even though in some ways it was over by the time I was with them in the early seventies. It was in their DNA, so to speak. I just feel with Miles and me, it was like how can you, Dave, do all that you do with your leg the way it was.

When you have something wrong as a kid, you don't know. You grow up with it as a part of your life. If you're blind, you're blind. I think Miles saw that, especially because he had leg problems then, with his hip and all. He saw that walking was pretty hard for me to do, and it is a pretty important thing to walk. Whatever it was, we always had a cordial relationship. I never had a bad moment with the guy, one on one. All the stories about him, like the way he was in the eighties to some of his musicians and so on, I just can't relate to them. For sure, he could be really spiteful, mean and petty, and a drag, especially when he kind of got the feeling you were leaving the band. But he never did that with me.

So, my take on Miles—the bottom line is that he was obviously a complex personality. I really think that in his heart of hearts, he was a shy, Midwestern, small-built, good-looking cat, serious as could be about everything, let alone music. A lot that happened to him was to me the result of outside forces: the conditions of being a black man in that milieu of the forties and on; the colossal effect of Charlie Parker's overwhelming personality; and even more into the fifties, Miles's status as *the* symbol of everything hip in the black world, which appealed to a certain breed of white people looking to break out of the middle-class coma they were in during that time period. Music doesn't exist in a vacuum—the times dictate a lot. I'm not a psychologist, but that's what I think. He was really a simple cat who just wanted to play the music—very much like Coltrane. I think that's where they met, in a psychological sense. In that way, I think Trane and Miles were kindred spirits, even though they had completely different lifestyles.

Lew: That's a good point. And absolutely, there is societal pressure that comes with being an icon.
Dave: Every cocktail party had Miles on the record player with the mute playing a ballad. The way he dressed, the girls, the car, and the way he looked—it was a complete package. The record company went right for it. The cover of *Milestones*, when he's in the green shirt, sitting on the stool in that relaxed position with the trumpet—they had never had a black male like that on a cover. That was groundbreaking. Black was hip, at least in the Northeast urban centers. Miles was the guy. You become what you are. You may not know it, but by five years, you become the thing that you're doing the most at the time. If you do something long enough, you become it. I believe that's why he became the crazy maniac he was. Of course, drugs fueled the whole thing. But without drugs, he was a nice guy. To this day, my experience with Miles still has resonance.

Miles died September 28, 1991. His funeral in Manhattan was by invitation only, and it was somethin' else. This was at St. Peter's Lutheran Church, the "jazz ministry," on Lexington Avenue, and I went with Caris. Speakers included Mayor Dinkins, I think Herbie, some of Miles's friends, and, most of all, I remember Bill Cosby. There was a giant photo of Miles in the back of the stage. In between speakers they played Miles's recordings, which really lent a heavy atmosphere.

Cosby said something to the effect of "Let's lighten the atmosphere. Miles would never have gone for this." He told some stories just to reinforce how influential Miles was—his clothes, his ladies, his car. All that was always a topic of discussion in the African American community. Cosby said he would hang out late at the Showcase club in Philly, and somehow "magically" everyone would be talking about what Miles had just played in his last set, up the road in New York implying that's how much everyone was on Miles's case, with news traveling down route 95 faster than light! Also Cosby said when Coltrane replaced Newk in Miles's band, all the cats in Philly, where Trane had lived, were signifying that Trane wasn't good enough to fill Sonny's shoes, etc. Then the band came to the Showcase to play, and Trane was, as we know, completely burning. All the guys were at the club opening night, shaking their heads, saying: "Miles is a genius—he knows everything," and so on. Cosby was fantastic at the funeral.

At the reception after, I saw Reggie Lucas for the first time since my last gig with Miles's band, and Mtume, which was cool. Wayne, whom I hadn't seen since that Tokyo concert in 1987, said to me something like, "Miles is fine, don't worry. I saw him yesterday"—or talked to him, something like that—of course, with that smile and look that Wayne has about him. And it occurred to me that when you looked around at the people attending the funeral, several dozen of us were there because our careers were made by playing with Miles Davis. We all owed him a lot—and still do.

Leo and Frances Liebman. *Liebman collection.*

With Mom and Dad at NYU receiving Maas Essay History contest award, 1966 (and on way to lesson with Charles Lloyd). *Liebman collection.*

With Brother Paul at Bronx Zoo. *Liebman collection.*

"Marshals" representing the boroughs of New York for the Mother's March on Polio, with Supreme Court Chief Justice William Douglas and unknown man, 1951. Dave is at the top. *Liebman collection.*

Wedding of Caris Visentin and David Liebman, 1986. *Liebman collection.*

Birth of daughter Lydia Nicole Liebman, 1991. *Liebman collection.*

With my family outside Lincoln Center for NEA Masters of Jazz Award, January 2011. L–R: Harold and Natalie Visentin, Lieb, Caris and Lydia Liebman. *Liebman collection.*

Caris and David.
Courtesy of Shelley Rusten.

With Jed Luchow, my oldest friend from P.S.99. *Liebman collection.*

With Steve Lipman, close friend from Lafayette High School, who often went with Lieb to see Coltrane in the '60s. *Liebman collection.*

With educator Jamey Aebersold. *Courtesy of Jamey Aebersold.*

Advance Music publishers Hans and Veronika Gruber. *Liebman collection.*

European record producers Jean Jacques Pussiau and Kurt Renker. *Liebman collection.*

Master saxophone teacher Joe Allard. *Liebman collection.*

With first mentor, drummer Pete LaRoca. *Liebman collection.*

Artist Eugene Gregan from Lookout Farm. *Liebman collection.*

With Elvin Jones from *Earth Jones* record date, 1982. *Liebman collection.*

Miles Davis greeting Lieb, sitting in at Savoy, NYC, 1981. *Photo by the late Julie Coryell, courtesy of Larry Coryell.*

Impromptu Quartet 1965–66; L–R: Lieb, Bobby Katz, Mike Garson, Gary Zehner. *Liebman collection.*

Ten Wheel Drive 1969–70; Top L–R: Bob Piazza, Steve Satten, Michael Zager, John Gatchell, Aram Schefrin, Lieb, Genya Ravan; Bottom L–R: John Eckert, Alan Herman, Dennis Parisi. *Liebman collection.*

Sawbuck, Tompkins Square Park, Manhattan, 1970. L–R: John Eckert, John Gatchell, Pee Wee Ellis, Lieb, Chris Qualles, Sky Ford, Jimmy Strassburg. *Liebman collection.*

Open Sky Trio with drummer Bob Moses, bassist Frank Tusa. *Liebman collection.*

With Steve Grossman during Elvin Jones years. *Liebman collection.*

Lookout Farm, 1974. L–R: Don Alias, Richie Beirach, Jeff Williams, Lieb, Frank Tusa, Badal Roy. *Liebman collection.*

With Pee Wee Ellis at the Palm, San Francisco, 1976. *Liebman collection.*

Dave Liebman Quintet, roof of Lieb's loft, 1979. L–R: Terumasa Hino, Adam Nussbaum, Lieb, John Scofield, Ron McClure. *Courtesy of Shelley Rusten.*

Quest. L–R: Ron McClure, Richie Beirach, Lieb, Billy Hart. *Courtesy of Kurt Renker.*

Davie Liebman Group, mid-1990s. L–R: Jamey Haddad, Tony Marino, Lieb, Phil Markowitz, Vic Juris. *Courtesy of Walter Bredel.*

Saxophone Summit with Joe Lovano and Michael Brecker, Montreal Jazz Festival, 1999. *Liebman collection.*

Current Dave Liebman Group, as photographed in 2003. L–R: Vic Juris, Marko Marcinko, Lieb, Tony Marino. *Liebman collection.*

Manhattan School of Music orchestra performing *Sketches of Spain* conducted by Justin DiCioccio, 2001. *Liebman collection.*

Dave Liebman Big Band, 2005. Top L–R: Jay Brandford, Pat Dorian, Jim Ridl, David Lown, Dave Ballou, Sam Burtis, Bob Millikan, Tim Sessions, Dave Riekenberg, Danny Cahn, Tony Marino, Jeff Nelson, Scott Reeves; Bottom L–R: Vic Juris, Marko Marcinko, Lieb, Gunnar Mossblad, Charles Pillow. *Courtesy of Eric Alberg.*

Saxophone Summit. L–R: Cecil McBee, Phil Markowitz, Billy Hart, Ravi Coltrane, Lieb, Joe Lovano. *Liebman collection.*

We3 with Steve Swallow and Adam Nussbaum. *Courtesy of Dario Villa.*

With pianist Marc Copland.
Liebman collection.

With pianist Richie Beirach.
Liebman collection.

Different But The Same. L–R: Jim Black, Lieb, Ellery Eskelin, Tony Marino. *Liebman collection.*

IASJ Executive Director Walter Turkenberg (left) and Chairman of the Board, Karlheinz Miklin. *Liebman collection.*

"Pan Piper" Lieb in Patan, Nepal, 1976. *Liebman collection.*

Teaching. *Liebman collection.*

Playing with Hukwe Ubi Zawose at awards dinner receiving Honorary Doctorate from the Sibelius Academy, Helsinki, Finland, 1997. *Liebman collection.*

Receiving French Order of Arts and Letters from presenter Claude Carriere. *Liebman collection.*

NEA Masters of Jazz Award ceremony, January 2011

Chapter 8

Beyond the Line: My Own World

Lew: After Miles, you led your own band, Lookout Farm.
Dave: This whole thing is definitely the beginning of my life away from the masters, on my own. Maybe I'm making more out of it, but it appeared to me that there was nowhere to go but down after Miles. Like I said, you were expected by the community to have a body of music and to represent yourself in that way. You got a record deal with a label, which in those days was still viable. You would go on tour, have a band, and make a statement. That was the supposed course of events, in a system that still worked at that time.

Lew: Before you left Miles in June 1974, the foundation for Lookout Farm was already in place.
Dave: There's an overlap in the sense of preparing the band, recording, and playing some gigs in little clubs in between tours with Miles in 1974. When I was with Elvin at the Berlin Festival in the fall of 1972, Manfred Eicher, the founder and producer of ECM Records, came up to me and said he wanted to record me. After a while, it got solidified. So in October '73, we did that first record, *Lookout Farm*.

Lew: And a big part of that is your relationship with pianist Richie Beirach, who became a close friend and musical colleague to this day. How did you two get started?
Dave: We met in '67/68 at a jam session in Queens College. I don't know exactly how we established a relationship, but we realized that as a kid he actually grew up in Brooklyn three blocks from me on East 3rd Street and Avenue P—I was on 5th Street and Avenue M. He moved to

Queens at ten years old or something like that. He became a regular visitor at the 19th Street loft while he was going to the Manhattan School of Music, studying composition. I think he played gigs at the time, but I'm not sure. In any case, we started playing. At the same time, there was a bass player from Queens that he was close with—Frank Tusa. So, we became friends in these years. We really hit it off. We were the same personality—city, Jewish, similar background and musical tastes, with a lot of commonalities even in the way we spoke and hung out. I often played drums with him and Frank at the beginning, when we all switched instruments in the loft during endless sessions.

He was around and on the scene—kind of up-and-coming, precocious, a real Brooklyn guy. Richie, Dave Holland, and Jack DeJohnette worked with Stan Getz in '73. In fact, my first record as a leader, *First Visit*, was done in July '73 in Japan when I was there with Miles, using Stan's rhythm section—they were there at the same time. That was Richie's period as a sideman. Eventually we started to put music together.

Lew: And then there was drummer Jeff Williams.
Dave: He was from Oberlin, Ohio. His dad was a newspaper publisher, at least for a while. His mother, Ann, was a jazz singer, so he kind of grew up around jazz. In fact, he started on drums at age eight. His parents separated a year later—his mother moved to New York and performed there, while he stayed in Oberlin with his dad, I think. He went to Berklee in '68 and moved to New York in mid-'71. I don't know how he got into my loft scene, but we started hanging out. He is a quiet guy and a complete natural with some similarities in playing to Jack DeJohnette. He was completely nonintellectual. I don't know where he got his training. He just came out of nowhere, and we liked him. There was another guy who was doing a lot of sessions with us. It was a real decision between the two of them, but we went with Jeff. So it was Jeff on drums, and Frank Tusa on bass. Also, we had different hand percussionists at times.

So we had a long history by the time we formed the band Lookout Farm. As far back as February 1970, back in my loft days, I recorded an LP with a poet friend of Chick's named Carvel Six—we freely improvised while he read his poems—and the band was me, Richie, Frank, and percussionist Armen Halburian, plus my friend Nancy Janoson on flute. On the *Lookout Farm* recording, three-and-a-half years later, I used exactly the same band, except for Nancy, plus Don Alias on congas and Badal Roy on tablas—Don and Badal did "live" gigs with us too. My old trumpeter friend Steve Satten also played some percussion, and Eleana sang a little.

A real unifying experience for us came through an artist named Eugene Gregan, who is still around. I met him through Barry Altschul and Eleana. He lived in upstate New York in a town called Napanoch on a piece of land called Lookout Farm, though it was not a real farm. He was renting from John Simon, the producer who worked with the Band and Dylan. Richie and I began going to Lookout Farm, hanging with Eugene and his lady, Beverly. We became really good friends with him, and he became one of the most influential people in my life. He's about ten years older than Richie and me, and as I speak, he is still doing what he always has done, which is to create a lot of great art with nothing pretentious about him at all. Down to earth as could be, a real street cat who was completely educated as far as art was concerned.

Eugene was from New Haven and went to the Rhode Island School of Design. He traveled to Europe to see all the masterpieces—the requisite tour for a budding painter. He was a Picasso kind of cat who could take a napkin or an animal bone and make something unique, beautiful, and useful as jewelry or whatever. They lived in a little house where we would stay with them, snacking on "brownies," drinking some wine, and most of all, talk, talk, talk. He would explain his paintings and expand everything to the spiritual realm. Eugene is an incredible cat, and Beverly also, beautiful, hospitable, and as hip as could be. My house is full of his paintings. His paintings are covers for my records *Drum Ode* and *Pendulum,* and Richie's first record for ECM. This was a guy who I got a lot of inspiration from, because he made me see what an artist does everyday. Of course, I wasn't a painter, but the info could easily be transferred. It was a world view, a way of perceiving things. This was the time when I was trying to find my way. I really didn't have a concept of what an artist was.

Lew: And this was around when?

Dave: This was '72, '73, '74—in that time frame. It was the Elvin and Miles years, all overlapping and all part of this. Of course, I was attracted to the *notion* of being an artist. It seemed so hip and different from what I knew—the mystery and voodoo of it. But I didn't know what that meant, though obviously it was different from what I had been brought up to believe. I was a "what you see is what you get" kind of person, quite meat and potatoes, though educated and highly curious. This art stuff was way beyond my purview. But because Geno was a street cat, like us in a way, I could dig it. Everything he saw was through the prism of art, of creativity. Of course, he loved music. Somehow Eugene was a big factor for Richie and me putting the music together in those years. We still play a tune called "Napanoch," for the town where Eugene lives. And to put the topper on it, I named my first band Lookout Farm, which was also the name of my first record as a leader.

Lew: Can you remember specific conversations with Eugene?
Dave: Conversations about everything. The first thing is that he was very much into Persian miniature art and seeing things below the surface. He painted in that way. You had to look closely to see what was going on.

Lew: With a lot of detail?
Dave: Yeah, with figures and faces. He also did nature, but he also just did things out of his head. He would say, "You see that over there? You see that?" He would point things out and say, "When I see something, this is what I think about." He would talk and we would listen. He was a teacher and a great hang. He wasn't stiff at all. He wasn't a cat in white robes.

Lew: He was just kind of sharing his stuff?
Dave: He was, and of course, he had an audience with us.

Lew: Did you ever play music at his place?
Dave: Oh yeah. I wrote "Lookout Farm" there and "Napanoch"—probably a few others. I would go into the fields with the horn and get into the vibe. Being there inspired and reinforced me toward a vision of what it is to have a body of music, to be a creative force, not just play saxophone. Slowly I could see the music transforming from craft to art. I always make the distinction when I'm teaching between a craftsman and an artist. One is a person who is adept and has the required tools of the trade down, while the artist possesses the requisite craftsmanship and expresses something of definitive value beyond mere technique. Artistry implies great craft, but vice versa is not necessarily true. One could just be a great craftsman.

Lew: The craftsman is kind of like the—
Dave: Nuts and bolts, but good at it.

Lew: What they say is necessary, but it's not enough?
Dave: It's enough for most of the population apparently, but not for me. This was becoming clear at this time to me and Eugene helped me get

there. I always tell one story: I give certain warm-up exercises to the students and tell them to do these every day for five to ten minutes, like a meditation, almost a Zen kind of silent time with yourself. I tell them how Geno would wake up in the morning, have a smoke and a coffee, then sweep his studio. I show the motion of sweeping with a broom. There could be shavings there or whatever. Not a big deal, but he would sweep the floor even if there was nothing on the floor or very little. "Well, what are you doing, Eugene?" "I'm into the motion. I'm thinking about what I'm going to create today." That was his meditation. By the motion of the arms, this brushing over the floor with the broom everyday, he would think about what his project was.

This cat lived like that—and, as well, very close financially to the vest. He and Bev didn't have much money at all. He couldn't stomach the gallery scene, which makes the record business look like fun in comparison, because of all the people you had to schmooze. Once in a while, he'd come down to New York. I remember we had an opening for him and a big party where we played. Then he and Bev went back to the mountain. They grew their own food, and she is a gourmet cook. The art world is really rough—very cutthroat. You've got to charm the people and everything. Eugene was a good-looking guy and really happening socially. He could play the part like Shakespeare when necessary and there would be a scene up there when potential buyers would visit, like Yoko Ono and other celebrity types. You got this great vibe, great food, and recreational smoke, only two hours from New York, with a master artist. He was known, but he never hit it and didn't give a damn about it, at least so it seemed to me. He just didn't want to deal with the art world. So he just hermited out and continued to create, as he still does today. He would sell a painting and that would be it for the next couple of weeks. He didn't just hand them out.

His fortunes have changed since then, thankfully. A couple of years ago somebody gave him a gift of land and a house, right down the road from the original Lookout Farm. He now lives in an amazing, great pad with a flower garden that seriously looks like Giverney, Monet's hang. All he does is paint now. Somebody realized how "bad" he was, how heavy. In summary, he's one of the godfathers of my life.

Lew: And Gregan's place, Lookout Farm, helped the band Lookout Farm come together.

Dave: Between his Lookout Farm and my loft, Richie, Frank, and I formed a real social and musical bond. The first record, *Lookout Farm*, was my best-selling and is still my most known recording. It has never been put on CD, except in Japan in the nineties. The LP has four tunes, and as befits a first-time record, it portrays all my influences up to that time—Miles, Trane, world music, and fusion, with additional musicians like John Abercrombie on acoustic and electric guitar, as well as congas, tablas, and percussion. It was a real production for a first record, though done in two days without much, if any, overdubbing, as I recall. It does show the beginnings of Richie's harmonic influence on the tune "MD," written, appropriately, for Miles. I followed up in May '74, just before I left Miles, with another ECM recording, *Drum Ode*, which featured a bunch of drummers in different settings and still seems to be a favorite among the listeners. So, I had these two records out already by the end of 1974.

Lew: The Japanese one, *First Visit*—I guess people didn't know about it over here so much?
Dave: Exactly. It has been released since on three labels, as companies got bought and sold. Also, I had the Open Sky recordings, and my first recording that I did in Sweden in 1967 with Lars Werner. But I would have to consider *Lookout Farm* and *Drum Ode* as my real firsts as a leader.

Lew: What was the music of Lookout Farm like?
Dave: Lookout Farm was an eclectic band. We played everything from funk and Miles-ish kind of stuff to Coltrane to standards. We had electric and acoustic piano, electric and acoustic bass, on occasion guys with exotic percussion. I used two Voice of the Theater Altec Lansing speakers as big as this room that we carried around for just *my* sound. And I used a chorus and Echoplex for effects. Richie used a Mu-tron and wa-wa pedal on the Fender Rhodes, which was an eighty-eight-key that we souped up by putting JBL speakers in the bottom cabinet. All this equipment was heavy as can be, but we traveled self-contained, in real rock-band style.

I will never forget our first gig in June '74 opposite Larry Coryell in Westport, Connecticut. We got on the bandstand, and suddenly somewhere near the first or second tune I realized that I couldn't look to Elvin, or Pete, or Miles for direction, that these guys on the bandstand were looking at *me* in that way. I was responsible for everything that would happen in the next hour, from what tunes to play, to who solos, to feeling like I have to inspire the cats—a million things *plus* my own playing—talk about a lonely feeling. This was an awakening into bandleader adulthood for sure, and there was no looking back. It was deep.

There was another gig near the beginning of the band that was a wake-up call to me, shaking me out of my post-Miles stupor, so to say. It happened the day Nixon resigned, so we are talking August 9, 1974, after the band had been together a few months. We're playing at a bar in Boston, a funky joint for students called Debbie's, which was run by an Irish cat. Somehow he had jazz in the club, probably rock or folk too, I don't know. Here's a lesson in humility coming up. Remember, we had a lot of equipment, and we were real *loud*! The word was out, and the joint is full of young folks because there's a buzz about the band. So we play our first set, and on the break I'm hanging out and enjoying being the star and so on. The Irish boss comes to me with a real strong Boston accent and says, "You should start playing." I said, "Well, I don't feel like playing yet," or something like that. I'm sure he probably doesn't even like the music in the first place and has no idea who the hell we are. He's selling a beer or two, maybe. I'm some little punk kid with a scarf on my head and I'm gonna tell him how to run his joint! I'll never forget the following: He takes me by the collar of my shirt, pushes me against the wall, and says, "You're working for me." I said, "Okay, we'll play!" This was a lesson that I obviously needed. It's like, excuse me, you're working for someone. I'm like, "Oh, I don't feel the magic yet," etc. I was being Miles again! Lesson number one in being a bandleader—work *with* the boss!

Anyway, we worked. Remember, it was the days of tour support, so Lookout Farm's tours were to some degree being subsidized by Polydor Records, which released ECM's records in the United States. We did a tour around the States, driving 10,000 miles, going everywhere. We had gigs lined up, staying in motels, the whole deal. We were a real band! It was the real deal. I hit on my parents, and they gave me $15,000 to buy a Trademaster Dodge van, which we used for gigs, most notably for a tour of 10,000 miles, going to the West Coast and Canada. That was three months of sleeping two or four to a room. There was also a tour of Japan, all over Europe—Munich, Hamburg, Yugoslavia, etc.—in June and July of '75, and in September 1975, for the State Department, we did India—eight cities—quite a deal.

Lew: I'll bet that was eye opening.
Dave: It appeared we were the first jazz band of our type to tour India—as far as I know, only Brubeck had been there in '58, and Duke in '63 and '72——not sure if that is 100 percent accurate, but it certainly was a milestone of sorts. Plus we had an Indian tabla player with us, Badal, on top of it. We went from Japan, to Hong Kong for one night, and then to

India. What a change. In Japan you didn't lift a fork! They did everything for you. And then we went to Hong Kong for a night. I even had suits made. In those days, all you had to do was put your thumb out, ask for suits or anything, and it was done in a minute. We had some great fun and the greatest Chinese meal.

I'll never forget landing in Calcutta from Hong Kong around midnight. Badal had bought a TV for his parents. Where he was born in 1945 was part of British India, and now is Bangladesh, but his parents had moved to Calcutta. We got out of the plane and there was nobody there except his parents. They were old and there were tears and a lot of emotion. They wouldn't let him take the TV through customs. They were screwing with him. It was a real drag and even the State Department guys couldn't do anything.

But the main thing is, we all got into separate cars with State Department cats. I was with the head guy, David. We became friends, by the way, and for some years I stayed in touch with him. "Why are we in four separate cars?" He replied, "For orientation, because you are about to see some stuff that you have never seen in your life." Sure enough, I could see trucks picking up bodies. And the streets were very dark with little candles, smoke, foggy, humid, misty—just uncomfortable. People were dying every day, that's all there was to it. Calcutta was like you were going to the end of the world—out of a movie. "We just wanted to have each of you individually to ease the way through," especially since we just came from Hong Kong and Tokyo. Talk about shock! I'll never forget this because we went to the hotel, the Grand something, supposedly the nicest hotel in Calcutta. It was a pit. I remember at breakfast you couldn't even eat the eggs. We came down to the lobby the next morning and everybody looked at each other in shock, like we were on another planet. We were really affected. Of course, as soon as we went out in the street to a van for rehearsal, there were ten beggars coming over to us with no arms, no legs. We were a target, for sure. The State guys told us, "Don't give them anything, because they'll never leave you alone." Badal was in tears, like "my country!" It was really a scene.

Unfortunately on these State Department tours you end up playing for diplomats, in a hotel lobby or a ballroom, or something like that. Maybe a couple hundred people in the audience. We were like entertainment night for the staff, I guess. They don't know jazz, so it was a little weird, but some of the concerts were better than others. We had two concerts in Calcutta that I can remember to this day, especially the first one. They were a highlight of my life because of the vibe. I remember getting a real vibe from the audience—so much feeling, intensity—it was something else. I could feel that the audience was on it, that they were knowledgeable, maybe not about jazz, but in general. Something about it was just different. I really felt that vibe that you get when you are playing your stuff in a foreign country that has a rich tradition of music and just knows the deal naturally, if not the specific music you're playing.

Badal playing tablas in the band was controversial. You have to remember this is before "world music" was on the table. Can you imagine? In the Indian tradition, everything is an agenda. Tablas in jazz! Blasphemy! So there were some articles about that, but most people were knocked out. For northern India, Calcutta is the intellectual center. Even though it was a poverty-stricken place and a hell-hole, it was also where all the arts and intellectual stuff was it seemed. Delhi was more of a government town, and Bombay was business. We also went to Bangalore, Puna, Madras, and we ended up in Goa, on the Indian Ocean.

Goa was like paradise. We stayed at the Taj Hotel. It was basically a Portuguese hippie colony, amazing because it's on the Indian Ocean and looks like the Garden of Eden—gorgeous—and the water is like a bath. I had an interesting incident in Goa. We were on the beach, and this guy came by with a long beard and a cane. I swear he looked like Father Time. He had a bottle of something with him, and he talked to Badal: "This guy says he can cure your leg. He says he's got pigeon blood and he'll give you a massage. Do you want to do it?" I said, "Hell yeah. I'll try anything." I'll never forget it, laid out in a blanket in the sand, naked or semi-naked, and this whatever is being poured on me. It was like that weird stuff in the movie *Soylent Green*! He rubbed my leg, outdoors, on the beach, and the cats were all gathered around. It was a scene. I gave him about ten rupees—who knows, probably a small fortune to him. But, needless to say, there was no change in my leg.

The tour was two weeks, and of course someone had to get sick. We were very careful—don't eat this, don't drink that. We tried to eat only in the restaurants and the hotels, definitely nothing off the street. No water, no food, no nothing. Finally, we were at a restaurant in Delhi named Moti Mahal. There was an incredible band with a clarinet, accordion, and some drummers that was burning. I said, "You know what? We've got to eat. Screw it!" We were cool and relaxed, sitting under the stars, eating chicken tandoori. The next day, Richie was way laid out. I think Frank or Jeff, too, to a certain degree. Somehow I was cool. Richie had it for six weeks because dysentery stays with you. Let's put it this way—I would look over and he wouldn't be at the piano. He would be running to the bathroom, then he would come back, he'd be playing and getting up again. That was the deal. Look, if you go to those countries, you're gonna get sick. It's kind of an occupational hazard—at least it used to be.

The musical experience of India was incredible. In Madras, some studio professional cats played for us on South Indian instruments—the clay pot on the stomach, vina, which is comparable to the sitar of the North, mridangam drum, and so on. We made a record in India, *Passing Dreams*. I certainly wanted to record with Indian musicians. Badal, through the help of a friend, arranged for a few musicians to record. One guy played sarod, which is like our lute—and, of course, a sitar guy, and the famous Sultan Khan on the sarangi, which is a fantastic violin-type bowed instrument. He completely burned, by the way. He's still around, because we did some gigs a few years ago. He recorded with Peter Gabriel, George Harrison, people like that.

Anyway, we did this record date. At eleven o'clock at night, we went into this building, walked up a dark staircase carrying the drums with us, and so on. We walked into a room not much bigger than this room we're in now, and there were like fifty people, seated very quietly, at attention it seemed. Dead silence! Obviously, the word went out. Everything was known somehow. I'll never forget it—upright piano with, I think, one microphone in the middle of the room, with a reel-to-reel two- or four-track machine, etc. Very basic. Nobody spoke English. Badal spoke to them. "Tell them to watch me. I'm going to point to them to play." Everything was in the key of A. We even played Coltrane's "Equinox." Each of us had a duo. Frank did one with the sarod player, me with the sitar, and so on. It was one of the best sessions I ever had, an amazing experience. We basically just jammed with these guys—not like Mahavishnu or any crazy stuff, just droning out and playing—a real meeting of cultures. Saxophonist Arnie Lawrence had a label and he released it as *Passing Dreams*. Then about ten years ago, Badal and I added some more music to make it CD length and released it as a home project.

After the tour, my mother, who by then was a retired assistant principal and loved to travel, wanted to go to India. My father wasn't interested, so the next year after my tour, we went together as tourists during Christmas week of '76. You know, a real tour with twenty regular people, not to play gigs, just be a tourist, which I have never done since by the way. We had done a bit of touring already, but ended up on New Year's Eve in a nice hotel in Bombay. So my Mom and I went into the ballroom and everyone was dressed to the nines, all Indians at the bar and the nightclub. I said, "Mom, we should dance or go have a drink." We walked in and the band starts playing "Pablo's Story" from *Lookout Farm*—my most well-known tune, a little sixteen-bar nothing ditty for

Pablo Picasso. On the recording of that tune, I quote "Andalucia," which was my mother's favorite song. She played it on the piano all the time. Here we were in Bombay, India, and the band was playing "Pablo's Story"! Sure enough, they came over: "Oh, we knew you were here because somebody saw you here in the hotel, and we expected you to come down and walk in." This was really out!

My mom eventually went up to the room, and I stayed with these guys, who took me back to their pad, which was on the beach, near Bombay. We sat all night and listened to tapes, especially the sitar master Vilayat Khan, whom they said was the main heavy cat at that time. Some Indians liked him better than Ravi Shankar, and at that time he wasn't well known in the United States. I was hearing the underground tapes! One was Vilayat playing at a gymnasium in a little school somewhere, a three-hour cassette. They let me keep them, so, in exchange, after returning home, I sent them a copy of a private tape of an amazing Trane performance at the Half Note, "One Up, One Down," which at that time was only known by the musicians—a good exchange, to be sure. So, that was India with my mom—very interesting. I haven't been back to India since—unfortunately, it just hasn't happened.

Lew: Now, in late July '75, a few months before the India tour, you did the recording *Sweet Hands*, which has an Indian influence, so you were into Indian music already—at least the classical tradition, sitar, bansurai wooden flute, etc.

Dave: I had been into Indian music since Bob Moses turned me on to it a few years before. I was aware of the great bansuri flute player named Pannalal Ghosh. Supposedly he even had the webs between his fingers cut so that he could have a bigger stretch. I loved his music and all the Indian stuff I heard. Later, when I went to California, I studied Indian flute with a student from the Ali Akbar School in San Rafael near Frisco. On top of my interest in the music, I just loved Badal. Our connection was and is strong, because he seemed older than the other cats and he was my go-to guy for advice and so on. He was definitely more mature than us, married, with a kid and responsibilities to his parents in India, making his way in America on his own. No kid stuff like us. We were basically kind of cloistered compared to him.

Not that he came from poverty or anything. He came from a good, well-educated family. Badal is very savvy. He didn't play tablas professionally until he got here to the United States studying statistics—he already had a master's in it and was planning to get a Ph.D. But he just has a great groove. He had no pretense to be an authentic Indian classical tablaist, even though everyone thought he was. He never said, "I'm the deal." He just hung out, playing when called for, hitting a cowbell once in a while. He has a great groove, a great vibe, and I just love being around him. Badal was a very important part of my life. He is a brother. He had that place in my life as the kind of elder statesman of Lookout Farm. So this was a whole Indian period—going to India and doing *Sweet Hands*, which was dedicated to Badal. If you have "sweet hands" it means you are talented. They say about a kid, "He has sweet hands." That means he will probably be a musician.

Lew: It doesn't have to be drums?
Dave: No. It just means that you've got the touch, you are musical, from what I understand. We recorded George Harrison's "Within You, Without You" on *Sweet Hands*. We also did a tune called "Ashirbad," which means "the Elders." It was like a long drone, with Badal's wife, Gita, playing tamboura. *Sweet Hands* is an interesting record with probably about the worst cover of my life—talk about literal interpretation. They put a saxophone with a lotus flower and a gigantic picture of a Buddha statue over a terrible garish yellow and green background—the most out, ridiculous cover of all times! It was A&M Records—a major label with an "art" staff—unbelievably bad taste. Hey, what do you expect from Peter Frampton-ville, who was their big hit then? They made up for it with the next record, *Forgotten Fantasies*, which has Chinese letters on it—that was very classy.

But, about Indian music, there is a lesson we all learn, which is about dilettantism, something to be avoided at all costs. I mean, McLaughlin really put his time into Indian music, and increasingly in our time, there are guys who truly study the music of a foreign culture. But in those days, you had a couple of Indian records, somebody showed you 5/4, and you thought you were cool. You know what I mean? I just liked the music and wanted to use it a little bit. But I realized this is a life study—you've got to live it, you've got to become it. For me, it was a stage and that was it. It was great and I learned a lot.

For my taste, Indian classical music is the deepest music in the world. Yes, it has no harmony, which as you know is my favorite game, but it has a serious vibe, period, from the get-go. There is no wading through any kind of bullshit. It is immediately spiritual and evocative, ceremonial and religious. It's ancient music on amazing-sounding instruments. As far as the rhythm goes, you cannot get any more sophisticated than the South Indian deal. In the world of drums and percussion, classical Indian music stands out. I realized that it was a good source for a period in my life, but you cannot think about doing something like that without really giving up your life for it.

Lew: Besides *Sweet Hands*, there were several other recordings during this period.

Dave: Well, first of all, on the *Drum Ode* date, I had a little problem with Manfred Eicher, which ended my relationship with ECM. The album *Lookout Farm* had seven guys on it. *Drum Ode* was more complicated, because I wanted a lot of drummers. We had Patato Valdez, Don Alias, Colin Walcott, Badal, Jeff Williams, Bob Moses, Barry Altschul, plus Gene Perla on bass. Also there was of course Richie, plus Abercrombie on guitar, my friend Steve Satten on percussion, and Eleana singing her own lyrics to my tune "Oasis"—so this was a big affair.

I had eight drummers sitting around, and after all, it was New York City, so you can imagine the vibe in the studio—not very German, to say the least. We're talking guys who were smoking and puffing away. Eugene, my painter friend, was the master of ceremonies because he had some good smoke. The vocal booth was completely filled with smoke. You couldn't see anybody through the haze. I was going to run it the way I wanted. ECM was the epitome of refined contemporary music—don't dare use the word jazz! It was actually amazing that I was even on the label in the first place, but *Lookout Farm* did very well, I guess. I don't know if Manfred had ever recorded in New York, usually opting for Germany or Norway. Anyway he was sitting in the booth and flipping out.

Finally, he came up to me screaming, "I can't stand this! You can't record like this! This isn't right! My studios are like laboratories. The wives don't even come!" I said, "Oh yeah? Look, Manfred, this is New York. You are in New York City. You're on my turf," etc., etc. I was with my boys, who were drummers, and they were going to smoke! Manfred was flipping, so that was it. I've seen him three times since then. That was the end of my relationship with ECM, though I did record on Steve Swallow's *Home* record for them in 1979.

The truth is I never could have gotten along with Eicher in the long run, from what I have heard about his relationships with even his longtime recording artists. It's his show, and the guys go along because they need him. He has been known to just cancel a date with everyone there already because he didn't like the music. That's his prerogative obviously, but it does seem a bit extreme. I can't believe that some guys have been with him for all these years. I'm sure he has some redeeming qualities and everything. He's extremely successful and done a great job, but with me it was oil and water. Looking in retrospect, if I had remained with him my career might've been quite different. Besides Jan Garbarek, there were no other saxophone players promoted over the years on ECM. It could've been me with Jan, potentially. But that's the way things go. A mistake of judgment—maybe? Anyway, that was the end of ECM for me.

Lew: So without a label, how did you keep the group going? In those days there was a system of promotion and so forth, between record companies and bands.
Dave: A&M came next. This was an amazing stroke of luck. I got a call from a producer, John Snyder. He worked with Creed Taylor at A&M; somehow they got him to start this Horizon line. I was his second call. I think Brubeck was first. He said, "I know you; I like you; I want you to be on this label." I didn't know the guy at all. He said that A&M was putting a million dollars behind Horizon. As I said, A&M had Peter Frampton, who was gigantic. It was *the* pop label at the time. Herb Alpert and Jerry Moss—A&M. The story was they were on the West Side Highway and they heard George Benson singing "Masquerade," which if you remember was a big crossover hit. "Why can't we do that?" Warner Brothers had beat them to it. By then, Herbie's "Chameleon" was popular, and "Masquerade" was even more popular to the general public.

This was the beginning of the time when some fusion was becoming popular beyond jazz circles, beyond Return to Forever or Mahavishnu or Weather Report. Benson's version wasn't jazz, but it was jazzy. Everybody was jumping on the bandwagon then. The height of it was '75/76. They started Horizon, giving Snyder free rein. He had the Revolutionary Ensemble with Leroy Jenkins—imagine that—and Brubeck, the Thad Jones-Mel Lewis big band, Ornette Coleman, a couple of others, and me. He did some nice stuff. Anyway, he asked me what I wanted to do. I was into Indian music pretty heavily at the time and had a lot of interaction with Badal through Miles, on McLaughlin's *My Goal's Beyond,* my *Drum Ode,* etc. We had a nice thing going when we played, especially since I played flute and loved Pannalal Ghosh. So I said I'd like to do a record using the Indian influence. I went out to A& M in L.A. They had a beautiful setup on the old Charlie Chaplin movie lot with little huts for each department, right in Hollywood. I went into Herb Alpert's office: "You know, we really love what you're doing with jazz, and we want to support this." He was a nice guy. I had an expense account!

Lew: Wow! Those days are long gone.
Dave: I had a deal for recording and for publishing, with advances, and pretty much whatever I wanted to do. I flew Abercrombie, Alias, and others in, staying for a week or two, mixing and mastering. It was the whole L.A. deal, if you know what I mean. It's as close to rock-and-roll style as I ever got. We did the record *Sweet Hands*, which had Lookout Farm as the nucleus of the group. What I'm painting here is a picture of heady days. We were pretty successful—or at least we acted like it! Sure enough, Lookout Farm won the *Downbeat* Critics Poll for Band Deserving Wider Recognition in 1976.

Lew: It was big time.
Dave: Well, it wasn't Return to Forever or Weather Report, but it was right under that. And for a New York musician, it was a lot. This was a successful band. We were playing opposite Weather Report, opposite pianist Bill Evans—like that. It was a great period for me musically. The next Horizon record, recorded in November 1975, after our India tour, was *Forgotten Fantasies*, my first duo with Richie—rather unusual in those days—which was very well received. Later I did *Lighten Up* with the Ellis/Liebman Band. And my first book, *Lookout Farm—A Case Study of Improvisation for Small Jazz Group* (1978), came out of this band experience.

Lew: It was very innovative, having analyses of the recordings by the performers themselves. And on the cover it is presented as being by the whole band, not only you.
Dave: We really did discuss the music a lot. We were all into it. It was really the way we related to each other. This relationship with Richie, Frank, Jeff, and Badal—but particularly Richie and me—was a unique situation where we were eager to talk and verbally could pull it off. We liked to describe what chord was the right one, or whatever. We would get a cassette from the gig and listen together after. I would say to Jeff Williams, "Well, what were you thinking at that bar?" I would fall asleep in my clothes, listening. It was a great period. That's why that book came out. I went to the head of publishing at A&M; his name was Joe Carlton. He was a heavy dude and had been around the business, music editor in the '40s at *Billboard,* then with various record labels including pop A&R head at RCA, etc.—older cat. He asked me if I had any ideas. I had an idea for a book discussing the process of how a band puts their stuff together. I said, "I don't think there's anything like it." And he answered immediately, "Catalogue item—I need it." I guess he figured it would

class the catalogue up or something. I guess he realized that jazz guys were another breed than the pop boys and girls.

Lew: He was thinking it was not going to be a hit, but it was going to be prestigious and it would sell slow and steady.
Dave: I think the intellectual side appealed to him. That was really a part of me for sure, that explaining thing. I said, "Okay, I'll take care of it. We'll talk into a tape recorder and I'll get somebody to transcribe it." I got Chuck Berg, who was writing for *Downbeat*. He was a very close friend and was living in New York at the time. I remember we used somebody's apartment in Manhattan and did three straight eight-hour days. That was the book! Almo Publishing did a great job with it. Fantastic pictures and nice thick paper, a beautiful cover. We included five recordings on two of those bendable plastic records, four from our various LPs and one, "Fireflies," from a live gig in early '76 that was not released otherwise until 2004, on our Mosaic Select set.

First there is a general intro about improvisation and about composition. Then, for each piece there are two discussions, composition and performance. For composition, each guy would talk about what the tune meant in any way, musically or extra-musically, including notated aspects of the leadsheet. Then a description of the performance as heard on the plastic disc, with transcriptions of the sax solo on one tune, tabla part on another, etc. In other words, a blow-by-blow description of the creative process. I was very proud of it.

Lew: I mention that book to a lot of educators because I've noticed that few of them are aware of your book. They are always telling me that writings about jazz are too focused on the individual solos, that there is almost nothing written about the interaction in the band. The other thing they want to talk about is the process from the leadsheet to the performance. For both subjects, I've been referring them to your book. And what about the personal relationships in the band?
Dave: Well, of course, there's a story. Richie got involved with a Canadian girl and ended up marrying her. Jeff ended up with her at some point. I remember it because Richie wrote a tune for the date he discovered them together called "October 10th," which we subsequently recorded on the duo record *Forgotten Fantasies*. Obviously, this put a certain "freeze" in the band.

This ends up being another nice Miles story too: Somewhere in the first year after I started the band, I went to visit him. Nothing special, just to check in with the chief. I rang the bell—he asked who it was, and he rang the buzzer. I walked up to the top of the stairs and he was just standing there. Out of nowhere, he gave me a quick right jab to the stomach. This is deep because it is something I bring up in relation to saxophone breathing, concerning having a strong center in your lower abdominal area. It's kind of an indicator of what kind of shape you are in physically and mentally—you know, yoga stuff, having a spiritual core and all that. So, he was checking me out. Then he looked at me and said, "I can tell you like being a bandleader." I said, "Miles, I've got a problem. The drummer is sleeping with the piano player's old lady, and it's going to poison the band." He said, "Herbie and Tony used to do it all the time. Don't do nothing."

Lew: He means, it's their problem.
Dave: What could I do anyway? The band went on with a weird feeling for awhile. Amazingly, after this, Jeff ended up being with this lady for a period. She was a nice girl—a little mysterious, but to be with jazz musicians a woman had to be a bit different. Richie's tune "Dark Lady" is for her, from the *Sweet Hands* recording. And "October 10th" is one of Richie's best tunes. He writes so many great tunes. This one has wonderful changes. You know, Lewis, when a tune has what we call great changes, it means that melodies just flow more easily. In fact, the tune is analyzed in the *Lookout Farm* book. I notated every nuance I played on the melody—how many vibrato shakes, when I slid in between notes, etc. It was an absolute in-depth analysis of expressive devices and nuances.

Lew: Why did Lookout Farm break up?
Dave: I got greedy and my ego took over. This was crossover heaven—'74, '75, '76. All kinds of cats were making fusion-like records and getting across big time. Some of the music was cool, but a lot was not happening at all. Miles and his bandmembers started something, and it got out of control. That's really what happened. I was hearing guys who couldn't play half of what my peers and I could do, and the record companies were dumping money into them. I'm not talking about the good ones, obviously Weather Report or Herbie or Chick, who were jazz guys, and most of what they played was always high level. But there were other posers or imposters coming through, and Lookout Farm wasn't rock enough to truly cross over.

I mentioned in Chapter 6 that I met saxophonist Pee Wee Ellis when I was playing in Port Chester early in 1971. We really got along well, and Eleana got on with Pee Wee's wife, Barbara, as well. They were living in the Bronx and we spent a lot of time hanging out there. They had a son named Junior, who was great. From that time, I had in my mind that it would be great to play with Pee Wee, because our styles could truly be complementary and very interesting to hear together. He had toured with James Brown from '65 to '69, writing or co-writing "Cold Sweat," among others. He was a great musician with a soulful style, kind of R&B meets jazz, Stanley Turrentine-like in a way. He also could arrange very well. Some of the rare studio dates I did were in '71 for Pee Wee, when he was arranging for the singer Esther Phillips. Later on he got known playing and arranging for the singer Van Morrison. In my mind, I was hearing what could be a good yin and yang, me with the Coltrane stuff, Pee Wee with the blues, etc. The opportunity presented itself in 1976, and I ended Lookout Farm in the spring of that year.

I think I was feeling like I really wanted to try and make it big. Somehow I found an investor who, if I remember right, was a sports lawyer and had something to do with the New York Knicks. In those days, there was a lot of money being thrown into record companies, with the tax write-off situation being popular then, which is probably what A&M did with the Horizon line in the end. A woman named Linda, in whose apartment we did the Lookout Farm interview tapes for the book, somehow connected me up with this lawyer. I don't remember his name. We had a meeting and he checked me out. He told me that he talked to the *Tonight Show*'s trumpeter and bandleader, Doc Severinsen, about me, who somehow gave his okay. I didn't know Doc personally, but the grapevine was smaller in those days, hence guys knew about other guys by word of mouth. In any case, I was perceived as hot and happening. The lawyer said, "I'll support whatever you want to do." I said, "Okay, but I cannot do this band in New York."

By now, I was really up to my head with New York. Those years with Elvin, Miles, and Lookout Farm—I'm talking about a five-, six-year period. I was burned out. I had moved already a few times in Manhattan and to Greenwich, Connecticut, and then in I think '74, back to Manhattan, near Gramercy Park. My relationship with Eleana was completely a drag by then. I was overindulging, just really wasn't taking care of myself, and needed a break from the Apple. Here it was, an offer I couldn't refuse. Also, I didn't want to do a fusion band in front of everybody. I couldn't get up and change so drastically from Lookout Farm to playing unabashed funky stuff.

Lew: So, you wanted to do it, but you were looking at it as a bit of a sell-out kind of thing?

Dave: I was a bit torn, but I also knew this was a chance because of the investor, because of what was happening on the scene, and because I was coming off of such a prestigious position. Artistically I figured Pee Wee and I would be great, because nobody was blowing like we blew. It was going to be real soloing—this was not going to be gloss, surface playing. I was going to do my crazy Coltrane lines while Pee Wee would play the real blues stuff that he did, and we were going to have good tunes. We were not going to have a chick singer in front just to be sexy. We were going to do this in a musical way. So, if you mean selling out in the sense that I wanted to get to the next level, so be it.

Another thing that was really in my mind was about San Francisco. The first time I went to San Francisco, which must've been with Elvin, I absolutely fell in love with it, like everybody does, and decided I had to live there sometime. Somehow I pulled it off, and in 1976, Pee Wee, Barbara, Junior, and I moved out to a houseboat near Sausalito, California. The drummer, Jimmy Strassburg, who had also been in the Sawbuck and Gotham bands, lived there and had been playing with Sly Stone for the past several years. He had a bass player, Tony Saunders, who was the son of Merle Saunders, a West Coast blues icon; and a young guitarist, Chris Hayes, who by chance went on a few years later to become the chief guitar/composer for Huey Lewis and the News. This was his first gig.

We had a secretary, a manager, a road cat, a band, and an office in San Francisco, with checks every week, paying salaries! This was the rock-and-roll dream—unbelievable. We started writing, rehearsing, gigging while I was still with A&M. I told John Snyder at Horizon that following up the last record, which was the esoteric duo with Richie, we should record this band. You can imagine his response: "Oh, they will be very happy about that," meaning A&M. We recorded two sessions, and half of the LP was from sessions in San Francisco recorded in May '76 with the Ellis-Liebman Band. The other half was from sessions that I went back to New York to make in September 1976, with Al Foster, bassist Jeff Berlin, guitarist Linc Chamberland, who had been with me in Sawbuck, and even Richie on a track or two. The record just has my name on the cover, and the title, *Light'n Up, Please!*, with a photo of Eleana and me hanging out of a car trunk in San Francisco's Chinatown. I have Leon Thomas on it, who was an amigo of Pee Wee, singing "Got to Work" and "Children of The Ghetto," which is augmented by a bunch of kids off the street from Harlem or somewhere in the city. Eleana pulled that together in New York somehow. "The Chicken" is Pee Wee's, which Jaco Pastorius loved to play. We did a version of it on the

LP called "Chicken Soup," where I added a vamp. We had a tune called "The Fonz's Strut." I loved *Happy Days* and the Fonz. We had a tune by Harold Williams, who played keyboard for the *On the Corner* date—Tranquility of the Protective Aura," a beautiful tune. There was one called "Exquisite Torture"—about my relationship with Eleana—using polychords on the guitar. It's a funky record and there's some great stuff on it. At gigs we also played "Cold Sweat" and "Mother Popcorn."

Sure enough, when the LP came out, I think in early 1977, A&M put me on a promotion tour, only interviews, no playing, in ten cities across America—those were the days! Atlanta, Houston, Detroit, New York—I stayed at the Essex House—San Francisco, L.A., Chicago, etc. A limo met me at the airport in each city with the company rep, because in those days there were sales reps and promo people all over the place for record companies. These guys had no idea who the hell I was. They just knew to take me to some interviews and get me whatever I wanted, if you know what I mean. I was like a rock star! Finally, by the third city, I got the point: "What are we doing? Is there a jam session around or anything to do?" The rep who was with me said, "Oh, I don't know. What's jazz?" These cats had no idea. Anyway, A&M released a single, and it sold pretty quickly. Somehow it got on the charts in Indianapolis or wherever and I think the LP sold ten to twelve thousand copies pretty fast—and then never sold another one again!

Meanwhile in six months or more on the West Coast, the Ellis-Liebman Band managed to spend about forty to fifty thousand dollars of this lawyer's bread for salaries and the like. The guy was in New York sending weekly checks, investing in the band. We even had matchbooks that said "Light'n Up, Please!" and had a picture of Pee Wee and me smoking. You can see that on my website's photo galleries. We recorded some tracks at George Benson's house in New Jersey. He had a studio in his garage and Pee Wee knew him.

We made it to L.A. and played the Troubadour on Sunset Strip. Stevie Wonder sat in with us on drums that night! I don't know how Stevie came in, but I guess he knew Jimmy because of Sly, or Pee Wee because of James, or me because of Miles. I'm not sure. Stevie was on the side of the stage and next thing I know he walks on and sits down at the drum set, feels them with his hands and says, "Let's go!" We had an arrangement of "Tequila" and he played the hell out of it. He absolutely burned. It was fantastic.

But that was the end of the band! It was the last gig the band had because the investor finally and rightfully pulled the plug. He wrote it off and we never heard from him again. That was it! Nothing happened. No gigs, no nothing. We weren't the next Weather Report or whomever. We were working California, but not much else. We disbanded.

We really tried. We didn't just squander the cat's bread. I really loved Pee Wee and I loved what we were doing and was into it. It was a real macho band. We were really strutting our shit. We were playing really raw and it was certainly over the top, which a lot of stuff was then. But the truth is, just like most fusion bands, we weren't this or that. We weren't a real pop band and we were not a jazz band. We were a little too wild for a pop band, but we were not deep enough for a jazz band because the beat was not a jazz beat, it was coming from funk and rock. The record was eclectic to a fault and had no legs. By the way, no one in New York ever heard of the Ellis/Liebman band. This band is, even to this day, like a state secret. Well, I saw how the other half lived for a minute—what a time!

So there I was, stuck in San Francisco with no plan. I started a group with all young guys: Mark Isham on trumpet, Mike Formanek on bass, and Mike Barsimento on drums. This was kind of my "loft" band, playing intense jazz and working small clubs and lofts in the area. It was a lot of fun. These guys, as you know, have gone on since in the business. I called the group informally the 3M Quartet because of their names—Mark, Mike, Mike. The group is on part of a record of mine called *The Last Call*. There is some confusion about this album in the discographies. It includes a few duets I recorded in Cleveland with Jeff Williams in '75 or '76, when we were touring with Lookout Farm. The rest of the LP is with the 3M group, from I assume 1977. I later sold it to a German label and they put it out, and some reference works say that it was recorded in Germany in 1976—that's totally wrong!

And I hooked up with the established Frisco jazz cats—trumpeter Eddie Henderson, drummer Mike Clark, bassist James Leary, trombonist Julian Priester, and on piano, Mark Levine—not a bad crew! Eddie used to sit in with Lookout Farm at the Keystone Korner, so we knew each other. I worked the next six months with Eddie in the Bay Area. We even did a small East Coast tour, including Buffalo, late in '77. It was a great band, but no one came to the steady gig we had—I think the club was called Christos. San Francisco wasn't really a hotbed of jazz at this time. It was frustrating and eventually, in spite of the great lifestyle, the lethargy drove me out of there.

The bottom line was that I knew I had enough after another six months. I had been there more than a year. The Ellis band had already died six months prior. This thing with Eddie Henderson was what it was, and the same with the young quartet, but it wasn't a life. And in the meantime, Eleana came and went, but it was ending. I missed New York. It was time to get back. I started again with Richie, talking, and over this period playing a few duo gigs. When I ended Lookout Farm, Richie went with John Abecrombie's quartet after doing some trio dates and a recording for ECM under his own leadership.

Then fate intervened in January 1978, when I got that call from Chick Corea to join for a world tour, which we discussed in Chapter 6. The money and opportunity meant I could cut San Francisco loose and get back to the Apple. Upon returning to New York, I finally ended my relationship with Eleana. I decided to start my next project, which was the Dave Liebman Group with John Scofield and Terumasa Hino. Within a short time, I got married to Dina, thus starting the next part of my life. This was basically 1978 and brings us to the recording *Pendulum* and the group Quest.

Chapter 9

Passages: The Ups and Downs

Lew: So you went on tour with Chick Corea from mid-April 1978 through early June, and then you were back in Manhattan again.
Dave: Yes. I'd found another loft, at 800 6th Avenue near 28th Street. It was a big space and pretty bare bones—basically one gigantic room. Today that address is a high-rise apartment building. My goal was to put together a new band. You know, "Lieb comes home"—the return of the prodigal son, and all that. Returning to New York, I wanted to form a band that was going to be different from what I had with Lookout Farm. I didn't want to go back at that point with Richie, who was involved with John Abercrombie's group at the time. I wanted to have a band that would have more single-line playing with less harmony and more power, through the electric guitar.

Guitarist John Scofield was relatively new. He wasn't unknown—he'd already toured and recorded with Billy Cobham and others—but he was in New York and was a fan of the whole Liebman/Grossman style, which by now already had a place historically in the jazz community. Around that time he lived in Westbeth, an artist's complex on the lower West Side where Gil Evans also lived. John and I met and maybe even jammed together at one point. He said that he listened to horn players, no guitars, and wanted to play like a saxophone. This is a common, but sophisticated concept of looking at your own instrument—how to come up with something different by trying to graft techniques from another, quite possibly distant instrument. I understood this, because in some ways I was trying to get some of Miles's trumpet stuff on the soprano.

Then there was the Japanese trumpet player, Terumasa Hino, whom I knew for ten years already because he was always visiting New York back in the early loft days and played a lot with me over the years. He would come once a year, often with his brother, who was a great drummer, Motohiko or “Toko,” and they would hang—the first wave of Japanese guys to come to New York. He was a star in Japan, but by now he was living in New York. I always loved his playing. And he and John had already worked together.

At first, the drummer I chose was Bob Moses. I figured this would be a chance to have my oldest mate in a group with organized music and a real presentation. For the bass I wanted Michael Formanek, who was in the 3M San Francisco group. He was a promising musician who wanted to get to New York, so I invited him, figuring an unknown young cat would be interesting and would be able to give me a commitment.

We started rehearsing. I wrote some music specifically for these guys and instruments. One tune was called “Move On Some,” another called “Doin’ It Again” for being back in the Apple, etc. These were all little letters to myself, which a lot of my tunes are. We rehearsed intensely for a week, getting ready to open at the club Sweet Basil, I think in September ’78. This was my return to New York, so everyone who knew me from my time with Miles, Elvin, and Lookout Farm was going to be there. I had cut quite a swath in the seventies in the city. Sunday night, before we were supposed to open the following Tuesday, Moses called me after rehearsal and said, “I don’t like the music, and I don’t like the bass player, and I’m not playing.” I can laugh now, but boy, I’ll tell you . . .

Lew: What were his reasons?
Dave: Moses is a kind of contrarian, or DA-type personality, meaning devil’s advocate. You say blue, he will say yellow. He’s since calmed down a bit, but he has a mercurial personality—temperamental and very picky, very choosy. He never liked playing with Richie, for example. He was very opinionated. I had a lot of respect for him because he was my first peer mentor, and in a way he brought me into the jazz scene. And he was experienced; he had played with everybody by that time. But he was a little off center in some ways and obviously couldn’t be counted on. Look, this was Sunday night and my big opening with a new band of basically unknown guys, combined with returning to New York, was in two nights. Hardly anyone knew Scofield. Nobody had ever heard Mike Formanek.

Lew: So, there was no talking with Bob to get him back?
Dave: I don’t remember the exact conversation, but he was emphatic.

The music was certainly more complicated than Lookout Farm or Open Sky. I mean, I really wrote! That was one of the reasons why I did this project. I wanted to write more intricate things. There were more interludes, unison parts, things like that, especially after being with Chick and hearing his very tightly organized music on a nightly basis. Lookout Farm was very improvised, as Quest became later on, because that's what Richie liked to do. But I wanted to write. I wanted to get the texture of the guitar and the trumpet and the sax; I was still playing flute, tenor, and soprano then, so I was after a lot of color and ambiance—all that stuff. Well, ace in the hole—I called Adam Nussbaum.

Adam had been around me way back to the Richard's Lounge days in the late sixties and early seventies when I played there a lot with Richie and Frank Tusa. It was a great little joint in Lakewood, New Jersey. Richard was a drummer and a kind of guru for everyone who knew him—a beautiful man. Adam was also often around when I was with Elvin and Lookout Farm. That coveted seat at the Village Vanguard to the left of the drums on the red couch—that was the drummer's seat. There was Adam copping that seat early in the evening when I was with Elvin, and then later on with Lookout Farm. I think he might have even sat in with Lookout Farm. He was fifteen, sixteen, maybe seventeen years old in those years.

So I called him that Sunday night: "Okay, here's your chance. I'm in a hole, opening Tuesday night, and I need you." He was in Norwalk, Connecticut, with his parents. "Come down now. We'll spend all night. I'm going to teach you the arrangements." The next day, I played everything for him on the horns and piano and we opened Tuesday night. That was the beginning of the Dave Liebman Quintet. Within the first few months, Formanek didn't work out or wanted to do something else—I forget. In any case, I went to Ron McClure, who was already one of the established guys and could play anything—a kind of Gomez vibe—extremely talented, versatile bass player who would bring some weight to the band, which I could use. Ron had played with everyone from Miles to Charles Lloyd to Monk and in the 19th Street loft as well. I had Hino, who was a heavy player, but was relatively a newcomer to the scene in a way; Scofield was basically a young cat, and Adam was even younger.

So, that became my band for the next few years. Adam was great. That was the beginning of our relationship, which is still active. He is a real jazz fanatic. He'll tell you everything about a recorded track from the time the track was recorded to how many takes, to what the weather was like when they did track #3 of "Bessie's Blues" or something like that. He's a great guy, and one of the most swinging drummers ever. He comes out of Elvin, which is right up my line. He was different from Jeff Williams with Lookout Farm, who was coming out of DeJohnette. It felt like a glove that fit my hand.

Hino was fantastic and lit up the audience. He had incredible fire and stamina, and a Japanese samurai intensity. McClure is the consummate professional. He brought tunes in for us to play—an excellent composer. And Scofield was having a great time, one reason being that he was the only chord instrument. In the back of his mind, he wanted to be Richie, 'cause everybody wanted to be Richie then. With those chords, Richie in the seventies was *the* New York guy, harmonically. Look, you had Herbie Hancock, Chick, and McCoy—the great triumvirate—and Keith Jarrett. But here comes Richie with those kinds of voicings, and people wanted to know what it was. Of course, the guitar isn't a piano, and this led to pretty intense discussions between John and myself: "Excuse me, only four fingers, maybe five. Let's not try to be a piano here, John." But everything worked out, and I really enjoyed that band.

Stylistically, I can't say fusion, but we did play eighth-note-type music at times. There was a sense of an electric feel because of the guitar with its inherent power, but also beautiful ballads and straight-ahead jazz—basically a lot of writing from everybody in the band. It went on for a couple of years until 1981 or so, and then eventually my relationship with Richie started back again. We made two records on the Dutch label Timeless: *Doin' It Again* in New York, August '79 and, in Holland, July 1980, *If They Only Knew*—the latter title referring to critics—a little message. Eventually Hino started getting busy with his own tours in Japan in about 1979 or 1980, some of which I did with him. That music was real fusionish, kind of smooth-jazz-type stuff, but well done. Gerry Brown was the drummer, Chuck Rainey bass, Leon Pendarvis keyboards, Janice Pendarvis singing, people like that.

When Hino got busy, I got pianist Kenny Kirkland, who was very good friends with Adam—I think they were sharing a loft together. He came on for about six months to a year with the band, which was very special. He was playing instead of Hino, so we had piano and guitar, the "dreaded" harmonic combination! We didn't record with him, but I have tapes. The one time I did record with KK was the record called *What It Is,* which I did for Japanese Sony—a fusion-style recording with Scofield, Don Alias, Marcus Miller, Mike Mainieri, Steve Gadd, and Kenny—in 1979.

Lew: Kenny died in 1998, when he was only forty-three, and it was reported as being due to a drug overdose.

Dave: Tragic. He was the hot guy then. Kenny was the most beautiful cat—a great guy and killer musician, and loved by everybody. This was before he toured with the Marsalis brothers, which of course raised his profile later on. He was just a New York young cat whom everybody dug. So I got him at the beginning. We had a really great relationship. He loved playing with Adam and me.

During this same time period I did other things as well. In February 1978, just when I was getting the band with Scofield going for real, I did a one-time gig recorded live at the Village Vanguard titled *Pendulum*, with Richie; Frank Tusa from Lookout Farm; Al Foster, who would become the first drummer with Richie and me when we reunited as Quest in a few years; and Randy Brecker. We played standards and it absolutely burned. The label Artist's House put out the LP, but now there's a boxed set of three CDs that has two nights of tunes. It was sort of the beginning of Quest with Al, Richie, and me.

Then Richie and I started getting together again with this Pendulum/Vanguard date and did some duo gigs here and there. We made our second duo album, *Omerta*, in June '78, after my tour with Chick. We started playing with Al Foster, and after Frank eventually moved to California, where he still lives, George Mraz became the bass player. He had been with Richie in the Abercrombie group—one of the all-time great bassists. Mraz is a giant. He's probably one of the greatest bassists who ever played. He could do anything and everything. He's a be-bopper in the end, but can be very flexible. Quest was playing pretty open music, but George loved it because it was a chance for him to do something different than his usual. And he loved Richie. Of course, Al loved George. All drummers love George. George is one of *the* choices for drummers. They loved his beat; they loved everything about him. He's like a drummer's dream. Kind of like how drummers feel about Ron Carter. Cats just loved having him.

Al was an extension of Elvin in some ways. The thing about Al was that if Richie played a rhythmic figure on the piano, he would hear it and give it back to you in one way or the other, all grown up, so to say. So, Richie was in heaven with Al, because Richie is truly a rhythmic player, and Al would just immediately seize the moment. This rhythm section was amazing with Mraz, heard on the first recording called *Quest,* in December 1981. If there was ever a time that I felt like I was Miles or Wayne, having Herbie, Ron, and Tony in the rhythm section, this was it! Here was a rhythm section that was absolutely on top of each other. For the first time in my life, I knew what it felt like not to have to think about what you were playing and with whom. By now, Richie and I had had a long relationship and I completely trusted his ability to lead the rhythm section, to take care of business, that it's going to be fine whatever it is. I could really just think about what I was playing.

Quest was booked for a major Japanese tour, with that first record to be released by a Japanese company. Al, who had been on salary for all these years with Miles, even when Miles was not working, told us that everything was cool and he would do our tour. This was important because Quest was four names, not the Dave Liebman Group or anything like that, so Al was an integral part of, let's say, the box office draw, whatever that is in jazz. Lo and behold, Bonnie Steinberg, the sister of Eleana, whom I was with in the seventies, was beginning to get close to Al and called me to say that Miles didn't want him leaving: "Al can't do it. Miles won't let him do it." In '81, Miles was touring again, after his five-year hiatus. This really pissed me off—not about Miles, but because Al didn't have the decency to call me, man to man, directly. That's something I just don't dig.

Anyway, it was six weeks till the tour, which must have been in early '82. I called the promoter, who naturally flipped out because in Japan everything is names. To Richie: "What are we going to do? We are in trouble here. We are going to lose this tour." He said, "I don't know." Me: "Look, the only one around with some credibility is Billy Hart." I had done a couple of records with Billy, including *On the Corner*, though I'd never played with him "live" much. But he was a New York drummer with a great rep who had played most notably with Herbie and McCoy. Richie was a little concerned, but we had no choice. That's where the relationship with Billy Hart began. He took Al's place. Later, Eddie Gomez took George's place with Quest, and it all settled with Ron McClure on bass in 1984. Musical chairs were a common thing in New York—nothing unusual.

Lew: Now, during these years of working with Richie, what is this polychord concept that he developed? It has become a huge part of your own style.

Dave: Well, it emanated largely from Richie. When we first met in the late sixties and started Lookout Farm, Richie was a combination of McCoy, Herbie, and Chick, who were the main contemporary influences at the time. We are all combinations of our first influences. Chick was especially important because we were around him at the 19th Street loft, and particularly the way he played the Fender Rhodes electric piano with

Miles. We used a lot of Fender Rhodes in Lookout Farm and it definitely had a Chick thing about it, which was great.

Richie had a way of playing that was his, but it was more derivative—as mine was at that time. In the seventies he really worked hard on getting the contemporary twentieth-century classical language into his playing. He's the guy who really did that, by listening, looking at scores, and exploring voicings. After all, he had done some of this music as a classical student with his teacher in Brooklyn when he was a kid, though I'm not sure how much he got past Chopin and Beethoven, the main repertoire. But now he definitely got into Scriabin, Webern, Bartók, Schoenberg, and others whose names I didn't even know yet—Xenakis, Mompou, and more. He really took it apart.

Lew: Was there a classical guru he was working with?
Dave: No, not that I know of. Richie is a very analytical, disciplined cat when he wants to be, and he figured it out. He's a great example of what a young artist is supposed to do, which is to absorb your influences, reexamine them, learn what is "them" and what is "you," filter out what's them, enlarge what's you, and hopefully find your own voice. That's the valid, time-worn path. You don't just get bored with your influences and overnight become Mr. New Style. You work your way through, which he did. By the eighties, he had his language down; he knew what it was. He went completely back to the acoustic and never touched the electric piano again.

Other guys had this twentieth-century classical influence also. You couldn't be a modern piano player if you didn't have some of that language in your playing, next to bebop, of course. But Richie went ahead of McCoy, Chick, and Herbie in this respect. He was scientific and very disciplined, about the harmony in particular.

So what did I do? I looked over his shoulder literally and figuratively: "What's that voicing? Is that your third finger on an E? Thank you. Can I write that out? What is that sound? What do you call it?" We had already worked on the Lookout Farm book and enjoyed our relationship of analyzing music together. We were pals and hanging buddies who loved to talk and get into the intellectual thing about music. We liked to discover things. Lookout Farm was a special thing; it was young cats playing the language of the day. But now, we were with George Mraz and Al Foster, Billy Hart—real jazz credentials—the legacy was now in our face.

It became a matter of how we could make this into a sound using the influences of the Miles and Trane groups of the sixties, which were our sources and inspirations. That's what Quest became. Quest was an answer to the sixties question: What do you do next? Wynton Marsalis tried to answer that challenge also, but left it pretty soon after he had the band with his brother Branford, drummer Jeff Watts, and Kenny Kirkland. They were dealing more with the Miles stuff—the implications in that great music from the sixties, especially rhythmically.

You're a product of your time. You can't negate it. You're going to deal with what's around you when you're young and that's going to stay with you. You'll learn more, you'll expand, you'll observe, you'll leave things out hopefully, but you are basically tagged by your period of history, especially musically, which of course changes every five to ten years. We were still in love with that music. Not that the music in the seventies was not good or anything like that, but overall it was the sixties that attracted us. The point was, we were still enamored by acoustic jazz. We still felt there was room to extend the language of Miles, Herbie, Wayne, Ron, Tony, and Trane, Jimmy, McCoy, Elvin. There was a way through ourselves to play like that in our own manner. That's what Quest became.

Lew: Now that polychord concept—you mentioned about looking over his shoulder and asking questions, but did you and Richie ever sit down and actually go through it in a methodical way?
Dave: Well, not exactly like what I do now in class, teaching my chromatic book, for example, not "classroom" methodical-like. But did we analyze? Absolutely! We did it like we did in the seventies. We were still able to do that, meaning talk about the music. By the mid-eighties, we stopped talking about it and rarely have talked in that way since, for a variety of reasons, including that we had kind of exhausted it and our relationship changed a bit by then. For one thing, by then the band had a life of its own. We didn't have to talk much anymore. But in this formative period we were still into discovering what was before us, especially in the twentieth-century classical field. He would come in and say, "Lieb, look at this from Schoenberg. Listen to it."

When I talk about this learning period, there's no question that Richie was my guide. After all, he's a piano player. You don't play that music with a saxophone. It's piano music and I had a guy who knew it. I knew that there was nobody else I could get it from, and this was a big opportunity. I was going to really milk it for what I could. From the harmonic standpoint that's what Quest was about. I hung in there for ten years, into 1991, sometimes against my better judgment, because I felt there was more to learn.

My book on the subject (*A Chromatic Approach to Jazz Harmony and Melody*, 1991) is the result of this period of study and analysis. It was intended to be written by the both of us. We had grandiose plans about writing the book. He would write about the harmony and I would write on the melody, but then he copped a plea, and it never happened. But anyway, what you call the polychord concept, we call a chromatic approach. It's a way of getting outside of the stated harmony, especially when the harmony is modal, pedal point, or non-chordal as in "time, no changes." What do you do harmonically? Other musicians were either very interested or not in this language, but in most cases they were playing by ear or following their tail—whatever. We wanted to have something that we could work on that came out of that sixties language and had some logic and rationale about it.

Outside of the one-and-a-half-year break in California, I had a running relationship with Richie from 1969 to 1991, musically and socially. Then there was a fourteen-year break, and then back together since 2005. He has been my longest associate, for sure.

Lew: During that time period of Quest, you had other projects as well.
Dave: Let me fill in some spaces. The band with Scofield did not take off popularity-wise. We worked; we trudged around Europe, like I still do; we played the Vanguard and so on. I obviously had a certain amount of cachet by that time because of my tenure with Miles and Elvin. And although Lookout Farm never attained the success of Weather Report or Return to Forever, we were known by the musicians and in the trade. The California break with Pee Wee was kind of an unknown thing, though. Being back in New York with a young band of relatively unknown cats was something, but I couldn't get it going business-wise. I even had management with Theresa Del Pozzo, who was Bob Moses's wife at the time. She went into business with Maxine Gregg, who at the time was Woody Shaw's manager and wife and was also Dexter Gordon's manager—and later, after Woody died, Maxine became Dexter's wife.

For whatever reason, it wasn't happening. By 1980/81, I was getting pretty disillusioned. I had returned to New York, was *Doin' It Again*—that was the title tune of the first release of my band with Scofield—but getting frustrated. I had gotten married to this lady named Dina. We had first met a few years earlier, around 1975 in Chicago. I remember the night we met because I was with Richie playing duo at a club outside of Chicago in Evanston called Amazing Grace. This beautiful woman came down to the gig and introduced herself as Diana Janis, who was doing an exhibition and a book in which jazz musicians contributed something artistic but outside of their music, like poetry, paintings, etc. It was a bona fide thing. Bob Moses did a painting, Ron Carter did something, so it seemed credible. I wrote a poem or story, I forget. Richie wrote a poem. Anyway, we were invited to the Janis house for dinner and met the teenaged daughters, one of whom was Dina. Somehow the family ended up living in lower Manhattan about two years later, and invited me to dinner when I was in town for my A&M promotional tour in '77. After that, Dina and I would sometimes see each other when I was in New York. Finally, in the fall of 1979, we ended up getting married and living in that loft on 6th Avenue near 28th Street. In fact, we had the wedding party at the loft, with the ceremony at the United Nations chapel.

Lew: You can get married at the United Nations?
Dave: Yeah, with the idea of ecumenism as the theme. Dina was Catholic, but obviously neither of us was religious, so I liked the idea of doing it at the UN. Reverend John Gensel, the famous jazz pastor from St. Peter's Church on 54th and Lexington Avenue, did the ceremony. I remember him using the color blue, it being Duke Ellington's favorite color, signifying peace as the main theme of the service, something to that effect. Everybody who I knew at the time was at the party—of course, a lot of musicians. Dina was around twenty and I was in my early thirties. She was studying acting at the famous Actors Studio and was very serious about it, working as a waitress like they all do. She was a lovely girl—very pretty, very nice. Her mother, Diana, also was a piano player, while her father was somehow hooked up with Hugh Hefner and the Playboy Club in Chicago. The parents were not together for quite a while at this time. I think I remember meeting the father once. It was a kind of dysfunctional family, the absolute opposite of my family in that respect.

Our marriage was ill-fated for a variety of reasons. She was too young, and I was too crazy. I came back from a tour and out of the clear blue just asked her to marry me—real spontaneous. By 1981, the marriage was already falling apart, coinciding with my frustration as I thought about the rest of my life. I was thirty-four, thirty-five years old. I believe very strongly in the concept of passages in life—stages we all go through in one way or the other, and this was definitely one of those crucial times. You start to think, "Now what? Am I going to be playing the Village Vanguard the rest of my life? Is this all there is?"

I had already seen the top. I had traveled all over the world. My knowledge was good; my ego was intact. I looked deeply at myself and noted that I had certain non-musical capabilities that were not being put to use. I had already demonstrated something to myself, by organizing Free Life Communication in the early 1970s, concerning organizational and leadership abilities beyond the music. I could verbalize, and I had a lot of energy, which is one of my trademarks. I just couldn't see doing only this music thing for the rest of my life. So, this combination—a relationship that was failing, disenchantment with the music scene, capped off by getting hepatitis A and then breaking my bad leg pretty viciously—all happening around the same period, definitely put me in crisis mode.

What could I do that would have some real consequence? I have to think that some of this concern was traceable to my upbringing. This sounds like a sweeping generalization, but I think it is valid—that a major emphasis in the secular Jewish tradition is to do something for the world, to be of service. We're not the only ones into this. I'm not saying we own the concept, but I felt a thread of this thinking. I was educated and my job was to give back. The Kennedy clan had this sense of obligation that I am referring to, but mine was obviously different. It wasn't just that your parents wanted you to be successful so that you could make money and be comfortable; they wanted you to be a doctor or a lawyer to help people, or a teacher. This was in the DNA, it seemed, for me.

Lew: It's a strong Jewish value, the giving back part. People miss that point.

Dave: I know they do. They think it's all just becoming a doctor because you can make a good living doing that. It's about education and making a contribution. In that respect, I didn't think I was really doing my job. By thirty-five years old, I didn't know if I had already or would contribute something of lasting value to jazz, so that was off the table, in this conversation with myself. Look, I was not Coltrane or Mozart, and I had to admit it. On the other side, it seemed that I wasn't meeting my full potential. Becoming a doctor was now out of the question, a vestigial thought from my childhood.

I thought about law and started asking around. My first mentor drummer, Pete LaRoca, had become a lawyer, practicing by this time, so I had a definite model to check out. He discouraged me, saying that it was a lot dirtier than it appeared. I attended a trial or two downtown and in general researched the scene, talking to lawyers and so on. Everyone dissuaded me. They said, "You think you're going to save the world, Dave? Oh, you're going to get into constitutional law?" This was because I loved history and all of that. "You're going to talk about the Second Amendment or the Bill of Rights and defend a right to vote in Tennessee or something? Or, are you going to defend the criminal who you know is guilty?" Real encouragement! They said it was not all it was cracked up to be, that you had to compromise your principles.

Lew: That you had an idealistic view of what it was going to be like?
Dave: Of course. That's why I was thinking about it, because there was this need in me to find something that would contribute to the world, probably utilizing my organizational and speaking capabilities. I'm not an intellectual, but I can get by with those kinds of things, and I can read pretty well. So, I got my college and high school transcripts out and took the LSAT test. I did get into three schools. One was Yeshiva University, right across the street from the New School in Manhattan. I even went to an orientation meeting there, and even asked the guy some questions. I also got accepted into New York Law and another, I forget. By May 1, you had to put your deposit in. I went right up to the minute with a check for $500 burning a hole in my pocket for the down payment at Yeshiva. My mother said, "I'll support you for a while. I'll help you out if you want to do this, if this is a crisis of life and you want to do something positive." But when the deadline came, it was the reality of all that school you had to do, which was quite onerous to think about. If there was another way around that inescapable fact, I probably would have done it. Check it out—I could have been a lawyer, right now!

When the law thing was done with, I decided I wanted to do something for the world vis-á-vis the Peace Corps–type stuff. I went to the library and looked up every charity organization such as Save the Children, Red Cross, and groups like that. I went so far as meeting in Washington, D.C., with Save the Children, and eventually got to know an artist there who used to go to Haiti with his work; we still keep in touch. His name is Benedict Tisa. Anyway, the head lady said, "I'll be honest with you. You are in midlife and you've accomplished something. You went to school, and you seem like an articulate young man. But we need people to teach how to grow crops, make water available, etc. We don't really need what you do." After all, they didn't need music in the practical sense of priorities. It was not like I spoke several languages or knew how to engineer water holes. So, that was a dead end.

This crisis went on for a good six months to a year. I didn't talk about it much to anyone. But I was thinking that I've got to find a way out of this rut. I just can't see myself at the Village Vanguard—meaning the top of the jazz line—and that's all there is for the rest of my life. All of this came together in one of the lowest years of my life, 1982. I left New York, basically forever as my living space, broke my leg, got hepatitis A, went through a divorce, and didn't do the law thing. I didn't know a way out of this quandary of what to do with myself. But something did save me and eventually brought me out of it. I have to back up a little because this story starts somewhere around the end of 1976:

One day I received a call from Jamey Aebersold. We all know his voice from the many play-along records that he has produced over decades—that Midwest twang: "My name is Jamey Aebersold, and I would like you to come to a clinic in Hays, Kansas, at the beginning of January." I said, "What's a clinic?" I didn't know what the hell he was talking about. He explained to me: "You have to talk to the saxophone players and play a set." I said, "With who?" "Bassist Rufus Reid and a drummer named Ed Soph." I didn't know Jamey at all and I was going to India with my mother during Christmas, right before the scheduled clinic.

In any case I got to Hays, Kansas, a day or so after getting back to the States from India. It was minus degrees, snowing and freezing. I talked saxophone to those students, which I don't think I had ever done before in a group meeting like that. I did the planned concert with Rufus Reid and Ed Soph, both of whom I ended up playing with quite a bit over the ensuing years—great musicians and teachers. As a sidebar, I got sick as a dog the night after the performance, getting ready to go home the next day. I don't know what happened, except it was intense stomach pain, terrible gas in the middle of the night, so they took me to the emergency room where it just cooled down. But it wasn't a disease or anything. Having just got back from India, crossing from one side of the world to another, especially in those days, was not easy.

Anyway, lo and behold, there were a bunch of kids sitting in a hall, waiting for me to talk. This was my first view of jazz education. I had never seen anything like this. I didn't know it existed. I had no idea who Jamey Aebersold was. After all, there was still no real organized jazz teaching in New York, at least that I knew of. As we've discussed, I had studied with Charles Lloyd and Tristano, but I wouldn't call that organized on an academic level. Schools? I knew about Berklee in Boston, but that was about it. So, here I was with the three guys known as the A, B, C's of jazz education: Jamey Aebersold, David Baker, and Jerry Coker. Jamey offered me some clinics during the summer, which he still conducts to this day. That's when the whole education thing really hit me. So, I did a couple of weeks that summer.

I never saw anything like those guys teach. You went from nine to six; you had dinner; then you played at night; and the same the next day, for five days. There were harmony, combos, and instrumental master classes. We're talking thirty-five to forty-five combos with ages ranging from twelve years old to mature adults, from complete beginners to some decent players. At night, the teachers played concerts. On Friday, the kids played from one in the afternoon to nine at night. Everybody played ten minutes. It went on forever, combo by combo. Jamey was a real personality, something really unique. They're all incredible teachers, and of course there is the hang with all the cats, a real crew of educators whom I got to know well, such as trombonist John Leisenring, Ed Soph, Pat Harbison, Ken Sloane, Dan Haerle, and others.

Now, I'm Dave Liebman, Mr. Ex–Miles Davis star, prototype New York hip jazz musician, blah, blah, blah. I knew nothing compared to these cats, at least for jazz up to 1960. They had codified everything and could explain it. They knew every chord, every tune, and every scale backward and forward. They could hear a pin drop and tell you what ii-V it was. Friday morning would be when Coker or on a few occasions trumpeter Tom Harrell, or eventually myself, would play the "Scale Syllabus" live for all the participants. Friday at ten in the morning! Jamey would start to comp chords and you had to improvise on the right scale and make music. I saw Harrell do the blues in twelve keys, one chorus after another. I saw Coker doing the scale syllabus completely by ear. I was taken aback. I never saw such teaching, and definitely not so well organized. This was a secret that I didn't know about, and it was happening at these clinics all over the country. What a revelation. I didn't know what they knew. No, because I had never gone to school for jazz. It had never been organized for me.

Lew: That kind of breaking it down and being able to spell it out?
Dave: From A to Z. Jerry Coker's book *Improvising Jazz*—it was and maybe still is the best-selling book of all time for jazz education, translated into fifteen or twenty languages. That little hundred-plus-page book—ii-V-I, side-slipping, tri-tone relationship, symmetrical diminished scale, etc.—some new expressions there. Jerry is the master of this stuff. He's on top of the food chain, the main guy. He taught Baker, and from Baker comes Jamey. He's the main cat. Plus, Jerry can play, kind of like old Trane. He is great and a perfect musician. Baker played cello, and Jamey could really play saxophone as well, kind of a Sonny Stitt type. Jamey also played piano and bass and knew every tune in the world. These guys were indefatigable, unstoppable when they taught. They made me look slow! They would teach, crack jokes, have the kids entertained, and at the same time were really giving them information. In David Baker's classes everybody was singing and laughing. They were

scatting "Groovin' High," singing backwards and forwards and moving at meteorite speed. It was unbelievable.

So, I was impressed and depressed at the same time. Two to three hundred people sitting there learning—from twelve years old on up. At sixty-five years old, they'd come back and learn with their kids. It still goes on now. So, the light went on. I saw my way to find something of value to do with my life, because the truth is that I'm a good teacher and I wasn't really doing it. I had had a couple of students here and there, like any musician, but I hadn't really taught. I certainly hadn't written it down, except for the Lookout Farm book, which was mainly done by interviews. With my natural organizational nitpicky personality, wanting to verbalize everything and understand it—a veritable note taker—I was perfectly suited for this jazz education thing.

So, a few years later, I finally realized that getting deeper into teaching was the answer for me, and that brought sort of an end to, shall I say, my mini-midlife crisis with law school and the international aid organizations, those balloons that I had floated around. The thing with education is that you're doing a service *and* you're making a living.

In 1980, 1981, Aebersold took the whole contingent overseas to Australia and to Europe. I met the Grubers, who owned Advance Music in Rottenburg, Germany. They hosted the Aebersold camp a few times, and after being distributors of jazz books, they went into publishing themselves, with a book of my compositions as one of their first projects, and many since. By 1983/84, I was offered the first big leap in upping the education ante, with Dave Holland, who became the head of the jazz program at the Banff Institute in Western Canada, inviting me to teach during the summer. This was much better pay than Jamey's clinics, and most important, at a much higher skill level of students.

Look. You've got to make a living. I was thirty-five years old. Jazz was not the biggest money maker in the world. So, what were the options? One possibility at that time was still studio work, which I had basically turned down when I didn't accept Joe Farrell's offer to play at the Plaza Hotel back in the early 1970s, when I was beginning with Elvin. I had already taught in the public schools, which by then was a disaster zone, especially in New York. This jazz education thing fulfilled a way to make extra money because, remember, this was really the beginning of widespread jazz education, and with it the musical scenario that you could teach in the afternoon and play at night. It fulfilled something in me that was missing. I took the ball and ran with it. After all, spreading the jazz ethos was for sure a positive thing, no matter the practical results of who ended up actually being a jazz player. We are messengers from another world and this is good, period. It saved me in the end.

Lew: So you got more deeply involved with Aebersold and his team. Tell us more about them.
Dave: David Baker was voted best trombonist in the New Star *Downbeat* poll at some point and then had an auto accident and hurt his chops, which meant he couldn't play bone anymore, so he found the cello and composition. Besides his personal teaching over the years at the University of Indiana and Aebersold camps, his books have made a major contribution. He wrote sixty, seventy, or eighty books covering the bebop language. Especially powerful was his monograph series, which was very instructional to me concerning how to use a transcription for my own advancement, not just as a tool for learning what came before. All these books I think were done by hand. This is the 1960s and '70s after all. He was *the* book guy along with Coker, and then Jamey for the play-alongs.

Lew: Jamey, as you said, is quite a personality?
Dave: Very special. I know that for a while he did Sunday sermons at a local church. It seems he was deep into Edward Cayce and at the same time one of the Yogi masters. Do not curse around Jamey! From what I have observed, he is absolutely straight as an arrow, peanut butter and jelly sandwiches, no alcohol, and works twenty-five hours a day, building an empire as he did. He is dedicated beyond belief, a great teacher and a great organizer. In fact, I just did my newsletter, which I always do at the beginning of every other month, and wrote about him as he turned seventy, in July 2009. We had our scenes to be sure. We couldn't be more opposite in some ways—New York meets the Midwest ethic. Look, I was one of the most well-known musicians on the staff. When I say staff, this is twenty, thirty, forty guys. It was like a traveling road show of teachers bringing jazz out to the sticks. They never saw that before in Australia or Germany.

Lew: Most of the regular staff—not including famous guest artists of course—were better known as teachers, not as performers like you.
Dave: Teachers, by and large, but they could all play. A lot of them, of course, were connected to the ABC boys. By then, it was starting to be more consistent that teachers could play well as well as teach. But I was kind of a star, and in a way I took it upon myself to represent the cats, not in a formal sense, but as far as commenting to Jamey about things that were not right in my mind and could be perceived as condescend-

ing—things pertaining to pay and basic interaction. One scene was very interesting and actually I learned a lesson through it.

I mentioned these Friday marathon afternoon concerts where every combo had to play their eight to ten minutes— I'm talking thirty or forty groups. Teachers had to be there from one in the afternoon through the evening in support, just waiting for your students' combo, and then to get going home in most cases, since this was the official end of the week. So, by then you definitely had had enough of bad playing. Being that I had among the top combos as far as level was concerned, my group would be near last, so I'm talking around 8:00 p.m. I had to sit there for about six hours. Some of these combos could not play at all. They were called, off the cuff of course, the Alligator Combos. They were playing with play-alongs, not even live rhythm sections, because their level was so basic.

Lew: Why did you call them Alligators?
Dave: They were slow, real slow. Nothing personal—just beginners. One day I said, "Jamey, it's ridiculous. They cannot play. Why do we have to endure this nightmare torture of these hours of listening to this completely nonmusical stuff just to get a kid up there?" He answered, "Liebman," with that way he had of speaking, which was not particularly full of warmth, "You never know when one of those kids will tell his grandson that he played in front of Dave Liebman." Dig it—he put me right in my place. And I'll tell you, if a cat puts me in my place, I am all for it. To paraphrase, "You don't even know the significance of what's going on here. You're just being selfish. You're worried about sitting around for six hours. You're not looking at it from that kid's standpoint. That twelve-year-old or fifteen-year-old has been working all week in Ensemble #89 to play 'Blues in B♭,' or I-vi-ii-V, and that's a big deal for him. It's not up to you to minimize it. How dare you do that on my watch. Plus it's your job!" He was right, and I learned something.

We still have a very good working relationship, and in a way I'm the David Baker of our time, with a million books out published by Aebersold and Advance Music. But check it out: Jamey is over seventy years old as we speak, and as I said in my newsletter, this is the guy who deserves the Medal of Freedom for contribution to American culture. You know why? There is nowhere you go on this planet where if there is any interest in playing a saxophone or another "jazz" instrument, you will not see a Jamey Aebersold play-along. I don't care where you go—if there's a horn especially, there's a Jamey Aebersold record. Remember, these records include the likes of Kenny Barron playing piano, Ron Carter on bass, and maybe Al Foster on drums, to name one all-star lineup.

Not a bad rhythm section to play along with in your living room in Jakarta or wherever you are. That guy has contributed a lot to culture. He's like Willis Conover doing the *Voice of America* on international radio. That's a contribution.

Lew: His weren't the first play-alongs.
Dave: No. MMO, Music Minus One, which I still have in my studio.

Lew: But they just had a few things—they didn't have a whole series.
Dave: Exactly. It was great, with Ed Shaughnessy and Barry Galbraith, etc. They also had Music Minus One Classical—a Vivaldi flute concerto, whatever. But it wasn't a series, and it wasn't organized. With Jamey, it's completely together, first of all, from the theory to every chord and scale. By now he has a volume for everyone from Bird to your grandmother. Everybody's got their own volume of tunes. Wait, there will be a Lewis Porter volume—you'll get one. It's up to a hundred and thirty-five or so recordings now.

But again, it's not just the play-alongs that Jamey has contributed, or the clinics, which are presently down to two sessions, each with several hundred participants, at the University of Louisville, near where he lives. It's his organizational abilities applied to the jazz literature. He organized the pedagogy—not that he wrote the books—it's that he organized the materials. He had a brochure that went out to thousands of people. This is before the Internet. You went to his catalogue under whatever topic and you could get what you needed. Nowadays, the argument for or against jazz textbooks is a pedagogical discussion. Do we need more, etc.? But man, in 1985, if you wanted to see a transcription of Coltrane, Jamey had it. If you wanted to see voicings for non-piano players, he had it. This is the point. He runs a successful business, and I give him a lot of credit.

Lew: Speaking of Jamey, he can be funny, too.
Dave: Oh, he's hilarious!

Lew: He has a dry Midwest sense of humor. Like if you say, "I'll see you later," he might say, "Not if I see you first!"
Dave: Not only that—he has kids laughing. He is up there with the projector machine cracking jokes, one after another. It's a comedy show, but with information. That's what I'm saying about the way these guys teach. Jerry was very soft spoken. Baker, very energetic, making everybody participate. Three different styles, three incredible teachers. Dan

Haerle, too. Incredible teachers who took care of the basics. Let's put it this way—they formalized the music from 1945 to 1960. You didn't get Dixieland or Louis Armstrong, and you definitely didn't get anything after "Giant Steps." But if you wanted to go from "Koko" to "Giant Steps," these guys gave you A to Z on how to do it. You walked out of there with the map laid out. Teaching creativity is the perpetual discussion about the value of teaching any art form, and we can go into that for hours. But information—these guys gave it to you logically and in order. You do this, you'll get that result. It was organized, it was entertaining, and it truly put jazz education on the map.

Jamey and his descendants—legions of students and teachers who are populating the schools, especially in America—this is the reason we are sitting here. It's the truth. I give him almost single-handed credit. To be fair, the Berklee College of Music in Boston had a major effect, but that's another more East Coast discussion.

Lew: So, this had a huge impact on you?
Dave: Yes, and it was cumulative. This "jazz ed" thing for me has been now over many years. By the mid- and late eighties, I started doing my books and getting into that aspect of it. You know this scenario better than anyone—being read, being discussed, being dissed, doing lectures on the material, being quoted. I became a source, and it contributed to my income and growth as an artist. But it was more than that. Jazz has a lot of intrinsic human values beneath the surface—individuality, socialization, the history, the black tradition, the link to American history. I don't care if the kid grows up to be a jerk—you gave him or her something life-affirming and positive. You know what I mean? The rest isn't your problem. You did something good for him or her that this person wouldn't have gotten elsewhere.

This turned me around and really gave me a reason to go on. To reiterate, before that, it was just the music and getting as good as I could, and hopefully as well known as I could—be the next Trane, be the next anything. But when that wasn't going to happen, as I started to realize by thirty-five years old, education kind of saved me.

Lew: And you also learned very quickly that you really are good at teaching. You were exposed to the ABC guys, but you were good in your own right. When I think of leading jazz educators, sometimes I think people forget you because they are looking for the cats who are full-time teachers. But in terms of someone who's out there teaching, you do more than most people. And you publish more than most people.

Dave: I am playing to the strengths I have. This is what I meant when I was having that crisis, or at least that aspect of the crisis. It was because my strengths were not being used. Leading a band was not bringing out those parts in me that I knew I had. Funny, but my mother knew all along. In the final result, I grew up with teachers. In my book *Self-Portrait of a Jazz Artist*, a short book that is kind of a precursor to what we are doing here, I say it right at the beginning. I grew up in a family of teachers. To explain, to verbalize, to understand, to repeat it, and to try to get it across—that's the mantra. And it's the best thing I do. I play good, but I teach better. I know that.

In the final analysis, once you are past the beginner stage, you are dealing with basic psychology: What makes a twenty-year-old work on something and find themselves? I'm good at this level and enjoy doing it. I feel I'm doing something good—a kind of missionary work. OK, I'm exaggerating, but the point is that I feel I'm performing a service while making a living, which has meant not selling out. It really did mean that I could become whatever Dave Liebman was career-wise, by my choice, for the most part.

Even when I did the rock-and-roll thing, the fusion thing with Pee Wee, sure, I jumped on the bandwagon of the time, but I really meant it. It would have been great if I had hit, but I probably would have gone back to what I'm doing now anyway. The point is, I could create my own terms. You can ask my wife about the following statement: If there's anything I have a problem with, it's authority. I have real trouble with somebody who is not qualified telling me what to do. I would be really tough in a country with a dictator—meaning, probably dead! I would be the head of the revolution.

It's not about being brave, but I just can't stand someone telling me what to do unless they are ahead of me in knowledge, experience, whatever. For me, having to have a boss, with my livelihood and personal development so dependent on that person's whims or ego, would destroy me. I don't want anybody telling me what to do, because usually they don't know what I know. That's the problem. This was the same gripe I felt about playing studio stuff—some guy was going to tell me how to play for eight bars. Come on! Okay, if you have a guy like Justin DiCioccio, who is my boss at the Manhattan School of Music, where I am currently artist in residence, it's alright because I respect his work ethic. I know we're going to be cool, because he knows what I know, and in some ways more. But with all the idiots you have to deal with in the world because of economics, from a bandleader whom you don't like because he has no idea of what art is, to playing a gig with a person who is just the opposite of your aesthetic—it's troublesome for me. The teaching thing enabled me to be free for the most part from these concerns, and it kind of fit my personality. I didn't know it at the time, but this is what it has become.

Lew: So, teaching became a major part of your career and solved that part of your crisis. But you also broke your leg again.
Dave: First some background. We're talking 1982 into '83. With all the events I am describing, the law school thing, marriage and divorce, etc., I was just completely fed up with living in New York City. Outside of that time in California, and some time in Eleana's scene in Greenwich, Connecticut, I basically had been living in New York since '69, in four different lofts. People were constantly coming over, and I had no time for myself. I stayed up too late, drank too much—you can imagine. I had had enough. I didn't want the doorbell to ring anymore. I didn't want distractions. I had sat in with everybody, I knew every club. This being fed up with my day-to-day lifestyle was also part of my so-called crisis.

Richie started hanging with a lady, Susan Sewell, who had a house on the North Fork of Long Island, way out past Riverhead, in Southold. I began spending time, hanging out there. It was beautiful, idyllic, and quite unknown at the time, populated by potato farmers, horse breeders, and eventually vineyards. Richie was basically living out there in a great house with a grand piano, overlooking Long Island Sound. My "brother" was living like King Tut and, by the way, wrote like eighty thousand tunes there—basically got his thing together musically. She loved him and gave him everything. She was completely independently wealthy, coming from Dallas, where her father was the first Cadillac dealer in town—something like that. We're still in touch. Great lady. She painted, but basically didn't have to make a living. Richie still kept his place on Spring Street in Manhattan right around the corner from the original Half Note Club, which was at Spring and Hudson.

Dina and I would visit Long Island and hang and play. I loved it out there. We all have that dream to escape into the woods or somewhere like that and wake up just playing music all day. Well, I did it. I found a house right around there in Peconic, New York—a little cape for $60,000. This just happened as my first wife, Dina, and I were splitting up—I have pictures of me and Richie on Long Island without Dina, since we were already pretty finished by that time. I brought the grand piano I had bought from Richie ten years earlier, and went out alone to stay. And then the shit hit the fan. I don't remember which was first, the broken leg or hepatitis A, but it all happened real quickly at the beginning of my time out there.

On my absolute first day, I was setting up the studio upstairs right at the top of the rafters. As you see here, Lewis, in my studio at home, I like to be surrounded by symbolic pictures. At the top of the highest beam there was a space where I wanted to put this great picture of a Japanese master leading his student up a mountain. You know—an image of eternal wisdom or whatever—iconic. I climbed up on the ladder to the top step, all alone, and I fell! I crawled down in terrible pain to call for help. I remember distinctly meeting my neighbors for the first time as they carried me out on a stretcher. Great intro to the 'hood! In any case, I broke my femur in the leg that had been bad since my childhood polio.

I did not wear a brace then like I do now, and had not since my teens. Because of the seriousness of the fracture, I needed a cast up to my arm pits, with a bar attached to a half cast on the good leg, so as not to have any movement at all for six weeks. I had to be completely immobile. I couldn't even go to the bathroom by myself. I sort of could walk on crutches. And I was getting divorced from Dina. The whole timing was terrible. I got hepatitis A around the same time—the list goes on. So the spring of '82 was a low point for sure, physically, mentally, and careerwise.

My mother came out to help me for the first days. Then somehow we found this angel caretaker, Candle Johnson, whom I'm still in touch with. I have a feeling she came through Eleana, but I don't remember. She is a beautiful woman in all ways. She definitely saved me out there. She cared for me for six months, nursing me back to health. Candle lived with me, cooked, and helped me get to the bathroom. I guess my parents were helping out or I had money—I don't remember. I owned the house, paying my mother like a small mortgage.

Susan, Richie's lady, was there also. By then, Richie was not with her anymore—he began a relationship with pianist LeeAnn Ledgerwood, whom he married soon afterward. I did gather a community of friends out there, some of whom I'm still in touch with. One guy, the late Frank Rizzo, came to visit because he had heard about me and knew I was a musician. He worked for the phone company out there. We became close. Also, a friend I'm still in touch with, Toby, is a singer and lives there. It actually ended up being a good period for the next few years.

When I got better, I would go to the beach, write music, just groove. When I met Caris, which is the next part of my personal life, she came out there also. *The Loneliness of a Long-Distance Runner*—that solo record—was put together out there. *Self-Portrait of a Jazz Artist* and the beginning of the saxophone book *Developing a Personal Saxophone Sound* were conceived and organized there. I started to get it together. My youth was basically over. I was done being wild. I was done looking for girls everywhere. I was done chasing the stardom trail. I was approaching forty. If there is a plan, I was going according to it.

Lew: What is the story on this hepatitis thing?
Dave: You can get it from food. Hepatitis B is more serious and C is coming on now for a lot of people of my generation, probably because of drugs, but type A is the light version where you're weak and your skin turns a terrible kind of sickly mustard yellow. My urine was yellow, and I had a high bilirubin count, but it dissipates by natural course. Unfortunately, I have to write down on every medical form that I had hepatitis A, even though it's long gone. It could have been from anything unsanitary, most likely food. The whole affair lasted six weeks. But it contributed to the whole vibe of that downward spiral. If there was a time for me to get it—if you believe that your immune system is affected by your psychological state—that was it.

I was definitely not in the best of spirits. When the divorce was settled, I think I had $5,000 saved in my bank account and medical insurance, though it's nothing like it is now, which I had for Dina and me. We had no kids; we had no belongings really; we had no possessions. She was a nice girl and it was nobody's fault the way it went down. But I certainly was pissed off that I had to give her the $5,000 and pay for her insurance for a time. I got a lawyer, who said I had no choice. I never saw her again. She was twenty-three when we got divorced. I wouldn't say it was a mistake. She was great and I had a lot of fun with her. She easily fit into the jazz life because of her parents, but we were just too young.

Lew: But your performance career started to pick up just after this rough period.
Dave: What eventually got me back on to the stage was that I started to do pick-up gigs. I would go around the States, cashing in on some of my teaching connections. For example, in Cincinnati I would play at night and teach in the afternoon—then on to the next city. I started to go back musically and play familiar standards, since these were all one-nighters with little or no rehearsal. I cemented some relationships with musicians in Chicago and New Orleans, in particular. This was the beginning of my resurrection because I also started to go to Europe where I had a reputation more than in the States, something quite normal for jazz musicians

historically. Those guys loved having me in their band, and I began several long-term relationships with European musicians, some of whom I still play with to this day. This scene started to really intensify in the mid-1980s. Plus, as I mentioned, the relationship with Advance Music began to develop further with workshops and publishing books. I got very close with the Grubers and introduced them to a lot of the guys in the field. If there's a dividing point in my life, it's the early 1980s.

Quest continued and really started happening by '84 or '85, especially in Europe, France in particular. If you wanted to hear the quintessence of New York jazz circa 1984–1988, Quest was the band. There was also Wynton's group with his brother, and the downtown guys at the Knitting Factory like John Zorn and Tim Berne, etc. But for the mainstream thing, at least in that particular burning style, it was Quest.

There were a lot of guys who came to New York at this time when Quest was *the* band to hear. New York jazz is cyclical—when Steve Grossman and I were with Elvin, we were the guys to hear in the early seventies. Every few years or so there are new saxophone kids on the block—David Sanborn and Michael Brecker; then Steve Coleman, Lovano, Chris Potter, Mark Turner. With Quest we had a little window of being truly representative of New York hard-core jazz and playing all the clubs. If you played in the Apple you were basically recognized everywhere, in jazz circles worldwide. We were a real New York band living the New York jazz life, hitting it hard.

We played at Sweet Basil a lot, but also Lush Life and the Village Vanguard. It was a kind of circuit that you had in those days. You knew everybody in the audience and played often until three in the morning. The jazz life still existed. People stayed out and hung for the third set. In fact, the third set was special, because the kind of people who would come later, say after 1:00 a.m. were shall I say, "people of the night"—guys who had made the rounds with "recreational materials" or whatever, other musicians, artists, etc. Let's put it this way—you wouldn't see your grandmother at that hour! The best audience was that last set. These were your friends.

Afterward you hung out in the dressing room or you went to a joint like Bradley's on University Place where cats jammed and hung till daylight—only insiders allowed. Cats only. At four in the morning, they locked the door at Bradley's. It was like Hernando's Hideaway—almost mythical. I don't think there was a secret password, but in general they had to know you to let you in. Richie was part of the Bradley's "mafia" at that time. It was primarily a duo joint for piano and bass—famously so. The drinks flowed, and so did other things, of course. Because of Beirach, I was treated like an honored guest. I had the corner chair, back to the wall, which is where everyone wanted to be. You could see everybody, and nobody could get behind you. You might be invited into the office for some private hanging. Guys would play and talk music—Herbie, George Shearing, a lot of guys would end up there talkin' shop and doing important networking for gigs. Bradley Cunningham, the owner, was an ex-Marine, tough-looking with all kinds of pock marks on his face—real Irish guy. He was real big and powerful looking, so no one messed around at the bar. He played piano by ear and could kind of play.

Lew: So, he knew changes?
Dave: Completely by ear! This big ex-Marine. He hated anything except straight-ahead jazz. But when Quest would play the Vanguard, because of Richie he would come down for the first set from time to time, and against his better judgment, Bradley would give it up to us. He liked me because I was real. He hated when I played, I'm pretty sure. After all, George Coleman or someone like that was his main guy. Of course, he loved Richie and George Mraz in those first years of Quest. George played with every duo in the world. He was at Bradley's all the time since it was the New York prototype duo gig for piano and bass.

Nobody bothered you at Bradley's. There could be thirty people there, mostly musicians. We had a great time. I was still living on Long Island, but by this time I was hanging with Caris, who was living at first on Waverly Place, and then eventually moved to Park Avenue South and 23rd Street, so I was in New York more. Plus, my parents still had their apartment in Brooklyn, which was empty for the winter months since they were "snow birds" in Florida at that time, before they settled there permanently.

But my house was two hours away on the busiest road in the world, the Long Island Expressway, so I was living a bit of a gypsy lifestyle, having to figure out where to stay and so forth. I was writing my books out of a briefcase and basically living out of a suitcase for a couple of years. There was no music out there, though there was a small community of players, but it didn't matter because I really enjoyed it on the North Fork, as it is called. Life was better by the mid '80s—I had the new relationship with Caris, I had the beach, and I had a band that I couldn't wait to play with, especially when the personnel solidified with McClure and Billy Hart. That was the ideal band for me, at that time. And as I said, we were successful in Europe and starting to do clinics, sometimes a week long.

Lew: And what about personal relationships within the band?
Dave: Richie played great, but I could see some effects of the drugs in the music—mainly rhythmical things. Look—rhythm has to do with what you feel physically. It's not your mind, it's your body. But we still played great together. We could turn that switch on and nobody played like us. It was really Richie and me with Billy, being the great drummer that he is, knowing he had the green light to do whatever he wanted. Ron did what he was supposed to do—he is the quintessence of a bass player. The mix worked.

It was a powerful and magical band, no question about it. What we did, we really did. Musically we never really had a problem. We'd get on stage and do the job. People loved it. But off the stage, it got harder and harder. By 1986, I was married to Caris. We bought the house in Pennsylvania where we still live, and we were thinking about having a family and all that. She'd say, "What are you doing? What's the story with Richie?" I would answer, "I've still got something to learn. I still need to play with this band." I wasn't ready to stop it, even though I should have. Let me put it this way—if it hadn't been for the musical reasons, I would have stopped the band two or three years earlier than I did.

Lew: So, it was difficult the last few years.
Dave: It was very hard—just the vibe. Even McClure would talk behind my back, because he also wasn't in the greatest shape. I can't describe what it was about, but it was a drag. Both Richie and Ron didn't look that good either. People could sense it, but fortunately the jazz community is very forgiving, and certainly in Europe. Not only are they forgiving in Europe, but they kind of dig it. I finally saw the Chet Baker movie *Let's Get Lost*. I never saw it before. The image of the fallen drug-ridden artist was perfect for Europe.

Lew: In a really negative way. It's kind of like, for them it's authenticity.
Dave: I guess so. Look, Richie was some kind of little genius. He was like this wunderkind. Plus, the way he looked, the way he acted—he was perfect, in a way. He played off of it. I stayed away from it. By then, I wasn't into that scene anymore. Caris was never involved with drugs and in fact hated that scene, and we couldn't keep going if I was around it—period. For whatever reason, I was getting away from all that and didn't care about it. I had grown out of it before this period, but it became an issue with Richie because a lot of our earlier, social relationship was predicated on that scene—not heavy drugs, but an assortment of things. Smoking pot was the most innocent aspect of all—that was like having a

Coca-Cola. With other stuff, we knew how much to take and when, usually pretty accurately, meaning you wanted to feel a particular way at a certain time of the night. We already had that down by the seventies. By the mid-eighties, it was old and we were in a pattern that really had no use anymore. I had outgrown it, but apparently he didn't.

Lew: How did all of this affect your playing?
Dave: Well, bad and good of course. I was certainly out of tune sometimes, which, given the soprano, is a problem no matter your state of mind or body. More so I was sometimes musically over the top, too much stuff, notes, vibe, energy, whatever. Other cats when they got high may play less, becoming more moody or introspective. We were definitely past that. We were professionals in that way, which most guys are by the time they've been around a bit. George Mraz could drink anyone under the table and still play perfectly. He was known for that. A professional is a professional, in all ways, and everyone reacts differently. In my case, I would get energized if I smoked, which for most people is the opposite, meaning they get more relaxed and dreamy. We used to call it "getting up on the down." Often I was the opposite of everybody around me in how things affected me.

You played games with chemicals, but you had to learn your body and how it was for you. My natural thing is energy. Although we always want to be relaxed in a musical way, I made it fit my scene. There were certainly nights when you didn't feel good, but there were times that were really nice. It was going for that perfect moment that occasionally you might glimpse, or have had, or think you had, or don't have but want to have—all those things—you went after it like a good meal: "I want the best steak." It was so innocent in a way. But like I said, there comes a point when there was nothing new to be learned from it. It gets old, it gets a little sloppy, and there is no reason to do it except out of habit. That's where it was at by the mid-eighties.

Lew: By the time you lost interest, it sounds like Richie was doing more?
Dave: I'm not going to do armchair psychology here, but in the nineties, when I hadn't seen him for years, he really went into a dark hole. I'm sure he was frustrated with the lack of recognition for his talents. Look, I felt the same way professionally, especially with such a great band. Much as we tried, Quest just never happened on a popular jazz level, especially in the States, and that was a source of great frustration. We even

had an expression to describe it—EBU, meaning "everybody but us" was getting recognition.

Lew: You had management?
Dave: I had some help here and there, but I couldn't get it going. We did the customary club route, but we couldn't crack through to the next level. Maybe the music was too intense? I was playing soprano exclusively, which warrants a little bit of a technical discussion. One aspect of the soprano is its absolutely grating quality in the high register, especially in the altissimo, the extreme high register. McClure would describe it as "a pet store on fire." This is not the greatest compliment in the world! I was trying to extend the range for myself.

Steve Lacy could do it, but not at the intensity that I was going for, so someone had to suffer for me trying to get above high F-sharp. This just added to the in-your-face attitude the band had, which in the eighties was not quite in the air, to say the least. We are talking the Reagan years, with the "young lions" returning to the roots and getting a lot of press for doing this dance. On the other hand, there were free jazz groups that made us look like a walk in the park as far as intensity was concerned. At any given time in history since the sixties, there's a band somewhere in the world that makes anything less than triple fortissimo for four hours seem completely wrong. But we were not a free band. In a way, we were mainstream and the intensity may have been a bit daunting.

Lew: For those kinds of venues.
Dave: Thank you. Yes—you had to pay attention when Quest played. And the harmony—dark as it was, certainly could be rough for the average jazz listener, who was accustomed to more "inside" stuff. When you refer to the term *polychord*, it's not the brightest harmony on the planet. I'm not going to say it's evil, ugly, tragic, or anything as general as that, but it's definitely not bright and happy.

Lew: So, this was serious?
Dave: We were trying for that sound. We were looking for Schoenberg in real time. Richie and I developed a way of speaking harmonically that we were proud of. At the same time, we played some beautiful ballads. The most famous tune of Richie's is "Elm," which is completely tonal and lyrical. We always played a beautiful ballad in a set, taking our cues from Miles and Trane, who no matter how intense the music always played something lyrical. But the majority of the way Quest was perceived was intensity personified, and a really heavy experience to hear.

You had to listen, and the audience wasn't ready for us in America in the eighties. They were more ready in Europe, as usual, being more sophisticated, open, and ready to pay attention for more than two minutes.

Lew: And more familiar with the threads of modern classical music.
Dave: Yes. There are many reasons why Europe became more accommodating for me, as it did for Dexter Gordon or other famous jazz expats. This EBU thing was cute, but it wasn't funny after awhile. You opened *Downbeat* magazine and realized that you were omitted. You could put on a show that you didn't care, but it hurt. Sure, we had critical acclaim. We were the real deal and the critics knew it. The eighties saw this whole Marsalis thing get really out of hand. I think it really got Richie down, maybe more than for me, due to his situation. And I can't blame him. He was such a heavy piano player, reputed for being a voice on his own, and he was being swallowed up figuratively by his students, meaning that the generation that learned from us, the guys who had listened to us to learn, were doing better than we were. By the mid '80s we had each been on the scene for fifteen to twenty years. That's enough time to make a statement. Everybody's heard you and has a take on you. It's not, "I haven't heard that guy yet." It's, "I heard him." We felt that other, less deserving groups were unfairly getting ahead of us, at least as far as material rewards, by which I mean work opportunities, breaks, press, polls—whatever.

I'm not complaining. I was always on the soprano poll since Miles. But Richie never made a poll. It's ridiculous. And the band was not recognized. We were overlooked, and though we could qualify it in our own minds by saying the music was too intense and we were ahead of our time, that we were just too sophisticated for them, the truth is it was a drag. Each of us took it in different ways. Billy played a thousand gigs and had a dossier as long as the dictionary, so maybe his view was less personal than for me and Richie. Of course he increasingly felt an allegiance to Quest, but Billy had a lot of other bands that he was part of, whereas for us, it really was a continuation of what we started together in the seventies.

Ron was also very frustrated because he, like Billy, had played with everyone from Wynton Kelly, Wes Montgomery, Monk, Charles Lloyd, to even Blood Sweat & Tears. He even played with Miles for a night or two. Ron was the real deal. When Ron came to New York at nineteen or twenty years old from Connecticut, he was the next guy, the next Eddie Gomez. He came to my loft in '69 or '70 and knocked everyone out. Remember, in those days that fast bass player style was not as common as now. He seemed to be the next one in line. But by our time together both with the Scofield group and Quest, he hadn't gotten recognition, for whatever reason.

You could say the same for Billy Hart, who, though widely respected, didn't have the status of DeJohnette or Tony Williams or Al Foster, which is still true in a way as we speak. Billy was known as Jabali, but we had a nickname for him because he was often late: WOB, "waiting on Billy," but endearing in his case. Work-wise, Billy's thing was that he never said no to a gig. He played with everyone, even student types. If there was a gig and he was available, he would take it. Sometimes he would take a few gigs in one night—double or triple booking, as it is known in the trade. Was it the music, or that he liked the guy, or the money? I don't know because it wasn't my business and I never talked to him about it. But in my opinion Billy was definitely overlooked and became the greatest sideman to everybody, making them sound better than they were, including me.

So, to finish this discussion, which is a bit depressing, here was a band of four guys with credits up the wazoo who just couldn't get the ball rolling on a popular jazz media level, at least to what it should've been, in my estimation. There was an inherent frustration within all of us, though the music was sublime no matter what.

Lew: For a while, starting in this Quest era of the '80s, you decided to play almost exclusively soprano sax.

Dave: During the seventies, I showed up on every gig, Miles, Elvin, Lookout Farm, whatever, with the full arsenal—C flute, soprano, and tenor, somehow playing all three in a set or on a recording. This was all well and good, and expected of a reed player, the doubling or tripling aspect of being a saxophonist in that period. It goes back to my first lessons at Bromley Studios with Nat Shapiro and him mandating that I play clarinet for at least one year before going to sax. So with the three horns by the seventies, I had a kind of formula: the tenor for intense Coltrane-type burning tunes, the soprano for fusion-like eighth-note material, and the flute for Indian-type stuff.

After California in the late '70s I was starting to feel that I wasn't doing the right thing by playing all the horns. After all, here's something that might not be noticed by anyone else, but when you play three horns in one set, let's say an hour and fifteen minutes, remember that a horn doesn't play every minute like a drummer or bass player. So in reality I was only playing maybe twenty minutes, if that. I wasn't taking thirty-minute solos like Trane, although I wished I could. Spreading that little time among three horns means I was dabbling, and an artist is supposed to continually raise the bar and be challenged. It was technical as well. You don't even have time to get the reed right if you play five minutes, put down one horn, and go to the other two. It was ridiculous, and it started to bother me. After all, nobody was telling me what horns to play, although of course on a record date someone might write a tune with the soprano or tenor in mind, which is understandable because of range considerations.

I started to entertain the idea of concentrating on one horn. Richie was very supportive of making this move from an artistic standpoint, but I had trepidation because of the associations that I, and to a certain extent my audience, had of me, from a musical standpoint. What would I do if I didn't have the tenor to "burn out"—you know, hit the music hard? But Richie was encouraging me. He said, "Lieb, give up something." I said, "How am I going to give up the tenor? How am I going to give up 'Impressions' as a symbol of Coltrane-inspired burning tunes? Or, how am I going to give up the soprano, of which I definitely am getting a reputation for and actually feel pretty comfortable on? And the flute—I'm not too bad on the flute." But, the truth is, I understood the rationale of spreading yourself thin and I was starting to be concerned with my legacy. "Who am I? Who am I musically?" It's one thing to have a band, but an individual style—that was another level. By then, a certain amount of Coltrane had been internalized, but overall, stylistically, I was still certainly coming from him. You can hear it on the *Pendulum* record from 1978—no question about it.

Nothing really was set in stone, but I felt that I had to make a decision. The reason for choosing soprano and leaving the tenor aside came from a few angles. The soprano really felt like it was more me, if only from a purely physical standpoint. I am not a big guy. I'm shrinking now, but I was never more than five-foot-eight. Truth is that the tenor on your neck is kind of a heavy thing. When you see Sonny Rollins with a tenor, it looks right, you know what I mean? You see Dexter Gordon—it looks right. Trane—it just about bordered on right, because he wasn't a giant either, but it looked fine. But on me and Johnny Griffin, for example, it looks a little big, which is okay, but the point is that there's something to this observation that is self-evident.

Another point, musically—in the late seventies, there basically were no soprano players except Steve Lacy and Wayne. There wasn't the plethora of people we have now, meaning there was room to find a voice on that instrument. The brutal truth was that on tenor I couldn't really get away from Trane. Actually, I really didn't want to get away from him because his music was still the best of all time for me. Also, by the late seventies—because generations were basically five years long in those days—here comes the next generation already, cherry-picking stuff, among other aspects, what Grossman and I did with Miles and Elvin—the stuff we played on the *Live at the Lighthouse* recording, which by that time became a sort of common saxophone language. These were good guys—Bill Evans, Rick Margitza, Branford Marsalis, and some lesser-knowns.

Steve and I were the first generation of post-Coltrane players—not Trane's contemporaries or peers or older—we definitely came after. For example, Joe Farrell, who preceded us with Elvin, was a contemporary of Coltrane. Michael Brecker, who went on to such popularity and influence, was a younger cat. I could go on and on with this placing of guys. I can't explain this point so well, but it kind of annoyed me to hear cats taking that stuff, practicing it till they were blue in the face, and spitting it out. Maybe I was envious; maybe I felt betrayed or violated. I don't know. But it was weird and it bothered me. The next generation usually technically perfects and extends what came before, by practicing the stuff relentlessly and creating a personal language from that vocabulary. Michael was a prime example of that. For all these reasons, the tenor lost the battle for me. The soprano was in.

I kept the flute until the mid-eighties, especially in the duo situation with Richie. But after *The Duo Live* recording in '85, I stopped the flute also. With the flute it was more obvious—to be great, you had to play it every day, unless you were like Lew Tabackin, Joe Farrell, Hubert Laws. These guys had conservatory training and were real flute players. I didn't like having a sound that was less than excellent. I didn't want to be like James Moody, Frank Wess, or even Eric Dolphy, who though they played great but had less than what I would consider a great tone on the flute. Sound was and is still numero uno, in my book, on an instrument. I couldn't stand the thin sound anymore that I got on flute. Technically I wasn't bad—I kind of had a Dolphy thing happening—but I couldn't stand the tone I was getting. It wasn't a good flute sound.

So, it was '79 or '80, and my last recordings on tenor at that time were with Steve Swallow as leader on ECM, called *Home*, and my fusion record titled *What It Is*. Then I made the *Dedications* record with a string quartet, Richie on piano and Gomez, which was soprano only. By '80 or '81, I stopped the tenor. I remember being apprehensive that for the next record date as a sideman, which at that time I was doing quite a bit of, I would have to say, "I just want to tell you that I'm not playing tenor." Sure enough someone, I forget who, called me for a date and I warned him. He said, "I'm not hiring an instrument—I'm hiring you." Thank you, whoever you were. But that's really the truth, especially in our music. It's not a tenor; it's Dave playing tenor or Dave playing soprano. That cooled me out, and then I hit the soprano hard. The recording that I feel captures my first stage of raising my game on soprano is *Quest*. By then, my soprano playing had literally doubled in skill, projection, sound, intonation—everything. I was playing more in tune, and my tone was better. I hit the mother lode by making the right decision.

Lew: So, you feel good about that?

Dave: Absolutely! I stayed with it until 1995. I never played tenor with Quest during the eighties. It was all soprano, and it helped make the sound of that group unique. It became emblematic—it's that sound! Pet store on fire? Yeah, but at least it's my pet store! It ain't someone else's. This was a good move that lasted for fifteen years. That soprano-only decision was very important for me because it's also about who I really was musically and the entire mid-life stage that I was dealing with at the time.

The whole theme of this part of my life was—not to be melodramatic—redemption. It was growing up, personally, socially, and musically. Part of it was that I finally had a real identity. I could say, "That's Dave." I could feel it. That's not something you cognize every day, but it's something in your life that you can identify when you look back. By '86 or '87 with Quest, what I and we did was established. What we played was what it was, and at least in Europe it was noticed by the outside world, to some degree. I mean the critics and people in the know. Like I said, I had been in the top soprano category since my time with Miles, sometimes higher in the Critics Poll than the Readers Poll, which of course was based on commercial viability to a large degree. There was no way I could ever get ahead of Lacy or Wayne, nor should I have. They were the masters for sure.

Lew: Are you saying that you became individually just more recognizable?

Dave: Yes. I became a stylist because by '86 or '87—we're talking five years of playing soprano by then—the music was not a finished product of course, but definitely something coherent and recognizable. That reed in your mouth, that mouthpiece, that horn in your hands, that weight, that feeling, every night with the same thing over and over again—that's what does it. Without that, I wouldn't be who I am. I tell my saxophone students who are at a high level, who are good, "Doubling or tripling—

I'm not for it." Not for art. For some gigs, you need it, for another tune, for color, variety, to play a show, or a bandleader wants the tenor or soprano because of tessitura or whatever. This I understand. But for you to get to the core of who you are, I would advise for a certain period—I don't know about fifteen years or fifteen minutes—but I would advise staying with only one horn and not spreading yourself thin.

Lew: For artistic reasons. But as you say, for gig reasons, it's understandable that you might need other horns as a saxophonist.
Dave: Correct. You are, by a certain time, good enough to do what is needed to play a part if needed on another horn. Surely you have to have minimum doubling skills, but this is expected and very doable, even by today's standards, though to a lesser extent than previous sax generations. You're good enough to do the job. But for you to practice equally on soprano and tenor over the course of a four-hour regimen, for example, I'm not sure that this is an effective use of your valuable practice time, at a certain point. By "certain point," I mean when you are really equipped and mentally ready to find out who *you* really are, not through your influences, but through your own introspection. Everything in its due time—that's kind of a mantra for life, ideally.

Lew: That's a good perspective because a lot of people wouldn't realize how successful that was, your switching to soprano. They might think it was just an experiment or whatever.
Dave: It worked for me because it really was closer to who I am. It's my voice. I think it's something to do with the Jewish thing. I really believe that snaky, wailing, Indian, Arabic, Bedouin sound—whatever it might be called as an influence—is real. I told you about visiting a psychic in Berkeley in the seventies, and she saw me in a desert vibe, dressed in white, dancing or something akin to that. I think there's something in there, in the way I speak, the way I talk with my hand movements, and the way I am. The soprano, it goes right there. The tenor is different and I of course love it, especially now that I've gotten back to a relationship with it. But the soprano is what I'm going to go down with.

Also, to be honest, I can't handle carrying the tenor physically like I used to. It's a pain in the ass. In ten years, when I'll have to probably be helped up on the bandstand because of the effects I still have of polio, believe me, I'll be just taking that damn soprano around. I don't take a tenor, anyway, even now. I'm famous for "tenor du jour." If I want to play tenor on a gig and it is not a car ride from my home, it will be borrowed. Soprano is my sound. I'm down with that. When the final line is drawn, one of the main soprano stylists will be Dave Liebman. That's something I've earned, along with three or four other guys, and that's about it in the end, nothing more, nothing less, because there are certain limitations with the soprano, though it does have certain charming qualities like a low register that's beautiful, for example. It has richness in the lows if you can do it. Also, as we know, it can cut through cacophony—the "pet store on fire." It has a speed thing for sure. It can have a trumpet or clarinet feeling, but it is what it is, meaning the soprano sax does not have the range of expressive possibilities that the tenor does. Not the alto—I'm talking specifically tenor. It's just the way it is. But I at least own a little bit of the soprano map, which is nice.

Lew: Steve Lacy played pretty high on soprano, and in tune.
Dave: He could. He went way up there. He had that stuff down—he was the master. There are some young cats now. Sam Newsome can do it. My friend from France, Jean Charles Richard, is great at the altissimo on soprano.

Lew: Can you play that high sometimes?
Dave: Sure, but I'm not as controlled as they are. These guys now, they have it down. I go up there screaming as a point of emotional intensity. I don't want to hear it clean. There should be a reason to go up there.

Lew: One other thing about soprano, because I and a few other people love Lucky Thompson on it.
Dave: He was very good and unique. Somebody recently turned me on to him. He definitely had a unique sound. John Surman is very good. He has a particular thing also. As mentioned, Wayne and Steve are on top of the soprano food chain, but we're talking certainly less than ten, if that, as far as soprano. On tenor saxophone, we'd be at ten in ten seconds.

Look, I wanted to escape Trane. "Yeah, but he played soprano great." True, but it wasn't his main thing, and he didn't play soprano much in his last two years. I never sat down and copied a Trane lick on soprano. I did only tenor, because I didn't play soprano until 1969 anyway, and by then a lot of my formative work had been done already. It wasn't that I picked up soprano because I saw it with Trane. I picked it up because Ten Wheel Drive required it. Maybe the fact that I didn't really do that much serious work on soprano, like on tenor getting the language down, resulted in it being a more open territory for me. The arena was not full and populated, which I think was to my advantage. Tenor was already marked for the ages by the seventies.

We might as well finish this part of the story concerning the soprano and tenor. Even with the new band I began in '91, I played only soprano until '95. It's a bit simpler why I went back to tenor. Despite the amount of great tenor players we were witness to in the fifteen years I didn't play it, it just sounded to me like no one had really stepped up to the plate and pushed the horn further. Okay, Brecker certainly did his share of spectacular things. But I still felt that it was not on the same scale as Trane or even Sonny in his heyday, or Wayne and a few others. Was I just thinking old fogey stuff like, "There will never be anything like the past. Everything new is lesser," etc.? I don't think I was being that way at all. It was just what I heard.

By the time I got to around fifty years old in the mid '90s, I couldn't have cared less what anyone thought. Also, I had taken the soprano as far as I could at the time. Sure, I could get more multiphonics, harmonics, altissimo, and so on. Get faster? Sure. But I was also growing as an artist and a human being, so I wondered what the effect would be going back to tenor with the fifteen-year hiatus.

Lew: Because you had such a long break from it you could be fresh again?

Dave: At least ostensibly. I had brought the tenor out for teaching in those years, because it was obviously more applicable—most students played tenor. By the late eighties or early nineties, I used it on a few recordings. But I really did stick basically to soprano only for that fifteen-year period. I kept it pure with only soprano. Believe me, with the power of the Quest rhythm section, I was tempted to bring the big boy out—that was a hard one to resist. I'm sure in a jam session with students I burned out on tenor, but not on the gig. In any case, by 1995 it was time to confront the big guy again. I brought out the tenor that year for my recording of Coltrane's *Meditations*, and then in '96 I did an all-tenor album, *Return of the Tenor.* As of the present, the tenor is part of the Lieb show, so to say, but the soprano is still closest to who I am musically.

Chapter 10

Turn It Around: Solidifying Art and Life

Lew: So tell me about your wife, Caris Visentin.
Dave: Caris was from Palmerton, Pennsylvania. In '79/80, she attended the Berklee College of Music for jazz performance on oboe and English horn, which of course was just about unique at a jazz school. Then in '81 she switched to pursue a composition degree at the then-new jazz program at the Steinhardt School of NYU. She had studied with Joe Viola and George Garzone in Boston, and George is very close with Joe Lovano in New York. It seems that she had initially tried to contact me for lessons since she first met me in Boston, when I was up there for a gig at Ryles with Pat Metheny in October '79 and one at Michael's with Mike Stern; during the time I was married to Dina. But because of my move to Long Island when I got divorced, I couldn't be found. So she called Joe in March '81, and it turns out he'd never really taught anyone privately, but he was willing to meet with her. It worked out, and she ended up being his first student, studying jazz improvisation with him privately for the next three years. In fact, through that, he got the gig teaching at NYU, because the head of the department knew she was studying with him and then later got in touch with him to be part of the staff.

So, starting in the summer and fall of '81, while she continued to study with Joe privately, she was as well officially studying with Lee Konitz and Jim McNeely through NYU, as part of her degree requirement. Two years later, she and a friend of hers came to hear me at a gig, and her friend suggested that Caris send me a recent demo of her original compositions, which she had just recorded with her group. So I gave her my address and phone number on the Island. The demo arrived without any contact information. I tracked down her phone number and called to tell her how much I liked the music.

Other than meeting at my gigs, we really hadn't known each other. It was strictly professional. After I called her, she came down to one of my gigs at the Vanguard a few weeks later to say thanks in person. She was nice, so soon after that I called and asked her out. This was December '83. She was twenty-two years old and I was thirty-seven. She was a stable girl and very different from Dina. After all, I was definitely gun-shy to be with a young girl again. But Caris was great. I met her family right away and they were very cool. Of course she was into the music big time. She was great and really beautiful.

Her favorite tune was Trane's "My Favorite Things." In fact, she always loved the soprano sax—she was familiar with me and my music—but she got attracted to the oboe and wanted to explore that instrument in a jazz setting, using the soprano as a model. She also played some alto sax but didn't feel an affinity for it. When we collaborated musically a few years later, I was able to take advantage of the blend of oboe and soprano sax. Her brother, Bob, who played guitar, was into jazz and gave her the recording *Live at the Lighthouse* when she was eleven years old. In fact, he has great ears and a natural affinity for the music. He attended the University of Miami studying jazz for a while, in the same class as Pat Metheny and drummer Danny Gottlieb. A few years ago he helped quite a bit with the sound on one of my recordings, *Back On The Corner.* He is a brilliant cat. He's seven years older than Caris. In addition to studying jazz, he did a lot of things in engineering and in business. He eventually got a master's degree in electrical engineering from the University of Illinois and married a woman named Amy, presently an attorney who came from his hometown. They ended up in Portland, Maine, where he held a position with National Semiconductor for years. He always loved jazz and has natural talent. A real nice guy—salt of the earth.

Her parents came to my gigs, which was nice. Her father, Harold, is from Pen Argyl, while her mother, Natalie, is from Palmerton, both towns in northeast Pennsylvania where the family lived. The father's name is John, but he is always called by his middle name, Harold. Natalie's parents were Ukrainian with a bit of Polish mixed in, while the father's side was northern Italian. His town, Pen Argyl, was in an area called the Slate Belt because it was one of, if not the highest, producers of slate in the country at the time. Immigrants from Italy and England were the majority population of that town. There were also tons of clothing factories run by Italians everywhere in this area of Pennsylvania, owned by contractors like my in-laws, working for primarily Jewish manufacturers in New York City in the Garment District around 7th Avenue and 34th Street, which was world famous at the time for textiles. Together, her parents ran a factory in Palmerton, Natalie Fashions, with a hundred people working, making women's blouses for the garment district in New York when it was still a viable business.

Palmerton is a small town that was built by Eastern European and German immigrants and developed by the New Jersey Zinc Company, which was the other industry there besides textiles. They processed zinc and literally had small hills of ash pilled up near the industrial plants, of which the town had two. It seems that the residue from the smokestacks completely destroyed a lot of the vegetation on the surrounding mountains. It is only recently that these mountains started coming back, since that industry is long over. Where Caris lived was beautiful, but near the zinc plants; the years of industry took its toll. I just remember so strikingly when you entered Palmerton, this mountain right in your face completely decimated—not one tree. Then finally the EPA got on it and it's growing trees again. They went after them! It's an American tale, as we know—completely killing the environment.

Her parents are very nice, hardworking people. Harold was really the brains behind the production end of things—putting a blouse together, maintaining the machines, etc. He knew the art of sewing, starting from the pattern to the machines, and running the operations along with Natalie, who ran the business end of it. These hundred people worked hard on sewing machines, stamping out blouses. It was a real factory. Every week Natalie would have to deal with 7th Avenue to get her price for the blouses. She was very smart and knew how to talk to the manufacturers. It had to be complicated, but my in-laws always remained straight-ahead business people. When my mother-in-law turned forty she went back to school and received a double degree in business and economics.

Harold was hard of hearing most of his life. He is the nicest guy and very mechanical—he could fix anything. They were very successful—enough to live very well, send their kids to school, and finance an amazing wedding for us. They had a prosperous business, which went on until the mid '90s, when they sold it and retired.

There was a lot of music on the mother's side. Natalie's father was Ukrainian and played violin. He had a collection of sixty violins. He was really into it. Natalie's Ukrainian-Polish mother was a singer and violinist, earning a living as a musician for years doing weddings and so forth until her mid-seventies. She had a beautiful voice, all ear stuff. She had a book of tunes from Yiddish to Polish to Italian—the whole ethnic club-date book. She grew up in New York—she sang and even played violin on the radio in Manhattan. Natalie also has a beautiful voice and likes jazz. So, there was music in Caris's background for sure. They were hip to musicians.

On the father's side, there was an appreciation for music but no musicians. Jazz music was encouraged in that house because of her brother's influence. When I walked in, being what I was with a bit of a reputation in jazz was good—they loved it! They enjoyed the music and have been very supportive all these years. I made a record for Natalie. She gave me a song list, which I followed pretty closely using Vic Juris and Steve Gilmore in a trio setting called *Classic Ballads*. This was after I knew her about five years. She liked me playing standards, like most civilians do. I said, "Okay, give me a list of tunes." She gave me "If I Should Lose You," "Green Dolphin Street," "Skylark," etc. I dedicated the recording to her. Her picture is on the cover, which is amazing—you can find it online—it's from when she was sixteen and looks like a movie star. Gorgeous woman—she's still very good-looking.

Lew: So you became close with Caris's family as well?
Dave: Very close—they are very cool, nice people. So, the relationship with Caris started to grow. Soon, I realized that living on Long Island just wasn't practical for any kind of life because it was too far, too isolated, and you had to deal with the Long Island Expressway. By this time, I figured I could probably buy a house and get a mortgage, actually enter the real world. I didn't want to return to New York. I certainly didn't want to live in Manhattan. I was done with that for sure. But I was still coming from the vibe of "New York—there's no other place." I had done San Francisco, lived on Long Island and Connecticut. Caris and I did look there, which was way too expensive. Upstate New York was not happening. For the most part, outside of a few enclaves, it was postindustrial and kind of funky. Jersey was just another version of Brooklyn.

So Caris said, "I know an area that's cool." Her parents had a summer house in the area. I happened to know Stroudsburg and Tannersville because of Mount Airy Lodge, which is now a casino. I knew it because guys had played there over the years, and I had visited in the '60s when my old friend from the Impromptu Quartet, pianist Mike Garson, was working there. I did a jam session one time and I remember the bandleader's name was Bob Newman. He was a saxophone player and his wife played trumpet. I remember one thing that stood out was that he could play anything in any key, which was amazing to me. He used to have jam sessions, and somehow I went out and played with Mike one night, so at least I had heard of the area. I also knew that Phil Woods lived in the first town over the Jersey border, Delaware Water Gap, which is the adjoining town to Stroudsburg. It was kind of on the "jazz map." I told Caris that I didn't want any redneck stuff. She assured me that it was cool in Stroudsburg. She also loved living in New York, so moving back to Pennsylvania was also a big step for her. She was very careful about where we settled—she'd become a New York girl in her heart. It was a mutual thing. Going to Pennsylvania was something big for me. I'm not joking—for a New Yorker, Pennsylvania could've been Ohio or Nebraska, whatever.

Lew: You could be the only Jew in the neighborhood.
Dave: Yeah, though I can't say that bothered me, but it ends up there is a temple here, since the '20s actually. Anyway, we looked with a real estate agent, and since Caris knew the terrain, she knew exactly where, and where not, to go. This general area is northeastern Pennsylvania, above the Lehigh Valley but below the whole Scranton–Wilkes Barre thing. It's the Pocono Mountains, which are part of the Appalachian chain. We found this house, which was great, around March of '86. I made the basement into a studio.

Caris and I were married on November 30, 1986. Who performed the ceremony is very funny and truly a full circle kind of thing: Lovano and his wife, the singer Judi Silvano, were married a couple of years before us. Judi's uncle was a rabbi, who married them, so he obviously was okay with officiating at a mixed marriage, since Caris is Catholic. You can't find many rabbis who would do that, at least in those days. So, he married us, along with a priest, at Garvin's, a really elegant restaurant that was right on Waverly Place in the Village. It's not there anymore, but it was right down the street from the Bottom Line. That's where we had the wedding and the reception—we did it all there. It was a beautiful wedding, and all my musician friends were there. If a bomb would have gone off, the jazz scene would have been pretty much depleted! I had sixty to eighty cats there. I don't have a big family, and neither does she, but somehow together we ended up with close to 150 guests.

Eventually we did go to a temple, when we moved to Pennsylvania, where Caris took conversion classes. She did it to gain a better understanding, although she didn't feel a strong desire to actually convert. I really didn't care one way or the other. But because I was Jewish and my mother was still alive—my father had just died right before we got married—to please my mother, I guess, we had a rabbi, Judi's uncle.

Lew: What about the priest?
Dave: The priest was recommended by the rabbi since they had done similar ceremonies together. Somehow the priest was in a Robert DeNiro movie, *Prizzi's Honor*, playing of course the role of a priest. We had an interview with him, and he was completely cool.

It was a real wedding. She and her family stayed at the Essex House. My immediate family was just my mother, brother, two nieces, Lisa and Cheryl, and one cousin, Steve Seltzer. The night before, her parents had a big family dinner, and they had a huge spread at breakfast the next day, following the wedding. Her parents, for those days, spent a lot of money.

Lew: You made up a customized ceremony? Did you do readings to each other, or whatever?
Dave: Caris spent a lot of time researching both Jewish and Catholic ceremonies, and we chose the best from both, along with Old and New Testament readings reflecting both traditions.

We wrote a very personal statement from the both of us that was read aloud. We definitely did the whole thing. For music, check this out—we had Bill Evans serenading us on soprano sax for the opening procession, and for the reception, the Steve Kuhn trio, with a singer and guitar player, whom we called "Baldy" because he was completely bald. He sang some '50s tunes among other pop-rock classics. It was great! Everybody was dancing. I loved it! After all, '50s was my first music, so we had a great time. How great is that—Kuhn, Coltrane's first pianist, serenading us? It was a real wedding with flowers, a great meal, and all that. Her parents really took care of their daughter the right way.

Lew: This period in your life, this relationship with Caris, besides the fact that it was a more stable relationship than you had had previously, it's also more of a middle-class scene. So, how was that for you?
Dave: Very good point. It was an adjustment and it took me a while, in that way. This was not living in a loft. This was, like, you've got a furniture set. You know what I mean? I had to mensch out and get on the ball. I'm a responsible person, so it's not like it was terrible. But once you've got the house, you've got a lawn and *things*. Suddenly I had all these responsibilities. So, this was the beginning of "mensch-hood." It was more than well worth it because Caris basically gave me a life and enabled me to move forward. You can only stay young so long. I have to say that I stretched out the youth period in some ways, always taking care of busi-

ness but never really settling into stability. With Caris, my life became a reality. I was lucky to meet the right woman at the right time. The bonus is that she is a great musician and a really good composer. I have recorded several of her tunes as well as used her talents on oboe and English horn on more than a few recordings. She writes very challenging compositions.

Lew: That's great. What about your self-image? That kind of stability incurs a different self-image.
Dave: Yes. This is a very good point. Was it just the inexorable movement of time and a personal maturing process, or was it somehow connected to what was going on in jazz by the mid- to late '80s as it became more middle class? See if you agree with me. What I'm suggesting happened possibly because there were more schooled, middle-class jazz musicians, college trained, and especially a lot of white folks.

Lew: Certainly when you started, and I'm just a few years younger than you, one never heard, "Where did you go to school for jazz?" Today, that's the first thing you ask them. There's not one of them that says, "I didn't go to school."
Dave: Not only school, but the environment in which they grew up. It's more stable than in past generations of jazz musicians, more middle class in general. Jazz was becoming a viable occupation, more than ever before. For whatever reasons, whether they are personal, having to do with passages in life, or partially because of the context I am describing, the fact was that in 1986 I became forty years old and it is a natural, inevitable course of events that makes a man at that stage finally just say, "Okay, I had my time. I had my fun. I'm getting married, I'm buying a house and having a child. Straighten up and fly right."

So, I'm a product of my time, but also of *the* time. It was an adjustment that I knew I had to make. Caris, the kind of woman that she is, wasn't going to go the other way. I had a good woman who cared for me and was taking care of business. When your love life gets solidified and you're not one-nighting it, with the anxiety and everything attached to that, you can finally get down to business. My most productive time began then and is still happening. When anybody looks at my life twenty-five years later and how productive I have been with gigs, books, records, etc., it really began then. Before that, although I had accomplished something, I was not rooted. When you get rooted, you can take care of things, like writing a book or organizing this educational association, IASJ, which we'll discuss.

Lew: Caris provided stability, and came from a family that was solid financially.
Dave: Yes, and I started really organizing my stuff toward making a living. The teaching thing became steadier, between the Banff Centre and Aebersold, while slowly my educational materials started coming out. My tax return was a normal tax return. Before that, it was always a loss, as most musicians will tell you.

Lew: And not much in terms of savings.
Dave: Of course not. Now I had an IRA account and things like that started. We bought the house, which is a big thing obviously—the same house we are in now. So, investments, mortgage, lines of credit to get a car, thinking about education costs—the whole deal.

Then in 1991 Lydia was born, which marks the beginning of another journey. Lydia is somethin' else, and I guess the expression "an apple doesn't fall far from the tree" is very true, in this case. She was the cutest kid—people would stop on the street. In 1994 I did an album for her called *Songs for My Daughter*, with her photo on the cover, and she even sings on one cut. She was always interested in reading about mythology, stuff like that. She had a talent for drawing, putting brochures together, even "producing" a movie every year with her cousin, Robbie, when he would visit from Maine. There is definitely a strong organizational thing in her, and she is very quick, with an outgoing personality. As a kid she did dancing, ice skating, painting stuff—you know, the whole deal—but she gravitated toward Broadway music and really developed her singing chops. She also did a few years of classical study. The jazz thing is interesting because as a kid, you know, when she'd come to a club or concert where I would be playing, she, like most kids, looked distracted and bored, naturally. There was also a stage where Eminem and those guys were heard all day, but one morning I heard her alarm ring and she had it set to Trane playing "A Love Supreme." I couldn't believe it, but it shows how the influences are absorbed in a home without maybe being recognized. Soon enough, she was studying with Nancy Reed, a really killing jazz singer in our area, and Lydia was singing standards and sitting in with me on occasion. I really enjoy playing piano for her in the house or wherever. I always say when they put me out to pasture I can have a gig playing for Lydia—a shriveled up cat on the piano that someone says, "Hmmm, that guy looks familiar…" Hey, you never know!

She started at Emerson College in Boston in the fall of 2010, also taking music courses at Berklee, aiming toward a degree in media production. I really do see her in that role, being able to produce/direct projects with an understanding of all the elements—lighting, stage design, sound, acting, and music of course. When she started Emerson, she immediately went to the radio station and did a jazz show, which they hadn't had for years. I told her that I had a show at NYU as a student that I called "Reeds and Deeds." Lo and behold, she has an ongoing Sunday night show, "Reeds and Deeds II." It's really happening, playing new guys, especially from Boston, of course, and classics. She did a show this year of underground Trane tapes. I am very proud of her. Notably, they made her manager of the college station, WECB—this in her second year of college, no less! Caris and I are lucky—Lydia is a smart young lady who will figure things out—we know that.

Lew: She's great! What else has changed for you? For example, do you still drink if you're on a gig or you're with the guys? Do you still hang with the guys all the time?
Dave: Oh, I like to drink. I like to get a little buzz going at times when I'm playing, as most musicians do. So, I found my drink. I have to thank Eleana for the vodka martini. I don't remember her drinking, but she introduced me to that drink. But not hanging as much as I did before was a slow devolvement. It took me a minute. Nothing dramatic, but psychologically, it was a lifestyle change. With Richie, who was my man for so many years in this respect, this got a bit difficult.

Caris wanted it straight. We had five years of marriage before Lydia was born, traveling and being together. Caris was with me all the time and we had fun. I totally advise all couples to have at least three to five years before they have kids, because that's what you're going to remember when times get rough, which they will inevitably, in one way or the other. Life is intense and it gets busy. Caris never had to get high to get hip. She's naturally very sociable, as you can tell, very easy to talk to and good with people. When she's there, I can recede into the background—I love it! She has a great sense of humor, which I see especially when she's in public.

It was and is a very compatible relationship. From the practical standpoint, something good happened business-wise with Caris. I had by now a personal relationship with Hans and Veronika Gruber, who owned Advance Music, which by the late '80s was doing very well and had published a bunch of my educational materials. They had begun by importing Aebersold play-alongs to Germany and eventually organizing clinics in their hometown of Rottenburg, near Stuttgart.

Caris actually had a company in New York at the time called Caris Music Copy, which did manuscript copying by hand of scores and parts for composers, which she was great at by the way. Since she has a degree in composition and had to write out all her own music, she developed a very good manuscript hand. This is before Finale or Sibelius notation programs were around. She submitted a sample to Advance Music to possibly be hired to do some work for their publishing company. That is how they first met. One thing led to another, and of course they wanted to have their materials distributed in America, at first through Jamey, but they wanted something more dedicated to their publications alone. Caris just spoke up and said she could do it. This way she could have her own business, and be a mother, while helping the authors, most of whom we knew and had recommended to Advance. She is still doing this, as well as distributing materials from other publishing companies, primarily from Europe. It all fit.

Our lifestyle centered around jazz, around creativity, but we didn't live the way I lived before, when it was the loft with music on all the time, smoking a joint, everybody hanging out and listening or playing. We didn't do that. In Pennsylvania there were musicians there, but in the country you kind of live by yourself. You see people on occasion, but it's not a daily thing, which is a big difference in lifestyle from the city. It enabled me to really become productive with things that take that kind of time, like writing books.

Lew: But there wasn't a part of you that said, "I wish I could stay in Manhattan"?
Dave: There definitely was, but on several levels it was impossible. Financially, New York was getting out of hand in the eighties. It was unlivable, unless you made a lot of money. In addition to the housing, it's $50 as soon as you walk on the street for coffee or whatever. I left New York because I really wanted a little peace. I didn't want to be on the scene all the time. I didn't want to be so accessible. Not from a reputation standpoint, but just time-wise! Playing in New York became more of a hassle obviously, and I still had to do that. It would be nice not to have to drive so far to get home after the gig, which is a problem I still have to deal with sometimes when I play New York, but we have found something to alleviate that situation. We have this property in Manhattan through the Hilton Club, like an urban timeshare, but not in the typical sense of reserving a week or like that. We purchased based on points, which you use when you want to stay in what is basically your own apartment house on 57th Street. You get a certain amount of days out of

the year. Let me put it this way: I don't have a second home, but I have property in New York. I have a place that I can use from time to time. Because New York is still the center of this music. That's why when we looked for a house to buy, it had to be within a certain zone. But no, I never missed it—not really. This period coincided with my traveling more and more to Europe for work, so I didn't need to be in New York on a daily level.

You need the airport, really. It's a two-sided coin. If you are in New York, you will do more record dates and clubs, etc. But I was making a living and I was being productive, so it balanced out. In fact, it more than balanced out. With more organized time, I began in the late eighties to work on the idea of an international association. It started to form in my mind after that episode with trying to get involved with an aid organization kind of thing in the early '80s. If you recall, I had been trying to find a way to satisfy a certain part of my personality that the music didn't take care of. To some extent the teaching did alleviate this, but there was more. I still had the thought that I wanted to do something that would have an influence in the world. It was about 1987 when I started thinking about it.

By 1984 or 1985, I was doing clinics in Europe alone, and sometimes with Quest as a group or maybe with Richie as a duo. Around 1987, I started thinking about the clinics I was doing in all these countries. I was definitely building a rep for teaching by this time, and interest in jazz education, especially in Northern Europe, was intensifying during this period. They had some schools there but not many, much like the States twenty years earlier. I was going all over the place: Israel, Japan, and all the European countries. I was getting to know the administrators as well as the instructors. One thing that seemed clear to me was that nobody knew each other from country to country. There was the Common Market at the time, made up of most of the western European countries, but that was more of an economic situation. In general the musicians didn't know each other. I had a good vantage point because I was going all over the place. The bottom line is that with teaching jazz, I don't care where you go, you're still going to teach Miles Davis or Duke, etc. It doesn't matter whether you're in Finland or Italy. Jazz is jazz. I thought that these people should know each other. Jeunesses Musicales does something like this in classical music from what I understand, so I looked into it. The National Association of Jazz Educators, NAJE, was happening at that time, but it didn't have an international profile at that point. It was national, geared toward educators and schools in the United States. They did later become the International Association of Jazz Educators (IAJE), and more recently, they went out of business. But back then I thought, why shouldn't there be an organization for schools worldwide? Like-minded people should know each other.

The idea of an organization with member schools was something that could be done on a world level and be a positive force, with the emphasis on student interaction. There were two friends who helped me formulate this in particular. Steve Lipman, my buddy who accompanied me to see Coltrane when we were in high school, was now at Berklee College in charge of admissions. Then there was my newer close friend from Israel, Leon Segal, who's just a great thinker. Leon is in a field called human factors. He develops ideas for businesses and products to make things around us work better, meaning more efficient and practical. He might be hired by an airport to develop better ways to communicate with customers through improved signage or whatever. He has worked on handheld devices and how they should feel. Hence the name human factors—very interesting. He is a brilliant cat. As for music, I would consider him a high-level amateur. He plays Coltrane solos by ear on soprano. He loves the music and really understands it.

So, between these two friends, we went back and forth about details concerning philosophy, practical questions, and so forth. I formulated the idea, with the bywords being *cross-cultural communication*—in other words, using jazz as a vehicle for promoting positive communication between cultures toward a better world. The cliché that music is universal definitely applies to jazz. People who study jazz have more in common than not. Human communication would be bettered by people knowing each other through the music, at least at first. That was my raison d'être—the fact that a school in Germany and in, let's say Israel, would get to know each other, foster exchanges through workshops, and so on. Good music would be the natural by-product. Teachers would get to know each other, enabling more performance possibilities because of the networking atmosphere that would naturally go on at an international jazz meeting. I saw that doing this would really be a very humanitarian as well as a good business thing to do.

I felt I was the guy to do this. This was all happening during the early years of my marriage to Caris and just around my turning forty, which was a watershed of sorts. It was the first time I thought about age at all. You are definitely halfway through on average, and it means that inevitably it is time to think a little about payback—I mean contribution time. I didn't see anyone else around who would do it, so I figured I was the designated driver. I felt confident enough to pull this off because by then I commanded a lot of respect in the business. There are two ways we are measured in this business. There is the popular and commercial aspect, which has to do with the public and is the result of many factors besides the immediate appeal of one's music, like timing, promotion, and so on. The other yardstick is peer respect earned through hard work. The highest reward is having your peers respect you, at least for me. That's what I was always after. You want to be one of the A-plus guys. With fifteen years, more or less, under my belt by the mid 1980s, with the cachet of having been with Miles and Elvin, and now with Quest, which was seen as a real artistic band, there was plenty of respect around for who I was, especially in Europe, since they are more serious about jazz than the American audience. I knew I could pull this world thing off.

For two years I wrote letters every couple of months to all the folks I had done clinics for, about how this could be a kind of United Nations of jazz, the cross-cultural angle, about aspects of brotherhood and service: "Let's play in hospitals and prisons," things like that. I got positive responses. By 1989, I decided to call in the chips. I asked Hans Gruber if I could use his premises for the first meeting, not sure who would really come. It was real dramatic in a way. I made a date, place, and time to meet with a hotel and phone number. "I will be sitting in this restaurant at one o'clock in the afternoon." It was April 22, 1989. It was a Yugoslavian restaurant that I loved in Rottenburg, Germany. I told everyone I would be at a table upstairs at 1:00 p.m. on this day, waiting for anyone who would come. I mean, this was like a movie. It was great. Lo and behold, men and women from thirteen schools from ten countries showed up including Israel, United States, France, Spain, Switzerland, Germany, Sweden, Netherlands, England, and Ireland. The guys from Spain drove twenty-four hours, and there were other stories like that—people I didn't even know. Remember, this is before email, cell phones, and common use of fax. It was just phone calls and letters that got this together. We met for that day, had dinner, and met the next day.

The main thing for me was to have a meeting every year in a different country. That's what I wanted to accomplish—having all the kids from the member schools and countries in one place for a week. I wasn't looking for a massive thing like IAJE became, which all these folks knew about by then. I kept repeating the mantra, "Kid to kid. The teachers and administrators will take care of themselves. It's the kids who have to hang together." I told everyone, at that meeting in April '89, that my interest was in the artistic end, not the business. I would do the musical part, but I needed somebody to run it. Out of the blue comes Walter Turkenburg from the Royal Conservatory in The Hague, Netherlands. I did not know him personally, as I did some of the others. He came because the head of the CIM school in Paris called and told Walter that he shouldn't miss this meeting. Walter introduced himself and basically said, "I'm your point man! I will come to your house, spend a couple days, and we'll put this together." And he did it, shortly afterward. He flew in for a few days in Pennsylvania, and we put the whole thing together.

We decided to have a meeting at his school in The Hague the next year, June 1990. If at least five schools showed up, we would go ahead. Any less and it was just a nice idea. At that first meeting we ended up with fifteen countries. Cats came from Russia because they heard about it. Everybody was dying for something like this, in Europe especially. A week spent with jam sessions, ensembles, concerts, and lectures all taking place at the school in The Hague, with local clubs taking part. We had one to two students from each school. I was very careful and still am for the IASJ that there should be no more than six combos, because for the final concerts I wanted everyone to have a chance to really play a full set —no little fifteen minutes or like that. I had learned the pitfalls of that from Aebersold clinics.

So this organization became a reality. We named it the International Association of Schools of Jazz, IASJ. The whole story is in detail on my website. This IASJ thing has been going on now for over two decades and it is a big part of my life. I'm very proud of it and always state that besides my relationship with my family, the thing I've done of most importance in my life is the IASJ. I feel this is my biggest contribution. It's small—maybe a few thousand people have passed through our doors—but it's high-quality interaction between cultures and musicians. Twenty years later, a guy will come up to me and say, "Man, that meeting—I'll never forget it. I met the drummer I play with now."

Lew: How did you deal with NAJE, later IAJE, being around at the same time as you were, doing a lot of similar things?
Dave: By the late 1980s, I had been to a lot of IAJE meetings, sometimes performing or lecturing. Let me put it this way—I was a known factor in that organization. I wasn't on the board, but I was a musician who was a teacher. Starting in 1988, I began going every year with Caris because she had a booth with the Advance Music products. When they got wind about the IASJ, there was definitely a draft. No question about it. I'm not going to mention any names, but it came down the pipeline like, "Why are you doing this?" We had a lot of European membership, about 70 to 80 percent of our total at the time; we had Japan, Israel, and of course some important schools in the States by the early nineties, all at the same

time that IAJE was trying to internationalize. So, I could see how they got bugged, but instead of trying to cooperate, they threw down the gauntlet, at least for a few years. When Walter Turkenburg, the chairman of our board, went to talk to them at one of their board meetings, they were actually rude. Walter would come, as a lot of Europeans started attending the yearly January IAJE convention more in the nineties. So he was there representing his school in The Hague and our organization. IAJE invited him to their board meeting and a couple of the guys were a drag. I knew who they were.

IAJE was the epitome of an old boys' network. It's known that the beginning emphasis was on big bands, evolving out of the Stan Kenton workshops in the '50s, I believe. It was more about the teachers and the administrators—*my* school, *my* band. The kids would come in uniform and play basically for themselves in the lobby, one band every hour. It had nothing to do with interaction. They had vendors on the convention floor with companies like Steinway, Yamaha, Selmer, Zildjian. It was a big commercial fair by the '90s, with thousands of people wandering around. The record companies were in bed with the board, exerting influence so that their acts could play the big concerts. IAJE had a million-dollar budget.

The IASJ on the other hand is small, artistic, nothing commercial. IASJ and IAJE were like David and Goliath at work. Finally, in 1994 or 1995, a guy from Detroit who liked me became president of IAJE. His name was Dennis Tini and he put out the olive branch: "This is ridiculous." I said, "Are you talking to me? Of course, it's ridiculous! We should be waltzing together instead of being at odds. We're all in the same game here." So we got it right in ten minutes. From then on, until the IAJE demise after their 2008 conference in Toronto, they gave our organization a stipend every year to bring a student from Eastern Europe, where there was no money in those days. Finally, we were on the same page, at least from this standpoint. We consulted with them on things, and from time to time a couple of the guys came for a day or two to our meetings. IASJ activities are limited to mainly our yearly annual jazz meeting, held usually in late June/July. As well, we encourage and facilitate, as best we can with limited administrative assets, teacher and/or student exchanges between member schools during the academic year, through a newsletter and a posting board on the Internet. This was and is mom-and-pop—very real and honest.

Lew: Did you ever consider just doing it through IAJE, instead of starting a new organization?

Dave: No, because of the reasons stated above as to the difference in the focus. Sometime in the '90s, there was a mini-revolt to try to change direction in IAJE, if you remember. A couple of guys called them on their thing—their small-town stuff, the money thing, who played at the convention, about not being run by musicians. Most of the presentations were stylistically straight-ahead with an emphasis on big bands. It was basically a Midwest organization—Manhattan, Kansas, was the headquarters, literally and actually geographically close to the middle of the United States, so what do you expect?

Lew: It's so funny that they picked a place called Manhattan.
Dave: Strange, but one of the founders I guess taught there and found an office at the very beginning, from what I understood, in a shopping center—a little building, like a couple offices—Suite 200 or whatever. But when they famously went bankrupt, that didn't happen as believed by many due to the executive director, Bill McFarlin, spending too much on the expense account. OK, he took guys to dinner—one time Kenny Werner and I had a lavish meal in the south of France. But to think the demise of IAJE was due to a bottle of wine or an executive suite at the yearly meeting is absurd. Maybe some of that is true, but it belies the main point. Besides bad management and sloppy bookkeeping, the real bottom line in my opinion was they didn't want to let the *guys* in. Guys like me. I went to McFarlin a few years before the end, 2003 or 2004. By then, the IASJ was a known entity and it was time for me to recede into the background a little bit. You never want to overstay your welcome, which every boss knows in the world. I told Walter, too, "You've got to recede. You become honorary executive director or something similar." I don't have to be at every meeting. If they want me at a meeting, they pay me separately to come. If they don't, okay. The IASJ meeting goes on anyway.

So I went to McFarlin and told him that I was backing off the IASJ and would be willing to take a more prominent role in the IAJE. "If you want me on the board, I'll do it," meaning someone like me who was a working jazz musician and educator. "You need somebody of my stature and experience." He said he was interested, but he was a PR kind of guy and would say anything to keep things smooth. It showed me that they just didn't want any guys like me. They didn't want the Marvin Stamms in. They didn't want the Hal Galpers—guys who really put some thought and muscle into jazz education. These are musicians/teachers who are on the front line of jazz education and have ideas and can play.

Lew: Marvin is a great trumpeter. He is a marvelous person too.
Dave: Absolutely. They didn't want the musicians in there. They wanted to keep it to themselves. Outside of any financial hanky panky, the bottom line to me was the mindset, because that's where it all starts in the final count. It was an us-versus-them thing—nothing personal, but it indicates a small-minded mentality. It started with the big band concept and they did not want to be more inclusive, except in a token way.

You want to talk administration and money? The bottom line is that musicians who are on the ground, like those I mentioned, would never let the money thing get too far away from reality, because that is what they do in real life every day! There's nobody more on top of it than a musician, who's watching every damn dime coming in, who's scuffling for a living. We would never let that happen. This will not happen to IASJ. We will not go bankrupt. We may run out of money, but we're not going to spend more than we have. I am not going to let that happen on my watch. I can tell you right now. Most working musicians who are at all on the case would never let that occur. The fact that they didn't let in any musicians is the real reason why some guy from the middle of nowhere had to say, "Oh, sorry, we don't have any money anymore."

Lew: So it wasn't just about wasting money, the way corporations do?
Dave: Surely, of course, but this is not on a Bernie Madoff scale. It's nothing like the corporate greed we see in the real world. Basically, nobody checked the books. Again, a dinner or an executive suite here and there is not the point. What I'm saying is that if you or I were in there, we'd be checking the books every day for major things, like where to have the convention or how many square feet are needed for the exhibitors, etc., because we live like that. These people were administrators who couldn't be fired. That's my point. They didn't let in the people who are the players, not just from the standpoint that the organization has the word "jazz" in its title for starters, but also the kind of mentality that we have, which is real-world, on-the-ground, an in-the-trenches way of existing. We're not sitting in some office marking papers. We are out there working and doing this every day and we're the reason this whole thing exists. They didn't want to let that reality in. That's what happened, in my opinion.

Lew: When you were first presenting your IASJ idea to the Europeans, did any of them say to you, "What about NAJE/IAJE?"
Dave: Of course. In fact some of them were in both organizations.

Lew: Did they all understand the need for their own organization?
Dave: They did. They were very glad to have a mostly European organization. Everybody has a vibe about America, especially about IAJE. You would go to this behemoth meeting with eight thousand people and Wynton Marsalis playing, or Herbie Hancock, and awards, gala dinners—the corporate world, which is resented in a lot of places. People were coming from Siena, Italy. They had a little school in a small town that a guy was killing himself to do on his own. Talk about fish out of water. But on the other hand they loved being around the glamour or whatever you want to call it, being around American star musicians. It's a two-sided coin.

Some of IASJ's members are state-supported schools, but we have members ranging from the prestigious London-based Royal Academy to the Tailler de Musicos in Barcelona, which gives five hundred lessons a week to people from ages eight to eighty. They were very glad to have a counter-group. They looked at me not as a turncoat but like, "He's one of us," which I was, because I was making my living in Europe and playing with their people a lot. I was and still am getting more out of Europe than from America, as a musician. All I did was the right thing for the people I knew and worked with, which was to organize them. Now, of course, we have more members in light of the end of IAJE, because there's nowhere else to join, except this new Jazz Education Network in America. But we are small and we're going to stay small. I don't want to have three hundred concerts going on at the same time like IAJE, where you had eighteen things at two o'clock in the afternoon and you can't decide where to go. People ended up walking out in the middle of concerts to catch a little of the other one. Bigger is not necessarily better.

For a while one of our founders, the late Graham Collier, put together a magazine called *Changes*. The magazine was very well done, with controversial topics and high-level writing. But in general we operated and still do on a shoestring, with one part-time person to help Walter, who after all is heading a major jazz department at the Royal Conservatory in The Hague, Holland. We do the best we can, and the meetings are like beacons of light. When you hear these kids play at the end of the week, after just meeting for the first time a few days earlier, from all different parts of the world, putting music together and hanging out, it's something else.

I insist on a real performance, not a fifteen-minute appearance—a fifty-minute set, more or less, which means I want these kids to feel they've worked on something by the end of the week. I pose it to them right at the beginning: "You are professionals for the next five days. You are going to do what musicians like myself do every day in the real world. You have a group of players who you may not even be able to talk to because of language problems." They don't know each other because I make sure that all groups are geographically spread out. That's one of my own requisites. I sit with a map, literally placing everyone by country, since for the most part the playing levels are uniformly good. "You have to put music on by Friday night, and believe me, I and others with great ears will be listening. What you have to do is get it together and help each other. We, the teachers, do the best we can in putting you in groups. Now it's up to you." The bottom line is every group has to put on a set as professionally as possible. The teachers at the meeting help, but I try to get them off the case as soon as possible and let the students do it on their own.

My next long-term goal is to have our own building, not just for jazz, but inclusive of the arts as a whole, with a seasonal program covering a lot from specific subjects like what Jimmy Cobb's brush stroke is, to the avant-garde techniques of Andrew Cyrille—whatever. Maybe the next week is a study of Trane and "Giant Steps," followed by the relationship between solo saxophone and a solo dancer—just being creative with combinations. Something like the Space for Innovative Development that I discussed in Chapter 5. Probably in Europe—France or Italy, a nice place. How about an old castle that somebody wants to give us? I need a guy to give me money! What I need is what Marsalis got from the Lincoln Center. I need somebody to say, "Liebman, what do you need? You deserve it. You've been working your ass off. You've been doing your job. What would you like to do if I could give you a couple of million dollars?" It takes one person to do that, just ten minutes from where we are sitting now, because we're in New York. "I need a million dollars to set up a home, a nonprofit endowment, etc., and here is what I've done." I can sell this to anybody. I need ten minutes and of course the follow-through. I could go to the president of the United States, I don't care. I know what I want, I know what I believe in, and now we have a track record at IASJ of twenty plus years. I hope before I go down, we'll have a home like what I'm envisioning.

Lew: Ideally, would the building be big enough that you'd actually have your annual IASJ concerence there?
Dave: Sure—a building with classrooms, performances—an ongoing home for ten months a year—clinics for eight-year-olds and for eighty-year-olds—whatever. With what we know about jazz education, we could really do it right. Plus, I am familiar with who the good teachers are. I know there's nobody better than you for a certain thing, or than Jim

McNeely for what he does, for example. I know what guys do because I've watched everybody in action. I'm a very astute observer and I know what makes a good teacher. I know my idea could be successful. Just give me some money. Give me a home!

Lew: Would you live there too?
Dave: I don't know, but it would seemingly coincide with the last part of my productive life, which wouldn't be a bad way to go down. Unfortunately, the philanthropic climate now is not positive for such a project. But there's somebody out there who could do it. What do I need, $500,000, a million? I don't think it's millions. At the end of every meeting, I always say the same thing. My last thing to the kids is, "You may be the minister of culture for your country in twenty years. Your uncle may say, 'Is there anything you'd like to do? I have extra money, and I'm looking for something to do with it.'" I say to them, "Remember IASJ."

I make a pitch every year. "You've just spent a week with people from twenty other countries. You had a good time, I know. You will really know how good this was in a couple of years from now. If you come across some money, call me up and I will be on the next plane to talk to your uncle, or your grandfather, or the head of your country, and I will convince them to do this, because I know about this and I'm on the right course here."

Lew: That sounds great and I certainly hope that happens. Now, another big part of your life since the late '80s is your annual summer master class.
Dave: Yes. These two activities, the IASJ and the East Stroudsburg University Master Class, got started as the result of a steady home life and working environment. These are things you can't do on the fly. You've got to be around. For sure, I became a lot busier. It's about using your time economically. That's important. You become very efficient doing something, even for an hour, that used to take several. On the other hand, you can't have everything. I can't always just sit down and listen to music like I did before I got so busy, or practice or whatever. That's a choice one makes concerning priorities. When I listen to something, it's in the car—things like that. These two projects, plus all the books I really wanted to do, became a priority. I wanted the chromatic book out of the way, the saxophone book, the *Self-Portrait of a Jazz Artist*. I wanted to get them done because I'm the kind of person who just has to finish stuff. I don't feel right until things are catalogued and documented, even if it

just stays on the shelf. I'm just that kind of person. It's that Virgo stuff, I guess.

So, in '87, almost immediately after moving to Pennsylvania, Caris said, "Go right to the nearby college and see if they do summer conferences." So I started the annual saxophone master class. I rent a music classroom and dorm rooms at East Stroudsburg University, which is the state school near our home. It's a Tuesday night through Sunday afternoon. The great thing is that I go home for lunch, meaning no travel. The students come to me for an intense week of study, which I really enjoy. I take about ten to twenty students. In the past ten years, I have been more or less alternating between the saxophone master class one year and the next year my chromatic harmony approach, from my book, which is open to all instruments. I wanted to see if the chromatic harmony course that I teach at the Manhattan School of Music over a two-year period can be boiled down to five days, and it can.

I've had participants ranging from teenagers to seventy years old. They all have to send me a tape of their playing because I don't want beginners. Beginners would do better at one of Aebersold's camps, where they have enough people to put together combos at different levels. There are plenty of camps and clinics that are specifically for beginners. I want guys who can already play jazz up to a decent level, middle and up. I don't advertise. It's all word of mouth. On my site it says to send me a tape after January 1. I have to hear them play if it is saxophone, or their compositional level if it is the chromatic class for that year. I do turn people down—at least two or three people a year, on average. I would like the full capacity, which could be twenty or so, but I don't want dead weight. Guys in my neighborhood are always welcome to come, because that's a service to the local jazz community. So, the participants send me a tape, I approve, they send me a deposit, I send them directions, and they come.

The music room at the college has a piano, sound system, music stands, drums—the whole deal. There's a professor of music there named Pat Dorian—his wife, Mary, helped to edit this book—who helps me get it all together there. He is quite a force for jazz in our area of the Poconos. He has become a great friend and plays trumpet in my big band. And at the end of the week I rent a little place at a hotel or whatever for a final hang. We also do a gig at the Deer Head Inn in Delaware Water Gap, which as you know is quite a famous place for jazz over many decades. I use guys like drummer Mike Stephans, Phil Markowitz, and my bassist Tony Marino to play with the students, doing their own tunes. This becomes part of the week, preparing, rehearsing, and performing.

And every year I have a guest speaker; George Garzone, Joe Lovano, Phil Woods, Steve Wilson, Mike Brecker, Steve Coleman, and many more have come as guest lecturers. They spend an afternoon lecturing about their music and approach.

Lew: When you do the chromatic course, what instruments have you gotten?
Dave: That could be anybody, as long as they write. I have to see their compositions. It's not based on their playing. I have to see what level of harmony they are at, which I can tell from their composing or a reharmonization of a standard. Maybe they are writing tunes in a '60s Wayne Shorter style or something like that, which is perfect for the class. But I don't want three-chord writing. I have to see that the level is high enough and they are ready for the chromatic approach material.

Lew: How did this whole chromatic approach become an actual course of study at the Manhattan School of Music?
Dave: This is important because the story chronicles some musical and conceptual things that I have been involved with over the decades. In 2000, Justin DiCioccio, a well-known educator and percussionist, became the head of the jazz department at the Manhattan School of Music, and he asked me to teach there. Justin is the real deal and knows what he wants and what he's doing. You have to remember that over the past decades I have been approached to sign on the dotted line and be part of a faculty on occasion but always resisted it because I didn't want the teaching to become routine, and honestly I was doing okay with what I was doing, which was mostly workshops and some private teaching. I told him that, and he came back with, "You can teach anything you want. The course is called Masters of Jazz. You can do a study of Coltrane, or you can do a study of your left pinky if you want. I don't care. I want you there." I started thinking about my book, *A Chromatic Approach to Jazz Harmony and Melody*.

When you write a book, and you, Lewis, know this better than most, you're kind of stepping on your own toes because you're giving away all your information. Why should they come to you if it's all in the book, assuming you did a good job? I thought about that with my saxophone book, *Developing a Personal Saxophone Sound*, because that one has everything I could tell you about saxophone, period. My DVD, *The Complete Guide to Saxophone Sound Production*, is not just describing, but actually demonstrating, so between the book and the DVD you get the whole deal. On transcribing solos, which is an important part of my pedagogy, I did a DVD, *The Improviser's Guide to Transcription*, which is also very complete. Finally, the chromatic book was the icing on the cake. I had spilled all the beans. I mean, there it is—it's all there!

But what I realized ten years later was that, although people buy the book and are interested in it, as I know from the grapevine, that doesn't mean everyone is reading it, or more to the point, understanding it. They go immediately to the hundred lines and voicings in the back of the book, which are easily accessible and can be copped right away without any understanding of what they are, no problem. I mean, how many people really read every word of Schoenberg's harmony book? Or every word of Hindemith's? Or even George Russell's, which we all bought in the sixties? Did I really read every word? Not really—but I wanted to have some familiarity with George's Lydian Concept, for example, in my library, because I considered myself a student of jazz. "Some familiarity" is quite different than true understanding.

First of all, just because the information is there doesn't mean anybody really ever reads it, especially in our period of history these days. Second, you've got to expound upon it and produce followers, students, for the book to have a real-world effect. Just because you wrote it doesn't mean it's going to be influential. You need followers. Schoenberg had his students. George Russell had his students. So with Justin's offer, I realized this is a golden opportunity. I can find some believers, spread some knowledge, and make what I spent time writing and figuring out viable, instead of it being some book on the shelf that somebody looks at the cover and opens up to one page, never getting past page ten. That's why I decided to take on the teaching at Manhattan School of Music for Justin. At first weekly, then for a few years I did it twice a month with longer hours, and finally I got Phil Markowitz to assist me, as I am doing at present. The real challenge was how to organize it on a weekly schedule, which then led me to think how I could do it in a five-day workshop, or even in two hours at a lecture. After ten-plus years, I have it down.

Lew: It's a different approach. I think what happens to most people with your book is they say, "I understand it intellectually, but it's not me. I can't think that way. I can't do it."
Dave: Exactly. And I tell them, "Ten years from now, you're more likely to understand it. Give it time." They can't actualize it. Not at twenty-three years old. Who could?

Lew: You're right about the teaching, because what happens is they read it, and then you get up there and tell them exactly the same thing, and they go, "Oh!" They look so surprised. You've probably seen it, when they looked so surprised. They already read it—why do they act so surprised? Somehow it didn't quite register earlier, just coming from a book.

Dave: That's why the whole thing about writing a book and giving it away is that it's like the appetizer at a meal. They really want you to be there, live and in person—the saxophone stuff particularly, even more than the chromatic thing. The chromatic thing is complicated and it takes time. You can't get it in one day. The saxophone thing—in two hours I can basically do the whole deal. Here are all of Joe Allard's principles—bam! Done. Even if I recited exactly what is in the book, which I don't, they would be happy. They still want you to be physically present. Thank God! They want to see the man who wrote the book. You are actually in a way more in demand.

Lew: You get more gigs instead of less, and that's what people always don't understand. You get more gigs because they know that you know. They see the book as, "Okay, I've got some notes I can take away with me." Not, "I don't need him."

Dave: Yes. And the other thing is, of course, this chromatic book is my life's work. It's a summary of ways of thinking. It's really a workbook more than anything. My original intention was that it would be my and Richie's explanation of how we play in that way.

Lew: Richie was supposed to work on the book with you?

Dave: He copped a plea—he didn't want to put it on paper, he didn't want to commit. I don't think he was in the state of mind to do it, in any case. For sure he was not in those days a typewriter kind of guy. Brilliant, but not about to sit for hours like I would. So by 1987/88, I became obsessed with finishing this thing.

Lew: But was it also Richie worrying about giving his ideas away?

Dave: I don't know if it was that, or if he felt he wasn't ready. Maybe he didn't want to make declarative statements because he didn't feel like it was credible enough yet. I'm not sure.

Lew: Or he didn't really have it organized in his mind that way.

Dave: That's what I think it was. He was supposed to do the harmony and I was obviously going to do the melodic concepts. He was going to do the connection to the classical stuff, show the roots, which I did a little of what I could, but I'm not a piano player like that. I'm not that versed in the classical repertoire, obviously. But when he copped out, I had to figure out what to do myself. It was a lot of work and I wanted it to be finished. By the time it got to the end of the '80s and I saw the writing on the wall that Quest was coming to an end, I thought, "You know what? I'll probably never play like this again, so I'd better get it down now, because this is a time-capsule thing covering a certain way of hearing and thinking that I have been doing for years. It's got to be done now, otherwise forget its relevance." Later, I wouldn't be around Richie. Basically, he was the conduit for this whole thing, although Phil Markowitz now knows the material inside out and can do it great. It's just that Richie and I were doing it in the formation stages.

Lew: Richie's an innovator.
Dave: Exactly. It's really his vocabulary, in the end. I mean, he owns the basic vibe. The piano has a lot to do with that. By 1988/89, the band was sounding better than ever, but the vibe was a drag. McClure was a little off, too. There was a lot of tension in the band and it just didn't feel good to travel. Caris was telling me, "What are you doing this for? Richie needs help. Stop enabling him." He was borrowing money from me. I was fronting him money, and she didn't like that, of course. To tell you the truth, the reason I kept it going for a couple more years than I needed to was because I really felt there was more for me to learn—not just from Richie, but also from Billy Hart. With Quest, I can't say I felt like Miles Davis, but I certainly had the chance to feel whatever he felt when he had a great rhythm section, which he always did. I knew this was probably not going to happen again in that particular "jazz" way because it was disappearing to play that way, meaning the kind of interaction we were doing. I could just play whatever I wanted to—in that vernacular. Richie, Ron, and Billy, they had the essence of that post-sixties way of playing, distilled from the Coltrane and Davis groups. We loved that music and still do. In a sense, this was my total postgraduate work. I *needed* those lessons on how to deal with a burning rhythm section. I would never get that cast of characters together again. Just like any great band. Weather Report was Weather Report with Joe Zawinul and Wayne; Coltrane with McCoy and Elvin was *that* sound, etc. You could substitute someone instead of Herbie in the Miles '60s band, but it wouldn't be the same. You have that magic that works. I knew that, which was part of the reason I finished the book, and part of the reason I just worked this band to the bone until I couldn't do it anymore—just grin and bear it, whatever the vibe was like. I took care of all the business, called the guys up, got

them on the plane, and everything like that, because I could and I needed it to finish my education. That's the truth.

Lew: So Quest actually ended when?
Dave: In 1991. I started to look toward this group that I still have at present, with the emphasis being more on writing. Richie just didn't want to read anymore. He honestly felt that whatever we wrote would not be better than what we could improvise, and he was right in that thinking for that situation. But I just felt the need to have more structure and composition, also more electric and color, in a way like Lookout Farm had been, sonically at least. I wanted to get more comfortable with the odd-meter craze that was just starting to happen. Of course, we played things in seven or whatever meter over the years—my *Lookout Farm* record has a long track in seven, "Sam's Float"—but the new generation was raising the ante a bit. Richie was definitely not interested in going in these directions.

Quest was primarily about harmony, pure and simple. That's why for the new group I wanted to emphasize color and rhythm, so the first thing I did was to get drummer Jamey Haddad, who is a hand drum monster, besides traps. I didn't want to get behind the eight ball with the rhythm game happening, the world music influence that was becoming stronger by the minute. I had seen Miles continuously changing to keep himself up to date, and that was my goal. I was forty-five years old. Was I ready to go out to pasture? Was I ready to be the classic musician who plays his way only? I still wanted to learn something, and that wasn't going to happen with Richie. I had to have a drummer who could play odd meter and loved it. That's how I got Jamey.

Jamey was freelancing around the area and was a buddy of Joe Lovano from Cleveland. He had studied in India with some drum master. Plus he had the Middle Eastern thing. He's Lebanese. He had a link to two different world cultures—very hip. So, he was number one for the new band. The bass player, Tony Marino, was from our area in Pennsylvania and was known in the 'hood. He's from the Scranton area and lives now in Moscow, Pennsylvania. I met him soon after I moved to the Poconos and he seemed to be doing a lot of the jazz gigs in the area. He had a musical relationship with Jamey, which was enough for me. I always take the drummer's bass man first, if possible, but I didn't know how great Tony was—he was the main cat for our area. I don't know how we met or first played together. There was Steve Gilmore, but he was Phil Woods's guy, so I wasn't going to touch him. Anyway, Steve was a bebopper in the end—one of the best by the way, especially as a soloist. But Tony seemed right.

For piano I wanted someone who could play synths. I wanted more texture, which we couldn't get with Quest and the acoustic piano. So, I needed somebody who could do that but also was a killer jazz cat. It happened to be that Phil Markowitz had a house out by us in Pennsylvania, and I knew him from our peer group, but not intimately. He had street cred from playing with Mel Lewis and Chet Baker, among others—a solid rep in the Apple. He'd been around the scene for decades like Andy LaVerne, Fred Hersch, guys like that—another great New York–based Jewish sideman piano player. Phil is a New Yorker. He was born in Brooklyn but brought up in East Hampton, out on Long Island. He and Davia, his wife, keep an apartment in Manhattan. They bought a place in Effort, Pennsylvania, about twenty minutes from me.

Guitarist Vic Juris, from Jersey, I met at a clinic. I think it was one of the Aebersold road shows in Germany for Advance Music. He just seemed like a really good guy, a nice cat, not totally unknown, who looked like we could do something good together. As I remember it, I got all the guys to my basement. Tony and Jamey didn't know Phil, and Phil didn't know them. Vic, I think, knew Tony but not Jamey or Phil. I'm not sure, but in any case you get the picture.

Lew: So, you really put that band together?
Dave: Oh, definitely. Hand-picked. This was my project. If I was more famous commercially, it would be Liebman's "New Band" with trumpets blaring: the *New* Lieb Group, ta da! Putting a band together with sort of known cats or the hot youngbloods. These kinds of moves evoke interest and for sure jazz media excitement. I had already done this, reshuffling a couple of times, but not as many as other bandleaders. By then, in twenty years, three groups—Lookout Farm, the Quintet with Scofield, and Quest—not counting the Ellis-Liebman band. When I do something, I'm going to keep it for a while. I wanted those elements musically that I described, with those guys. I wrote specifically for that band, and then of course I realized how good Phil was at writing, and things grew. It's still together now, with some minor changes.

Lew: That's a good, long stretch. It's unusual these days.
Dave: It's very unusual. I have loyalty—they stay with me. I definitely had a concept and I was very enthusiastic about it. I got the first record out on a French label with whom I had a relationship for years, Owl Records. It was called *Turn It Around*, meaning turn it around: the music,

and by extension my life. That's what it meant to me. Most of my titles have some personal significance.

Lew: Vic is a marvelous player, and I've loved his music since I first saw him with Barry Miles in the 1970s. I said, "Wow, this guitar player is great!" I recommended to Rutgers that they hire Vic, based on his music and his teaching reputation—I didn't know him personally then. He has since put out two valuable books of advanced ideas for guitarists. And it's my sense that he's almost like a protégé of yours as far as the chromatic harmony.

Dave: Definitely. He didn't play like that at all. Essentially he was a bebopper, organ trio kind of guy, like standard guitar stuff. He was coming out of Grant Green and Pat Martino. Vic was a straight-ahead player and had the rock and blues thing down. Jersey guitar, man! That's a real thing, you know. I've never seen a musician change more. Our relationship is now over twenty years. I'd say it can be marked off in three periods. The first seven years when Phil was in the band, Vic was like the second horn behind me. For the next few years as a quartet, with Jamey still playing drums, Vic of course had more to do as the second main soloist *and* accompanist. Finally, when Jamey split and Marko Marcinko came in, Vic's role increased in responsibility because the music got freer and more texture oriented. I asked for and got more sound things from Vic. Also when Phil left, I needed more compositions from Vic. I've never seen anybody work harder on music.

He really took care of business. If necessary, we would and still will sit at the piano for voicings, knowing of course that the guitar is not a piano keyboard and notes have to be left out, especially for many of my chords. It can often be easily accomplished by letting the bass obviously cover the bottom note and me assume the top note. But honestly, you'd be surprised at how many complex chords can be done on the guitar. They are not common-language chords necessarily, but with study there are a lot of possibilities. The great guitarist and teacher Mick Goodrick, kind of the godfather of all the modern cats, told me that a long time ago. In fact, he was one of the first guys to love my chromatic book. When I jokingly apologized for the book being so piano-biased, he assured me that it wasn't an issue.

Anyway, with Vic, we figure things out. He will tape the first rehearsal and he really works on the music. We are faster now, but he is and has been the most diligent musician I've ever been around. It's not because he has a weakness. It's because he wants to get better and learn more—absolutely no ego. It's not like this band plays so much of that chromatic harmony as compared to Quest, for example, or in my duos with different pianists, where it is more readily available exactly *because* of the piano. I try not to put a square in a circle, so to say. The guitar has other advantages on which to capitalize. It is not a piano, pure and simple. I wanted the power of the guitar with some bits of rock in there. That was my first intention with the new group, with Phil on keyboards as the glue.

Lew: So you got them together and said, "I'm thinking of putting a band together. Let's have a session at my house."
Dave: We played standards. That's the way I do it with everybody at the beginning of a relationship, because that's the common language you are supposed to know to some degree. It's like a musical validation. In any case, guys like this know it all, so it's not a problem. It's just a good way to begin a musical relationship. Because we all know that stuff and it provides a means to communicate from the get-go, even if I don't verbally communicate details of what I am intending. It's the same with the IASJ meetings. The kids get together and play standards—that's the way to begin, and go from there if you wish to.

Lew: So when you got them together, they knew that for them this could be big?
Dave: Well, *big* I don't know, but musically interesting and challenging, yes—enough to be able to envision some work and recording. No big deal, because in this country I am not a big-ticket item, but with a decent reputation for honesty and good music. I would say without being egoed-out that the vibe was, if you're going to be with Lieb, the music is going to be good.

Lew: What if it turned out you'd made a wrong judgment on one of those guys?
Dave: Like I did with the band with Scofield in the late seventies when I had Mike Formanek. It didn't work out, so McClure came in with that band. You have to change. That's part of being the leader.

Lew: So, you were ready for that, but you had a good sense that these cats were going to work out?
Dave: Yeah, I could tell. I don't remember if we did the standard thing more than a few times. The process moved pretty fast. If I remember correctly, the first time I think Vic came down and met Jamey and Tony, I

think we played like ten minutes and said, "Okay, that's enough. We're done."

Lew: Really? You just wanted to hear it.
Dave: I just wanted to see the vibe. Also, when you form a group with anybody, let alone music, you have to, at least as much as you can in the beginning, "read" the personalities involved. I could see that Jamey was a certain kind of person, a real drummer personality, very loose and open—quite the opposite of Phil and pianists in general, who are so organized. Tony was this very quiet guy who just did everything perfectly. You didn't have to say a word to him. And Vic was wide-eyed: "What do I do?" Look, a band is made up of individuals and my job is to blend it all together. Phil was already a mature musician; Tony was a natural but not with a lot of experience at the highest level; Vic and Jamey were ready for anything. *Nice!*

Phil learned the chromatic harmony stuff by himself. I never sat him down, but he obviously knows everything I'm talking about. He probably knew most of it before, but just got used to my way of describing, that way of conceptualizing. Phil is one of the two best musicians I've ever known. I put Chick Corea up there, but I've never seen a musician more equipped than Phil Markowitz. He can write—every tune is a masterpiece, from fusion to great chromatic stuff. He can do synthesizers, and he understands all that computer stuff. He can play fusion; he can read anything; he writes for big band; he did his first orchestra piece at Manhattan School of Music, which was fantastic; and he's a great teacher—just a massive musician.

Lew: And Jamey was playing the drum set with you?
Dave: Oh yeah, but also hand drums. He had a drum he co-developed, called the Hadgini drum, a combination of tablas and electronics, which was fantastic. Like I said, he helped me develop in that odd-meter language that was just becoming the big deal at the time—nothing new, just getting more exposure on the jazz map through guys like Dave Holland, Steve Coleman. Five-four became the new three-four, they would say, or after a few years of playing in eleven, it was like the new three, etc. Each generation added something and I didn't want to get behind. Not a lot of guys from my generation do it that well. It's a way of hearing, and like anything, concepts come easier when you are young, meaning learning it when you are older is a challenge. I'm not going to tell you I'm as good as Steve Coleman is at it, or as my students, but I must say that at my ripe age I can get by with this crazy shit, more or less. Do I enjoy it as

much and all that? That's a different discussion, an aesthetic one. But I want to be able to get on a gig and do it, not be just like, "He only plays 'All the Things You Are.'" I don't want to be the old man, you know. That's an ego thing, besides musical—you don't want to be typecast.

With the new band, things came together. The first record worked, the arrangements worked, and I was thrilled. We had a really great beginning and got some work—Europe, of course. I have a booking agency that I started with in the seventies when I was with ECM; Saudades is the name, from Austria. They do some things with me from time to time with the American groups I have. In general I do my own booking, through the musicians themselves who invite me to join them. By the late 1980s, I was working with Scandinavian guys like Bobo Stenson, Jon Christensen, and Lars Danielsson—piano, drums, and bass—in a band we called Far North. Another group was with the French trio of Joachim Kuhn, Daniel Humair, and J. F. Jenny Clarke, and at times Michel Portal—all top European cats. So, I had to balance being a leader, keeping my guys at work, and making a living. When I worked with my band, I made less money. It's the same deal now. Nothing much has changed.

Lew: Sometimes you're touring as a single and sometimes…
Dave: Exactly. That whole European thing in general made me a better musician. I am so thankful for all the work I've done in Europe, not just because of making a living, which goes without saying. It's more than that, because they play different. The bottom line is—and I am generalizing, because obviously there are exceptions—they are just not that interested in playing straight-ahead jazz.

Lew: They feel that's the American thing.
Dave: They do. Of course, Bob Stenson can do it. Daniel Humair played with Bud Powell, and so on. But the point is that they want to have their own music. By the late 1980s into the '90s, they had developed their sound quite deeply, with differences between countries. The Scandic cats had a certain way of playing rhythm very open and loose, the French gravitated toward a time, no-changes style, while the Germans could be counted on for very free stuff, and so on. I think now it's more homogeneous because of the Internet and everyone has access to the same stuff. But in the 1990s there was still a lot of individuality from country to country. It was intense for me and still is when I go over there. I'd walk off a plane and go directly to rehearse or record. I didn't need a day off. I like to work. I have learned to be really fast in the studio. In fact, it's part of my rep. It fits that aspect of my personality—I speak fast; I move fast;

I am very fast with comprehending music. You put something in front of me, I've got it.

Lew: They'll give you original tunes?
Dave: Absolutely, and in those days there was no MP3 stuff to check the music out. You had to be fast. You got off the plane and had to get the music down. You walked in and sight-read. I'm not an ace like a New York studio guy, but I'm good, and I can get the concept down, which is the main thing. I brought my experience to the plate, and they appreciated that. I might be with the Italian cats for a day or two and then go three days later to the Dutch brothers. I think playing with Europeans has been a major contributing factor to my style of the past decades. It has made me wider, more flexible, and a better musician than I would've been without these experiences—real hands-on stuff. Beyond the actual music, it gets down to the restaurant, the hotel, and in those days even the currency, meaning you had to get into the scene and absorb what was around you. This went along perfectly with the IASJ, the international aspect of my musical experiences in this period. This all seemed to be a plan that worked. Here I was, starting the IASJ, trying to unite folks, being like Gandhi and all that, and at the same time out in the real world in the trenches doing it. Going from France to Italy, getting off the plane and having to say *ciao* instead of *bonjour* or whatever. I worked hard at it.

This was a great period with the European stuff and the new band. The nineties were great for me and in general it was a very good time for jazz musicians. I think that when we look back, just from the business standpoint, the 1990s were the best years. Certainly not the 2000s—we know that. And the eighties were just the beginning, a preamble to the nineties. In the seventies, jazz was still a secret. But the '90s with Wynton and the Young Lion thing getting the media going over here, with subsidies from European governments so that every town could have a festival, with record companies doing well enough to keep recording—it was a fertile time for sure. Especially in Europe, the whole philosophy that the state supports arts was entrenched in six to eight countries, which was enough to keep things really moving for American and eventually European musicians. Now we still go, but we're not making that kind of money and it's much different. That was the heyday of working jazz and I was in on it big time.

Lew: So your band was just called the Dave Liebman Group?

Dave: Dave Liebman Group—tres simple. I didn't want to say quartet or quintet, which turned out to be a good decision because by 1997, for a variety of reasons—some musical, some personal, and some economical—I let Phil go. First of all, Phil and Jamey had a basic conflict of personality from day one, some of it the natural drummer versus the piano player M.O. Dig, piano players, and especially Jewish piano players—now what I'm about to say is not an ethnic slur on my own people, but it's because they are so intellectual, so educated, so punctilious in everything they do with knowledge ranging from Bach to Schoenberg—are naturally among the tightest cats around. They're also the best musicians on the bandstand. They have to be. Jamey was from another culture, a hand drummer, a funky, down-home, talented, extremely street-smart man. So we had: "The drums are too loud. Less monitor. Use brushes in this place," etc. Whatever. Jamey: "The piano—I can't see you man. Could you move it over?" Phil: "Well, this is the best position for me to be in." Now, not out-and-out war, meaning the guys could have dinner together, but definitely a vibe, and a conflict that was oil and water. There's nothing to be done about it and nothing to say. The first few years it was cool because of me. Nobody ever messed with me of course. But finally the guys got more confident and they became who they were. That was a factor dictating an inevitable change in the band.

The other was economical. I don't have to tell you, Lewis. You're a pianist. You've got to have a piano everywhere you play, which limits work to some extent. Finally, there was the Vic factor. He had jumped leagues in this five- to seven-year period. He wasn't just the second soloist anymore. He was really burning it up. I could see, not that he ever said it to me, but I didn't want him leaving me. Whether he could've or should've or would've, I don't know, because we never discussed it. But I could tell he was ready to move on unless I made more room for him. In a way, when I stopped Lookout Farm back in the seventies, although we did discuss the Ellis/Liebman Band and how that situation motivated me to end Lookout Farm, there was also the fact that Richie was ready to move on by them. And sure enough, he had a trio with Frank Tusa and Jeff Williams from Lookout Farm, which recorded for ECM and toured a bit when we broke up in '76. I knew Vic loved playing with me, so I had to move on this inevitable step. Obviously without a piano, the guitar would have to step up to the plate, big time.

Phil and I have continued our relationship and he is with me in Saxophone Summit, which we'll get to. Once again, overnight it seemed, Vic became another musician, rising again to the occasion as well as contributing great compositions. When I know guys write tunes, except for Richie, I have to approve the tune. I don't just say, "I'm going to definitely play what you bring in." It's got to be the right tune for the repertoire. With Vic, I will ask him for a bunch of tunes and pick one or two. He has a lot of songs.

This personnel, sans Phil, with Jamey, Tony, and Vic, went from 1997 to 2000. Then in 2000, Jamey got the gig with Paul Simon on percussion. How can I compete with $5,000 a night when I'm making $50 a night? You know what I mean? I have a view about this that I want to tell you, a tangent—nothing personal concerning Jamey.

It's like the plantations in the South used to be. The white guys would come along and get the good-looking black chicks from the other side of the tracks. Those rock cats—Paul Simon, Sting, and others in this period were like that in a way. Everybody had to have a jazz musician to make them cool. It made them kosher—no kidding! The bottom line is, who is going to say no to soloing for eight bars somewhere and get paid like that? Mike Brecker kind of started it with Simon, and later Branford and Kenny Kirkland with Sting. You can't compete with the money, the glamour, the fame, private plane. To be honest I sort of resent the fact that they just go and pick the cherries and get the benefit of our hard work and years and years of on-the-ground, in-the-trenches work and learning, playing these $50 gigs, playing "All the Things You Are" a million times and all that stuff, and then here you go to play a big eight bars on a G-minor seventh. I'm obviously exaggerating, but point made.

I really loved Jamey, so what was I going to do? Well, of course, there was this kid in the area, kind of like Adam Nussbaum had been in the seventies. He lived around where Tony was and played in the area. Marko Marcinko graduated from the University of Miami and represented the new generation of college-educated musicians. He came from a musical family, could play a couple of instruments, and basically came through rock and jazz, as his generation did for the most part. He had chops, imagination, and pedigree, so I hired him. This is around 2000, 2001, and I'm so glad. He learned faster than anyone and has become a real jazz drummer, no question. Also, he had a natural inclination toward free jazz playing, a bit more than Jamey, which meant I could go in a different direction, which we have pursued since then. I was getting influenced by my European visits. As I said, the musicians there like to play free in one way or the other, and I wanted to get some of that into my group

I knew with a young cat I could train him because I would have more of an empty blackboard. Also, because he was younger, he would have heard the music I had in mind more in his formative years, because it was part of the vocabulary in the nineties. So, that was another thing that Marko enabled me to do. A new guy enables you to change direction. You can't play the old music. You do that for a minute, but you've got to change it eventually to fit the new reality. To bring the band basically up to date, the music has changed a few times in the past ten years. My job is to keep it challenging and on the edge so that the guys want to stay with me. I always reiterate this when people ask, "What is it to be a bandleader?" You've got to be on top of all the business stuff and be absolutely clean with money and all that. You've got to keep your word of course. That's just good mechanics. But musically, you must keep the music going so that the guys always know that they're being challenged. Of course if one is being paid a lot of money, they may be a bit more, shall I say, "forgiving" with regard to this point about musical challenge, meaning if you're making a lot of money, that will hide all sins.

In my case, it could only be that guys give me their commitment based on the fact that they love playing with me, and they can't love playing with me if I do the same music over and over again. My responsibility is to keep the ship moving. These little things that happened—Phil leaving, Vic stepping up to the plate, and Jamey leaving, which turned out to be positive because Marko truly stepped up to plate—all add up over the years. With Marko, he didn't come from the jazz tradition as much as a mixture of fusion and rock drumming, so there was a matter of touch. I mean every drummer can't be like Billy Hart or Al Foster. I have to say that for the most part white guys don't have, shall we call it, the "lightness of being" that the brothers have when it comes to touch. I know this because to some extent I had to deal with it also on the horn. It's in the DNA or something like that. There are some exceptions, like Adam Nussbaum or Ari Hoening, but I'm talking touch. One thing about Marko that holds true across the board—you are who you are. I've never played with a drummer who's more consistently creative than him on a night-to-night basis. That's the truth.

He's high energy and he's fast. People love him for that of course. But musically, he's just very creative. He's a real musician. He can play piano, arranges, sings in rock bands—his own bands, by the way. He's like the nineties whiz kids who went to school and can do everything. He even tap dances. He's also going to be mayor of Scranton at some point, or something like that, because he's politically involved. He runs the Scranton Jazz Festival and organizes a workshop for the local kids at the same time. He also is involved in a clinic for already accredited high school teachers to get some info on how to teach jazz. Marko is a very powerful guy, outgoing, funny, and extremely entrepreneurial.

I did feel at the beginning of our relationship that he should've made the move to New York to be part of the scene there, which he would've done very well in. I pushed him a lot because I could see his talent and didn't want him to "waste it" in the coal regions of Pennsylvania. But he stayed and is really a big force for live music of all sorts in that part of the country. Hey, I wanted my drummer to be on the scene! It makes me look better!

Lew: It's true, because people don't know who he is. If he was in town, he'd be getting a lot of work without a doubt.
Dave: Thank you. But people have a way of finding out what is right for them in the long run. As an older cat, I feel responsible to make some suggestions, but water seeks its own level in the end.

Lew: It's a different life plan.
Dave: Yes, sir. Not mine, he's got his own. Somehow this band, together since 1991, basically has a book of nearly a hundred tunes, unheard of for most bands. I have a large body of music with these guys, and a lot of recordings. I'm probably going to hold it together till the day I die—at least for as long as I can. We know each other very well. We get along on the road and actually have fun. Marko is a ball of fire—a lot of fun who doesn't shut up. He's like a lot of drummers—they just love to talk. But you know what? You need to have somebody to keep the fire going; otherwise, guys would be nodding out all the time. Tony is very quiet. Vic reacts to Marko and it's great. I'm like kind of the outsider, 'cause I'm the old man. So, it's cool and it works out.

Lew: Guys who play with you have to absorb at least some of the harmonic language you enjoy playing. With Vic, it seems like he has really done that, because I've heard him do that stuff on his own gigs. At Barney Kessel's memorial in 2004, out of all the guitarists performing, he was the one who had us all standing there with our mouths open! He does really interesting stuff. He has absorbed that language and I think he really loves it.
Dave: He has, and in his original writing also. This harmony is an acquired taste. That's why teaching it is kind of hard, because you can't expect somebody to get it in ten minutes, or ten weeks. Musicians differ in how they learn new material. Vic is a methodical, slow, and a thorough learner. Markowitz is very fast—he looks at it once and he's got it. Some guys are like that. I'm pretty fast. Vic needs to absorb it; he wants to go home and check it out. I know that about him now. With this play-

ing, it grew on him. He got to like it and was able to do it. At first, of course, it was intimidating.

In some ways, I think a lot of folks from our generation were intimidated by me and Richie. We've been playing in this way since the early 1970s, so several generations of musicians who would come to New York had to deal with our language. These days you have to deal with all the metric stuff going on. That's New York and that's what you do. On each instrument there's a "new" guy that you are indebted to check out. That was the thing you did. When guys get a taste of something strong at a certain point in their life, more dramatically when they come from somewhere else to New York, it makes a strong impression, especially if it is a band thing. They're going to walk away saying, "Holy shit, man, I don't know if I could ever do that. Could I?" In the seventies and eighties, with Lookout Farm and especially Quest, I can imagine that Vic, being a guitar player, had some similar kind of reactions, like Scofield did to the music of Richie and me from the '70s, meaning wanting to understand it but being a bit puzzled. Being a guitarist just put more oil on the fire. It's to Vic's credit that he did the work. Otherwise he could have floated and coasted and gotten the surface of it, but not as deep as he has become. Now he writes tunes that even I have to practice because they're so hard harmonically!

Lew: Not in terms of how fast the line is?
Dave: No, harmonically, but different than from a piano standpoint. The material is still double triads and so forth, not much more, but challenging. Here's a story that dramatizes what I'm talking about in relation to Vic:

This is about one record I did with Pat Metheny, which is very interesting vis-à-vis this guitar/piano chromatic harmony discussion. In the mid-nineties I got a record deal with a label called Arkadia. We did a CD with my group, a kind of Brazilian thing with the percussionist Café and the original group with Phil and Jamey, called *New Vista.* This producer, who turned out to be a complete drag eventually, went along with me at first about recording a series of CDs covering the four elements: earth, air, fire, and water. We never got past this first project on water.

For the first of this intended project, I asked Pat. He had told me around that period when he saw me play one time that he would like to record with me, and I took him at his word. I decided to do the element of water first and use Billy Hart and Cecil McBee, who as a team were very special, since we had done a trio record earlier called *The Seasons* that I loved. I really liked the way they worked together and I thought it would be interesting with Pat and me. The main musical point was not to use piano but still include some of my chromatic language. It was definitely necessary for me to see Pat after I wrote the music and well before the recording because I knew it would demand some time to look at it. He was very agreeable. I showed him the stuff months before the date, and when we got to the recording it seemed that he had a different concept on how to approach the music. All the tunes were based on one primary theme. Each tune employed a part of that theme in different idioms—Latin, eighth note, straight-ahead jazz, free, etc.—and would require a different guitar sound. The music was hard and it was necessary to prepare. So we rehearsed one afternoon at my house, played at the Deer Head Inn that night, and then recorded for two days.

Lew: Wow. At the Deer Head Inn?
Dave: Amazing, for sure. We didn't let the word go out until a week before, but it was packed for two shows. Then we recorded at Red Rock Studios, the one near my house in Pennsylvania that I have used so much over the years I've lived there. The record's okay, but let me put it this way—the water was pretty deep, no pun intended since the title of the record is *Water: Giver Of Life.* Pat's a great melodicist. Next, his time is very good. But he, like most guitar and keyboard players, doesn't leave much space in his playing, and when you deal with a rhythm section with the likes of Billy Hart and Cecil McBee, there are some matters that if addressed can really raise the level of the music. It didn't really work that great on the record. Pat and I spoke about it right after the session because we decided to do a marathon mixing session, after Billy and Cecil left, in the afternoon of the second day. He had stipulated to me prior to the date that he wanted to be able to fix things after the tracks were down, but when we got to that, he didn't want to re-record anything and just added some chords behind his solos, which was great. We did fifteen hours the second day and finished it.

During the mix we talked about the recording and how it felt with Cecil and Billy. I said something concerning leaving space, and that from my experience with Billy you're not getting all you can from him when you play a lot of eighth notes. Pat played a lot with Jack DeJohnette, who is the greatest of all time for me, but he is a different experience as far as accompanying is concerned. Billy is a conversationalist. "It's good to leave the cadence at the end of the phrase open for him, because he will set you up. That's something I learned from Miles." Pat understood.

Lew: You don't always talk to people about that.

Dave: You don't lecture a guy before you play. The discussion came up. As far as the music itself, he definitely had time to consider how to approach it, but of course it was different when he was actually there with the others. Look, I'm responsible because I wrote the music for those guys. Cecil actually kind of got it, as did Billy. Maybe Pat couldn't leave much space because he wasn't sure of where the music was heading. When that happens, you usually play more, not less, by nature.

Lew: It was sort of a pick-up group. Maybe it was too ambitious.
Dave: I miscalculated. But I really thought that he and I would be the glue, and we would let Billy and Cecil kind of do what they do. Anyway, the point concerns the guitar and the inherent difficulties of playing this so-called chromatic language. That's why Vic is so great, because he works on it.

Lew: Yes—he's amazing. So you've had a long time with this great group, and you've made a few changes in the band over the years. But Jamey Haddad's departure was a little different. You're very understanding, but it seems to me there's a side of you that says, "What about loyalty? What about really playing the music?" Because with Paul Simon he's not playing jazz.
Dave: Look, you're either a jazz musician or you're not. This thing with Jamey did something good for me. When it happened, I was about fifty-five years old, so I wasn't a baby anymore. It made me more aware of the jazz culture, the pride you should feel if you're a jazz musician, and the necessity of being loyal to the tradition. Forget the Dave Liebman Group—you're a jazz musician.

Guys sweated and killed themselves—mostly African American guys. There were drugs all around them, living in unspeakable hotels, playing in bars with bad pianos, no sound systems, gangster boss mentalities, etc., traveling by car or whatever, and sometimes not being allowed to eat in a restaurant. And why? To bring music to the people and develop this art, without which you and I wouldn't be here. So it bothers me when someone who should know better goes over to the other side because of money . . . and then to say well, it's really great and all that. Maybe it's well done and honest from the artist's standpoint but there's a lot of money tied up in that music and the raison d'être of commercial music is to get people out of their seats and buy product. Sorry, but to me that's what it is. Jazz is about enjoying yourself also but equally to raise consciousness.

Hey—I want people to like me, too, but I've got to play what I've got to play! Don't get me started! Maybe I'm exaggerating to make a point, but when you go to the other side, you have given your fucking heart to the devil. It's Goethe; it's Faust; it's that shit. Sorry, but that's how I feel.

Lew: So, it's really about selling out?
Dave: It is. I'm not innocent—I've done it, too. We've all done it. But you've got to get up sometime in your life and stand up for what you believe in, if you do believe in anything at all.

Lew: And there's always the question: How much money do you want to make? If it's about money, why are you in the jazz field? Just go to another business. There are businesses where you can make money—you know what I mean?
Dave: It's just knowing who you are, which you're supposed to have down by a certain age, I would think. And it's standing behind it, being loyal to those who have done that trip before and will after. You're part of a culture, and for you to just sell it out like that, because somebody comes by with some green paper, to the other side of the tracks—that's my metaphor—is to me, weird, strange, and I don't have respect for it. If Lady Gaga came up to me and offered me ten million dollars for an eight-bar solo, would I say no? I'm not sure. So, we all have the problem. I'm not standing up here like God. There is the temptation, of course. Is it ten million or would I do it for five or one? I don't know if it's a matter of degree or if I'm being unfairly prejudicial, but I have to state the case as I see it.

I certainly can't judge for anybody else, but I feel a certain loyalty to the cats in the trenches, which is what we are. You know, especially some folks more than others in our jazz world. Look at Lee Konitz, whose book in your series was my original inspiration for doing this book with you. He is *still* in the trenches and doing it as we speak! And he's an innovator and one of the main guys for sixty years. So, yes, I do feel a little bit of a draft concerning this crossover stuff.

Lew: Jazz is part of the music business.
Dave: Yes, and it's entertainment whether I like it or not.

Lew: So, where do you draw the line?
Dave: Between entertainment and art for art's sake? This brings us back to my discussion with Chick Corea, because Scientology says the value

of an art—maybe I'm oversimplifying here—is in its communicative power. So, in other words, something that communicates more is more artistic? I'm not sure. If that's the case, then quality doesn't mean anything because high quality doesn't necessarily communicate. Sure, sometimes it does. Even Trane had a so-called "hit" with "A Love Supreme," but often great quality doesn't equate to big box office. That doesn't mean that what one communicates isn't artful; it just means that it may be less artful than other things that do not commercially hit.

It's a timeless question and there's a line that each individual draws in the sand for him or herself. I always say to students, "What size of an audience will make you feel okay, so you'll go home and say, 'I'm all right'? Ten folks hearing the most esoteric music in a basement on Avenue A? Three hundred? Or three thousand? I can tell you right now that whatever that number is that makes you feel good about yourself will have a lot to do with determining the music you play. You better think about that at twenty-five years old."

I am dramatically oversimplifying the numbers of people and so on, but the point is valid. It has to do with your horizons. If you want to be a household name in this particular business, I can tell you right now that you had better play some specific kind of music. Don't be playing some chromatic stuff in eleven/fourteen meter. You should be looking at something that most people can get to. If you don't care about that, then you're not looking for a lot of people in that audience. That's the way it has been since the beginning of time. It still bothers me to this day when I don't see people out there, but that can't be the barometer of your self-worth. It shouldn't be, but you can get confused, because it's human nature and ego and one's psyche and one's surroundings all mixed together. At twenty-five years old, it doesn't matter. If you're working for the door but playing what you need to do, it's okay. Should you desire a manager, promo agent, tour manager, and all that? Sure, if you want. But let's not confuse reality with dreaming, although one must imagine what *could* be.

Lew: Then there's the aspect of showmanship. That's a tough one to draw the line for also because some jazz cats are uncomfortable with the idea of showmanship. But other cats say, "As soon as I step onstage, that's showmanship. That's not a problem for me."
Dave: Absolutely! Even what you wear. This is why you must really create your own picture and step into it. The challenge in teaching this conceptual stuff is to tell a twenty-five-year-old or a thirty-year-old to build a mental picture and then construct the landscape. Do you want to be up there in a suit and tie? Do you want to be in jeans and portray what

that conveys? Do you want to say to your audience, "Love your neighbor," like what Chick was doing on that Australian tour? Do you want to go there? Or do you want to be like, "My name is Dave Liebman. This is Vic Juris. Thank you for coming, and our first tune is such and such"? Or Coltrane, who didn't say anything? See, no show can be a show. Monk dancing around when he "strolled" from the piano. Was that a show or just what he did? People certainly came and were entertained by his antics. People loved when Miles turned his back on them. That was part of the deal. But those guys could back it up.

So, you've got to make this decision on your own. It appears to me that if you feel that what we do is art for art's sake, there are some people who do love it and you should treat both the music and the audience with the highest respect. That means simple things like being prepared, showing up on time, looking nice, playing the music to the best of your abilities, saying thank you, hello, and goodbye. It's just being cordial. To be mysterious, to be in dark lights and have sunglasses on and hats on, I don't think that works anymore. And definitely you shouldn't talk down to the people.

Lew: As long as you're onstage there is showmanship—even announcing the tunes and introducing the players are aspects of showmanship. What you have to decide is how far you want to go in relation to that and your audience.

Dave: Some guys don't care, while some guys make clear decisions in this regard. For me, I know when it's too much. I don't know when it's too little, but I know when it's too much. Here's an example. Caris has commented to me about the IASJ final concerts and how the kids for the most part dressed. In this one particular case, it was obvious that the students had not considered their appearance at all. As we know, we live in an era of dressing down—ripped jeans and so on. I like to encourage individualism and that young artists should make their own decisions and back them up, but the truth is, I should make it clear to them that they're on the stage and that the way they look reflects on the respect due to them from the audience. Somebody once told me a long time ago that you should look better than your audience. The kids kind of look like their audience these days. But aren't we supposed to be a little above that in the sense that *we* are presenting something that *they* came to hear? On the other hand, suits and ties?—I don't know about that. But please dress accordingly and with respect to the music. Period. It's the music, the tradition. Would you go out and play Mozart like that? No. That's the point.

I'm just asking for balance and good taste—not the easiest things in life to attain.

Chapter 11

While We're on the Subject: On Others

Lew: Let's take some time now to discuss some of the major jazz artists who have played a role in your musical development. To start with, you've mentioned our friend Lee Konitz a few times, and in 2010 you recorded the CD *KnowingLee*, on OutNote Records, with him and Richie Beirach.

Dave: Lee came when Bird came, but he was different from the start. He was his own man immediately and pursued that track. Lee has never been a household name in jazz. As we speak, he is still playing with young cats on the road, gig to gig—the essence of the "jazz warrior," doing what I and others like me do. In his eighties now, Konitz is a survivor who has basically, with the exception of a few like Roy Haynes and Phil Woods, outlasted everybody from that era. The main point is that he has stayed true to his creed. From what I can tell, he has pursued his path relentlessly.

He is emphatic about his musical beliefs, which he so clearly enunciated in his book *Conversations on the Improviser's Art* with Andy Hamilton. You were the series editor for that, and when I read it, it inspired this one we are doing here. His book is not as biographical as this one, but what inspired me was the clarity of his thoughts about music, and the honesty, even about himself, which is something you don't usually hear from artists of that stature. Most remain neutral, for obvious reasons. Lee speaks his mind, and I must say, I for one agreed with him on a lot of points concerning the music. That book reveals a way of looking at music that I found so fascinating and very real. I respect Lee for his convictions as well as his incredible playing, which has retained the key elements of his style, regardless of his using the same tunes over and over.

He is always fresh and clearly values true on-the-spot/spontaneous improvisation—no licks, no clichés, no matter how many times you hear him play "All The Things You Are."

Lew: You've told me that you feel some connection with Lee.
Dave: Well, besides our being Jewish, which might be something, there are I think some similarities in personality. He is from a different era than I am—twenty years older. But the challenge of evolving in the shadow of a massive artist—in my case, Coltrane, in his case, Charlie Parker—is something I think we share. The other unfortunate aspect we share is the white/black thing, he much more than me. If anybody suffered from a kind of reverse prejudice, it was Lennie Tristano's school of playing. "They're not swinging, too intellectual," etc. In the middle of Bud Powell, Charlie Parker, and Dizzy Gillespie—the heroes of bebop, of a new language—were these white cats who, though they didn't turn their back on bebop, definitely came up with another way to perceive it. After all, Tristano's favorites were Prez and Bird. But Lennie was ostracized by some critics throughout his career, and Lee, Warne Marsh, and others suffered from it, I'm sure. The tracks "Digression" and "Intuition" had complete free playing in 1949. They just did it a different way and stuck to their guns for the whole journey—talk about balls. Damn!

Lew: Don't you think things have changed in this regard? Now cats, including African American musicians like Mark Turner, will check out, for example, someone like Warne Marsh.
Dave: Yeah, it's in vogue now, finally. You know, everything comes around. It took eighty years to discover Bach, for which you have to thank Felix Mendelssohn, though it was probably inevitable. I think some of the flak was not musically based, though it might be couched in terms like "not swinging," "too intellectual," or whatever. It was reverse racism—"white guys can't play"—usually advanced by white critics, by the way. This is a strong general statement, but it appears that way to me, and Lennie may have taken it to heart, becoming a recluse as far as performing and recording were concerned. This is all arguable, but I think there is something valid about what I am saying. I am not comparing this scene to my situation at all, because by my era things had changed in that respect, compared to the '50s and '60s.

In reference to Lee and myself, when you grow up in a period where there's such a monster like Charlie Parker or John Coltrane staring you in the face—though I wasn't contemporaneous with Trane the way Lee was with Bird—the shadow looms large. The way for one to deal with that, because you can't escape it, is by finding a path that's yours. This is what I feel is something similar between Konitz and myself. He's certainly a much more obvious example of what I'm talking about than I am, but I still think there's some common cause in this way between us.

Musically, if there's ever been a guy more dedicated to the essence of pure melodic invention, along with others like Chet Baker, Paul Desmond, Stan Getz—note an abundance of white guys, by the way, in this approach—surely Lee Konitz stands on top of the pinnacle for creating melodies on modulating harmonies. His time swings so hard—that behind-the-beat thing for which he is emblematic. One of the acknowledged classic recordings in the history of jazz is his *Motion,* with Elvin Jones and bassist Sonny Dallas in 1961. Elvin, who plays so tame compared to his usual style with Coltrane, allows Lee to pursue that feeling of just hanging on the cliff of the pulse. He does it ceaselessly throughout his career—something that is really hard to do, which I alluded to earlier regarding what I learned from playing with Elvin. Plus his sound—that dark, almost tenorish tone from the alto, without the normal bright timbre we usually hear from that instrument—is from the saxophone standpoint a unique attribute.

Surprisingly, Lee is also a wonderful "free" player, stylistically not something one would associate with his basic harmonic and rhythmic style. He enters that arena like he does with standards, without an agenda, incorporating his mastery of melody and time playing, refraining from the crazy free playing that my generation came up with, which stems from the sixties avante-garde, meaning the squawking, squeaking color stuff. No, for Lee it is pure melody even without chords, which in a certain way is closer to Ornette's style than one might think, though they sound completely different in the end result.

Lew: It's kind of like that same melodic approach, applied to a free context.
Dave: Exactly. Of all people, Lee Konitz playing free from direct harmonies—a guy who can play so great on chord changes—it's unbelievable. As a true artist, he's at the top of the heap for me.

Lew: Now, did you want to say something more about Bird?
Dave: To my mind Bird appeared to have come from another planet. It's like he landed from Mars or something like that. He was just so different, creating a universal language, yet indebted in some ways to his predecessors, Benny Carter and Lester Young for sure. Bird is definitely the mark-off point for the modern age, as was Armstrong for the beginning.

Louis Armstrong came from zero, so of course that was the creation of a new language. But Bird changed it all, and from then on everything was an extension, including my hero, John Coltrane. You hear Bird today: "How did he play that?" You hear Lester Young and you can figure out how he played. But Bird, he just seemed to come out of nowhere in a certain sense—the rhythm, the technique, the sound, the speed, all of it. By the way, why was he called "Bird"?

Lew: It's a funny story—one of these things where you might think it's some very sophisticated answer. But it turns out he liked to eat chicken, or what they called "yardbirds," so they called him "Bird" for short.
Dave: That's funny because "Bird" seems so appropriate for his playing—he sounds like he's soaring above the planet, light as a feather, floating in the air. He sounds more like that than anybody I've ever heard. Plus, the sophistication and complexity of his rhythm, along with note choices, is astounding, especially in light of what was happening at that time around him. He is *the* man, in the end. Like Mozart? Bach? Rembrandt? I don't know—he's one of those kinds of guys. To put a little more significance on it, from the little I got from Miles about Bird, it seems that he was the typical jazz personality. He wasn't the prototype, because everybody kind of gives Lester Young that prize. But just the vibe, the mercurial nature of Bird's life—incredibly down, incredibly up, incredibly generous, incredibly would-sell-your-wife vibe—the complete contrary personality—the beautiful way he played and the terrible dues he paid. The story is beyond romantic. It's the yin-yang deal personified—day and night, in front of your eyes.

Lew: It's like so perfectly tragic, you can't believe it's true. You'd have to make this up, you know. What about your neighbor Phil Woods, a definite follower of Bird? He lives not far from you.
Dave: Literally ten minutes. I can't really say that before my moving to Pennsylvania he was a major influence on me, which has something to do with him being an alto player. Having some interaction with him over these past twenty-five years does bring home the point that he is one of the great musicians playing that instrument. Stylistically, it's not exactly my cup of tea, but for what he does, he is the top of the line. The most amazing thing about Phil Woods to my ears is that when you stand next to him, you can't hear yourself!

Lew: Because he's got a big sound?

Dave: The biggest in the world on that instrument! It is unbelievable how loud he can be and yet kind of sweet. He is amazing. From a saxophone standpoint—and you understand this since you used to double on alto—his breathing apparatus, meaning the path of the airstream beginning in the abdomen through the chest and ribs, into the oral cavity and larynx, finally vibrating the reed and exiting through the horn, is absolutely unified, smooth as glass. There is no break, which is the goal. He speaks and sings the sound, so to say. Stylistically, one thing that I did hear out here over the past twenty-five years is that he's got a little Eric Dolphy and quite a bit of Cannonball Adderley in him—a wide interval leap like Eric, or a turn like Cannon might've done.

From a personal standpoint, he's a very astute, literate guy who writes prose with great clarity, combining a sense of humor, accuracy, verve, and once again, like Lee, complete honesty—truly an amazing combination, separate from his playing. I wish I could write like that. I can't put that kind of sense of humor into prose like Phil can. He has that sarcastic but humorous kind of way of communicating that belies the wisdom in what he is saying. I cannot say that I have agreed with his utterances through the years, not as much as I do with Lee, and he can be a bit heavy at times. I am guilty of this critical aspect as well, which is why I can spot it so easily. But he is honest as the day is long and knows the real deal. When you hear Phil Woods either play or speak, he is for sure there, big time, in the room. He does not circle around the subject, musically and personally.

Lew: That's true about writing—you can be a funny person, but to write funny? That's a whole other thing.

Dave: It's very difficult. Phil's not so much like that as a person, though he is quite witty and fast on the draw in real-time conversation. He can be a little distant, not off-putting, but you don't get in deep conversations with the guy. He's the kind of cat who says something and doesn't really wait for you to comment on it—you just take it or leave it—actually a bit like Miles was in that respect. He's not about to get into a deep give-and-take with you. At least, I haven't seen that. But his prose writing is much more introspective. It's done in a manner that suggests it's not deep, but it really is deep. The reason I have such a vantage point is because for many years he has written a column for the journal *The Note*, which is the publication of the Al Cohn Memorial Jazz Collection coordinated by Bob Bush and housed in the Kemp Library at East Stroudsburg University. His column has a great name, since he lives in Delaware Water Gap:

"Phil in the Gap." Just his way of describing going to the airport was a riot. He has a take on everything—a true improviser.

Comparing these two masters in this way, Lee is another kind of animal—subtle, winding around the point, there but sometimes kind of ghost-like. Lee's sound is lighter in general, though it can be very strong. Once again it is the persona. Phil Woods is the center of attention when he plays—there is no mistaking that. The hamburger light is on him, and I love him for that. Lee becomes the background. From the standpoint of the musical community where I live, Phil is the capo. He is and has been for forty years the main guy. He's the inspiration for what's going on in our area, which is something beyond the norm in America. The Pocono area where we live has turned out a lot of musicians because Phil Woods lives here. In the end, he's the reason.

Lew: What's going on with Phil now?
Dave: He's got emphysema.

Lew: Was he a smoker?
Dave: Yes. But he's cool and still has that giant sound when he plays. He is eighty and beat prostate cancer. Phil is still active and his usual cantankerous self. Everybody knows him for that. But he's a heavy guy, and in history he is *the* sound of the lead alto for the sax section. I'm not a big-band-section musician, never have been, so for me it has never been a big deal. But in the big-band tradition, which probably 99 percent of saxophonists have dealt with, Phil Woods was the voice of the saxophone section, the lead alto responsible for the phrasing and general tone of the section. Lead alto, like lead trumpet, is a real thing that guys are known for specifically. In the sixties, when there was so much big-band recording going on, Phil was invariably the main player. He was *the* studio sound of New York. If only for that, he would still have a place in history.

Lew: That's a great point. Now, you already mentioned Cannonball, so let's go there for a second.
Dave: I was fortunate to see him live a lot. I saw him with Charles Lloyd and without him. You have to remember in the '60s there were often two bands on the bill. I saw a lot of groups opposite Coltrane. Cannonball is the epitome of *joie de vivre*. What a vibe—what a feeling of bubbling all over! It's the champagne bottle opening—a joy of life, even when he plays blues licks—just happy, period. On "So What" from *Kind of Blue* with all that minor, introspective stuff coming from Miles and Bill Evans

and Trane cascading over, Cannon finds a way to sound up, bright, even cheerful—an amazing power to create a mood. All those guys had it. I mean mood, let alone the differing styles and tones and all that.

Look at these three alto players above. Lee is melancholy, with an introspective kind of getting-to-the-gut thing. Phil is like: "Let's go hang, baby!" Cannonball is a real blues player, out to get the people dancing. His job is to make you get up on the tables. Cannonball is a very sophisticated level of that spirit on the saxophone—the sound, the notes, and the vibe. One thing about Cannonball, when you saw him play, he was a big guy and the alto looked like a toy. He played it like that, like picking up a spoon. No effort, just boom! You felt like the saxophone was nothing to him. Even more than somebody like Phil Woods—effortless. And if you want to talk swing, this was one of the most swinging guys of all time. He's in the top five swingers—Dexter, him, a couple of other guys. True eighth-note swinging jazz. I would put Phil there also.

Lew: That's great. What about pianist Bill Evans, since you mentioned *Kind of Blue*?
Dave: We have to absolutely bow our heads to Bill Evans for bringing harmony up a big degree from the Bud Powell era. He is responsible. Whether it's the influence of Impressionism or whatever is said about it, the point is he raised the bar big time. I was just playing "Turn Out the Stars" at the piano at eight o'clock this morning. This is harmonic sophistication, written big. I was looking at it because my daughter, Lydia, is playing it. She read his biography and everything. Lydia is quite into the music and very interested in all the players.

I'm not going to say Evans changed harmony, but he really raised the ante. He is one of the reasons why there is a Herbie, why a Chick, and why a Keith—why everybody except maybe McCoy, who is a separate tree unto his own. Just the sound that Bill got from the piano, the breathtaking sensitivity, is amazing. When he wanted to hit, he could hit hard. Some people dismissed him as a kind of sophisticated cocktail piano player. I'm sorry, but this guy could hit the piano, too. It's just that he really understood dynamics. This is a guy who lived the fact that every note is supposed to be a different color. Trio was the best format for that, for obvious reasons, so that's what he did predominantly. He was a magnificent colorist—harmony as color. This is what harmony is, in the final analysis, no matter the level of sophistication. My first lesson for the chromatic class I teach is a quote from the *Harvard Dictionary of Music* stating that chromaticism used to be thought of as "color modification." Harmony isn't just a stack of notes or whatever. What does the word *color* mean in music? It means sound. And if there was anybody who controlled sound through harmony, it was Bill Evans.

Lew: Interesting. You saw him live?
Dave: Many times. I played with him once, sitting in with Philly Joe and Eddie Gomez. I don't know what we played, probably a blues. All I remember was that it was rushing like crazy. You know, it happens to the best.

Lew: Wow! How did it happen that you played with him?
Dave: Richie was friendly with him. I have a story that's great with Richie and Bill. We played opposite Bill's trio, Richie and me, at the University of Michigan, or somewhere up there. It was the trio with Marc Johnson and Joe LaBarbera, toward the end of Bill's life. Richie and I have a way we play "All Blues," which to say the least is a bit different than the original. We played first, and in a tone of voice that I can't describe, not hostile, just a bit quizzical, Bill says to us in the dressing room, "Interesting version, gentlemen." This cannot be translated properly on paper.

Lew: That's great! He said "gentlemen"?
Dave: Something like that. Anyway, the best part is the following: We all know how famous those voicings in fourths are on "So What" that Bill played. I can't tell you when the first fourth voicing appeared in jazz, way after Scriabin's "mystical" chord in classical music, but let's just say when it appeared on *Kind of Blue* it made history. The interesting question: Why did Bill Evans put it on the map and then not follow that road? He never really incorporated those voicings, which in essence became the foundation of McCoy Tyner's playing with Trane in the sixties. Richie asked him why, right there in the dressing room. He said, "Bill, just a question—how come you didn't pursue the fourths?" Bill said, "Not lyrical enough."

Lew: Interesting. That's the answer?
Dave: From that standpoint, absolutely. And as I tell the students, "Remember one thing about fourth voicings: You're not going to get the same melodic juice that you get out of thirds." You're not going to get that beautiful lyricism. You're not going to get the same harmonic thing because of the overtones—there are all kinds of reasons. On another track, similar to my thoughts on Phil Woods, Bill was also extremely literate when he wrote or talked about music—complete clarity and

depth. You know that film *The Universal Mind of Bill Evans*, when he is talking and demonstrating things to his brother? It's amazingly clear and deep. He would have been the teacher of all time, if that was the period to do it. Literate, intelligent, sophisticated, just so knowledgeable and artistic. Bill is what you mean when you say *artist*.

Lew: Very true. Which of his other trios did you see, besides the last one?

Dave: I never saw the trio with DeJohnette, but I definitely saw the one with Marty Morell and possibly Arnie Wise on drums. In any case, it's mostly the Gomez period because that's my time in the clubs listening. I did have a lot of interaction with Eddie over the years—recordings and gigs—so the conversation would inevitably turn to Bill. On another note, you have to give it up to Gomez—the way he played the bass at the time—talk about changing the role of an instrument. Sure, Scotty LaFaro was first, but Eddie took it to another level beyond, after Scotty passed. So that was another astounding thing concerning Bill Evans, which is the bass players. When you saw Bill, you heard a bass that sounded like a horn—maybe more than a horn.

I have great respect for Bill Evans. I must say that at this point in history for me, Bill doesn't get his due the way Monk or others do. Again, I think it was a bit and still might be a bit racial. I hate to keep going to that, but it just seems that this kind of thing was a factor in those days and the stench remains, however slightly. It's not as obvious as, "He's white. Forget about him." It's much more subtle, but unfortunately, Bill doesn't get the notoriety that others who have passed do, and he should because he was and is a serious influence on everyone.

You can't mention Herbie or others in that style without bowing to Bill. I just think he should be more applauded for what he did. Okay, maybe it got a little rough at the end. Maybe it got a little boring. Maybe it got a little workman-like. Maybe it got a little like, punch the clock in, punch the clock out—the trio doing the same tunes. That's possible. Nonetheless, it doesn't take away from his body of work. To say that he couldn't play the blues, which was another of those "wonderful" clichéd statements going around—to anybody who says that I go, "What?" Because he didn't play a blues scale the way Wynton Kelly played a blues scale? What about his vibe, the touch, and the sound he got out of the piano? You want to talk melancholy? You want to feel sad? You want to feel the essence of the blues? Listen to Bill play a ballad!

Lew: That's a great point. After all, he does play the actual twelve-bar blues once in a while and sounds great on it. Now, how about Rollins?
Dave: For my generation, it's Sonny and Trane. For the generation before on tenor, it was Hawk and Prez—two sides of the same coin in some ways, completely different in others. What Sonny could do with a simple trite tune using the simplest of harmonies, by manipulating the pulse and rhythm, as well as what he played technically on the saxophone, nobody has ever matched. I put him at the top of the line as far as the saxophone goes. I even put him above Trane.

Lew: Really?
Dave: Technically, yes. It's not like you hear it on every recording, but there are instances, like the title track from the recording *Alfie*, where he plays so much saxophone, it's scary. It's a different kind of technique. Sonny could turn on a dime—change up in a minute. He could change the color, the sound, the rhythm seemingly from note to note; the articulation might vary from phrase to phrase; his ability to play saxophone harmonics, even when he would do it casually, was extraordinary. His offhandedness is actually genius in a way because it fools you into thinking how easy it sounds. You know what I'm saying? Trane was a disciplined, practiced, fingering kind of guy. Sonny, you never get a feeling that Sonny's fingers were going ahead of his brain. With Trane, sometimes it's the fingers, great as it is. With Sonny, it's like you just hear him going with the flow and he can do anything on that instrument, at any moment. Not in total as much as John did, I think for reasons I will mention about originals and personnel, but for what he did and what he intimated, Sonny is king. His prime time is really the fifties and sixties, from *Night At The Village Vanguard, Saxophone Colossus* through *The Bridge*, *Alfie*, *The Standard Sonny Rollins*, and a bunch of bootlegs that have come out, especially *Live at Ronnie Scott's* from 1965. After that period, for my taste, it's another story.

Lew: What was it about Sonny's playing in those years?
Dave: In the fifties, the way he played bebop—the flow, the rhythm, the smoothness, and the absolute agility on the tenor saxophone—was the pinnacle of that music, refining Bird, taking it to its logical conclusion. Besides the fantastic control of the language, Sonny often presented his ideas using motivic and episodic thinking, clearly evidenced on the track "Blue Seven" from 1956, which was so well analyzed by Gunther Schuller in 1958. It's true that he was playing the language of the time and didn't change it as Trane would a few years later, but the way he put

it together was virtually flawless. He could have stopped with *A Night at the Village Vanguard*, the one with Elvin in 1957, and he would've secured his place in history. But instead, he went into the sixties full steam and seemingly shaken, or at least influenced, by the leaps and bounds his friend Coltrane was making on the horn.

In 1959 Sonny famously took a hiatus and practiced on the Williamsburg Bridge in Manhattan, returning with a fresh approach that incorporated some new saxophone techniques, a different way of phrasing and interacting with those around him, resulting in, for me, the loosest and most advanced rhythmical approach to time playing ever heard. *The Bridge* from 1962 was a major statement, as were the ensuing recordings named above.

The challenge when listening to Sonny Rollins is his seeming offhandedness, almost to the point of losing attention—a certain kind of flightiness, a sense of being distracted, often embedded within a palpable sense of irony and humor. This can be either off-putting or not, depending on how you listen to him, especially if you put him next to Coltrane, where there isn't ever any doubt of where the "train" is going, so to say. Sonny will go in a direction and suddenly stop and change it, which suits his style since he is the epitome of Mr. Spontaneity. It is well known that Sonny is not at his most comfortable in the recording studio, which makes sense if you can dig that recording jazz is a kind of contradiction.

I digress, but dig it: Exaggerating one moment over another, the moment that is recorded, is kind of anti-jazz in a way. In jazz, every moment is equal to the next or last one. It's all about present time. The studio exaggerates *one* moment over another, forever. There are the positive trade-offs that we all realize about recording, the most obvious being that people who are not present at that time and place can hear it forever, anywhere on the planet. With Sonny, who is so into the moment, this freezing the moment could be a drag, which is to me understandable.

Sonny could also be a bit inconsistent from night to night, or even tune to tune, but when you went to hear him, you knew that. For sure, it never fell below a high level, true of all professionals. The reality was that in Rollins's case, when it was great, it was the best ever and you knew it really was happening, right there in front of your eyes. Sometimes with Trane, you might get the feeling that he had an agenda, meaning he was going to play what he was working on, come hell or high water. Rhythmically, Sonny at his best is the loosest of anybody I've ever heard play music, any music. You really hear this on that Ronnie Scott collection, though the band is not the greatest.

Sonny is a real bebopper, in the sense that there could be a tsunami happening around him and he could still play his deal. He is in another place. Nothing bothers him, it seems. Once again, highlighting a few: *The Bridge* with Jim Hall with them both in a true conversational mode; *Our Man In Jazz* with, of all people, trumpeter Don Cherry, which even has moments of avant-garde playing. Then there's *The Standard Sonny Rollins*, where you have a great harmonicist on piano, Herbie Hancock, which is very revealing because a lot of Sonny's work was with trios, sans chording instrument. But one thing that I just never understood was that Sonny didn't keep high-level bands together on a continuous basis. In the end, jazz is group music, where the expression "the sum is greater than its parts" is absolutely true. Sometimes when he had great bands, he disbanded them. I don't know why—it's not my or anyone's business—but I think it hurt the overall effect of the music, in the final analysis. Imagine if he had the equivalent of McCoy or Elvin on a nightly basis. Who knows what it would've sounded like and where it could've gone?

Another point is that though he wrote some of the most famous jazz songs—"Airegin," "Doxy," "Oleo," to name the most notable, and "St. Thomas," which is his arrangement of a folk tune—for the most part, he played standards. To my mind, framing one's style in the context of original music is another aspect of what we do and helps to focus whatever is notable about one's playing. On the other hand, Sonny is the repertoire man of all time, in a certain way. He could take a standard, twist it and reshape it, wringing every ounce of juice from even the simplest, most rote of tunes like "The Sheik of Araby" or "There's No Business Like Show Business" and many, many more.

The last forty years or so, with all due respect, I have no idea what to say about Sonny, except of course I'm glad he's still alive. He's a lovely person, great to talk to, very open, very respectful, not at all pretentious. I just don't understand these last decades as far as the personnel is concerned, or the music, or even his saxophone tone. But who am I to say? I feel like I'm talking about God. It feels like blasphemy to talk this way. It has just been perplexing to me. He still goes on a gig, and much like Miles in the eighties, he will play something that kills you, but what goes on around him, I don't know. He played that Carnegie Hall fiftieth anniversary gig in 2007, commemorating a concert fifty years before, with Roy Haynes, joined for the first part by bassist Christian McBride. They played okay, nothing remarkable, but the second set was with his group playing three or four tunes that were as I recall all calypso-ish stuff at the same tempo. I just didn't get it.

On the other hand, he just did his eightieth birthday concert at the Beacon Theater, which I heard was supposedly great playing on his part and notable because Ornette and Jim Hall sat in. So, who am I to say? All I know is that if you take his playing from the mid-fifties through the late sixties, it is some of the greatest jazz of all time, period! He took the language from Bird and extended it as far as it could go, while still maintaining the common vocabulary from that great period of history.

Lew: Do you think it is inevitable for an artist that there will be a natural decline of creativity or whatever, if he or she has a long life?
Dave: In our business, it's tough because the thing is to keep going, even if you don't want to. First of all, we have to make a living, and performing is the main income stream. So, the belief, though it hardly exists in reality anymore, was that you were supposed to play every single night and be "on" all the time. This is virtually impossible, and inevitably something has to give. Classical guys, even pop guys, don't have that as a premise, but *we* do because of the, what shall I say, folk aspects of the music, meaning for the people in bars and taverns, etc., at least as it came down to us through the tradition. The pop guys do a world tour and then take off for three years to "record." We're supposed to get out with that horn every damn night. I love it—that's what makes us what we are, and every one of us would like to play every night if we could. But how can you expect continuous creativity over a sixty- or seventy-year career, on a daily or near daily level? In the case of Phil and Lee, this is a moot point—they seem to be able to do it—but I pose the question anyway. Some people can sound fresh every night. Others recycle, but there is the quality of the music that doesn't lie, in the final analysis. It's really a demanding thing to be creative on call when the bell rings.

Lew: Okay. Let's talk about Wayne Shorter.
Dave: For me, he's the third part of the equation of heavies on the tenor saxophone, with Trane and Sonny. He's number one as far as composing. Wayne is the voice of the last fifty years as a composer. Basically, he is the Duke Ellington of our time, as far as a body of work representing the history of jazz from 1960 to now. Duke was, in the end, about the song form, diatonic, classical melody and harmony. Then comes Wayne, who says let's change the modulation just a little bit; let's change the order of events; it doesn't have to be ii-V-I, it could be to another V to a different I, maybe not a I, maybe to a iii chord; and with a different harmonic color, maybe a sharp 5 or whatever; upper structure triads became the actual chord, rather than as an appendage to a given chord; unevenly

phrased melodies with unusual interval shapes; the list goes on and on. He is completely unique as a composer, and he influenced everyone compositionally, if not improvisationally, speaking.

Lew: How do you play on his songs?
Dave: You have to figure out a whole other way to do it. As a saxophone player, he is a Sonny in a way, in the way he can twist on a dime, articulation and dynamic-wise, harmonic content, especially in his time with Miles in the sixties. *Live at the Plugged Nickel* is the bible of how far you can take standards, and it is truly Wayne's session. He really brought intervallic thinking into ordinary time-worn harmonic situations, and swinging above all. Also, his expressiveness on the tenor and later the soprano is remarkable, speech-like—he's talking to you.

There is a quirkiness certainly evident in the early sixties with Art Blakey and to some extent with Miles that eventually gets smoothed out, but to be honest when you converse with Wayne, you get that kind of vibe. He will transform any conversation to another plane immediately, a little like Ornette talks, but unique to Wayne. He looks you straight in the eyes with a beatific countenance, lovely, wide-open facial expressions, nothing to hide or guard, and always smiling. That's kind of the way he plays.

This is true of all the cats—you play what you are, somehow, maybe deep down, but one way or another. Wayne will play a note and you'll think, how could he do that in the middle of that? So ungraceful. So out of character. So unsmooth. So honky and raunchy. So splurty, or whatever the word is. But on the other hand, how expressive. Who else would do it except him? Wayne is the kind of guy who at any moment could jump out of the car and just stop on the road. You'd say, "Why'd you do that?" He'd answer, "I don't know. I just felt like it." Then he'd get back in the car.

If there is anybody who represents the composer as improviser, Wayne is the one in the history of jazz. This guy is composing when he improvises—a compositional mind when he plays. You hear the thought pattern; you hear him building; you hear him motivic-ing out, not in an obvious kind of A-B-C elementary way. I really can feel his thoughtfulness, his use of space, which I'm sure he got a lot from Miles because he didn't play like that before with Buhaina, Art Blakey. There's a logic that's intrinsic to his playing. That is what I mean by a composer at work. Coltrane is not a composer at work—he is the improviser as composer. Charlie Parker, the same. Now Monk, he's a composer at work, especially because there was such homogeneity between how he played and what the composition was like, even somehow when he played standards, the way he transformed them. Some guys are more like that. Wayne is, to me, the master of the composer as improviser.

Lew: What can you say about finding an original voice, the way Wayne and the others discussed in this chapter have done?
Dave: You bring up a philosophical question. Where is the line between great talent, understanding the vocabulary, knowing what came before, having great abilities—and an original voice? I was just discussing this in my class yesterday. I played drums with the sax students, which I do all the time. "Get up and play a tune." After a while: "Okay, we just heard ten of you play. What's the story? How many of you will even remember what you or anyone else played after you left? What is individuality? How do you get it? Why is it important? What are you really doing if you are not telling a story?" Answers like: "Oh, I don't know, I don't think about it, I think it will happen if it's supposed to happen," etc.

So, is this something that one must strive for? Should we be worried? Should we be neurotic about it? The bottom line is that it's about desire; it's about wanting it. It has to be priority number one at some point, this finding oneself, or it will not happen. It does not fall from the sky, even to so-called geniuses. You have to look outside the box, outside of jazz, to other arts, the humanities, life in general. It's about a worldview in the end, though it may not be articulated as such. It takes hard work weeding things out that are not yours, that are really coming more from your influences than you. Two and two is four, but sometimes two plus one plus one is also four. Creativity is how you mix and match. It's not about inspiration. That's a different question. It's about desire and hard, disciplined work.

Chapter 12

Tomorrow's Expectations: The Legacy

Lew: Let's talk about where you are today in 2011, as we speak. We talked about your current group. What about the CD of Ornette Coleman's music released in 2010?
Dave: With this group, after twenty years, we've recorded sixteen CDs, everything from original music, to repertoire projects like Puccini arias on *A Walk in the Clouds*, to a Miles dedication called *Miles Away*, to *The Unknown Jobim*. So this record, called *Turnaround: The Music of Ornette Coleman*, is another in that repertoire series. I like translating my musical concepts to a relatively known body of music.

Lew: When you say repertoire or repertory, you mean…
Dave: I mean not originals—somebody else's music providing the content for a project.

Lew: How do you get ideas for these albums? To a lot of people, I think the *Jobim* one was maybe a little bit of a surprise: "Is Lieb a bossa nova player?"
Dave: He's one of the greatest composers who ever lived. In fact, his combination of melody and harmony is probably about the top of the line in my opinion, along with Cole Porter, meaning specifically how the harmony enriches the melody. Also, though I don't understand the Portuguese lyrics, the sound of that language sounds so charming and fitting to the music. When the lyrics are in English, whoever's done them, they sound great also.

Lew: It sounds very natural. But in people's minds, I don't think they associate you as a bossa nova player.
Dave: Well, of course, I didn't do the tunes in that idiom. I used all kinds of feels and so forth to encase the material.

Lew: Right. Now, the Puccini—that sounds interesting. Our friend Bob Belden did a Puccini album in '92, but it wasn't released. Yours was recorded in '97.
Dave: I was with Caris, doing a workshop in Lisbon. They gave us a video machine and one morning, getting ready to teach, I put on a tape. Coincidentally, it was the John Abercrombie Quartet playing a concert with Richie in the group, but afterward came on the New York Metropolitan Opera. I was showering, and I heard these great melodies, I believe sung by Placido Domingo. It was "Tosca" and it really stayed with me. When I got home I asked the resident classical teacher, Professor Larry Fisher, at East Stroudsburg University, about Puccini. Lo and behold, he gave me all the scores and recordings, so I spent a whole winter listening to Puccini. I picked out twelve tunes that I liked, reorganized and arranged them for different instrumentations using my quintet with Markowitz and Haddad at the time as the core, along with cello and woodwind quartet, which included Caris on oboe and Phil Woods on clarinet.

On the other hand, with Ornette's music, it has always interested me from a historic standpoint. We all know that he's an innovator and a gigantic influence. I can't tell you that Ornette was one of my favorites as far as listening goes. I never really loved him like some people do and I'll tell you why. It's very specific: There's no direct harmony, for the most part. I know that's a categorical and sweeping statement that's not quite accurate, but in general I believe strongly that one of the greatest things Western culture has contributed to the history of music is the notion of harmony.

Lew: And your whole chromatic concept is strongly geared toward the harmonic content.
Dave: Exactly. I just like harmony. I think it enriches the expressiveness, the feeling of a melody, of the music all together. This is not only because we improvise over harmonies in jazz, but just in general for all music. Look, for most of the history of the human race and even at present, the majority of the world's cultures do not include direct harmony as a musical element, but we do, thankfully. I always missed that in Ornette's music, meaning direct, *intentional* harmony, not harmonies that

arise while you're improvising together. There's a concept that Richie and I always talked about, which we call the slack theory—if one musical element is emphasized, or in this case de-emphasized, some other musical element will be heightened in importance.

Lew: Another element takes up the slack.
Dave: Perfect. It goes even further in this case because Ornette's melodies are profoundly lyrical and pass the "stand-alone" judgment in my opinion, which means exactly what it says: One of the criteria of a great melody is that it sounds "good" without the support of harmony. In other words, the harmony, when present, truly enhances what is already a wonderful melody. Therefore, what I wanted to do with Ornette, for at least a few tunes, was put some harmony to the music—not every tune, but a few that I chose out of a hundred and fifty I reviewed. I don't know how many he has—there are just so many great melodies—but I picked ten or twelve for the recording. It was very rewarding because having the guitar created another challenge as well.

I like this record a lot and it was awarded best of the year in 2010 by the German Jazz Journalist Association—not an easy audience to please, by the way. Again, concerning repertoire versus original music, it isn't like I try to switch one after another sequentially, but I do like to offer those listeners who follow me something familiar on occasion, for obvious reasons. Even with Quest, we did a record of standards in 1988 called *N.Y. Nites*; and as we speak, Quest just recorded some of the Miles Davis Quintet mid-sixties tunes after a week playing at Birdland in New York. Those are the classic Shorter songs like "Nefertiti," "Pinocchio," "Vonetta," and others. What a great repertoire—incredibly sophisticated music and quite a challenge to transform to the style of Quest, but I think we did it well. This is coming after two CDs that we did in the last few years since we reunited in 2005, which had a few repertoire tunes but consisted of mostly originals.

Lew: It's interesting because there are guitar players who are influenced by Ornette. It would be possible to do something with a guitar player and not have the harmony.
Dave: Definitely, but guitarists can go both ways, and Vic did both harmony and single-line stuff on the recording. We did "Kathelin Gray" and "The Blessing" with harmony, just adding a few things to what Ornette already had there.

Lew: "The Blessing" is one of the early ones that included changes.

Dave: Right. Our repertoire ended up being a lot of the early Ornette tunes from around 1960, which are so classic now. They probably are among his most well known, but they attracted me, maybe because I am familiar with them. We did "Lonely Woman" and "Una Muy Bonita" with a Latin feel arranged by Vic. With "Lonely Woman" I used a wooden recorder that I have been playing for years, and Vic had some great sounds from the synth. Every tune was arranged a certain way.

Lew: What gave you the idea to do the Miles 1960s repertoire with Quest? Where do these ideas come from?
Dave: I have kept a repertoire list for years. Steven Sondheim is on it, as well as Jerome Kern and a few others that I haven't done yet.

Lew: That's interesting! This is an aspect of your art that we haven't really talked about—arranger. In jazz there's this whole thing about an arranger. People ask how this is different from a composer.
Dave: Very different. When I teach, I note that there are several processes involved. There's writing the tune, then arranging the tune, followed by orchestration. Each area exemplifies a different mechanism. Composition is obvious; arranging is the form that the tune will take—who will play what, where, and when. Orchestration, even if it is a duo of horn and piano, has to do with tessitura—that is, range, as well as doubling lines and other matters of colorings. Arranging, in this case, is taking known material, like Puccini, like Jerome Kern, and casting it in your light, in what you personally hear and enjoy playing in your particular style.

Of course, purists could object to, for example, altering the melody as I do, or the form, and other techniques I might use. To me, that's part of what we do. It's a great way to perceive an artist's creativity, by how they alter a known quantity like a standard. There's something for the listener to relate to. In a certain way, one's artistic tastes are seen in a more stark light when you have a known quantity.

Lew: You have something to compare it to.
Dave: Certainly in jazz because of the amount of what we call "common language" repertoire—standards. You say "All the Things You Are" and we have something in our head that we all know together. If I say a Puccini aria, you sort of know it, and classical fans know it well. This rearranging sheds a new light, in contrast to the known quantity.

Lew: One of the things I learned from studying Coltrane was, it's okay to change the form. When I first started hearing Trane's version of "My Favorite Things" for example, and he discarded the chorus structure, I thought it was not allowed, like this was a crime or something!
Dave: I'll tell you the first time I encountered changing the actual written melody on purpose—not as a consequence of phrasing alterations, which was always part of jazz from the beginning—was "Without a Song," from Joe Henderson on *The Kicker* recording. He changed the melody—talk about irreverent! He changed the melody by a half-step, and of course the harmony to complement this variation. I thought, "If Joe Henderson can do it, I can do it."

Lew: It does help to have a role model, to have someone who says, "It's okay. You can do that."
Dave: Someone who breaks the rules. Like with the Miles '60s project, we were having a discussion about "Pinocchio." "Pinocchio" has an eighteen-bar form, but I wanted an extra two bars. Someone noted that it is exactly the eighteen bars that makes the tune so special. I understand that, but I wanted two more because then it would be a four-bar phrase, which would allow me to either finish a statement or begin a new one. Two measures feels too short. I understand the challenge of doing what was originally written, and I'm not taking away from that because twenty bars, rather than eighteen, is still a challenge. But I just feel that my solution is a little more conducive to what I like to play. So, we added two bars to Wayne's tune. Okay, so kill me—sue me!

Lew: The other thing I noticed is with your groups, you make a decision—this material is for the quartet with Vic, that one is for Quest, and so on. How do you choose? Or is it just whatever you're doing at that moment, and that's who you're gigging with at the time?
Dave: It's a little bit what I'm doing at that moment, and a little bit of what we need for that particular group. Like I mentioned, since Quest reunited, the last recording had one "repertoire" tune—Coltrane's "Brazilia"—but the other seven tunes are original. I said to Richie, "I think we should do some repertoire tunes, next project." Besides the musical reasons to do repertoire, there is the obvious, let's call it the "commercial" aspect, which simply means that the listener has some reference point to notice what the artist is doing. I'm not against being liked or comprehended, you know. This reference point of something they have heard before helps them listen, and in the case of Quest that could only

help our listeners. Obviously, you need pretty hip listeners who recognize "Vonetta" or "Hand Jive," but that's another discussion.

Lew: It's interesting because other groups might just do a couple of tunes by someone else and a couple of originals. They may do that on every album, rather than do a whole repertory album. But if you do that, then every album seems kind of the same, in a way. This way, there's something really different.
Dave: Also, don't forget we learn something by delving into the repertoire of a master. I did Kurt Weill and Alec Wilder in the past few years, and I really got into these guys.

Lew: That's a good point, that there's a difference between really doing a repertory project or just saying, "Well, I've got a couple Kurt Weill tunes in the book." You really make a study of it.
Dave: I become immersed in it, and I like that, because then I learn something. I really learned from the Ornette project about triads because I'm not by and large a triad player, although a lot of my favorite type of harmony has triads implicit in it. My lines just don't come from that source, for the most part.

Lew: What about what they call triad pairs?
Dave: I don't do that. George Garzone and Gary Campbell, two really good players, have approaches on triads that really work for them. I have never really used that. It sounds a little too patterned for me. But I must say that Ornette is way into triads—and in major keys a lot. Even when he plays a blue note, a minor thing, it still sounds like major—hard to explain why. Like "Lonely Woman"—it's minor, but it feels major.

Lew: Different from Trane. Trane's a minor guy.
Dave: Big time. And the emotion—this is important—if you are hip to it and sensitive enough, you truly get into the guy's being and persona. Ornette's music is absolutely like the sun coming out. It's uplifting, it's joyous, it's *joie de vivre*—fantastic—and completely different from Coltrane or from Wayne, or any of the people we've spoken about. I appreciate that certain form of expressiveness that I find within a person, that I can then absorb and react to, or at the least reflect upon.

Lew: Well said. Now, let's talk about the different projects that you're involved with these days. The quartet is still your main thing, yes?

Dave: For sure. But there are several groups besides the Quartet, and Quest: Saxophone Summit with Joe Lovano and Ravi Coltrane, Different But the Same with Ellery Eskelin, We3 with Steve Swallow and Adam Nussbaum, and duos with several piano players, besides the European groups. In most cases I have to plan a year to two in advance with these very busy musicians. We block out a time—for example, we already know we have a European tour with Different But the Same in March 2012; we know that Quest is going on tour in the fall of next year, and so on. I try to work at least several times a year with my steady quartet in some concentrated way, meaning enough that I can say to the guys, "Give me those two weeks." It could be a date in New York and then maybe Boston. Coming up is the Midwest—we're going to go play Chicago, the University of Indiana, University of Michigan, etc., places that have been very generous with me every couple of years. These are not great money-making gigs, but we're on the road and we'll make some music—plus drive a lot!

Lew: So, each time you do a project with one of these groups, you already start saying, "When can we do this again?" and it just kind of works out. If it's going to have to be a year and a half away, that's all right.
Dave: Exactly. Logistics is always a problem. I'm a bit of a juggler. I have a lot of things going on at the same time. I spend a lot of my time juggling these things. I don't have anybody doing it for me. I keep all the guys informed as to what is transpiring and so on. I don't call a guy two days before and say, "We're going out." I really try to treat everybody with respect. That's part of what I do. I'm a leader, and that's what a leader is supposed to do. He must be responsible to his sidemen or peers, whatever the case may be, which varies in these situations for me—give them the right time, the correct pay—just do the job right.

Lew: So, you do all the business yourself, like most cats do.
Dave: In jazz, we're in a marginal business. We don't make enough money to pay someone a salary or commission, which they deserve if they do their job. It's only fair. They want 10 to 15 percent, which is absolutely reasonable. I can't afford to give away 10 to 15 percent. I could if I was making $10,000 a day, but this is not my reality. Another thing I have to acknowledge is that in the final result no one does as good a job as you will for yourself. I'm not saying nobody's good enough, not being judgmental. The truth is that it's your business, and no one is going to care about it as much as you do.

Even if you say to your best friend, "Could you take care of this?" they'll do the best they can do, but it's not like you taking care of it because you're checking every detail since it's your life. I've learned that when I did have people helping me, it always ended up that I had to tell them what to do. So what was I saving?

Lew: Half the time you end up saying, "Well, let me get on the phone with the concert hall manager."
Dave: That brings up a subtle point about communication in the business end. In jazz, people want to talk to you. This is not the entertainment business per se. It's more personal. A booking guy doesn't want to talk to a manager. He will, but he would much rather talk to me because he wants contact with Dave Liebman. And I appreciate that. So, I try to take care of as much as I can on a variety of levels. I am extremely organized and a very hard worker. These days, I'm on email all the time. It takes a lot of my time. I'm not happy about it because it takes away from music time, especially if you factor in the obvious family commitments and so forth, but I just don't see any way around it if I want to work, which I must. So I end up doing everything, from booking, to PR, to sending out photos, to getting the CD to the right guy, to doing an interview. When I've had formal help, it just ended up that I did these things anyway.

Certainly I have some people around the world who help. In the States a guy named Mike Cherigo, whom I've been working with for many years, takes care of some things. He will, for example, call Birdland, instead of me, to negotiate. In Europe I have two booking agents for the different bands, but with all my individual projects, like when I go to teach or do stuff on my own, that's all me organizing. I do "stringing," which is putting gigs on top of gigs, meaning consecutively. Next week I'm going to France, but maybe I can get something in Holland before that. This is what takes all the office time.

A manager, in my mind, is not supposed to be a glorified secretary, taking care of logistics and all that. They would and should do that, in the final analysis, but a manager is really supposed to find outlets for you that you can't do on your own—to enlarge your potential and possibilities. They're supposed to put their finger in the wind and say, "This is an opportunity for Dave Liebman to be a part of this project," etc. I have plenty of ideas for expansion beyond just playing, like being a motivational speaker, meaning telling my story to inspire others, musicians and lay people alike, to follow their dream and make it real. I want to do an interview type of show, TV or radio, whatever, where I interact with other known artists in a "Q and A" setting. I just don't have the time to explore these avenues, so I need someone who will tap into these possibilities in a creative manner, seeing the big picture. That's the function of a real manager, to be creative with the material, my life's work, that's being handed to them. I know it's jazz, which means not a big profit margin, even with so-called success, but I still think that with some creative thinking, more can be done with an artist like myself. Helen Keane, who managed pianist Bill Evans, comes to mind. She really raised his professional stature. Musicians and jazz aficionados knew how "bad" Bill was, but Helen got him Grammy awards, best-selling records in the jazz sense, by putting him into creative contexts like the one he did with three overdubbed pianos and so forth. She could see the potential and acted on it. I can dream, right?

Lew: Let's hope it comes true! Now, what about Sax Summit. How, where, and why?
Dave: We spoke about the concert called "Live Under the Sky" that I did with Wayne Shorter in 1987. Well, in 1997 the Japanese did a concert called "Live at the Sea," taking place, if I recall correctly, on Tokyo Bay in some Yamaha Disneyland resort-type thing. It was sort of a ten-year anniversary of the 1987 concert, celebrating Coltrane once again. They invited me, Joshua Redman, Michael Brecker, Joe Lovano, and some great rhythm section guys. You know, an all-star bash. It ended up that Joe couldn't make it, so George Garzone did it. It was very nice, with several combinations. Joshua played with Metheny, and I did a quartet playing "My Favorite Things" with Jack DeJohnette, Dave Holland, and Joey Calderazzo. Of course, we had the tenor portion where we played "Impressions" and other Trane tunes. So, a few months later, Brecker's manager, Darryl Pitt, called and said that the Red Sea Festival in Israel was interested in something similar—Mike, Joe, and me playing together.

We did the gig, which was great, but most important, I had a chance to sit down and talk with Mike Brecker, something we hadn't done since the seventies when he bought my 19th Street loft from me. We just had busy lives. Michael and I had a very good relationship, always cordial and friendly and always deeply personal, whenever we did have time together over the decades. After all, Coltrane was for both of us the real deal and had affected our lives immensely, so there was that common bond. In Israel, I suggested we make something out of this saxophone meeting, with an emphasis on the late Coltrane period, which in my mind has been perpetually underappreciated by listeners and musicians alike. Underperformed, under-everything. When it was performed, it wasn't at the highest level, maybe because the music had a large element of cacophony, without a consistent harmonic framework, all encased in free pulse, with no steady rhythm. This style of free jazz could be and was easily misconstrued as a green light for playing *anything*. I've always felt that that period has been neglected and that this stage of Trane's playing had an emotional element that went beyond the pale.

To Mike: "We were in the lofts playing this stuff together. Do you remember? We are the people who should be playing this music and bringing it now to the people because of who we are, as well as what we are musically." This didn't mean that we were only going to play Coltrane, but that the main point should be the collective energy of Mike, Joe, and me with a high-level rhythm section of peers. He said, "They'll kill us!" "What do you mean, they'll kill us?" He answered, "The critics." "But if you and I and Joe don't do this, who will? The other thing is that it's time to take a stand. We are getting near our sixties and we should do it. Who else is going to? I know it's three white guys, but that's the way it goes, bro, and I think we should do it." He went for it. I felt that he had to be on board because of his status, his playing, and his presence. Next, we went to Joe and he was completely down with it. The first rhythm section, which I basically put together, was with Billy Hart, my compatriot from Quest; Phil Markowitz, whom I just felt was the right guy to take care of the three horns; and on bass it was Rufus Reid, to be replaced a few years later by Cecil McBee. This is the same rhythm section today, fourteen years later.

Lew: You definitely didn't want to have to pick up a rhythm section in each city when you traveled?

Dave: No, that was out of the question. It had to be guys who carried as much or more weight than us, from a historical standpoint. That was certainly Billy and certainly Rufus, followed by Cecil and Phil. That was part of the premise—that we're going to keep a first-class rhythm section that's equal or even above us in stature, even age in the case of Cecil and Billy, and most of all in experience and depth. That was the decision. The three of us were united in that thinking, though management might've liked less expensive guys. Financially, when Mike worked with us, obviously he made less money than when he was on his own. We split everything equally after paying the rhythm section, which was pretty high compared to most bands. I didn't want to be up there with young guys.

For the first few years, the repertoire consisted of standards, when we played several times at the New York club Birdland. But we did play

Coltrane's "Meditations" and some pieces from that period. What we brought from the late Trane period was the idea of a good deal of collective playing together somewhere during the set. We made the first CD in 2004, called *Gathering of Spirits*, where we recorded "India," which we performed a lot. The point of the group was an attempt to really say something meaningful by three well-known guys who are individual stylists but all coming from the same sources.

Lew: Understood. With Brecker, the interesting thing is, though he was deep into the stuff and played brilliantly, the way his career was perceived, it would seem that people wouldn't picture him in such a group because he was at that point almost like a pop star. Of course, he was an amazing saxophone player, but Brecker playing outside, so freely—was that a surprise for some people?

Dave: It certainly was. This was also true in Joe's case. After all, he was making CDs of Sinatra and Caruso tunes! Believe me, there was definitely a mystified look on some faces out there in the seats of Birdland. But Michael had a lot of respect for my views and felt that the direction was something that he could latch onto. He felt good about it. The manager told me, "Mike likes to be with you."

Of course there were business matters that had to be sorted out. Sometimes I would have to go to Mike and get him to move the management in a certain way or whatever—no big deal, but it needed to be done. Michael was always straight with me and respected what I was trying to do with this group. In 2004 we did a great European tour and that first recording. His last real gig was with Sax Summit at Birdland, right before he stopped playing and then eventually passed. It was a long illness, and at some point I know that Mike reconciled himself to the reality. When he passed on January 13, 2007, many people were at the IAJE conference in New York. It was late that very night that I found Jabali Billy Hart at the hotel. Billy was like Badal Roy had been for me in the seventies—he was my go-to-for-wisdom guy. He came up to the room and we talked. We were obviously very upset. I said that we have a duty, even more so now as a memory to Mike, to continue Saxophone Summit, meaning that we would have to find a replacement.

By this point, we had played a few gigs during the preceding summer that were contracted for Sax Summit, which we were obligated to do. As Mike was unable to play, we had to get substitutes. There was a festival in Burlington, Vermont, the Playboy Festival, and Newport, all done during the summer of 2006. So, we ended up for those three gigs having Chris Potter at one, Joshua Redman once, and Ravi Coltrane.

Lew: Wow, that's amazing! You got to try them all out.
Dave: Well, the first level of interaction was that we had to cover our bases and get someone with a reputation. Of course, there was no substitute for Mike Brecker, but these guys were credible, both as known quantities and musically on a high level. With the decision-making being primarily just Joe and myself, obviously with input from the rhythm section, we eventually felt that Ravi was the right guy for a few reasons. My discussion with Billy was whether it might be construed as opportunism if we had John Coltrane's son in Saxophone Summit. Billy reassured me that it was fine.

Lew: Now, the current situation with Sax Summit?
Dave: Well, as we speak here in February 2011, we just recorded after a week at Birdland and a tour last November. On the tour, Sax Summit played Trane's "Meditations" every night, a piece I have been presenting for years on the anniversaries of its original recording. My wife, Caris, did the original transcriptions from the actual recording, which I have used in different performance situations. Most recently I recorded the suite with full orchestra at the Manhattan School of Music, arranged by my good friend and leader of my big band, Gunnar Mossblad.

Lew: You wrote an article about that piece for a journal some years ago.
Dave: Yes, an analysis, available on my website too. This present summit recording features one tune by each of us, all in a very free style with a lot of rubato and so forth. I felt it was time for us to have all originals since the second recording, *Seraphic Light*, with Ravi in 2007, featured a few late Trane tunes. I really worked hard getting everyone on the same page for this new one, making sure the music had an overall concept to it stylistically. We ended up with a beautiful, very free-flowing record. There's no steady time, very few chord changes, but it's not chaotic crazy either. It's half ballads and half open jazz. I don't know what else to call it. I don't know who will release it, especially with the record business seemingly dead, but we will deal with it and hopefully get it released, one way or the other. I'm quite proud of it. It is very personal and unique, and most of all, truly a group sound.

Lew: Let's talk about some of your other projects, starting with We3.
Dave: This is family. Adam Nussbaum was in my group in the late seventies as you know, and Steve Swallow goes back with me to the Open Sky Trio with Bob Moses, as well as my first heavy gig, with Pete La-

Roca. Steve is really one of my first compatriots, even before Richie. Actually, I shouldn't say compatriot, implying peer, because he is master level, ahead of me for sure.

Lew: How did the three of you get together as a trio?
Dave: I think Adam asked me. I was open to being with old friends and playing in a pretty straight-ahead style, as befits these guys. The chordless trio format is one of my favorite combinations. We have two recordings out and have done a few European tours, but we haven't worked in New York or the States at all. Like all the groups we are discussing, these are projects you try to do every year or two, just juggling things around to make schedules work. In the old days, it would more likely be one group that everyone would work with, but the situation now demands that everyone is a juggler.

Lew: But not every group works out to be a continuing thing.
Dave: No, not everything's a go. You might walk off and think, "I had a nice time. See you."

Lew: In this case, it must have been something that felt good.
Dave: It felt great. These are the most comfortable guys to play with. Steve's compositions are classics, as anyone in jazz knows. He's up there compositionally with Wayne in some ways, since his tunes are played everywhere. They are like little jewels, miniature puzzles to work out, which people enjoy playing—simple, but deep. For drums in a trio situation, the orchestral possibilities are heightened, bringing out the full sound and colors of the drum set itself—something Adam, coming out of Elvin, knows real well. In this particular situation, Adam really has a chance to shine. He's a great drummer.

Lew: He's a marvelous drummer and a nice, funny guy.
Dave: Great guy. He's something else—a truly unique personality.

Lew: Very cool. Now, saxophonist Ellery Eskelin?
Dave: When Ellery came to New York, he hung with me for a minute, taking lessons and playing together. He definitely picked up some of my stuff in his playing, and even today sometimes I have to do a double-take as to whether it is him or me when I listen to what we are doing, much like it was with Steve Grossman in those early Elvin days. Over the years I've always been very supportive of Ellery. I have a lot of respect for him because he's made a name for himself in the avant-garde wing with a

sound and style that is completely individual. But he can play anything—changes, time, whatever. Ellery is a real artist, no question, in a category by himself.

Lew: In a way, maybe people would be surprised to see you with him, not in terms of "outness," because you are open to everything, but in terms of the scene. He's known more in the "downtown" scene, which actually *is* in downtown Manhattan. You know one of his famous groups is himself and an innovative electronic accordionist—
Dave: Yes, Andrea Parkins—and the drummer is Jim Black.

Lew: The accordion! So, it's not like Ellery is known for doing straight-ahead stuff.
Dave: Let me tell you how we put the group together. I had heard Jim Black on a tape and I got in touch with him to invite him out to my home to play with bassist Mike Formanek, who at that time was living in the Pocono area. We had an old-fashioned session, which was fantastic. Somehow this morphed into putting the group together with Jim and Ellery, who were buds from that group with Andrea. I brought in Tony Marino on bass from my group, who can play anything. I also decided that, at least for now, we would have the front line just be two tenors—no soprano for me.

Lew: The two-tenor sound—a grand tradition!
Dave: Johnny Griffin and Eddie Lockjaw Davis; Al Cohn and Zoot Sims, and so on. Why not? Much like We3, we get together every so often. We call the group after the name of the first record, *Different But the Same*, which I think is very appropriate in light of the way Ellery and I play. In a way, it could be my most fun group because it's so open, the musicianship is so good, and Jim Black is a phenomenon on the drums.

Lew: On any kind of repertoire.
Dave: Jim can do it all. It doesn't matter. He is completely creative, one of a kind, on the case, a real force. I can't tell you how much I love that guy's playing. I always say that he's like Bob Moses, updated. He has a lot of similarities to the way Moses plays, but he's taken it further, as the younger generation does. The group is great. Again, Tony, after all these years playing with him, is the most flexible guy I've every heard in my life in any style. He just fits right in—free jazz, no problem! This is perfect for him. Finally with Ellery and me, we have a lot of similarities and a lot of differences, so I am enjoying it immensely.

I'm surrounded by saxophones, if you throw Saxophone Summit into the mix. There's nothing like having guys on your own instrument, because you know the same secrets. There's mutual respect and differences, but the same ethos. I just think there's a compatibility when you have guys of your own instrument, with a little competition, friendly jousting, shall we say, in the mix. One-upmanship—yeah! But that's great.

Lew: And repertoire-wise with Ellery?
Dave: We do some standards. We do this thing on "What Is This Thing Called Love" where Tony plays that melody, I play "Hot House," and Ellery plays "Subconscious Lee"—you know, those great contrafacts based on Cole Porter's chord changes. We play Dolphy's "Out There." We just recorded Albert Ayler's "Ghosts." But we do mostly originals, which in Ellery's case are very musically distinct. He writes exact rhythms to play, but with your choice of pitches up to the moment.

Lew: Are they hard rhythms?
Dave: No, but they're hard in the sense that everybody may be together or not at the same time, and you really have to concentrate trying to avoid finger cliché responses to filling in the pitches. In fact, for the recent Sax Summit recording, I used that idea a bit, dividing the twelve tones into four each for me, Joe, and Ravi, to deal with using some rhythmic motifs. It came out quite nice. I call the tune "Partition."

Lew: Speaking about your originals, when you write a piece, do you think, "This is only for this specific group," or would you do it with any one of the projects?
Dave: When I write a tune it depends on what the center of the tune is about. If it's harmony, it's obviously meant for quartet, with either piano or guitar, there being a slight difference. Is it meant for open situations—chordless trio or quartet, like we're talking about with Ellery? Is it meant for a twentieth-century-type harmonic setting—me and Phil Markowitz, or me and Copland, or me and Richie? Is it meant for a fusion situation with electric bass? I have categories. My three to four hundred tunes cover a few genres and are mostly adjustable to different idioms. I might take one tune from one genre and make it into a trio with Swallow and Nussbaum. But basically I think of a tune as already molded for a certain instrumentation, which for me is mostly small group. I don't really go beyond five musicians.

Lew: So, people should know that that book of your tunes called the *David Liebman Anthology*, from Advance Music in 2006, is just the tip of the iceberg.
Dave: Those are just sixty tunes. Also, I recycle and revise. We recorded a tune last week with Ellery and the original date said 1974, also 2000 and 2010, meaning that I continually might work on a song. Three times I brought it back, but I never recorded it until now. A composition is like a living creature. When you address the tune, the issue again, because you have changed, because you are different, because you hear differently, you might say, "Why did I write that? It doesn't belong," or needs to be changed, etc. If you were a student and brought me a tune, I would say, "That A-flat is not right." I see that in my own stuff! I see that I can make a better musical decision here or there in the composition. I'll revamp the tune with no problem at all, whether it is old or whatever. It's fine with me. All tunes live forever.

Lew: Very true. Now, how about the Dave Liebman Big Band?
Dave: The big band was a natural for me because over the decades I've had so many people arrange my tunes for that setting, mostly as an outgrowth of being a clinician. You know, the usual scenario is you go to a school, do a clinic, and play with a big band, for which the guy in charge asks whether he can write a chart for you. I encourage them to take one of my originals, which they are happy to do. I not only encourage it, I give them a CD with maybe sixty tunes, just the heads. I tell them to pick what they like by number on the CD. They don't even know the names at that point. Then I will send the full recorded versions with the lead sheets, and they should whittle it down to the one they like the most.

Last night, one of my former Manhattan School students came to the club. He's arranging one of my tunes, "Negative Space." He was ready to have it played by the BMI workshop, and I said, "Let me see it first," not because of specific notes or chords, but for the overall shape of the form and so on. I don't monitor what the guys write. In fact, I encourage them to be as creative as they can, but on form and structure I like to put my opinion in. I have purposely kept it to all soprano sax, so that the sound of the big band can be identified, like Woody Herman or Benny Goodman did with the clarinet—sounds like a corny idea, but it works.

By around 2000, after having begun this process with arrangers in the seventies, I had nearly forty of my tunes arranged for big band and several recordings, including the University of Miami and McGill University big bands, various radio bands in Europe, a group from Sweden called Tolvan, and one with the Brussels Big Band that we did in 2006.

I'm not a big-band kind of guy, having not spent much time in them outside of the early days in the Catskills and a few assorted record dates over the years. But with all these arrangements, I had a whole book for my own big band, and we've recorded two CDs, *Beyond the Line* and *As Always*.

As far as writing for big band, it scares the shit out of me. I just don't know how anyone does it, with all those available choices of instruments and so on. I have a lot of respect for Jim McNeely, Vince Mendoza, and Maria Schneider, just to name a few great contemporary writers. I am not a giant fan of the big-band sound in general or an aficionado, but being in front is like being the quarterback in football. The energy that you feel is definitely intoxicating. There's a feeling of power and unity that is about numbers, sheer numbers in this case—seventeen musicians! I enjoy it very much.

Lew: So, there may be somebody out there arranging some of your tunes who you don't know about, but whenever you do know about it, you like to be involved. You don't just say, "Go write it. I'll see you later."
Dave: I give them complete artistic freedom, but again my concern about form is most important, since form is like the frame around a painting, strongly influencing how the work is perceived by the listener. The elements in between, like who's going to play the melody, where you're going to put the second trumpet—that's the arranger's business. That is something I don't know how to do.

Lew: I would guess that they would like that because that means they are getting input from the artist.
Dave: They love it. Here's what happens as a side effect though—the band's music is very difficult. Why? Because the arranger is putting his best foot forward. It's his one chart that will definitely get performed, so he goes for the gold star. They are doing it for no fee at this point, so apparently the "respect" quotient, meaning they are writing for Dave Liebman, whatever that means, must be at least part of the motivation to work on my tunes. I'm not saying that the arrangers make the music hard for hard's sake, but they will write challenging stuff because it's Dave Liebman, and it's only going to be one chart of theirs that gets played, although sometimes someone will have several. So, the band's repertoire is tough music. But I have the best New York musicians, some with solid reputations as improvisers, with my quartet as the core rhythm section.

Lew: What about Gunnar Mossblad?

Dave: He is the actual leader of the band, on first alto. Gunnar is my long-time associate who has helped me on many projects—books, teaching DVDs, chamber music, several recordings, etc. Could I say he is my aide de camp who has made many of my creative projects a reality, as well as a good friend? He is a consummate musician and knows how to take care of serious business. He did that arrangement of the "Meditations Suite" for orchestra and did an arrangement of it for Sax Summit and big band a few years ago, which we played at Symphony Space. By the way, these kind of large-scale projects all come to fruition through my association with Justin DiCioccio at the Manhattan School of Music, who has a conservatory pool of musicians to choose from.

Lew: Justin is great. I was there for the orchestra performance of "Meditations"—beautiful.
Dave: Gunnar is my man and has helped me beyond description. I owe him a lot.

Lew: And he's a former student of yours? He's a protégé?
Dave: He studied with me. He's now in charge of jazz at the University of Toledo.

Lew: Would you say in the big band he's what they used to call a "straw boss"?
Dave: Yes. He organizes the charts, sets the tempos, and rehearses the band. He's the leader.

Lew: If there's a held chord at the end…
Dave: You got it—he cuts it off, conducts it.

Lew: But that's not a touring project then, the Dave Liebman Big Band?
Dave: Well, it is virtually impossible to go anywhere with that number of musicians, considering travel, per diem, and fees. We figured the least we could get away with for one gig is $20,000. It's impossible! There are others who can get that for a big band, but I can't, unfortunately. But I and the other musicians, some of whom are in several more well-known big bands, know the music we play is unique and very powerful.

Lew: Now, there is something called the Dublin Project.
Dave: The Dublin guys are Ronan and Conor Guilfoyle on bass and drums, with guitarist Mike Nielsen. This is just one of several European projects I have been doing on a more or less regular basis. I have another

group called the World View Trio with Jean Paul Celea, bass, and Wolfgang Reisinger, drums. And my relationship with Bobo Stenson, piano, Lars Danielsson, bass, and Jon Christensen, drums, resulted in a band we called Far North for over twenty years, playing that Nordic style of jazz.

Lew: Wow—what a trio! That's a great album, that *Far North* one.
Dave: Over the years I have initiated, sustained, and encouraged relationships with European musicians, trying to keep it steady for both practical and musical reasons. The Dublin guys I have been hitting with since the late '80s. I have a rhythm section in Italy that's like my standard straight-ahead group with Roberto Tarenzi, piano, Tony Arco, drums, and Paolo Benedetinni, bass.

Lew: Those guys are great! I know those albums.
Dave: I enjoy these groups because they all bring out different parts of my playing. And as we know, European musicians and audiences are very appreciative of the music when you go there, and especially when you play with them. They have real respect and take good care of you when you are touring. This performing and being able to benefit both musically as well as financially in Europe is not new in jazz. We know about Coleman Hawkins, Sidney Bechet, and later on, Johnny Griffin and Dexter, etc., all sojourning for different lengths of time in Europe. Jazz musicians have been doing this for decades. I really enjoy it. These various groups are ongoing and they may kick up every couple of years and then go to sleep for a minute, but overall these are ongoing projects with European musicians.

Lew: And there's the Dutch trio.
Dave: The Dutch trio is just bass and drums—Eric Ineke, and Marius Beets on bass. I use them as my repertoire group. We've recorded the music of Kurt Weill, Alec Wilder, and we just did one featuring blues pieces played by Trane. Ineke's from my generation and he's been for years the go-to guy for putting together straight-ahead local rhythm sections in the Netherlands, to back soloists, usually American. In fact, we are doing a book in which I interviewed Eric about the guys he has played with over the decades, which is absolutely everyone in jazz. He would organize the rhythm section and the tours for Dexter, Frank Morgan, Freddie Hubbard, etc. Talk about stories! He's a real swinger in the traditional sense—no funny business—real jazz.

Lew: I've been to Europe, I've recorded with the fabulous Furio Di Castri on bass in Italy. You don't have to tell me this, but a lot of American cats will say they don't have world-class players in Europe. What's your answer to this?
Dave: It's apples and oranges. It's different, but the same in the final analysis, as far as quality of music goes. Here we go again with that expression that explains so much—different but the same. Are they rooted in tradition as much as American musicians? Obviously not. New Orleans is a long way from Rome, geographically.

Lew: And there are not as many African American musicians there.
Dave: Yes, the musicians are mostly white. So instead of the blues as a familial root, they have the world music influence, from all the countries they controlled for years in the imperialist days. And we know they certainly have the classical tradition from Monteverdi to Ligeti, etc. I mean, let's put it this way: Ludwig B. is on your doorstep there! You had Bach with all that church stuff. The list goes on. This is where that music originated from—ground zero for the classical tradition. In America we have R&B, pop, jazz, and country—people's music, which is entirely different from what they have. Many European musicians were and are enamored by pure jazz, but not necessarily to play in that style.

This is not to say that there aren't some great swinging, killing, straight-ahead jazz guys there. Rhythm sections used to be a problem, but now everything is equalized throughout Europe, and to some degree the rest of the world, wherever jazz is played. With the International Association of Schools of Jazz, I am in touch with twenty to twenty-five countries yearly in this regard at our meetings. It used to be more true that the European musicians played from their immediate context, which means there were differences between, let's say, the Italian and the Dutch cats or between the French and the Norwegians, and so on. There was even a difference between the Norwegian and the Swedish musicians, although they are all Scandinavians. They all brought in their influences and traditions, so to say that it was or is less legitimate is wrong. It's good music. Improvisation is the core of it and jazz is the root, period. Now with the Internet and YouTube, differences are becoming, for better or worse, smoothed out, with everyone having equal access to the same information. In other words, regional differences, though still heard, are less apparent than just a decade or two ago. Nothing you can do about that.

Lew: Good points. Now you've also got duos with piano players. There's Beirach, and more recently Phil Markowitz and Marc Copland. You even did a record with a young guy, Bobby Avey, that's classically oriented. Why duos with piano? Where does the idea even come from?
Dave: It starts with me and Richie with the record called *Forgotten Fantasies* in 1975, which in that day was not so common to have a whole program with just horn and piano. It's ongoing with Richie but has expanded to Copland and Phil in the last decade or two. Like all the groups we are discussing, each brings out another aspect of my personality. The central point is that the piano duo is in some ways the most challenging. You have to account for every note; you have to be in tune; every nuance is heard from the beginning to the end of the note. If you make a trill, if you do a vibrato, if it's a slow vibrato or a fast vibrato—everything counts.

That is not true when you have drums around because a lot of nuances get covered up. With the piano, you have to be exact. I don't want to say perfect, but really correct. The expertise level is raised quite a bit when you play with piano, especially these piano players we are mentioning who go beyond bebop and use the piano like a painter uses colors, sound and touch being major components, as well as the entire range of harmony. You've got to blend in. I have to not be too loud, get the right note, get the right color. It is a supreme challenge to play duo, basically because there are no drums. You don't hire a drummer and then tell him to play soft all the time. That would be counterproductive for what a drummer naturally does, which is *hit* skins with a stick! If you want the drummer to play polite, why have the drummer there? You want him to hit hard, at least some of the time.

Richie and I have a record coming out in the next few months titled *Unspoken*, which is absolutely gorgeous. With Phil it has been on occasion, and with Copland a bit more because he likes to get work and tour. I enjoy each one of them. I am privileged. It is incredible to be playing with three such distinctively different piano players. Beirach's harmony, Markowitz's harmony, and Copland's harmony are very different, even though it's a combination of twentieth-century and bebop since they all know the jazz tradition very well, what came before. In a way, like anything, it has to do in the final result with temperament. Richie is a dramatist, a storyteller. He's like Rachmaninoff. You are going to get the concerto of the day—grand, sweeping, orchestral. Copland is coming out of Herbie and Bill Evans, with very subtle voicings, a softer touch, light, very sympathetic, and an incredible ear that can shift in a minute, with a wide variety of voicings. But high energy is not a large part of his M.O., though he can get there if he wishes to. Marc is like a big, beautiful curtain—a sunrise or sunset. Phil is in between the two. As I've told you, he's one of the best musicians I have ever known. He can do everything and can go anywhere. Emotionally he is more in the middle, very controlled, calm, and efficient. The bottom line is that I, as a horn player who is to some degree completely subservient and controlled by this massive eighty-eight-key piece of wood weighing a ton or two, am very fortunate to be in such august company. They bring out different aspects of my playing for sure.

For each duo there is original music, but we all enjoy playing standards in our convoluted way. I may have some tunes that cross between the pianists. Marc has some twentieth-century stuff and in some ways like Swallow, little and economic conundrums to decipher. Phil is a remarkable composer on a grand scale, with sections and a lot of rhythmic angles to consider. Richie has a great combination of harmony and melody, very meticulous. They are all very harmonic players, which is what I love.

Lew: Great. I think we've covered all your different musical projects. On the personal front, what have you been up to? Could you talk about this mission trip you did to El Salvador and the visit to Mauritania?
Dave: This missionary thing was a trip to El Salvador in 2004 with the main Catholic Church in Stroudsburg. I have attended St. Luke's with Caris and Lydia for holidays since we lived there. In fact, Lydia went to Catholic school until she was in eighth grade, not necessarily because of the religious thing, but because it was a better primary school, we thought. When she got older, we put her in the public high school because there are more opportunities for extras, like musicals and other extracurricular activities.

Lew: Was Lydia bat-mitzvahed?
Dave: No. We did the Catholic route for her, though we observed Jewish holidays, even the Friday night Shabbat on occasion, with the candles and some prayers. We have discussed my view on religion, but suffice to say it doesn't much matter to me. The Force is the Force, no matter what you call it. She was baptized Roman Catholic and had Communion and Confirmation, all that stuff, but she also received a Hebrew name when she was born. What is relevant here is that the church in our town does a good job. I am on a first-name basis with the two priests in charge, who are extremely nice guys and very well educated. We actually had one of them over for dinner. Caris, Lydia, and I are on the rotation for doing the

soup kitchen on Saturday afternoons; I play for the free Thanksgiving dinner offered to the community—no big deal, just trying to help out.

Anyway, as churches do, they were involved in missionary work in El Salvador. Each year a group would go there to see what the people were doing with the donations that were made and how they were progressing. I joined them for a week, and as you can imagine, it was very enlightening. It is third world, dirt poor, and like any other rookie in these things, I was both depressed about that, of course, but also inspired by the spirit and kindness of the people. I had to get malaria shots, other immunizations—the whole third world scene in all its glory. It was ten to fifteen people—a couple of students, but mostly adults. The church sponsored projects there. It wasn't proselytizing or anything like that—these people are Catholic anyway. It was charity work, giving money to put a reliable roof on instead of tin, or whatever, to try and better the people's lives, one person at a time. The church pays for these projects to go on, which in some loose way they monitor. The visiting group kind of checks out the scene, but in the end you just hope that good work is happening. The guy in charge, Henry, was a great cat, doing the right thing. He was responsible for activities in Honduras also, where we went for a visit during that week. We stayed at a church-run home with barbed wire and concrete walls—one shower, fried food—like that. They had prayers every day, but also a lot of singing. But of course on the street there were guys with guns everywhere, even at the local joint we went to for breakfast everyday. These places are dangerous, there's no question.

This was quite a trip for me. I was certainly the oldest person there and getting around was tough because it's all mud and dirt roads. But I had the little wooden flute that I always take, and of course I played. There were kids in these villages we would visit, and I would play and hang with them. No Dave Liebman, jazz saxophonist—just some cat with a toy flute. The trip was about a week long and it's all on my website under Special Projects. You can see the pictures and a day-to-day log.

Lew: What about the Sahara visit, which is also on your site?
Dave: For my sixtieth birthday, I decided to follow through on my early exploration of the afterlife stuff—specifically, this feeling that I had had in my life of having been somewhere in past lives in a desert situation. When I say desert, it's only by the process of elimination because the whole picture that was in my head took place in an atmosphere of brilliant, white hot sun with sand all over, so I guessed it was a desert situation I was envisioning. Probably the Middle East because of the Jewish

connection, where we most likely began this journey with Abraham or whomever. Who knows? But for sure it wasn't Las Vegas! I'm talking white sand and dunes as the backdrop to this scene in my head.

I have a very good friend in France, saxophonist Jean-Jacques Quesada, who is like a brother to me. When I spoke about this desert thing he suggested the Sahara, especially the part that is French-oriented, deciding on Mauritania. After talking for a few years about it, we went to a travel agent in Paris and put it together. He was also friendly with the saxophonist Rick Margitza, who by that time was living in Paris. We invited him to come also. It's in the western Sahara just above Senegal. It's a big country land-wise but only three million people. I just felt it was time for me to spend some bread on myself fulfilling a dream I had, regardless of the harshness of the environment, or weather, or living conditions. I wanted to go out there and see what the sand is like, what that heat feels like, all for one time in my life.

We spent a week out there with these two guides driving around endlessly in the middle of nowhere, stopping every few hours to have mint tea and eating whatever they brought with them, some salad, bread, and a piece of chicken or lamb—definitely not gourmet. Somehow in the middle of the desert these guys would boil up water for tea, which you had to drink. Talk about sweet—there was enough sugar in one of those cups for an army!

Lew: So it was the three of you and two guides?
Dave: Two guides, all of us living in the bush, sleeping in the desert. We had a tent eventually, but the first night we didn't. It was freezing. It had been like ninety degrees Fahrenheit and then it went down to forty, and we couldn't sleep. We were on the ground in a sleeping bag, freezing the whole night, the three of us lined up. The guide bros were cool—they were used to it. I said, "I think we've got to be in a tent from now on." Jean-Jacques was speaking French, so we got it together the next day. It was still freezing at night, but at least you didn't have the wind blowing, which was all the time.

We also went inland to one of the oldest "libraries" that had the Koran—really just a shack. But mainly they just drove in the sand. We had the requisite van breakdown and had to wait under a tree for five hours while they somehow got it together—no phone, no nothing, but these guys know what they are doing out there. All you would see were a few Bedouins walking around with sheep and goats everywhere. The main city, Nouakchott, is a complete zoo. Chaotic. It's just what you'd think an African city is like. Impossible—cars everywhere, people on the street "bathing" themselves with bottled water. Way out! I didn't take a shower for a week. I came home with sand on me for the next four months. It's still in my main bag! The sand is everywhere—it's the Sahara Desert.

But, I have to tell you, Lewis, I really felt that this was a place I had been before! I felt great. I loved it! I loved the heat, I loved the blinding sun. I dug it. I felt comfortable. I really did. I felt like in another life, I could definitely be there. And of course, we heard music. We didn't play, but we found a village by accident with some music at night. Men and women, separate dancing, incredible moves. The people were completely cordial, with no bad vibes at all. The Arab way is to treat strangers with kindness. "*Insallah*"—God willing—that's their greeting and goodbye. The men are very tall and thin, dressed in blue robes, while the women are all heavy with colorful garb. Men danced with each other and looked like giant birds strutting around. Guys played on pots and pans, on the floor, whatever, with some small guitar or ukulele-type thing going on constantly, slightly out of tune. I know this sounds a bit off, but I could see myself there in another life, playing with the cats. If I had been born there, it would have been no problem. It really felt right. Not that I don't feel right in the here and now, but it felt even "righter." I just felt comfortable. I am probably romanticizing, but it felt free, truly free. I just felt like that life would have been fine if I had either been there in a past life or will be there in a future incarnation. Maybe I will return to that place the next time around?

Lew: What other music was there?
Dave: Singing, big time. We found out who the big deal was in that part of the world. Her name was Dimi Mint Abba, who passed on at age fifty-two in June 2011. She was like the Aretha Franklin of the western Sahara region. We didn't find her physically, but we heard her everywhere. The guides had her on the cassettes in the car and I had researched her before I went to Mauritania. You can find her on YouTube. We somehow arranged a series of concerts in Paris with her group and added Jack DeJohnette along with Rick and Jean-Jacques. Incredibly, I couldn't do it because I was featured with the Ensemble Intercontemporain the same week. The ensemble, which is considered the premier new music group, founded by Pierre Boulez, had invited me to be a soloist, the first time they ever had a jazz guy. That was great, but it conflicted with this Dimi/Jack concert.

But I did hang with them in Paris for one afternoon and played in the hotel room with Abba and the band. Her son and her daughter generally performed with her, as is the way in these cultures. She had already buried two husbands. She chain-smoked Camels and was really a nice down-to-earth lady with a definite blues feeling in her voice. Very friendly, smiling all the time, just sitting in the middle of a hotel room in the heart of Paris, receiving guests, singing, smoking, and eating for *eight* hours on this one afternoon. We had a soprano with us, and Rick, Jean-Jacques, and I took turns playing. Also, I had the little wooden flute with me. Once you're in their circle, you don't leave. This is village life. You have to eat with them. Life is present time. There are no appointments! It was an afternoon for the ages.

The whole trip to the desert was incredible. I'm really glad I went and I hope I can go back. The places we went to could hardly be called cities—it was completely desert—just driving around. You don't know where you are because everything looks the same. These guys follow the wind and the sun. We had destinations, but we were basically just driving. There were mountains also, and the last night we barbecued some fish on the ocean since Mauritania is on the Atlantic.

Lew: That's wild. What an amazing experience. It was as good as you hoped it would be?
Dave: Absolutely. Now the government just changed and it's crazy, so it's not safe. In these places, things can change on a dime. The truth is Mauritania was fairly stable, and by the way, the only country in that part of the world that had official relations with Israel. But I think the new guy came in and stopped that by now.

Lew: It's good you went when you did. Now, you have won some very distinguished awards over the course of your career, but recently some very big-deal awards like the French Order of Arts and Letters and the National Endowment for the Arts Jazz Masters.
Dave: The first award I got for this type of thing was the Sibelius Academy Honorary Doctorate in Helsinki in 1997, which up to that time they had never given to a jazz guy. I think they recognized that the formation of the IASJ was important, along with my playing, I assume. This most recent French Order and the NEA Masters—well, they were just big surprises for sure.

I have definitely put my time into France, meaning I have played with everyone there and taught a lot. It has been my best place for sure, as far as work and interest goes. It has a lot to do with that French label that I was associated with in the nineties, Owl Records, and the producer, Jean-Jacques Pussiau, who really did a lot for me. I guess they felt I had contributed something to French culture. I'm very comfortable there, that's true. As far as the audience, as far as my stature, the amount of work I do, France is number one. Italy next, but France is the most. One thing about the French, whatever you want to say negatively about their attitude, they *do* really respect artistry, and once they accept you as an *artiste*, you are good forever there. They are faddish like everyone, but they also have a loyalty thing going on. I read this once in a Josephine Baker bio. Remember, she was an African American dancer from Harlem who became quite famous in France. I totally agree with her observation in this regard. Once they like you, it's for life. They respect you, and they don't judge. You're an artist and you can do what you want. The drummer I have played with a lot, one of the most famous in Europe, Daniel Humair, was very supportive of my getting the award. Other Americans have received it also in the past. Roy Haynes just got one.

Lew: What about the NEA award in January 2011?
Dave: The big thing is that I'm thrilled and privileged to be in the same company as the past recipients, who are my idols, and in the case of Miles and Elvin, my bosses. The past recipients are true masters. I can't believe that I'm up there with them. I'm younger than most of them by five to ten years. The luncheon had forty of these guys in one room, and it was amazing. The presence of such humanity, brotherhood, feeling, and talent in one room on a given afternoon in January was something else.

I'm glad to be part of an honored circle. I feel that I'm the first representative of the seventies generation, meaning maybe that time wasn't as much a wasteland as it has been reputed to be because of the so-called fusion era. We are carrying the flame for better or worse into the future, and honoring me recognizes that fact. One contemporary remarked that I represented those who have passed on early or will never be noticed by the establishment. In a way, I can see what he meant.

Lew: That's great. They were also saying, "You don't have to be eighty to have made a contribution." I mean, you've been out there a long time now.
Dave: I'm very gratified.

Lew: It's great to see you getting such recognition. Now, let's finish up with some closing thoughts from you.
Dave: Two things I want to say that are important, if students read any of this book. They have to do with maintaining a balance between your professional and personal life, which is not a walk in the park. Life is an on-

going cycle of ups and downs. I certainly have found some sense of equanimity in the last twenty-plus years, mostly due to Caris, having a great daughter, an established home, and love. You have to tend the plant and water the flowers. It's a balancing act because we are by nature obsessive—musicians and artists in general.

Our lifestyle is obviously not a routine, our financial situation is precarious, and we have to deal with a lot of unpredictable events. In some ways, we have to be in twenty places at the same time. It is a gigantic balancing act. So far, I'm okay and my health is fine in general, but what I would say to anybody who is pursuing this life is you must be ever vigilant. There is no time off. You have to be 100 percent on, 24/7 as they say. That's the way it is to be an artist, and to be in the world to boot. If you want to live in a garret alone, with crackers and cheese, you can do that, but it's probably going to affect your music eventually, and not in a positive way. There's a time to be in the garret, and there's a period when you must live with some sense of normalcy so that you can relate to the real world, which is after all your audience.

Lew: When you say there's a time to be in the garret, that's when you're young and wood-shedding?
Dave: Yes, to be suffering, practicing, dealing with the art and yourself. It might mean living on chips and coffee. You're struggling and you should be. It's the nature of maturing. You are finding out who you are, facing the basic questions, not hiding in an office or somewhere to avoid these matters, which are in the end about human existence—why we are here and what to do in our allotted time.

Lew: And the other closing thought?
Dave: The other thing I wanted to end with is that we are responsible—you, me, the people of my generation—for keeping this music alive. I don't mean just funding it, teaching it, and obvious practical things like that. I mean that the spirit of this music; its tradition; the people who came through it and what they created; the blood, sweat, and tears literally that were put into this—we are now left with the flame that's been handed down to us, and we have to be true to the cause. We are missionaries from the other side, and we have continuous work ahead of us.

This Miles story is a good way to end: When I was in his house one day during his hiatus in the late seventies, he said, "Come over here, I want to show you something." He went behind the couch and there was a blow-up picture as big as the couch. It was a photo from 1970, I believe. Miles was very close to Louis Armstrong's shoulder, looking at Pops with a big smile on his face. He took the picture out to show me—very uncharacteristic of Miles. He said something to this effect—I don't remember exactly: "Look at that. From him, to me, to you." That's all. I took this statement as meaning the line begins with Louis, through Miles, to guys like me.

And that lineage is important. We have to uphold it any way we can—teaching, playing, talking, whatever. It's something we really have to respect and keep together, which I am proud to be part of. I'm bound to the end, and that's because it's given me a life. If there are redeeming qualities that I have brought to this world, besides my parents and loved ones, it is the music that enabled me to be who I am. Without music, I wouldn't know very much about beauty and truth, two of the heaviest qualities one seeks. I thank the music and have a responsibility to it, which is what I have to do with my time left.

Lew: The music gives to you and you give to the music.

Dave: You get a lot from this music. I can't talk expertly about other music or other art forms, but I would expect a writer or painter would say the same thing. All I know is that this music is a living, breathing organism. You go out with your horn and you play. It's not something you hang on a wall or hold in your hand. You are involved in it on a physical level. That organic, present-time nature of jazz makes it really clear that *you are that,* nothing more, nothing less, every time you pick up the horn.

That's something really special about jazz. It's in the here and now, big time. Because it is group music, you are in conversation with other people—at times in deep conversation. I love that contact with other human beings. I don't want to have that conversation necessarily on a bus with just anyone—I'm not looking to touch everyone. But when I get on the bandstand to talk, I'm down. This is the deepest talk I can have with someone in present time, and I have great respect for that aspect. We pay dues for this knowledge and insight, but, in my mind, that is what the whole voyage of life is about.

Appendix I

Selected Discography by Dave Liebman

Since recordings are the way jazz musicians document their work, they provide a running commentary on an artist's interests and evolution. What follows are short summaries of my choices of fifty notable recordings from my catalogue (a few items include more than one CD), beginning in the early 1970s. Notwithstanding any considerations vis-á-vis record company directives, a particular producer, or what have you, an artist's choices as to what to record reflects his or her goals. The bottom line for recording is that, whatever past and future listening formats may be, one's music can be heard anywhere, anytime. I have recorded for dozens of labels, choosing flexibility and freedom of choice over stability. With several hundred recordings to choose from, my criteria for this list are that they be musically notable and/or worth mentioning from the standpoint of my career. The order is chronological and there is a mixture of live and studio recordings, which measure in different ways what one's art is all about. A complete discography is on my website, davidliebman.com.

1. MY GOAL'S BEYOND/JOHN MCLAUGHLIN. 1970: This was my first notable recording along with Elvin Jones's *Genesis* a few weeks later. With an illustrious cast of musicians, the music was Indian flavored and was important toward ushering in the whole world music phenomenon, as well as introducing McLaughlin's mastery.

2. LIVE AT THE LIGHTHOUSE/ELVIN JONES. 1972: This live recording captures the essence of the two-saxophone/bass-drum combination that I was part of with Elvin and has become a minor classic, especially for saxophonists, as a study of the way Steve Grossman and I interpreted and continued the Coltrane tradition.

3. ON THE CORNER/MILES DAVIS. 1972: Being on this record raised my visibility toward having a solo career. Musically, it was a forerunner of many ideas heard in pop music since then. This was yet another recording that portrayed Miles as a perpetual innovator.

4. LOOKOUT FARM. 1973: My first major recording as a leader, this became the name of my first group on the then-young ECM label, representing what my first musical interests were and to a certain extent still are—a mixture of rock, Coltrane influence, chromatic harmony, and world music.

5. DRUM ODE. 1974: Definitely one of my best-known recordings; featuring a notable cast of drummers/percussionists, this was my ode to the legacy of the drums and their importance to me.

6. FORGOTTEN FANTASY. 1975: With my long-time partner, pianist Richie Beirach, this was our first duo outing, recorded on A&M records, setting the style we would pursue for the next decades.

7. PENDULUM. 1978: Live from the fabled Village Vanguard in New York City, this recording features Richie Beirach, Al Foster, and Randy Brecker playing mostly standards in the post-modern style that members of our generation had developed up to that time. Mosaic has released a three-CD version with lots of extra material.

8. DEDICATIONS. 1979: With bassist Eddie Gomez and Richie once again, this music with string quartet represented my most extensive writing to date.

9. IF THEY ONLY KNEW. 1980: My second band formation featured John Scofield as a sideman, mixing idioms in differing stylistic formats.

10. MEMORIES, DREAMS AND REFLECTIONS. 1981: My first solo recording, playing all the instruments, with compositions of a very personal nature, inspired by Carl Jung's book of that name.

11. QUEST. 1981: The first record by this group featured me exclusively on soprano sax, with drummer Al Foster, bassist George Mraz, and Richie, beginning a ten-year run with Quest.

12. EARTH JONES. 1982: Nearly ten years after I was in his band, I felt more confident to play with Master Elvin Jones under my direction, featuring the late Kenny Kirkland on piano.

13. THE LONELINESS OF A LONG DISTANCE RUNNER. 1985: This recording is the most personal solo statement of all my work. Using only overdubbed soprano saxophone and a lot of compositional devices, portraying the metaphor of the artist as a long-distance runner, it was dedicated to the soprano king, Steve Lacy. This was at the height of the period when I was playing soprano sax exclusively. It also marks the beginning of my ongoing relationship with German engineer Walter Quintus and producer Kurt Renker.

14. THE DUO LIVE. 1985: More duo with Richie Beirach, representing both our jazz and twentieth-century musical interests, also transcribed meticulously in a book format by Bill Dobbins.

15. QUEST II. 1986: The band had solidified in personnel a few years before this date, with Ron McClure on bass and Billy Hart on drums. This recording captured the band in its first stage of development.

16. LIVE UNDER THE SKY. 1987: For a live tribute to John Coltrane in Japan, I had the opportunity to play opposite Wayne Shorter with a stellar rhythm section of Eddie Gomez, Jack DeJohnette, and Richie performing Coltrane classics. This was a momentous event for me and is captured on DVD as well.

17. HOMAGE TO JOHN COLTRANE. 1987: I finally felt that I could interpret Trane's music in my own fashion, using two different rhythm sections, acoustic and electric. This record helped especially to raise my stature in France, where it won an award, and it was the beginning of my fruitful relationship with producer Jean-Jacques Pussiau.

18. MIDPOINT. 1987: This live recording from Copenhagen's famed Montmartre showcased the further evolution of Quest.

19. TRIO + ONE. 1988: With Jack DeJohnette and Dave Holland, along with my wife, Caris Visentin, on oboe, this music was a look back at the free jazz that I had grown up with several decades earlier.

20. NATURAL SELECTION. 1988: Made for a short-lived American label, once again Quest's evolution is traced, here with some more developed writing and arranging by band members.

21. CHANT. 1989: The last duo recording with Richie Beirach from this period. By this time our language was telepathic, and harmonically speaking, the influence of twentieth-century modern classical music had solidified.

22. WEST SIDE STORY. 1990: In duo with Gil Goldstein, I took this most American of scores and rearranged it for the two of us. Gil was incredible on the synths and keyboards that were available at that time.

23. THE TREE. 1990: A completely improvised solo soprano recording depicting the evolution and metaphor of a tree and artistic growth. The music had no themes, just specific interval sets and textures.

24. OF ONE MIND. 1990: The last Quest recording from that era, a completely improvised repertoire based on formats we had been exploring for years, with no written music as such.

25. CLASSIQUE. 1991: With three quartets—woodwind, sax, and string—and featuring myself playing over the composed parts, this was by far the most extensive composing I did for a recording up to that time.

26. TURN IT AROUND. 1992: The first recording of the new Dave Liebman Group, this repertoire reflected more developed compositions than previously with Quest, along with the use of electric instruments and percussion, which would be the core of the group's sound for the next few years.

27. THE SEASONS. 1992: A completely free recording portraying the seasons and daily cycles of sunrise, sunset, etc., this featured masters Billy Hart on drums and Cecil McBee on bass.

28. SONGS FOR MY DAUGHTER. 1994: Once again the DL Group in all configurations, playing my original compositions and one from my

wife, Caris, commemorating the birth in 1991 of our daughter, Lydia, and her first years. You can even hear Lydia singing "You Are My Sunshine."

29. MILES AWAY. 1994: Celebrating all the eras of Miles, using my group and rearrangements of songs recorded and written by Miles, this was a deeply felt tribute record.

30. FAR NORTH. 1994: Since I had already enjoyed a ten-year relationship with masters of the so-called "Scandic" sound—Lars Daniellson on bass, Bobo Stenson on piano, and Jon Christensen on drums—this music captures my immersion in another way of improvising that these musicians represented at the highest level.

31. RETURN OF THE TENOR. 1996: This recording of standards with the DL Group was my first featured tenor performance in fifteen years, marking a return to the big horn.

32. WATER: GIVER OF LIFE. 1997: With Pat Metheny, Cecil McBee, and Billy Hart, this programmatic music celebrates the element of water in its various manifestations, featuring Metheny on a variety of guitars.

33. A WALK IN THE CLOUDS. 1997: An ode to the music of Puccini, this recording featured a variety of instrumental settings and re-arrangements of classic operatic material.

34. COLORS. 1998: Another solo outing, completely improvised on tenor, exclusively depicting six of the primary colors, two takes each.

35. THANK YOU, JOHN. 1998: This is a "various artists" collection from the label I was with at the time (Arkadia). I am only on a few tracks, but it is included here for my performance of "My Favorite Things," which garnered a Grammy nomination for Best Solo.

36. MONK'S MOOD. 1999: With Eddie Gomez and Adam Nussbaum, I arranged Monk classics sans piano.

37. MILES DAVIS/GIL EVANS COLLABORATIONS: SKETCHES OF SPAIN (2001); MILES AHEAD (2005); PORGY AND BESS (2008): I was able to record these legendary pieces at the Manhattan School of Music, conducted by Justin DiCioccio, on three CDs. Substi-

tuting the soprano sax for the trumpet, I attempted to walk the thin line between personal interpretation and respecting the heavy karma that the classic original recordings represent.

38. BEYOND THE LINE. 2001: The first Dave Liebman Big Band recording garnered a Grammy nomination for the performance of Jim McNeely's arrangement of "Sing, Sing, Sing," written for me.

39. BOOKENDS. 2002: A duo setting with pianist Marc Copland of originals and standards marked the beginning of an ongoing musical relationship.

40. CONVERSATION. 2003: With the DL Group's original members Vic Juris on guitar and Tony Marino on bass and a new addition, drummer Marko Marcinko, the sound of the group began to go in a freer musical and compositional direction than previously.

41. GATHERING OF SPIRITS (2004); SERAPHIC LIGHT (2007)/ SAXOPHONE SUMMIT: *Gathering,* with Mike Brecker and Joe Lovano, captures the power of this all-star band doing originals and Trane compositions. For *Seraphic*, Ravi Coltrane replaced Mike, while we retained the rhythm section of Phil Markowitz (piano), Cecil McBee (bass), and Billy Hart (drums), following a similar direction.

42. REDEMPTION. 2005: This live recording from Europe showcases a reunited Quest with Beirach, McClure, and Hart playing originals and standards in the classic style of the band.

43. THE DISTANCE RUNNER. 2005: A live solo set at the Willisau Festival in which I play drums and piano as well as the saxes (including alto), this was truly a special event for me.

44. THREE FOR ALL. 2005: With old friends Adam Nussbaum (drums) and Steve Swallow (bass), this trio plays a real "song" repertoire featuring many of Steve's compositions.

45. BACK ON THE CORNER. 2006: Adding to the DL Group guitarist Mike Stern and bassist Anthony Jackson, I commemorated the spirit of Miles's *On The Corner* with originals, as well as some selections from that period.

46. RENEWAL. 2007: Another setting that I am part of is named "Different But The Same" with Ellery Eskelin on tenor, Jim Black on drums and Tony Marino on bass. This was the group's second recording of music, and it ranges from straight-ahead to free bop to all-out free jazz.

47. RE-DIAL: QUEST LIVE IN HAMBURG. 2007: The second recording of the reunited Quest, this live date really captures the mature power of the group as well as the very lyrical side.

48. RELEVANCE, WITH EVAN PARKER. 2008: Accompanied by drummer Tony Bianco, this live meeting with one of the free jazz icons is a complete burn. This was recorded for a BBC radio broadcast from London.

49. QUEST FOR FREEDOM. 2009: With the high level arrangements of several of my original "chromatic" tunes by master arranger Jim McNeely, along with Richie Beirach and the German HR radio big band from Frankfurt, this is a high-class recording from top to bottom.

50. TURNAROUND/ THE MUSIC OF ORNETTE COLEMAN. 2009: Employing my steady group, I rearranged classic Ornette tunes, creating my own harmony in some cases and using a variety of instrumental combinations. This CD was selected as Record of the Year by the German Jazz Critics.

Appendix II

Selected Educational Materials

The following works were authored by Dave Liebman.

Aebersold Publications:

How to Approach Standards Chromatically: Techniques of Superimposition (with CD).

Maximize Your Practice (DVD). A concise summary of what good practicing involves.

Scale Syllabus Volume 26 (with CD). A complete guide to improvising on all the required scales.

Standards and Originals Play Along, with the David Liebman Group, Volume 81 (with CD). A collection of challenging tunes for students to play along with.

Ten Chromatic Compositions (with CD). Lead sheets, played on the CD by Phil Markowitz and David Liebman.

Advance Music Publications:

A Chromatic Approach to Jazz Melody & Harmony (with CD).

David Liebman Anthology (original compositions).

From Student to Jazz Artist: Talks with David Liebman (MP3). Relevant for students leaving school and embarking on a career as a jazz musician.

Self-Portrait of a Jazz Artist. A book about the process of becoming a jazz artist.

Caris Music Services Publications:

The Complete Guide to Saxophone Sound Production (DVD).

Improviser's Guide to Transcription (DVD).

Understanding Jazz Rhythm: The Concept of Swing (DVD).

Miscellaneous Publishers:
Developing a Personal Saxophone Sound (64-page book). Dorn Publications (available in English, German, Japanese, Czech, Chinese, French).

Master Class with Dave Liebman (DVD). Roberto's Winds.

Appendix III

Two Compositions by Dave Liebman

"What It Is"
This tune was intended to be a bit easier than my other material for my group with John Scofield in the late '70s. It really is "what it is" and nothing more—kind of a funk tune, with some blues and harmony.

(See next page.)

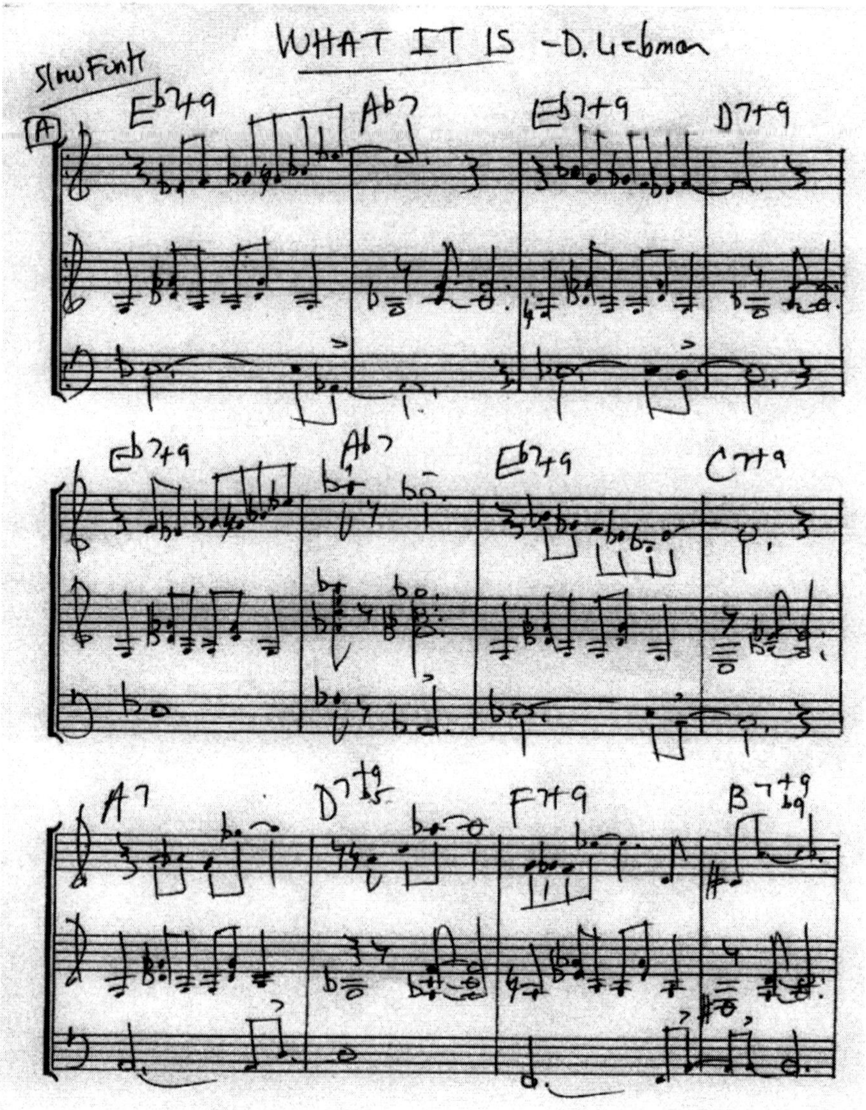
WHAT IT IS -D. Liebman
Slow Funk
A
Eb7+9
Ab7
Eb7+9
D7+9
Eb7+9
Ab7
Eb7+9
C7+9
A7
F7+9

WHAT IT IS - 2
(Fine)
(to B)
B
© Liebstone Music
(all rights reserved)
D.C. al 2nd ending

The tune "WTC" was written to memorialize what happened at the World Trade Center in New York City on September 11, 2001. The work is a twelve-tone, quite dissonant piece, with several layers superimposed.

Index

3M Quartet, 211, 214
A Chromatic Approach to Jazz Harmony and Melody, 220, 270
A&M Records, 202, 204, 205, 208, 209, 210, 340
AACM, 113, 114
Abercrombie, John, 106, 212, 213, 310
Adderley, Cannonball, xvii, 72, 297
Aebersold, Jamey, 183, 225, 229
Ali, Rashied, 45, 73, 111, 118
Alias, Don, 160, 171, 192, 203, 216
Allard, Joe, xvii, 51, 55, 56, 58, 61, 72, 112, 120, 126, 130, 140, 142
Altschul, Barry, 126, 193, 203
American Bandstand, 30
Arco, Tony, 327
Arkadia, 285, 343
Armstrong, Louis, 231, 295
Baker, Chet, 123, 147, 238, 275, 295
Baker, David, 112, 225, 226, 228, 229
Balakrishna, Khalil, 164
Barkan, Todd, 176
Barron, Kenny, 229
Barsimento, Mike, 211
Basie, Count, 40, 52
Beatles, the, 88, 94, 107, 154
Bechet, Sidney, 106, 327

Beets, Marius, 327
Beirach, Richie, ix, xiii, xvii, xxi, 110, 112, 115, 121, 131, 191, 236, 293, 329, 340, 341, 342, 345
Benedetinni, Paolo, 327
Benson, George, 204, 210
Berg, Bob, 110, 114, 185
Berg, Chuck, 206
Berklee, xii, xv, 120, 192, 225, 231, 249, 256, 260
Berlin, Jeff, 209
Berne, Tim, 236
Bianco, Tony, 345
Birdland, 3440, 41, 42, 43, 44, 46, 137, 144, 155, 311, 316, 318, 319, 320
Black, Jim, 345
Blakey, Art, 40, 84, 181, 306
Bley, Paul, 135, 136
Blood, Sweat & Tears, 105, 154, 241
Blue Note Records, xii, 142
Blue Note, 72
Booker, Walter, 70
Boustedt, Christer, 66
Brackeen, JoAnne, 134
Bradley's, 236, 237
Braxton, Anthony, 114, 126
Brechtlein, Tom, 128
Brecker, Michael, 56, 99, 106, 118, 236, 244, 270, 282, 317, 320, 344
Brecker, Randy, xv, 64, 70, 77, 78, 83, 110, 112, 118, 217, 340
Bromley, Buster, 24
Brookmeyer, Bob, 40
Brown, Cameron, 65, 66, 67, 77, 115
Brown, Gerry, 216
Brown, James, 38, 105
Brubeck, Dave, 86, 197, 204
Budapest, 1
Burton, Gary, 38, 64
Butler, George, 142
Cables, George, 63, 77, 134
Calderazzo, Joey, 317
Campbell, Gary, 314
Carlsson, Jan, 66
Carnegie Hall, 19, 56, 58, 61, 304
Carter, Benny, 295
Carter, Ron, 72, 146, 217, 221, 229
Catskills, 6, 25, 26, 27, 28, 29, 30, 31, 33, 35, 39, 47, 105, 106, 137
Celea, Jean Paul, 327
Chamberland, Lic, 138, 139, 209
Cherigo, Mike, 316
Cherry, Don, 304
Chicago, 105, 142, 154
Christensen, Jon, 66, 279, 327, 343
Clark, Mike, 211
Cobb, Jimmy, 138, 267
Cobham, Billy, 106, 213
Coker, Jerry, 225, 226
Coleman, George, 140, 143, 237
Coleman, Ornette, 204, 309

Coleman, Steve, 236, 270, 278
Collier, Graham, 266
Coltrane, John, 21, 38, 39, 40, 41, 42, 43, 44, 45, 46, 49, 50, 53, 54, 55, 56, 59, 61, 64, 66, 68, 69, 72, 73, 74, 77, 78, 80, 86, 88, 101, 106, 107, 110, 111, 113, 118, 119, 120, 121, 122, 123, 134, 141, 144, 145, 146, 147, 151, 153, 154, 156, 157, 196, 200, 208, 209, 219, 220, 226, 231, 240, 242, 243, 244, 247, 248, 294, 296, 312, 313, 314, 317, 318, 320
Coltrane, Ravi, xvi, 314, 319, 344
Columbia Records, 106, 142
Conversations on the Improviser's Art, 293
Copland, Marc, 329, 344
Corea, Chick, xii, xvii, xix, 102, 103, 108, 125, 126, 131, 212, 213, 278, 288
Coryell, Larry, 196
Cosby, Bill, 189
Cosey, Pete, 168, 169, 171, 173
Cream, 88
Dallas, Sonny, 295
Daniellson, Palle, 156
Daniels, Eddie, 27
Danielsson, Lars, 279, 327
Dave Liebman Big Band, 324, 326, 344
Dave Liebman Group, xvii, xxii, 212, 218, 280, 281, 287, 342
Dave Liebman Quintet, 215
David Liebman Anthology, 324
Davis, Miles, xii, xvii, xxi, 19, 45, 46, 58, 70, 77, 84, 102, 103, 105, 110, 111, 115, 120, 121, 123, 126, 128, 133, 134, 141, 146, 148, 150, 153, 154, 159, 160, 161, 162, 163, 164, 165, 166, 167, 168, 169, 170, 171, 172, 173, 174, 175, 176, 177, 178, 179, 180, 181, 182, 183, 184, 185, 186, 187, 188, 189, 190, 191, 192, 193, 196, 197, 204, 206, 207, 208, 210, 213, 214, 215, 217, 218, 219, 220, 221, 226, 240, 241, 242, 244, 245, 259, 273, 309, 311, 312, 313, 335, 336, 337, 340, 343
DeJohnette, Jack, 71, 72, 110, 136, 148, 160, 192, 286, 301, 317, 333, 341, 342
Desmond, Paul, 295
Developing a Personal Saxophone Sound, 58, 234, 270
DiCioccio, Justin, 232, 270, 326, 343
Dixon, Bill, 114
Dolphy, Eric, 41, 42, 120, 244, 297
Donner, Otto, 66
Dorian, Pat, 269
Downbeat, 41, 205, 206, 228, 241
Earth Wind and Fire, 87

East Stroudsburg University, 269, 297, 310
Eckert, John, 138, 139
ECM, xii, 126, 136, 137, 181, 191, 193, 196, 197, 203, 204, 212, 244, 279, 281, 340
Ellington, Duke, 180, 222
Ellis-Liebman Band, xvii, xxi, 128, 139, 205, 209, 210, 275, 281
Ellis, Pee Wee, 138, 139
Eskelin, Ellery, 314, 321, 345
Evans, Bill, 41, 42, 46, 125, 205, 298, 299, 300, 301, 317, 329
Evans, Gil, 213
Far North, 279
Farmer, Art, 135
Farrell, Joe, 143, 145, 227, 244
Fields, Lanny, 110, 111, 112, 119, 121
First Visit, 192, 196
Forgotten Fantasies, 329
Formanek, Michael, 214
Formanek, Mike, 211, 277, 322
Foster, Al, 138, 148, 164, 171, 173, 187, 209, 217, 219, 229, 242, 340, 341
Foster, Frank, 140, 142, 143
Frampton, Peter, 202, 204
Free Life Communication, 107, 109, 112, 114, 116, 117
Fried, Donny, 27
Friedman, Don, 72
Gadd, Steve, 216
Garbarek, Jan, 65, 66, 204
Garrett, Kenny, 185
Garrison, Jimmy, 39, 73, 134, 145, 146
Garson, Mike, 25, 26, 34, 38, 50, 63, 66, 77, 134, 252
Garzone, George, 249, 270, 314, 317
Gatchell, John, 139
Geist, Judy, 128
Getz, Stan, 38, 86, 176, 192, 295
Ghosh, Pannalal, 201, 204
Gillespie, Dizzy, 294
Gilmore, Steve, 252, 274
Gomez, Eddie, 218, 241, 300, 340, 341, 343
Goodman, Benny, 85
Goodrick, Mick, 276
Gordon, Dexter, 65, 146, 147, 176, 221, 241, 243
Gordon, Max, 161
Gottdiener, Sam, 1, 3, 11
Gottlieb, Danny, 250
Green, Grant, 276
Griffin, Johnny, 148, 243, 322, 327
Gross, Julie, 41, 46, 91
Grossman, Steve, xvii, 56, 58, 63, 77, 84, 98, 110, 111, 112, 118, 119, 124, 140, 144, 161, 183, 321
Haden, Charlie, 134
Haerle, Dan, 226, 230
Halburian, Armen, 192
Half Note, 43, 44, 50, 72, 122, 201

Hall, Jim, 75, 304, 305
Hamilton, Andy, 293
Hamilton, Chico, 64, 75
Hammer, Jan, 143
Hancock, Herbie, 72, 146, 160, 216, 266, 304
Harbison, Pat, 226
Harlow, Larry, 31
Harris, Eddie, 163
Harris, Ratzo, 184
Harrison, George, 200, 202
Hart, Billy, 160, 218, 219, 237, 242, 273, 283, 285, 286, 318, 319, 341, 342, 343, 344
Havens, Richie, 90
Hawkins, Coleman, 183, 327
Haynes, Roy, 293, 304, 335
Heath, Jimmy, 169
Henderson, Eddie, 211
Henderson, Joe, 183, 313
Henderson, Michael, 160, 164, 169, 173
Hendrix, Jimi, 88, 90
Herman, Woody, 85
Hersch, Fred, 275
Hessle, Sven, 66
Hill, Calvin, 110, 118
Hino, Terumasa, 110, 118, 212
Hochhalter, Paula, 128
Hoening, Ari, 283
Holiday, Billie, 38, 52
Holland, Dave, 65, 70, 102, 109, 115, 121, 125, 127, 134, 135, 192, 227, 278, 317
Houston, Clint, 110
Hubbard, Freddie, 63, 134, 327
Humair, Daniel, 279
IAJE, 259, 261, 262, 263, 264, 265, 266
IASJ, 255, 262, 263, 264, 265, 266, 267, 268, 277, 280, 290, 334
Impromptu Quartet, 26, 32, 39, 47, 63, 252
Improvising Jazz, 226
Ineke, Eric, 327
Isham, Mark, 211
Israels, Chuck, 42
Ives, Charles, 125
Jackson, Anthony, 344
Janis, Diana, 221, 222, 233, 234, 235, 249, 250
Jarrett, Keith, 71, 73, 181, 216
Jenkins, Leroy, 204
Jenny-Clarke, Jean-Francois, 156, 279
Johnson, Marc, 300
Jones, Elvin, xii, xvii, xxi, 38, 58, 78, 84, 107, 120, 139, 140, 145, 148, 150, 151, 152, 158, 162, 164, 181, 295, 339, 341
Jones, Hank, 143
Jones, Philly Joe, 148, 152, 300
Joplin, Janis, 106
Jordan, Clifford, 143
Juris, Vic, 75, 252, 275, 290, 344
Kelly, Wynton, 241, 301
Kern, Jerome, 312
Kerper, Mitch, 27
Khan, Vilayat, 201

Kirk, Rahsaan Roland, 38, 64
Kirkland, Kenny, 184, 216, 220, 282
Konitz, Lee, xvii, 50, 53, 85 249, 288, 293, 295
Kuhn, Joachim, 279
Kuhn, Steve, 135, 254
LaBarbera, Joe, 300
Lacy, Steve, 106, 240, 243, 247, 341
LaFaro, Scott, 301
Lafayette High School, 33, 34, 37, 41, 49, 83
Laird, Rick, 128
LaRoca, Pete, xvii, 70, 93, 131, 133, 136, 150, 156, 157, 172, 173, 181, 223, 320
LaVerne, Andy, 275
Lawrence, Arnie, 200
Laws, Hubert, 110, 244
Lawson, Cedric, 164, 173
Leary, James, 211
Leisenring, John, 226
Levine, Mark, 211
Lewis, Mel, 275
Liebman, Abraham J. 1
Liebman, Celia, 1, 3
Liebman, Dave, 215, 218, 226, 229, 232, 246, 316, 325, 331
Liebman, Frances, 12
Liebman, Leo, 4
Liebman, Lydia, 256, 257, 299, 330, 343
Lincoln Center, 130
Lincoln, Abbey, 37, 39
Lipman, Steve, 260
Lloyd, Charles, xvii, 62, 71, 72, 73, 74, 77, 81, 113, 156, 215, 225, 241, 298
Lockjaw Davis, Eddie, 322
Lookout Farm, xvii, xxi, 128, 191, 192, 193, 194, 195, 196, 197, 200, 202, 203, 205, 207, 208, 211, 212, 213, 214, 215, 216, 217, 218, 219, 221, 227, 242, 274, 275, 281, 285
Lookout Farm (album), 181, 191, 192, 195, 200, 203, 205, 274
Lookout Farm (book), 205, 207
Lovano, Joe, 236, 249, 253, 270, 274, 314, 317, 344
Lucas, Reggie, 164, 169, 173, 189
Macero, Teo, 160, 179
Mahavishnu Orchestra, 154, 200, 204
Mainieri, Mike, 216
Mangelsdorff, Albert, 156
Manhattan School of Music, xii, 232, 269, 270, 271, 278, 320, 326, 343
Mann, Herbie, 38, 86
Marcinko, Marko, 276, 282, 344
Margitza, Rick, 332
Marino, Tony, 269, 274, 322, 344, 345
Markowitz, Phil, 269, 271, 273, 275, 278, 318, 323, 329, 344
Marquette, Pee Wee, 40
Marsalis, Branford, 244
Marsalis, Wynton 87, 219, 266

Marsh, Warne, 50, 54, 294
Martino, Pat, 276
Mathewson, Ronnie, 65
McBee, Cecil, 71, 73, 285, 286, 318, 342, 343, 344
McBride, Christian, 304
McClure, Ron, 184, 215, 218, 341
McFarlin, Bill, 264
McGregor, Chris, 65
McLaughlin, John, 94, 141, 160
McNeely, Jim, 249, 268, 325, 344, 345
Mehegan, John, 51
Mendoza, Vince, 325
Metheny, Pat, 249, 250, 285, 343
Miller, Marcus, 184, 216
Mitchell, Blue, 126
Mobley, Hank, 147
Monk, Thelonious, 45
Montgomery, Wes, 241
Moody, James, 244
Morell, Marty, 301
Morgan, Frank, 124, 327
Moses, Bob, xvii, 37, 38, 39, 40, 46, 49, 63, 64, 72, 73, 83, 98, 109, 113, 114, 118, 121, 132, 133, 135, 201, 203, 214, 221
Moss, Ron, 128
Mossblad, Gunnar, 320, 325
Motian, Paul, 42
Mraz, George, 217, 219, 237, 239, 341
Mtume, 164, 169, 170, 171, 173, 185, 189
Mulligan, Gerry, 40
NAJE, 259, 262, 265
National Endowment of the Arts, xi, 334, 335
New York University, xii, 3, 49, 50, 63, 64, 68, 72, 76, 88, 92, 136, 249, 257
Newman, Bob, 252
Newman, Randy, 106
Newport Festival, 74
Newsome, Philly, 32
Nielsen, Mike, 326
Nussbaum, Adam, 184, 282, 283, 314, 320, 343, 344
Ohio Players, 87
Omerta, 217
Open Sky Trio, 132, 196, 215
Owl Records, 275
Palmieri, Eddie, 32
Parker, Charlie, xvii, 152, 188, 294, 306
Pastorius, Jaco, 209
Pearson, Duke, 78
Pendarvis, Janice, 216
Pendarvis, Leon, 216
Pendulum, 193, 212
Pepper, Art, 124
Pepper, Jim, 63, 64
Perla, Gene, 84, 109, 110, 112, 132, 140, 154, 203
Peskin, Joel, 37
Phillips, Esther, 208
Pine, Courtney, 156
PM Records, 132
Polydor, 106
Porter, Lewis, 230

Potter, Chris, 236, 319
Powell, Bud, 54, 66, 125, 279, 294, 299
Priester, Julian, 211
Puente, Tito, 137
Pugh, Jim, 128
Quest, xvii, xxi, 212, 215, 217, 218, 219, 220, 221, 236, 237, 239, 240, 241, 242, 245, 248, 259, 261, 273, 274, 275, 277, 285, 311, 312, 313, 314, 318, 341, 342, 344, 345
Rainey, Chuck, 216
Ravan, Genya, 106
Redman, Joshua, 317, 319
Reid, Rufus, 225
Reisinger, Wolfgang, 327
Return to Forever, 126, 154, 204, 205, 221
Riddle, Nelson, 52
Riley, John, 184
Rivers, Sam, 177
Roach, Max, 38, 147, 148, 152, 157
Rogers, Barry 32
Rolling Stones, 89
Rollins, Sonny, xvii, 75, 122, 123, 134, 183
Rome, 67
Roy, Badal, 160, 164, 173, 192, 197, 198, 199, 200, 201, 202, 203, 204, 205, 319
Russell, George, 65, 135, 271
Rusten, Shelly, 117
Rutstein, Lonnie, 77
Sanborn, David, 7, 59, 106, 236
Sanders, Pharaoh, 73, 111, 120
Satten, Steve, 27, 83, 193, 203
Sawbuck, 107, 109
Sax Summit, ix, xiii, xvii, xxi, 317, 319, 320, 323, 326, 344
Schefrin, Aram, 106
Schenk's, 31, 32
Schneider, Maria, 325
Schuller, Gunther, 302
Scientology, 125, 127, 129, 131
Scofield, John, 156, 184, 212, 213, 340
Seed, Lenny, 137
Self-Portrait of a Jazz Artist, 232, 234, 268
Severinsen, Doc, 208
Shankar, Ravi, 38, 201
Shapiro, Nat, 24, 55, 62
Shaw, Woody, 110, 221
Shearing, George, 237
Shive, Carol, 128
Shorter, Wayne, xvii, 70, 106, 111, 186, 270, 305, 341
Silvano, Judi, 253
Silver, Horace, 38, 111, 112
Simon, Paul, 282, 287
Simone, Nina, 112
Sinatra, Frank, 52, 155
Skidmore, Alan, 65
Sloane, Ken, 226
Slug's, 140
Smith, Kate, 11, 23
Smith, Lonnie, 122
Sondheim, Steven, 312
Soph, Ed, 225, 226
State Department, 197, 198

Steinberg, Eleana, 124, 138, 159, 161, 162, 163, 170, 174, 175, 177, 193, 203, 207, 208, 209, 212, 218, 233, 234, 257
Stenson, Bobo, 74, 279, 327, 343
Stephans, Mike, 269
Stern, Mike, 184, 185, 344
Sting, 282
Stitt, Sonny, 75, 163
Stone, Sly, 108, 209
Strassburg, Jimmy, 138, 209
Stroudsburg, 252, 268
Surman, John, 65, 247
Swallow, Steve, 132, 133, 135, 156, 203, 244, 314, 320, 344
Szabó, Gábor, 72, 75
Tabackin, Lew, 244
Tarenzi, Roberto, 327
Taylor, Art, 123
Ten Wheel Drive, xvii, xxi, 95, 102, 105, 106, 107, 108, 109, 110, 116, 137, 139, 247
Thad Jones-Mel Lewis Band, 133, 184, 204
The Complete Guide to Saxophone Sound Production, 270
The Improviser's Guide to Transcription, 271
Thompson, Lucky, 247
Tower of Power, 105, 154
Tristano, Lennie, xvii, 49, 50, 51, 53, 54, 58, 225, 294
Turn It Around, 249, 275
Turner, Mark, 236, 294
Turrentine, Stanley, 208
Tusa, Frank, 110, 115, 132, 192, 215, 217
Tyner, McCoy, 300
Valdez, Patato, 203
Van Gelder, Rudy, 141
Van Morrison, 208
Veal, Charles, 128
Village Vanguard, 41, 43, 56, 58, 135, 153, 161, 164, 184, 215, 217, 222, 224, 236
Village Voice, 98, 137
Visentin, Caris, vii, xvi, xvii, xix, xxi, 186, 189, 234, 237, 238, 249, 250, 251, 252, 253, 254, 255, 256, 257, 258, 260, 262, 269, 273, 290, 310, 320, 330, 336, 342
Vitous, Miroslav, 132, 134
Vizzutti, Al, 128
Walcott, Colin, 160, 203
Ward, Carlos, 164
Watts, Jeff, 220
Weather Report, 154, 204, 205, 207, 211, 221, 273
Weinstein, Mark, 31
Weisz, Carrie, 1
Weisz, Julia, 1
Welk, Lawrence, 23, 27
Wess, Frank, 244
What It Is, 216, 244
White, Lenny, 63, 86, 103, 77, 121
William Paterson University, 183
Williams, Harold, 160

Williams, Jeff, 192, 203, 205, 211
Williams, Tony, 72, 136, 144, 146, 148, 242
Wilson, Steve, 270
Winter, Paul, 164
Wise, Arnie, 301
Wolff, Frank, 142
Wonder, Stevie, 87
Woods, Phil, xvii, 252, 270, 274, 293, 296, 297, 298, 299, 300
Woodstock, 89, 93, 154
World View Trio, 327
Young, Larry, 160
Young, Lester, 52, 147, 295, 296
Zager, Mike, 106
Zawinul, Joe, 273
Zorn, John, 236
Zottola, Bob, 128

About the Authors

David Liebman (DavidLiebman.com) is one of the leading forces in contemporary jazz. Prominently known since the early 1970s from his performing with Miles Davis and Elvin Jones, and for his leadership of noted ensembles since then, he has exerted considerable influence as saxophonist, bandleader, composer, author and educator, mentoring many of today's notable young artists. In addition to his recognition as a National Endowment for the Arts Jazz Master, he has received the Order of Arts and Letters from France; is the founder and Artistic Director of the International Association of Schools of Jazz; Artist in Residence at the Manhattan School of Music; granted an honorary Doctorate from the Sibelius Academy in Helsinki, Finland; and garnered multiple Grammy nominations.

Lewis Porter, Ph.D. (Lewisporter.com), long known as a jazz educator at Rutgers-Newark, and as the author of books including a celebrated volume on John Coltrane, is also very active as a jazz pianist, keyboardist and composer. He has written a three-movement concerto for Liebman and orchestra, and has performed or recorded with Liebman, Badal Roy, Wycliffe Gordon, Ravi Coltrane, Marc Ribot, and many others.